CONNECTICUT
REVOLUTIONARY PENSIONERS

Compiled by:
The Connecticut Daughters *of the* American Revolution

Southern Historical Press, Inc.
Greenville, South Carolina

This volume was reproduced
from a personal copy located in
the Publishers private library

All rights reserved. No part of this publication may be reproduced,
stored in a retrieval system, transmitted in any form, posted
on the web in any form or by any means without the
prior written permission of the publisher.

Please direct all correspondence and book orders to:
**SOUTHERN HISTORICAL PRESS, Inc.
1071 Park West Blvd.
Greenville, SC 29611**

Published Washington D.C. 1919
ISBN #978-1-63914-617-8
Printed in the United States of America

Pension Records of the Revolutionary Soldiers from Connecticut.

FOREWORD.

The copying of the pension records of the Revolutionary soldiers from Connecticut, which are herein published, was due primarily to the initiative and efforts of the Connecticut Daughters of the American Revolution.

In 1913 it was brought to their attention that the original records on file in the Pension Office in Washington, D. C., were in danger of destruction by fire, exposure, and careless handling, and that copies should be made before it was too late. Accordingly, at their State conference in March, 1914, it was voted to petition the Connecticut Legislature of 1915 to make an appropriation for this purpose. To carry out this vote the State regent, Mrs. John Laidlaw Buel, appointed a committee, known as the Pension Records Committee, Connecticut Daughters of the American Revolution, with Mrs. George Maynard Minor, vice president general, National Society Daughters of the American Revolution, from Connecticut, as chairman.

Mrs. Minor's committee drew up a bill for presentation to the legislature and enlisted the organized effort of all the chapters of the Daughters of the American Revolution in Connecticut in its behalf by urging them to approach their local representatives and to attend the hearing on the bill before the appropriations committee. The interest and cooperation of Mr. George S. Godard, librarian of the Connecticut State library, was also secured by the committee.

The result was an appropriation by the legislature of $1,000, the expenditure of which was placed in the hands of Mr. Godard, who requested that the Connecticut Daughters of the American Revolution Pension Records Committee remain in existence as an advisory committee to him in the work to be undertaken.

It was under the able and enthusiastic direction of Mr. Godard that the work of copying these invaluable records was instituted and brought to a successful conclusion. The copies are safely housed in the Connecticut State library at Hartford, to which institution we are indebted for the photostat copies from which this publication is made.

[Revolutionary pensioners who served from Connecticut and whose applications are on file in the Pension Office, Washington, D. C. Copied by Mrs. Amos G. Draper, formerly registrar general, D. A. R. Volume I: A–I. Hartford Connecticut State Library, 1918.]

NOTE.

Cont. (Conn.) means that a man was paid by the United States Government but enlisted from the State of Connecticut.

Cont. and Conn. means that he served in the Continental, also in the State regiments.

Rejected widows' claims.—Where there is nothing after the name that means that either the soldier did not apply or was rejected. In list beginning "E" notice is made where soldier was pensioned and the widow alone was rejected.

The service for which a man was pensioned is not necessarily all of the service that he actually performed. Often, from old age, a man neglected to mention part of his service; and again he might be unable after the lapse of years to prove it.

S means survivor's file; W, widow's file; and R, rejected file. Often a man was pensioned and the widow's claim rejected for technical reasons, she may not have been married before 1794, or not have been a widow at the time of the passage of the act, etc. The case is marked by the last action, so that most of the cases marked R are really proven claims as far as the soldier is concerned.

BLWt. means bounty land warrant. Those issued before 1804 are marked first with the number of the warrant; then with the number of the acres granted. Those issued later are marked first with the number of the warrant, second with the number of acres, third with 55, indicating that the act under which the warrant was issued was passed in 1855. This act allowed children as well as pensioners to obtain land.

REVOLUTIONARY PENSIONERS WHO SERVED FROM CONNECTICUT, AS SHOWN BY THE PAPERS IN THE OFFICE OF THE COMMISSIONER OF PENSIONS, WASHINGTON, D. C.

There are 776 drawers in the files, 12 of which are filled with other material or are vacant, leaving 764 drawers. These are divided as follows:

Letter.	Number of drawers.	Number of cases from Connecticut.	Average.	Letter.	Number of drawers.	Number of cases from Connecticut.	Average.
A	23	400	17	N	12½	166	13
B	83	1,451	17½	O	7	111	16
C	67	1,030	15	P	43	732	17
D	39	466	12	Q	1	7	7
E	13½	183	13	R	35	507	14½
F	26½	424	16	S	77	1,106	14⅓
G	36	545	15	T	30	456	15⅕
H	66	1,018	15	U	1	19	19
I	2½	35	14½	V	9	21	2⅓
J	15½	271	17	W	60	923	15⅓
K	17	222	13	X [1]	....	....	....
L	34	414	12	Y	4	25	6¼
M	60½	617	10½	Z	1	1	1

[1] No pensioner from any State.

The greatest percentage to a drawer is in those whose names begin with the letter "B."
The smallest in those whose names begin with the letter "Z."
The total number of names from Connecticut are 11,150.
According to drawers the letters are graded as follows: B, S, C, H, M, W, P, D, G, R, L, T, F, A, K, J, E, N, V, O, Y, I, U, Q, Z, the last three being equal.
According to number of pensioners from Connecticut, B, S, C, H, W, P, M, G, R, D, T, F, L, A, J, K, E, N, O, I, Y, V, U, Q, Z.

Revolutionary pensioners who served from Connecticut as found in the Pension Office, Washington, D. C.

A.

ABBE, ABBEE, ABBEY or ABBY.
Eleazer........ BLWt. 267-100
George........ S 11931
Hezekiah, Conn. & Conn. Sea service........ S 21034
James or Joseph James........ R 1
Jeduthan (Qr. Mr. Serg't. 1818)........ W 12225
Lucretia Roberts, former wid. of.
Joseph James. (See James.)
Nathaniel........ W 26215
Nancy Little, former wid. of.
Richard, wid. Lydia........ W 17197
Samuel, BLWt. 101726-160-55........ W 5150
Margaret Mitchell, former wid. of.
Thomas, Cont. (Conn.)........ S 38105
(Pensioner, 1818).
William Conn. & Cont. wid. Lydia........ W 20556
(N. Y. in 1818)

ABBAT, ABBATT, ABBOT or ABBOTT.
- Aaron (Conn. 1818; 82 in 1840, New Canaan.) .... S 38101
- Asa, wid. Elizabeth .... W 20558
- Benjamin, Conn. & N. Y. .... S 11933
- James (Fairfield Co. in 1832) .... S 17229
- John .... W 22434
  Temperance Tarbox, former wid. of.
- Joseph, wid. Nancy .... W 20553
- Stephen (Fairfield Co. in 1832) .... S 17231

ABEL or ABELL, Abel (Pensioner in 1818; Middlesex Co. in 1832; 77 in 1840, Chatham.) .... S 11930
- David, Conn. & Cont. .... S 10314
- Elijah .... S 17805
- John .... S 4257
- Simon, wid. Betsy .... R 7
- William, wid. Lois .... W 20559

ABORN. Samuel (Conn. in 1818) .... S 38103
ABRO. Benajah (Conn. in 1818) .... S 38104
ACHMET, Hamet (81 in 1840, Middletown) .... S 38107
ACHOR, ACOR or ACRE. .... S 39144
- Jacob .... BLWt. 1145-100

ACKELEY, ACKLEY, AKELEY or AKELY.
- Ahira, wid. Miriam .... W 4872
- Champion, wid. Abigail .... W 5197
- Edward .... S 11935
- Elihu .... S 44544
- Isaac (Chalker) .... S 17232
  (Middlesex Co. 1832; 80 in 1840, East Haddam, known in later life as Chalker, according to his grandson.)
- Ithamer .... S 28614
- Nathaniel .... R 20
- Simeon .... S 18680
- Stephen, wid. Mehitable .... W 17198
  (Middlesex Co. 1832.)
- Thomas (Conn. in 1818) .... S 38106

ACOR or ACRE. (See ACHOR.)

ADAMS, ADDAMS or ADDOMS.
- Abijah, Conn. & R. I. .... R 24
- Abraham (Fairfield Co. in 1832) .... S 14914
- Benjamin, Conn. & Cont., wid. Susan .... W 20570
- David (Serj't. in N. Y. in 1818) .... S 45171
- David, BLWt. 30-400, Surgeon was issued Jan. 28, 1790. No papers.
- Deliverance, Conn. & Penna .... S 45170
  (Penna. in 1818).
- Ebenezer, Conn. & Cont. .... S 37647
  (Conn. in 1818)
- Elijah, wid. Sarah .... W 21604
- Elijah, Conn. & Mass .... S 2494
- Elijah, Conn. & N. Y., wid. Sarah .... R 46
  BLWt. 34592-160-55
- Elisha .... R 28
- Gideon, Conn. & Cont., wid. Rhoda .... W 23395
  (N. Y. in 1818).
- Hitty, former wid. of Asa Hoskins .... W 25366
- James .... S 11937
- Jedediah, Conn. & Cont. .... S 49293
  (Penna. 1818).
- John .... S 11947
- John (Orleans Co., Vt.) .... S 15728
- Joseph (Windham Co. in 1832) Wid. Rebecca .... R 45
- Joshua (Fairfield Co. in 1832), BLWt. 13201-160-55 wid. Sarah .... W 25337
- Levi, Conn. & Vt. .... S 11941
- Luke (Conn. in 1818) .... S 37652
- Mary, former wid. of John Hutchinson .... W 20571
- Moses (Ohio in 1818) .... S 45174
- Reuben, wid. Abigail .... W 23399
- Reuben, wid. Lydia .... W 20568
- Roswell, Conn. & Privateer, wid. Eunice .... W 23411
- Samuel (Vt. in 1818) .... S 38483
  Vt. res. & Agency .... BLWt. 955-100
- Samuel C. (Windham Co. in 1832; 76 in 1840, Canterbury) .... S 11948
- Shubael .... S 28615
- Silas .... S 12905
- Timothy, wid. Susannah .... W 21600
  (Soldier in Windham Co. in 1832; wid. 98 in 1840, Canterbury.)
- Titus .... R 50
- William (N. Y. in 1832) .... S 11946
- William (Lisbon, New London Co., in 1832; 87 in 1840, Lisbon) .... S 45173

ADDEE or ADYE, Caleb .... S 6465
- John .... S 21595

ADKINS, David (80 in 1840, Plymouth) .... S 12012
- Isaiah (Corp. N. Y. in 1818) .... S 49292
  BLWt. 649-100.
- Jabez .... S 33248
- Luther, wid. Azubah (Mass. in 1818) .... W 23400
  (See also ATKINS.)

ADYE. (See ADDEE.)
AERY. (See AVERY.)

3

AGARD, Hezekiah	S	23092
John	R	62
Joseph, Conn. & N. Y.	S	45179
Noah, Conn. & N. Y.	S	45180
AGGLESTON. (See EGGLESTON.)		
AIKEN, AKIN, or AKINS, James, wid. Amy, Conn. & N. Y. service	W	1349
Seth, wid. Sally	W	25341
Thomas	S	4258
Thomas	S	16595
AINSWORTH, Edward, wid. Polly	R	67
AKELEY. (See ACKELEY.)		
AKEN or AKINS. (See AIKEN.)		
ALCOCK, ALLCOCKS, ALCOX, or ALLCOX.		
Asa, Conn. & Cont. (N. Y. in 1818).	S	23513
David (as Alcox in N. Y. in 1818, as Serj't)	S	45186
John Blakesley, wid. Lois.	W	17209
Samuel, wid. Lydia.	W	17211
ALDEN, Judah, Cont. (Conn.)	BLWt.	1150-300
Roger, wid. Elizabeth	W	4113
ALDERMAN, Ephraim	S	45185
Gad, Cont. & Conn	S	32639
Timothy, wid. Ruth	R	77
ALDRICH or ALDRICK, John, Conn. & Navy	S	21601
ALEXANDER, Benjamin, Conn. & Cont., wid. Elizabeth	R	84
James (N. Y. in 1818)	S	38490
James, Conn. & R. I.	S	16599
(Voluntown, Windham Co. in 1832.)		
ALFORD or ALVORD.		
Alexander, Conn. & Green Mt. Boys	W	20600
(Vt. in 1818.) Wid. Elizabeth or Eliza.		
Benedict, Conn., Mass. & Vt.	S	8016
Eber (Hartford Co. in 1832; 79 in 1840, Canton, as Aber)	S	11966
John (N. Y. in 1818)	S	39932
John (90 in 1840, Fairfield)	S	15314
Phineas	S	18295
Seth (Middlesex Co. in 1832)	S	11959
ALGER or ALGIER.		
Asa, Conn. & Mass., wid. Sarah	R	94
Elijah	S	11962
Nathaniel, wid. Dorcas	W	5612
BLWt. 30593-160-55.		
ALING. (See ALLEN.)		
ALLCOX. (See ALCOCK.)		
ALLEN, ALLIN, ALLING or ALLYN.		
Abel, Conn. & Cont., wid. Phebe (Conn. in 1818)	W	20595
Abiel, Cont. (Conn.), wid. Lydia (N. Y. in 1818)	W	16807
Abner, Conn. & Cont., wid. Lucy (Mass. in 1818)	W	20588
Amasa, Conn. & N. Y. (N. Y. in 1818)	S	44547
Amos, wid. Hannah	W	20582
Amos, Conn. & Mass.	S	28619
Asahel, wid. Eleanor	W	25346
(Tolland Co. in 1832.)		
Asher, wid. Elizabeth	W	9325
(Ohio in 1818.)		
Azor, wid. Anna	W	20592
Benjamin (N. Y. in 1818)	S	46171
Cady, wid. Parthenia	W	16094
Charles (Hartford Co. in 1832)	S	14916
Cyrus, wid. Eleanor	W	8094
Daniel	S	11956
Daniel	S	37656
David	S	5241
David, wid. Desire	W	15533
David	S	39930
David, wid. Lydia	W	17212
Diarea	S	12917
Ebenezer	S	11968
Ebenezer	S	37662
Ebenezer, wid. Huldah	W	8095
Edward, wid. Abigail	W	20596
BLWt. 682-100; BLWt. 87-60-55.		
Eleazer	S	35171
Elias, Conn. & Privateer.		
Wid. Amy	R	99
Eliphalet	R	109
Enos, wid. Mabel	W	17207
(New Haven Co. in 1832; wid. was 75 in 1840 in Wallingford.)		
Ezra, Conn. & Mass.	W	27268
Catharine Hunt, former wid. of.		
Gabriel, Conn. & Conn. Sea Service	S	12915
(New Haven Co, in 1832.)		
George, Conn. & Cont., wid. Sabra	W	21606
(Conn. in 1818.)		
Heman, Cont. (Conn.) & Green Mt. Boys	W	18285
Abigail Wadham, former wid. of.		
Hezekiah	S	23093
Howard (N. Y. in 1818)	S	45204

ALLEN, ALLIN, ALLING or ALLYN—Continued.
  Isaac, Cont. serv. Conn. res. & Agency... S 37654
    (Conn. in 1818, as priv. Hazen's reg't. d Oct. 8, 1818.)
  James... R 12085
  Jared, Conn. & R. I.. S 11967
    (Windham Co. in 1832.)
  Job, wid. Abigail... W 17210
  John, Conn. & Cont. wid. Electa... W 25347
    (Wid. was 79 in 1840, Plymouth.)
  John, Conn. & Mass... S 17235
  John, Conn. & N. Y... W 23429
    Persis Coolidge, former wid. of.
  Jonathan... S 12910
  Jonathan... S 32094
  Jonathan, Conn. & Cont.. S 45203
  Joseph... S 11963
  Joseph, wid. Lucy.. R 130
  Lathrop, wid. Abigail... W 17208
    (N. Y. in 1818 as Capt.)
  Levi... S 11969
  Luke.. S 16030
  Luke.. S 18296
  Othniel, wid. Phebe.. W 17202
    (Conn. in 1818.)
  Parley, wid. Catherine... W 17206
  Phineas or Phinehas... S 45200
  Phineas, Conn. & Mass.. S 45199
  Reuben, wid. Rebecca.. R 136
  Reuben, Conn. & N. Y... R 137
  Robert, BLWt. 29-200 Lieut. issued Aug. 3, 1796. No papers.
  Samuel, wid. Susan... W 17201
    (N. Y. in 1818.)
  Seth... S 11952
  Sluman, wid. Hannah.. W 20576
    BLWt. 32226-160-55.
  Stephen.. S 11964
  Stephen.. S 12920
  Stephen, Conn. & R. I... S 11965
  Stephen, Cont. (Conn.).. S 37664
  Timothy, Conn. & Cont.. S 29580
    BLWt. 82-300.
  Titus, wid. Abigail B... W 25367
    BLWt. 19760-160-55.
  William, wid. Rebecca.
  William, wid. Rebecca... W 10353
    (Fairfield Co. in 1832; 75 in 1840, Westport.)
  William Cornelius (N. Y. in 1818).. S 4519g
  Wolcott.. S 18687
ALLIN, ALLING or ALLYN. (See ALLEN.)
ALTON, William, wid. Sarah.. W 17205
  (Wid. was 77 in 1840 in Thompson.)
ALVORD. (See ALFORD.)
AMADON. (See AMIDON.)
AMBLER, James, Cont., Conn. & N. Y... S 11977
  Peter, Cont. service, Conn. res. & Agency, wid. Hannah........................ W 25369
    (Hannah was 77 in 1840 at Danbury.)
  Squire, Cont. service, Conn. res. & Agency, Jerusha Beers, former wid. of, BLWt. 194-60-55. W 205
    BLWts. 5373 & 12727 were issued June 27, 1791. Her former husband was Squire Ambler.
    Her later husband, Phineas Beers, was also pensioned, S 16635.
  Stephen, Cont. (Conn.).. S. 37665
    (Conn. in 1818.)
AMEDON. (See AMIDON.)
AMES, Amos, Conn. & Cont., BLWt. 2396-100... S 45505
  Asa... S 11973
  Asahel... S 45207
  Daniel.. S 17237
    (New London Co. in 1832; 84 in 1840, Montville.)
  David... S 11975
  Elijah, wid. Cynthia, BLWt. 50810-160-55... W 5615
  Everit or Everitt.. S 37666
    (Conn. in 1818, as Everit.)
  John, Navy (Conn.), wid. Sally or Sarah, BLWt. 28544-160-55.......... W 20601
  Joseph, wid. Hannah, also EAMES.. W 17213
    (New London Co. in 1832; wid. 80 in 1840, Norwich.)
  Nathaniel, BLWt. 5215-160-55.. S 11979
  Samuel, wid. Axsa or Acksa.. W 25348
    (New Haven Co. in 1832.)
  Zebulon (Vt. in 1818)... S 41413
  See also EAMES and EMES.
AMIDON, AMADON or AMEDON.
  Asenath, former wid. of Simon Skeels, Cont. (Conn.).......................... W 20605
  Jacob, wid. Hannah.. W 23438
  Jedediah or Jedidiah.. S 14917
    (Windham Co. in 1832.)
  Jonathan, wid. Keturah.. W 23441
    (Vt. in 1818, Amadon.)
  Moses.. S 11976

ANDERSON, Asa	S 15732
Daniel (Fairfield Co. in 1832)	S 14919
James, wid. Abigail	W 23451
(Wid. was 81 in 1840 in Hartford.)	
James, Conn. & Cont	S 37671
John, wid. Linda	W 20621
Lemuel, wid. Rachel, BLWt. 14662-160-55	W 20615
Robert (Middlesex Co. in 1832)	S 10325
Samuel	R 200
Thomas (Conn. in 1818)	S 37668
BLWt. 28-200, Lieut., was issued Feb. 5, 1790. No papers.	
Thomas, Conn. & Vt., wid. Alice, BLWt. 12849-160-55	W 17216
Timothy, Conn. & Privateer	S 31522
(Hartford Co. in 1832; 78 in 1840.)	
ANDREAS, ANDRES, OR ANDRESS. (See ANDREWS.)	
ANDREWS, ANDRES, ANDRESS, or ANDRUS or ANDRUSS.	
Abner Cont. (Conn.)	S 19899½
(Middlesex Co. p. 648.)	
Amos (Conn. in 1818)	S 37679
Andrew, wid. Mary	W 15538
Benjamin	S 17239
Benjamin	S 11988
Clement, Conn. & Mass	S 44304
(Ohio in 1818, as Andrus.)	
David	S 5244
David	S 46495
Ebenezer	R 221
Eli	S 11989
Elijah	S 12935
Elijah	S 11983
Elisha	S 11985
Elisha, wid. Anna, Cont. (Conn.), BLWt. 587-100	W 16172
Ephraim, wid. Asenath R	W 1795
(Tolland Co. in 1832.) BLWt. 26503-160-55.	
Ethan	S 23515
Giles	R 1493
Hezekiah, wid. Rhoda	W 17215
(Wid. was 83 in 1840, Berlin.)	
James, wid. Lois	W 15542
Jeremiah, wid. Cynthia, BLWt. 36630-160-55	W 25350
John, wid. Sarah, BLWt. 16257-160-55	W 5621
John, Conn. & Cont	S 11990
John	R 214
John, Cont. (Conn.) & Mass	S 38501
John, Cont. (Conn.), wid. Lydia	W 23442
Jonathan, Conn. & Cont., wid. Sopphia	W 17214
(Conn. in 1818; wid. was 76 in 1840 at Canton.)	
Joseph, Mercy	W 20612
Josiah	S 16032
Josiah, Cont. (Conn.), BLWt. 86-100	S 37670
Moses, Conn. & Mass	S 30247
Nathan, Conn. & R. I	S 19525
Nathaniel, wid. Jerusha, BLWt. 19753-160-55	W 4117
Phinehas	S 12928
Richard (N. Y. in 1832)	S 12931
Richard, wid. Catharine (1818)	W 21616
(Wid. was 87 in 1840, Simsbury.)	
Samuel, BLWt. 15424-160-55	S 45218
Samuel, wid. Mary Lee	W 25351
Conn. & Privateer.	
Samuel, Conn. & N. Y	S 11980
Samuel, wid. Elizabeth	R 222
Samuel J., Cont. (Conn.)	S 11982
Theodore (Conn. in 1818)	S 37669
Thomas	S 12933
Thomas, Conn. & Cont	S 45219
Thomas, Conn., Cont. & Privateer	S 5247
Timothy, wid. Mary	W 20620
(N. Y. in 1818.)	
William	S 11981
William	S 37678
William, wid. Rosetta	W 23450
William, Conn. & Cont., BLWt. 19-200.	
Lieut. in Crane's reg't. Art. issued Aug. 12, 1789. No papers.	
ANNABIL, Ebenezer, Conn. & Conn. Sea Service, wid. Ann	W 5629
ANNIS, Elizabeth, former wid. of Jason Harris	W 23443
ANSWERT, Appollos	S 32657
ANTHONY or ANTONY, Jack (colored), BLWt. 297-100.	
Samuel	S 14918
APLEY, Josiah (Litchfield Co. in 1832)	S 16607
APPELL, Peter, French Navy, Sea Service (Conn.), U. S. Revenue Service	R 235
ARCHER, Amasa (Middlesex Co. in 1832)	S 17242
Crippen (Conn. in 1818) wid. Jemima	W 21617
Obadiah	S 28623
ARES. (See AYRES.)	
AREY. (See AVERY.)	
ARMSBEY. (See ORMSBEE.)	

ARMSTRONG, Daniel (Conn. in 1818).. S 37681
   Ebenezer, Conn. & Cont.. S 44298
   Jabez... R 250
   James, wid. Miriam, Conn. & Cont... W 25360
      (Wid. was 84 in 1840, Washington.)
   James, Conn. & Cont., wid. Nabby.. W 25372
      (Wid. was 75 in 1840, Franklin.)
   Jeremiah... S 21610
ARNOLD, Fenner.. S 5250
   Isaac (Tolland Co. in 1832; 76 in 1840, Mansfield).. S 31526
   Jabez, Conn., Cont. & Mass... S 14922
   John.. S 19183
   Jonathan, wid. Polly, Conn. & N. Y... W 8102
      BLWt. 887-100. BLWt. 212-60-55.
   Jonathan, wid. Lucy, Cont... W 17218
   Levi, former widow, Fanny Harris... W 9050
      Conn. & Privateer, BLWt. 67536-160-55.
   Samuel B. P. (Middlesex Co., 1832)... S 31524
   Seth, Conn. & Privateer.. S 18690
   Timothy, Conn. & Mass., wid. Anna.. W 15549
ASHCRAFT, William, Conn. Cont. & Navy.. S 37687
   (Conn. in 1818, as ASHCROFT; New London, 86 in 1840.)
ASHER, Gad (New Haven Co. in Conn. Men, p. 648)... S 17244
ASHLEY, Abner, Conn. & R. I... S 18298
   Daniel, Conn. & R. I... S 14928
      (Windham Co. in 1832; 82 in 1840, Hampton.)
   Joseph, Conn. & R. I... S 14926
      (Conn. in 1818; Windham Co. in 1832; 84 in 1840, Hampton.)
   Samuel, wid. Lucy.. W 17219
ASK, Samuel... S 10327
ASPENWALL or ASPINWALL, Aaron (N. Y. in 1818)... S 44556
   Samuel, wid. Jane.. W 20634
ATKINS, Chauncey or Chauncy... S 10328
   David, Cont. (Conn.)... S 12013
   David, Cont. (Conn.)... S 45224
   Isaac... S 22092
   Josiah.. 45223
   Josiah, former wid., Sarah Culver... W 17673
   (See also ADKINS.)
ATTWATER or ATWATER.
   Holbrook, Cont. (Conn.), wid. Mehitable.. W 16494
      (Conn. in 1818.)
   Ichabod, wid. Electa... W 699
      (80 in 1840, Norfolk.) BLWt. 26184-160-55.
   John, wid. Lucy.. W 698
      BLWt. 26949-160-55.
   Jonathan... R 298
   Russel or Russell.. S 28238
   Stephen.. S 12014
ATWELL, Oliver, Cont. (Conn.)... S 19526
   Samuel, wid. Betsey.. W 1205
      BLWt. 19805-160-55.
   (Soldier in New London Co. in 1832; & 80 in 1840 in Montville.)
ATWOOD, Ebenezer, wid. Demarest... W 23469
   BLWt. 36626-160-55.
   Elijah... S 39945
   Isaac, Conn. & Mass., wid. Elizabeth... W 20636
   Jesse, Conn., Cont. & Mass., wid. Rachel... W 17222
   John, wid. Candace... W 15718
   Jonathan... S 15361
      (79 in 1840, Mansfield.)
   Philip, Conn. & Mass... S 18689
   Samuel, Conn., Mass., & Vt... S 14930
AUGER or AUGUR, Felix, wid. Esther.. W 20610
   Justus, Conn. & Cont... S 38507
AUGUSTINE, Joel, wid. Ann Taylor.. W 23166
   Also given GUSTENE.
AUSTIN or AUSTEN.
   Aaron (Conn. in 1818, as Capt.).. S 37692
   Amos... S 22626
   Andrew D... S 5257
   Apollos, wid. Sarah, BLWt. 56512-160-55... W 20644
   Benjamin, wid. Susannah.. W 2514
   Catharine, former wid. of William Wooldridge or Woolbridge, BLWt. 80028-160-55........................ W 10359
      Conn. & War of 1812.
   Dan.. S 29594
   Ebenezer, wid. Amy... W 20642
      (N. Y. in 1818.)
   Edward, wid. Mary.. W 16171
      (N. Y. in 1818.)
   Elias.. S 12019
   Eliphalet, wid. Sibbell.. W 3918
   Eusebius, Cont. (Conn.).. S 45221
      (N. Y. in 1818.)
   Hannah, former wid. of Abel Tharp.. W 20641
   James, wid. Hannah... W 20643
   James, Conn., N. Y., & R. I.. S 19186

AUSTIN or AUSTEN—Continued.
 Jedediah, Conn., N. Y., & R. I. .... S 21616
  (78 in 1840, Stonington.)
 John, wid. Esther .... W 15674
  (Vt. in 1818.)
 John, Conn., N. Y., & R. I. .... R 322
 Nathan .... S 14932
 Nathaniel .... S 19902
 Nathaniel, wid. Margaret .... W 1695
 Phineas .... S 44557
 Richard, former wid. Mary Phelps .... W 17445
 Samuel, Conn. & Cont .... S 2931
 Seth, wid. Hannah .... R 320
AVARY. (See AVERY.)
AVEREL, AVERELL, AVERIL or AVERILL.
 Daniel (Conn. in 1818; New Haven Co. in 1832) .... S 12027
 Ebenezer, Conn. & Privateer .... S 28625
 Jonathan, Conn., Navy & Privateer .... S 29333
 Nathaniel .... S 12938
 William, wid. Abigail .... W 20645
  Conn., Navy & Privateer.
 See also AVERY.
AVERY, Abel, wid. Elizabeth .... W 23476
  (79 in 1840, Cornwall.)
 Abner .... S 12025
 Abraham, Conn., Cont., Mass. & Privateer .... S 28626
 Amos, wid. Betsey .... R 12189
 Amos, wid. Eunice .... R 305
 Amos, wid. Mary .... W 25374
  He had a disability pension under act of 1816; and she lived in New London Co.
 Amos, Conn. & Cont .... S 12023
  (Mass. in 1832.)
 Benjamin (Conn. in 1818) .... S 44558
 Caleb, wid. Mary .... W 25363
  (New London Co. in 1832.)
 Charles, wid. Mary .... W 23478
 Christopher .... S 22627
 Christopher, Conn. & Cont .... S 49280
 Constant, wid. Zipporah .... W 1696
 Daniel .... S 19903
 Daniel .... S 44560
 David .... S 12022
  (New London Co. in 1832; 75 in 1840, Lebanon.)
 Denison, wid. Hannah .... W 23474
  (Tolland Co. in 1832 as Deneson.)
 Ebenezer .... S 19006
 Ebenezer or Ebenzer, BLWt 782-160-55 .... S 12021
 Elihu, former wid. of Thankful Rogers .... W 15955
 Elisha, wid. Sybil .... R 310
 Ezekiel .... S 5261
 George, Conn., Mass., & Vt., wid. Mary, BLWt. 26129-160-55 .... W 23477
 Griswold .... R 306
 Jonathan, wid. Parmelia or Parmela .... W 20646
  Conn. & Cont.
 Jonathan, Conn., Navy & Privateer .... S 29333
  (Also given AVERILL.)
 Joshua, wid. Rachel, BLWt. 11391-160-55; BLWt. 36616-160-55 .... W 9335
  (Mass. in 1818, as AREY.)
 Miles (Mass. in 1818, as Serj't.) .... S 32666
 Nathan .... S 10331
 Nathan, wid. Rebecca .... R 308
 Nathan, Conn. & Cont., wid. Aliff .... W 17223
  (N. Y. in 1818 as AVARY.)
 Nathaniel .... S 18693
 Nathaniel, Conn. & Cont., wid. Amy, BLWt. 34521-160-55 .... W 700
 Oliver (New London Co. in 1832; 83 in 1840, North Stonington) .... S 16613
 Park .... S 19904
 Peter .... S 12024
 Roger (N. Y. in 1818) .... S 44561
 Rufus (New London Co. in 1832; 81 in 1840 in Groton) .... S 12939
 Samuel, wid. Lydia .... R 307
 Simeon, BLWt. 1143-200.
 Simeon, former wid. Sarah Bigelow .... W 23615
  Cont. (Conn.). BLWt. 5210-160-55.
 Stephen .... S 12026
 Stephen, Conn. & Cont., wid. Mary .... W 6890
  BLWt. 19764-160-55.
 Thomas, Conn. & Cont .... S 5260
  BLWt. 313-200.
 Uriah, Conn. & Navy .... S 16612
AYER, AYERS or AYRES or ARES.
 Ebenezer, Cont. (Conn.), wid. Achsa, BLWt. 26027-160-55 .... W 8589
 John, former wid. of, Abigail Pelton, Rej. BL. This woman was pensioned as wid. of Joseph
  Pelton, Conn., W 26303, and that is why the BL was Rej.
 John, wid. Martha, BLWt. 27614-160-55 .... W 1357
 Peter, wid. Temperance .... W 15872
 William, Conn. & Cont .... S 37685
  (Conn. in 1818 as ARES.)

8

NAMES OF MEN MENTIONED AMONG THE CONNECTICUT PENSIONERS BUT NOT SO CONSIDERED BY THE AUTHORITIES AT THE PENSION OFFICE IN WASHINGTON; ALSO NAMES MISPRINTED IN CONNECTICUT MEN IN THE REVOLUTION.

NOTE.—The service for which a man was pensioned is not necessarily all of the service that he actually performed. Often, from old age, a man neglected to mention part of his service; and again he might be unable a_ter the lapse of years to prove it.

S means supervisor's file; W, widow's file; and R, rejected file. Often a man was pensioned and the widow's claim rejected for technical reasons—she may not have been married before 1794, or not have been a widow at the time of the passage of the act, etc. The case is marked by the last action, so that most of the cases marked R are really proven claims as far as the soldier is concerned.

BLWt. means bounty land warrant. Those issued before 1804 are marked first with the number of the warrant; then with the number of acres granted. Those issued later are marked first with the number of the warrant, second with the number of acres; third with 55, indicating that the act under which the warrant was issued was passed in 1855. This act allowed children as well as pensioners to obtain land.

ACKART, Solomon, 90 in 1840, Canton, Hartford Co., Conn.
    N. Y. not Conn. service, although pensioner lived in Conn. after the Revolution.
ALDRICK, Noah, Hartford Co. in 1832.
    This man served from Mass. and was pensioned in 1832, while a resident of Hartland, Vt., where he died. The mistake is found also in the Report of the Secretary of War in 1835.
ALEXANDER, Thomas, East Hartford, Conn., Conn. Men, p. 666.
    This man served in the Continental and Mass. service, but lived in Conn. after the Revolution.
ALLEN, Arnold, Hartford Co. in 1832; also 71 in East Windsor in 1840.
    This man served in Mass. not Conn. Line.
AMES, Smith, Hartford Co.
    No such name in files of Revolutionary pensioners. Probably served at a later date.
ANDREIS, Ephraim, Tolland Co. in 1832.
ANDREWS, Ephraim, Tolland Co. in 1832.
    Only one man pensioned of that name. He lived in Tolland Co. and spelled his name Andrus or Andrews.
ANGEVINE, Lewis (Conn. Men, p. 649.).
    No such name in files of Revolutionary pensioners. Probably served at a later date.
ARNOLD, Nathaniel, Windham Co., in 1832.
    R. I. not Conn. service.
ASHLEY, Elisha, Middlesex Co. in 1832.
    Only one pensioner of that name in the files. He lived in Vt. in 1832; service given as Green Mt. Boys and Vt.

B.

BABBET or BABBIT, or BABBETT.
    Edward.. S 31545
        (Conn. Men, pensioners 1832; also 77 in 1840.)
    Seth.. S 12956
        (Conn. Men, pensioners 1832, also 80 in 1840.)
BABCOCK, Amariah, wid. Sabra; Conn. & N. Y. BLWt. 3753-160-55............... W 25198
    Beriah, Cont. (Conn.)... S 12034
        (Conn. Men, pensioners, 1818; pensioners, 1832.)
    Caleb, Conn. & R. I... S 23112
    Daniel.. S 12102
    Daniel, wid. Tryphena.. R 345
    Daniel, Conn. & R. I.. R 340
    Elisha, wid. Anna, BLWt. 26693-160-55.. W 681
    Ephraim... S 37709
        (Conn. Men, pensioners, 1818.)
    George, wid. Content, Conn. & R. I., BLWt. 2350-160-55................... W 5210
    Horace, wid. Elcey.. W 23513
    Job, Conn. & Cont.. S 44576
    John, former wid. Lydia Barnard.. W 25187
    John, former wid. Lydia Edgerton (Egerton)................................... W 17749
    Nathaniel... S 2367
    Oliver, former wid. Marcy Brown.. W 16865
        Conn. & Cont.
    Reuben.. S 28978
    or BADCOCK, Roger.. S 12107
    Sherman, Conn., R. I., Vt.. S 17246
BACK, Elisha.. S 44605
    (Conn. Men, pensioners, 1818.)
    Lyman, wid. Eunice.. W 23540
BACKUS, Abner, wid. Jemima, BLWt. 3794-160-55................................... W 2049
    (Conn. Men, pensioners, 1818, 78 in 1840.)
    Elijah... S 38514
    (Conn. Men, pensioner in Vt. 1818.)
    Josiah.. S 8058
    Ozias, wid. Elizabeth... W 17227
        (She was 74 in 1840, Conn. Men.)
    or BAKUS, Samuel... S 16036
    Stephen, Conn. & Privateer.. S 18704
BACON, Abner.. S 37728
    (Conn. Men, pensioners, 1818. A BLWt. 2639-300 Capt. was issued Mch. 27, 1794, to Samuel Dorrance, assignee. No papers.)
    Ebenezer.. S 30849
        (Conn. Men, pensioners, 1818.)
    Ebenezer, 2nd., Conn. & Cont... S 44569
        (Conn. Men, pensioners, 1818.)
    Francis (Conn. Men, pensioners, 1832)... S 12981
        91 in 1840.
    Henry... S 29604
        BLWt. 2138-100; Conn. & R. I.
        (Conn. Men, pensioners, 1818.)

BACON, Jacob, Conn. & Privateer.. S 15306
    (Conn. Men, pensioners, 1832.)
    Joseph, wid. Betsey... R 355
    Joseph, Cont. (Conn.), wid. Eleanor... W 25190
    Josiah, Conn. & Mass... S 17263
        (Conn. Men, pensioners, 1832.)
        (Conn. Men, 84 in 1840.)
    Nehemiah... S 45239
        (Conn. Men, pensioners, 1818.)
    William... S 23525
    William, BLWt. 101-100.. S 37694
    William, Conn. & Cont... S 45566
BADCOCK, Amos.. S 44577
    Jonathan... S 12108
    Robert... S 23105
BADGER, Benjamin, Conn. & Mass... S 12121
BADGER or BAGGER, John.. S 15301
    Jonathan... S 22104
    Joseph, Conn. Cont. & Mass.. S 44336
BAGLEY, Barnard, BLWt. 73588-160-55... S 10341
    John, Conn. Cont., Mass., N. H.. S 12096
BAILEY, OR BAILY, or BALEY.
    Caleb, wid. Elizabeth.. BLWt. 77804-160-55
    Christopher... S 12098
        (Conn. Men, pensioners, 1818 & 1832.)
    David, wid. Eunice, BLWt. 71016-160-55... W 18552
    Eliakim.. S 17264
        (Conn. Men, pensioners, 1832.)
    Elijah... S 44573
        (Conn. Men, pensioners, 1818.)
    Enoch... S 12072
BAILEY, Henry... BLWt. 1594-100
    Hezekiah, Conn. Cont., wid. Adah, BLWt. 30596-160-55.............................. W 9340
        (Conn. Men, pensioners, 1818. Conn. Men, pensioners, 1832. Conn. Men, 85 in 1840.)
    Ichabod, wid. Patience... W 20667
        (Conn. Men, pensioners, 1832.)
    Jacob, wid. Sarah... W 15875
    James, wid. Thedee or Theede... W 1799
        Conn. & Cont. BLWt. 3795-160-55.
        (Conn. Men, pensioners, 1832.)
    Jared, wid. Elizabeth, Conn. & R. I... W 4884
    Joshua... S 10347
    Loudon, Conn. & Navy.. S 37703
        (Conn. Men, pensioners, 1818.)
    Robert... S 39953
        (Conn. Men, pensioners, 1818.)
    Timothy.. S 44574
        (Conn. Men, pensioners, 1818.)
    William, former widow, Rachel Goodsell... W 25640
        Conn. & Cont. (Conn. Men, pensioners, 1818.)
BAILEY. (See also BALEY.)

    NOTE.—Silas Bailey of N. H. R. F. 390 had a wife (name not stated) who was the former wid. of Joseph Marks, who served in the Rev. from Conn. No papers in regard to his claim except what are in this envelope.

BAKER, Abel.. S 10338
    Alpheus... R-
    Andrew, former wid., Mary Walden.. W 22524
    Asa... S 12127
    Asa, former wid., Zilla Pangburn.. W 21893
        Conn. & Cont.
    Daniel, wid. Jerusha.. W 3922
    Elijah, wid. Olive, Cont. (Conn.).. W 18569
        (Conn. Men, pensioners, 1818.)
    Enoch... S 17250
        (Conn. Men, pensioners, 1832.) (Conn. Men, 86 in 1840.)
    James... R 416
    Joshua... S 12074
        (Conn. Men, pensioners, 1832.)
    Lovel, Conn. & Cont.. S 37715
    Nathan.. S 12118
    Rebecca, former wid. of Marvin, Nathan... W 18558
    Robert, Cont. (Conn.), wid. Sarah... W 704
        BLWt. 255-60-55 & 286-60-55.
        (Conn. Men, pensioners, 1818.)
    Rufus, Conn. & Vt... S 16622
    Samuel, Conn., N. Y., & 1812... S 9271
    Seth, Conn. & Conn. Sea Service.. S 23106
    William.. S 44323
        (Conn. Men, pensioners, 1818.)
BALCH, John, wid. Lucy... W 20685
    (Conn. Men, pensioners, 1818.)
    Joseph, Conn. & Cont. BLWt. 3641-160-55... S 12106
BALCOM (Balcam), Azariah... S 16039
    (Conn. Men, pensioners, 1832.)
    Elias... S 44348
        (Conn. Men, pensioners, 1818.)
    Nathaniel.. S 22108

BALDWIN, Aaron, Conn., Cont., & N. Y.. S 12090
  Abel, wid. Molly... W 20677
  Abiel (Abial), wid. Elizabeth... W 8351
  Abner... S 12126
  Asa, Cont. & Conn. wid. Dolly.. W 10372
    (Conn. Men, pensioners, 1832.) (Conn. Men, 84 in 1840.)
  Ashbel.. S 22629
  Asil (Azel)... S 19196
  Benjamin, wid. Lydia... W 16498
  Brewen (Brewin).. S 12073
    (Incorrectly given Brewer. Conn. Men, pensioners, 1832.)
  Caleb, Conn. & Cont.. S 45517
    (Conn. Men, pensioners, 1818.)
  Daniel.. S 12036
    (Conn. Men, pensioners, 1832.)
  David, wid. Ruth... W 23524
    (Conn. Men, pensioners, 1818; Conn. Men, soldier d 7-10-1819.)
  Desire, former wid. of Negus, John, who had Conn. & Conn. Sea service..................... W 17228
    Only one Desire wid., was in files. (Conn. Men, 83 in 1840.)
  Eleazer... S 2046
  Elijah, Conn. & Cont... S 22103
    (Conn. Men, pensioners, 1818.)
  Elisha.. S 44306
    (Conn. Men, pensioners, 1818.)
  Elizabeth, former wid. of Gorham, Joseph... W 17247
    Cont. (Conn.)
  Henry, wid. Jane, Conn. & Cont.. W 17240
    (Conn. Men, pensioners, 1818.) (She was 81 in 1840, Conn. Men.)
  Jabez, Conn. & Mass., wid. Hannah... W 17261
  James, wid. Sarah.. W 12241
  James, Conn. & Cont., wid. Nabby.. W 25203
  James, Cont. (Conn.)... S 12124
  Joel.. S 12067
  John.. R 447
  Jonathan, wid. Keziah.. W 25202
    (Conn. Men, pensioners, 1832.)
    (Conn. Men, she was 76 in 1840.)
  Jonathan, wid. Submit. BLWt. 26258-160-55.. W 10402
  Joseph.. S 31530
    (Conn. Men, pensioners, 1832.)
  Joseph, wid. Rosanna... W 17256
  Josiah, former wid. Martha Hill.. W 21326
  Nathan, Conn. Sea Service, wid. Avis.. W 25209
  Nathaniel... S 28982
  Peleg, wid. Anna or Anne... W 2050
  Philemon, Conn. & Cont.. S 18305
    (Conn. Men, pensioners, 1832.) (Conn. Men, pensioners, 1840.)
  Phineas, wid. Abigail.. W 17235
    (She was 77 in 1840.)
  Samuel.. S 10335
  Samuel.. S 12081
  Seth, Conn. & Vt... S 44307
  Stephen... S 23111
  Theophilus, Conn. & Mass... S 37719
  Thomas... BLWt. 377-200
BALEY, John, Conn. & N. Y... R 454
  (See also BAILEY.)
  Stephen... R 392
BALL, Benjamin, Conn. & Cont.. S 12059
  Humphrey... S 39176
    (Conn. Men, pensioners, 1818.)
  John, BLWt. 143-200, Lieut., issued Feb. 4, 1797. No papers.
  Jonathan.. S 44320
    (Conn. Men, pensioners, 1818.)
  Wait.. R 460
BALLARD, Daniel, wid. Ruth. BLWt. 17702-160-55... W 474
  John, Conn. & Cont... S 44596
    (Conn. Men, pensioners, 1818.)
BALLOU, Jeremiah, Conn. & R. I.. S 23102
BANCROFT, Oliver.. S 12980
  (Conn. Men, pensioners, 1832.)
BANISTER, George, Conn., Cont. & Penna... S 9095
BANKS, Benjamin... S 12954
  (Conn. Men, pensioners, 1832.)
  Daniel.. S 9811
  Ebenezer.. S 12038
  (Conn. Men, pensioners, 1832.)
BANKS or BANK.
  Elijah, wid. Mabel... W 20675
  Ezekiel O... S 18303
    (Conn. Men, pensioners, 1832.)
  Gershom (Gershon) wid. Ruth.. W 20669
    (Conn. Men, pensioners, 1832.) (Conn. Men, she was 86 in 1840.)
  Hyatt (Hyat).. S 12040
    (Conn. Men, pensioners, 1832.) (Conn. Men, 76 in 1840.)
  Jonathan, wid. Molly... R 476
  Joseph.. S 12973
  Joseph, wid. Esther.. W 20680

BANKS or BANK—Continued.
 Moses O.. S 12035
  (Conn. Men, pensioners, 1832.)
 Nathan, wid. Mabel. BLWt. 26131-160-55.................................. W 17236
 Nehemiah.. S 12974
  (Conn. Men, pensioners, 1832.)
 Obadiah, Conn. & N. Y.. S 12050
 Obadiah.. S 28272
 Thomas.. S 44602
  (Conn. Men, pensioners, 1818.)
BANNET (BENNET), Samuel... S 15747
BARBER, Abraham, wid. Sarah... W 16832
 Conn. & Cont.
  (Conn. Men, pensioners, 1818.)
 Amaziah, Conn. & Cont... S 44340
 Bela, Conn. & Cont.. S 12071
  (Conn. Men, pensioners, 1832.)
 Benjamin, wid. Sarah.. R 484
 Daniel, Conn. & Cont... S 8052
 David, BLWt. 154-150 Ensign, issued Aug. 7, 1789, to James Noyes Barber, Adx. No papers.
 Job... S 15309
 Job, Conn. & Cont... S 12083
 Joel, Conn. & Cont.. S 12099
 Jonathan, wid. Abi... W 17259
  (Conn. Men, she was 73 in 1840.)
 Michael Conn. & Cont... S 31531
  (Conn. Men, pensioners, 1832.)
 Obadiah... S 15300
 Rebecca, former wid. of Simons, Thomas............................... W 20679
 Reuben... R 485
 Reuben, Conn. & Cont. wid. Elizabeth.................................... W 24624
  (Conn. Men, she was 86 in 1840.)
 Reuben, Conn. & N. Y. wid. Hannah...................................... W 10291
  BLWt. 11277-160-55.
 Simeon... S 16037
  (Conn. Men, pensioners, 1832.) (Conn. Men (Barbour), 87 in 1840.)
 Stephen.. S 12030
BARCE, or BEARSE, or BASS, or BORCE, or BERCE.
 Josiah, wid. Freelove.. R 489
BARDEN, Abraham... R 1448
 Ebenezer S... R 492
 Samuel, Conn. & Cont. wid. Mary.. W 16833
BARDSLEE (BEARDSLEE), Thaddeus..................................... S 14952
BARDSLEY (BEARDSLEY), William, wid. Elizabeth.............. W 23584
BARKER, Archelaus, Conn. & Conn. Sea Service, wid. Mary... W 17225
  (Conn. Men, she was 78 in 1840.)
 David, Conn. Privateer, Conn. Sea Service & Vt..................... S 6573
 Ethan... S 15308
  (Conn. Men, pensioners, 1832.)
 Hananiah... S 38519
 James, wid. Lydia.. W 21628
 John, Cont. (Conn.) wid. Huldah... W 25215
  (Conn. Men, she was 80 in 1840.)
 Jonathan.. S 28636
 Joseph, wid. Susannah... R 504
 Oliver, wid. Ruth... W 1698
  (Conn. Men, pensioners, 1818.)
 Phineas, Conn. & Privateer.. R 501
 Russell (Russel), wid. Elizabeth... W 23528
 Samuel... S 12977
 Samuel... S 33990
  (Conn. Men, 1818.)
 Samuel.. BLWt. 220-300
 Timothy... S 16615
 William, wid. Phebe, BLWt. 9467-160-55................................ W 24629
 William, Conn. & Cont... S 45223
  (Conn. Men, 1818.)
BARLOW, Aaron, wid. Rebecca... W 20665
 David, wid. Lucy... R 510
 John, BLWt. 1416-100... S 37732
  (Conn. Men, pensioners, 1818.)
 Samuel, Conn. & Cont... S 6585
 Tempa, former wid. of Carter, Jonah, BLWt. 113035-160-55.... W 10383
BARNABE, or BARNABEE, or BARNEBE or BARNEBEE.
 Chandler, wid. Esther, Conn. & R. I.. W 20661
 James, wid. Ann.. W 20687
  (Conn. Men, pensioners, 1818.)
BARNARD, Cyprian, Conn., Cont., & Navy.............................. R 512
 Dan.. S 23532
 Grove, wid. Mary Ann... W 17224
  (Conn. Men, pensioners, 1818.)
 John, BLWt. 133-300, Capt., issued May 4, 1795. No papers.
 Lydia, former wid. of Babcock, John.. W 25187
 Moses, wid. Hannah.. W 16817
 Moses, wid. Reliance... W 4634
 Rufus, wid. Mary... W 3644
 Timothy, wid. Phebe, Conn. & Cont.. W 25214
 William.. S 12125
(See also BERNARD.)

BARNEBE or BARNEBEE. (See BARNABEE.)
BARNES or BARNS, Abel... S 44317
   Abel.. S 12055
   Abel.. R 514
   Ambrose.. S 44316
      (Conn. Men, pensioners, 1818.)
   Amos, Conn. & Cont... S 44333
      (Conn. Men, pensioners, 1818.)
   Amos, wid. Elizabeth Cont. (Conn.)... W 17238
   Benjamin, former wid. of Abigail Clapp... R 1957
   Daniel.. S 12084
   Daniel, wid. Sarah.. R 527
   David... S 12944
      (Conn. Men, pensioners, 1832.)
      (Conn. Men, 76 in 1840.)
   Elijah... S 12976
      (Conn. Men, 77 in 1840.)
   Eliphalet, Conn. & Cont... S 37695
      (Conn. Men, pensioners, 1818.)
   Enos, wid. Lucy, Cont. & Conn... W 20650
      (Conn. Men, pensioners, 1818.)
   Hartwell or Heartwell... S 44312
      (Conn. Men, pensioners, 1818.)
   Israel, wid. Susanna, Conn. & Cont.. W 25201
      (Conn. Men, pensioners, 1818, 1832, & 82 in 1840.)
   Ithiel, wid. Grissel.. W 23504
      (Conn. Men, pensioners, 1818.)
      BLWt. 5447, issued 1790.
   Jared, wid. Silence.. W 25197
      (Conn. Men, pensioners, 1832.)
   Jared... R 516
   Joel, wid. Dolly, BLWt. 3611-160-55... W 3497
   John.. S 2047
   John, wid. Rachel... R 525
   John, Conn. & N. Y.. S 12105
   John, Conn. & N. Y.. S 23110
   John C., wid Abigail, Conn. & N. Y.. W 10385
   Jonah, wid. Abigail... W 20692
   Jonathan... S 44330
      (Conn. Men, pensioners, 1818.)
   Jonathan... S 44603
   Joshua... S 18302
      (Conn. Men, pensioners, 1832.)
   Josiah, wid. Olive, Conn. & Cont... W 25213
      (Conn. Men, pensioners, 1818.)
   Moses.. S 2356
   Nathan.. S 15307
      (Conn. Men, pensioners, 1832.)
   Nehemiah, Cont. (Conn.).. S 39965
      (Conn. Men, pensioners, 1818.)
   Orange, wid. Olive.. W 21647
      (Conn. Men, pensioners, 1818.)
   Reuben, Conn. & Cont... S 12104
   Samuel.. S 44318
      (Conn. Men, pensioners, 1832.)
   Simeon.. S 37731
      (Conn. Men, pensioners, 1818.)
   Thomas, wid. Sibel, Cont. (Conn.).. W 4123
   Warner, wid. Elizabeth, Conn. & Cont. BLWt. 30611-160-55........................... W 25218
BARNET or BARNETT, Moses, Conn. & N. Y... S 15303
   Nathan.. R 536
BARNEY, Luther, wid. Ruth, Conn. & Privateer... W 4124
   Samuel, wid. Sarah, Conn., Sea Service.. W 17233
BARNS. (See BARNES.)
BARNUM, Amos... S 37707
      (Conn. Men, pensioners, 1818.)
   Daniel, wid. Hannah, BLWt. 3812-160-55... W 1123
   Eli. BLWt. 144-200, Lieut., issued Oct. 12, 1789, to Eunice Barnum, Adx. No papers.
   Ezbon, Conn. & Cont... S 12979
      (Conn. Men, pensioners, 1832.)
   Jehiel.. S 44334
      (Conn. Men, pensioners, 1818.)
   Josiah, wid. Abigail... R 549
   Levi.. R 552
   Noah, Cont. & Conn.. S 37722
      (Conn. Men, pensioners, 1818.)
   Samuel, Conn. & N. Y... S 44335
   Seth, wid. Abigail... W 21625
   Stephen, Conn. & Green Mt. Boys.. S 39960
      (Conn. Men, pensioners, 1818.)
   Stephen... S 4917
   Zenas.. BLWt. 1074-100
BAROTT. (See BARRETT.)
BARRET. (See BARRETT.)
BARRET, BARRETT, BARRIT, BARRITT, BAROTT.
   Bartholomew... S 44579
   Benjamin, Conn. & Mass... S 18697
   Hezekiah... S 10353
   Jacob... S 6576

BARRET, BARRETT, BARRIT, BARRITT, BAROTT—Continued.
Jeremiah	S 37711
Jonathan	S 2049
Joseph, wid. Sally	W 21627
Oliver, Conn. & Mass	S 4920
Smith	S 29605
William	S 12048
(Conn. Men, pensioners, 1832.)	

BARROWS, Eleazer.. S 23101
 Isaac.. S 17248
 Isaac.. S 39162
 Jacob, wid. Emela, BLWt. 32224-160-55........................... W 2515
  (Conn. Men, pensioners, 1818.)
 Lemuel, wid. Abigail, BLWt. 7445-160-55............................ W 5780
 Thomas.. S 15297
BARRUS or BURRUS, Thomas, wid. Esther, BLWt. 57751-160-55........... W 8402
 (See also BURROUGHS.)
BARSTOW, Ebenezer.. S 15740
 Job, Conn. & N. Y... R 571
 John.. S 12039
  (Conn. Men, pensioners, 1832.)
 Michael... S 45519
  (Conn. Men, pensioners, 1818.)
 Samuel, wid. Lucinda, BLWt. 10241-160-55.......................... W 25196
  (Conn. Men, pensioners, 1832.)
  (Conn. Men, 80 in 1840.)
BARTHOLOMEW, Charles, wid. Lenda or Belinda, BLWt. 1006-160-55...... W 25195
 Isaac, Cont. (Conn.)... S 44590
  (Conn. Men, pensioners, 1818.)
 James, Cont. (Conn.)... S 12943
  (Conn. Men, pensioners, 1818.)
  (Conn. Men, pensioners, 1832, & 80 in '40.)
  Only James Bartholomew from any State.
 Jonathan... S 12068
  (Conn. Men, pensioners, 1832.)
  (Conn. Men, 85 in 1840.)
 Joseph, wid. Lina, BLWt. 61241-160-55.............................. W 9345
 Moses.. S 15314
 Luther, Cont. & Conn.. S 21625
 Oliver, Conn. & Cont.. S 12086
 Samuel, wid. Elizabeth.. W 20651
  (Conn. Men, pensioners, 1818.)
 William.. S 37717
  (Conn. Men, pensioners, 1818.)
BARTISS, John... R 575
BARTLET, BARTLETT, BARTLIT, BARTLITT.
 Abraham.. S 28629
 Christopher.. S 10340
 Daniel C... S 12077
 Isaac (or W.), wid. Sybel, Cont. (Conn.), BLWt. 33570-160-55....... W 517
 Levi, Conn. & N. Y.. S 12082
 Otis, Cont. (Conn.).. S 10346
 Samuel... S 12982
  (Samuel 2nd in 1832, Conn. Men.)
 Samuel... R 585
 Stephen, Conn. & Cont... S 44589
BARTMAN, Joseph, Conn. & Mass. & Sea Service & War against France & against Algiers & 1812... R 593
BARTON, Caleb, wid. Elizabeth, Conn. & Mass......................... W 15565
 Elkanah, Cont. & Conn.. S 37712
  (Conn. Men, pensioners, 1818.)
 Ruth, former widow of Josiah Conant................................ W 17260
 William, wid. Clarissa Cont. (Conn.), BLWt. 19779-160-55........... W 10375
BARTOW, John, Cont. (Conn.)... S 37718
 (Conn. Men, pensioners, 1818.)
BARTRAM, Isaac, Cont. (Conn.)... S 12110
 (Conn. Men, pensioners, 1818.)
 (Conn. Men, 88 in 1840, as Isaac H.)
 James.. S 12066
  (Conn. Men, pensioners, 1832.)
 Job. Discharged. No papers.
 Noah... S 12043
BASCOM or WARD, Urial... R 597
BASS, BARCE, BEARCE, BIERCE.
 Joseph, Conn., Cont. & N. Y. Sea Service........................... R 666
 Josiah, wid. Freelove.. R 489
 Samuel, Cont. (Conn. residence in 1802)—BLWt...................... 87-100
 (See also BEARS.)
BASSET or BASSETT, Abel... S 45227
 (Conn. Men, pensioners, 1818.)
 Abraham, wid. Mary.. W 17253
  (Conn. Men, pensioners, 1832.)
  (Conn. Men, she was 81 in 1840.)
 David, wid. Sarah.. W 17241
 Edward, wid. Damarius, Conn. & Cont............................... W 12234
 Isaac.. S 12062
  (Conn. Men, pensioners, 1832.)
 James.. S 17259
  (Conn. Men, pensioners, 1832.)
  (Conn. Men, 83 in 1840.)

14

BASSET or BASSETT, Joshua, wid. Lydia, Conn. & Cont.. W 21634
  Nathan... R 603
  Samuel... S 15746
    (Conn. Men, pensioners, 1832.)
BATES, Benjamin, Conn. & Cont... S 12148
  Eleazer... S 23991
    (Conn. Men, pensioners, 1818.)
  Elias... S 12949
  Ezra... S 12117
    (Conn. Men, pensioners, 1832.)
  Hinsdale.. S 16043
  John... S 40738
    (Conn. Men, pensioners, 1818.)
  Joseph, Cont. (Conn.)... S 34642
  Phinehas, wid. Keziah... R 618
    BLWt. 84508-160-55.
  Samuel, former widow Deborah Wright.. W 16798
    BLWt. 1534-100.
BATTERSON, BATTESON, Abijah... S 12075
  George, wid. Mary, BLWt. 2356-160-55.. W 17257
    (She was 77 in 1840, Conn. Men.)
  James, wid. Nancy... R 624
  John, wid. Sarah.. W 17239
  Joseph, wid. Rebecca, BLWt. 1404-160-55.. W 23536
    (Conn. Men, pensioners, 1818, Penna.)
  Stephen... S 40737
    (Conn. Men, pensioners, 1818.)
    (Conn. Men, 89 in 1840.)
  William... R 625
BAXTER, Aaron.. S 37714
    (Conn. Men, pensioners, 1818.)
  Benjamin, wid. Hannah... R 633
  Nathan... S 6594
  Nathan... R 637
  Simeon, Conn. & Mass.. R 638
  William, wid. Deborah, Conn. & Vt... W 25207
BEACH or BEECH, Adna, wid. Sarah, BLWt. 16270-160-55.................................. W 1212
  Asa... S 10362
  Asa, Cont. & Conn.. S 35187
    (Conn. Men, pensioners, 1818, Ky.)
  Ashbel... S 12173
  Daniel.. S 12178
  Daniel, wid. Comfort.. W 17290
  Daniel or Dan, wid. Abigail.. R 649
  David, wid. Elizabeth... R 650
  David, wid. Anna, Conn. & Cont... W 15823
    BLWt. 146-200 Lieut. issued June 9, 1709, to Ezekiel Moore. Assignee. No papers.
  Edmund... S 10367
  Elihu, wid. Mary... W 4889
  Elnathan.. S 12162
  Ezekiel, wid. Azubah... W 4130
  Francis, Conn. & Mass. Sea service.. S 15323
    (Litchfield Co. 1832; 85 in 1840.)
  Israel.. S 12160
    (N. Y. in 1818.)
  Jabez, wid. Parthenia.. W 17279
    (Fairfield Co. in 1832.)
  John.. S 12138
  John, wid. Rhoda.. W 23559
  John, Conn. & Green Mt. Boys.. S 12200
  John H. wid. Phebe.. W 18575
    (Phebe was 82 in 1840.)
  Jonathan, wid. Martha, BLWt. 26392-160-55... W 5806
  Joseph, former wid. Hannah Harrison... W 23187
  Julius.. S 12182
    (Litchfield Co. in 1832.)
    (75 in 1840.)
  Miles, wid. Sarah.. R 653
  Nathaniel, Conn. & Cont., wid. Ruth.. W 21655
    (1818 in N. Y.)
  Obiel or Obil... S 4264
    (1818 in Ohio.)
  Reuben... S 46366
  Robert, Conn. & Cont... S 16046
  Roswell or Rosewill.. S 45315
    BLWT. 15412-160-55.
  Stephen, Conn. & Vt... S 28998
  Thaddeus, Navy (Conn.)... S 37741
    or Mial Camp.
    (Marine, on frig. *Alliance*, Conn. Men, 1818.)
  Thomas, Conn. & Conn. Sea Service.. S 14946
    (Hartford Co. 1832.)
BEADLE or BEDEL, Benjamin, wid. Rhoda.. W 20705
BEAMAN, BEAMONT, BEAUMONT, BEEMAN, BEEMONT, BEMAN, BEMENT.
  Benjamin... S 12179
    (New Haven Co. in 1832.)
  Caesar.. S 39190
    (Conn. Men, 1818.)

BEAMAN, BEAMONT, BEAUMONT, BEEMAN, BEEMONT, BEMAN, BEMENT—Continued.
 Dan, wid. Lois. .... W 20703
 Daniel, Conn., Mass., Green Mt. Boys, wid. Mary .... W 17295
  (Litchfield Co. 1832.)
 Deodate, Cont. (Conn.). .... S 12334
  (1818 in N. Y.)
  (1832 in New Haven Co.)
 Friend. .... S 12140
 Isaac. .... S 6623
 Isaiah, Cont. & Conn. .... S 9099
 Lemuel. .... S 40741
 Matthias, Conn. & N. Y. .... S 37775
  (Conn. Men, 1818.)
 Oliver, wid. Jane, BLWt. 2182-160-55. .... W 7361
  (1818 in N. Y.)
 Samuel, Conn. & Cont. .... S 37736
  (1818 in Ohio.)
 Tracy, wid. Polly, BLWT. 26663-160-55. .... W 10404
  (1832 Litchfield Co.)
  (78 in 1840.)
 Truman, Conn. & N. Y. .... S 23121
 William. .... S 32111
 William, BLWt. 145-200, Lieut., issued Sept. 24, 1790, to Peleg Sanford, Assignee. No papers.
BEAN, Thomas, Conn. Sea Service & Mass. .... S 21065
BEARCE. (See BASS.)
BEARD, Abijah, Conn. & Cont. .... S 28640
 Andrew, wid. Susan. .... W 17288
  (New Haven Co. 1832.)
 David .... S 12204
BEARDSEE or BEARDSLEE or BEARDSLEY or BEARDSLY, or BARDSLEE.
 Aaron, wid. Sally. .... W 25237
  (Wid. was 73 in 1840.)
 Abijah. .... S 17278
 Abijah, wid. Elizabeth or Betsey B. .... W 8133
  BLWt. 5475-100 issued July 2, 1790. No papers.
  BLWt. 131-60-55.
 Abijah (1750-1789), wid. Drusilla. .... W 17289
 Benjamin, wid. Amelia. .... W 24649
 David, wid. Huldah. .... W 25238
 Elijah. .... S 45265
 Gershom, Conn. & Cont. .... S 44622
 Ichabod. .... S 12995
 James, wid. Ruth, BLWt. 15180-160-55. .... W 1364
  (Fairfield Co. in 1832.)
  (83 in 1840.)
 John, wid. Margaret. .... W 17265
  (Fairfield Co. in 1832; wid was 78 in 1840.)
 Joseph. .... S 14939
  (Fairfield Co. in 1832.)
 Josiah. .... S 16631
 Moses, Conn. & Cont. .... R 675
 Robert Chauncey, wid. Huldah, BLWt. 26687-160-55. .... W 20710
 Salmon Wheeler, wid. Abigail. .... W 23585
BEARDSLEE, Silas, former wid. Catherine Whitaker. .... W 3370
 Thaddeus (also given BARDSLEE). .... S 14952
 Thomas, Conn. & Cont. .... S 12142
  (85 in 1840.)
 Whitmore, wid Dolly .... W 24650
 William, wid. Elizabeth. .... W 23584
  (Also BARDSLEE.)
  (See also BIRDSEYE and BIRDSLEY.)
BEARS or BEER or BEERS or BIERCE or BIERS, or BERIS.
 Ann (see Samuel). .... S 17267
 Daniel. .... S 12132
 David. .... S 10365
 David, wid. Molly, BLWt. 2055-160-55. .... W 25212
 Ezra. .... S 12181
 Fanton or Fenton, Conn. Line. .... S 37750
 Gershom .... S 18314
  (Fairfield Co. in 1832.)
 Isaac. .... S 39182
 Isaac. .... S 12198
 Jabez. .... S 12171
 James. .... S 12209
 Jerusha, former wid. of Ambler, Squire, Cont. service, Conn. residence, BLWt. 194-160-55. ... W 2056
 Joel, Phebe Gardner or Gardiner, former wid., Conn. & Cont. service, BLWt. 3765-160-55. ..... W 19482
 John, Conn. & Cont. .... S 14949
  (Conn. Men, 1818, & 81 in 1840.)
  Only John Beers from any State.
 Joseph. .... S 16632
  (Fairfield Co. 1832.)
 Josiah, Conn. & Conn. Sea Service. .... S 12197
 Lewis, Conn. & Cont. .... S 31547
BEARS, Matthew, wid. Phebe. .... W 8355
  BLWt. 26317-160-55.
  (Fairfield Co. in 1832.)
 Nathan. .... S 12999
  (New Haven Co. in 1832.)
 Nathan. .... S 15335
  (Fairfield Co. in 1832.)

BEARS, Nathan, wid. Mary Conn. & Cont... W 17269
    BLWt. 147-200 Lieut. issued Oct. 6, 1789. No papers.
    (Soldier was pensioner in 1818, and 87 in 1840.)
  Phineas (Litchfield Co, 1832)... S 16635
    Jerusha, wid. of the above received a pension as former wid. of Squire Ambler (Cont.).. W 2846
  Samuel, Conn. & Mass... S 17267
    (Fairfield Co. in 1832.)
    Ann, wid. of the above, was pensioned as former wid of Thomas Phillips............... W 25233
  Silas... S 14935
    (Hartford Co. in 1832.)
  William... S 4265
  Zachariah or Zacheriah... S 4946
BEAUMONT. (See BEAMAN.)
BECKLEY, Daniel... S 12199
  Richard Cont. Conn. residence in 1818... S 39188
    (80 in 1840.)
  Solomon... S 31583
  Zebedee, Conn. & Cont. wid. Elizabeth... W 15579
    BLWt. 26807-160-55.
  (See also BUCKLEY.)
BECKWITH, Abner.. S 12158
    (New London Co. in 1832.)
  Amos Conn. & Cont. wid. Susanna.. W 17299
    (1818, Vt.)
  Jesse (New London Co. 1832)... S 16633
    (88 in 1840.)
  Job.. S 12168
  John, Conn. & Cont... S 28643
  Joseph.. S 9278
  Joseph, wid. Esther.. W 17286
  Lemuel.. S 12167
  Nathan, Cont. (Conn.).. S 39189
  Phineas... S 40745
  Roswell, Conn. & Cont.. S 10358
  Samuel, Conn., Cont. & Sea Service, Polly Tinker, former wid. of...................... W 25485
  Seth, wid. Esther.. W 25234
    (New London Co. in 1832.)
  Silas, Conn. & N. Y.. S 32115
  Thomas, Conn. & Conn. Sea Service.. S 12149
  Timothy, Conn. & Cont., wid. Lydia... W 25226
BEDEL. (See BEADLE.)
BEDEN or BEDON, William, Conn. & Cont.. S 44620
BEDIENT, John, wid. Betsey.. W 18576
  Mordecai or Mordica, wid. Polly... W 9354
    BLWt. 42882-160-55.
BEEBE, Amon, Conn. & Mass.. S 49302
    (1818, in N. Y.)
  Asa or Asahel, wid. Annabell Cont. (Conn.), BLWt. 1751-100........................... W 23576
  Daniel, wid. Jane.. S 21656
  David... S 16045
  David... S 40746
  Hopson, Conn., Mass. & N. Y... S 4262
  Joel.. S 40742
    BLWt. 5482-100, private issued Oct. 26, 1789. No papers
  Joseph.. S 12997
    (Fairfield Co. in 1832.)
  Lemuel.. S 9097
  Paul, Conn. & Cont., wid Mary.. W 17274
  Peter, Cont. (Conn.) & Green Mt. Boys.. S 12157
  Reuben... S 22638
  Richard, wid. Nancy, BLWt. 24608-160-55... W 2053
    (1818 in N. Y.)
  Richard Jeduthan, wid. Rachel, BLWt. 26330-160-55... W 5808
  Ruel.. S 12169
  William... R 705
  Zaccheus, Cont. (Conn.)... S 12196
BEEBEE, Comfort, wid. Lydia... W 17268
  David, wid. Sarah.. W 16838
  James, wid. Mehitabwl... W 10408
  Joseph.. S 17257
BEECHER or BUCHER, Jonathan.. S 36455
  Moses, Conn. & Privateer, wid. Dorcas.. R 707
  Nathan, Conn. & N. Y., wid. Lucy, BLWt. 6390-160-55... W 20707
  Wheeler.. S 14943
    (Litchfield Co. in 1832.)
BEEMAN. (See BEAMAN.)
BEERS. (See BEARS.)
BELCHER, Elisha, Conn. & Cont., wid. Lydia... W 9725
  Joseph, BLWt. 2113-100.
  Nathan, wid. Lucy.. W 17281
    (New London Co. in 1832; 82 in 1840.)
BELDEN, Azor, wid. Hannah, BLWt. 13737-160-55... W 8356
  Benjamin, wid. Sylvia.. W 5819
  Bildad, Cont. (Conn.).. S 40744
    (Conn. Men, 1818.)
  Charles... S 10355
  David... R 714
  Ezekiel Porter, wid. Mary... W 17280
    (Ezekiel in 1818, prob.)

BELDEN, John (Hartford Co. in 1832) .... S 12137
   Joshua .... S 15326
   Leonard, wid. Anna .... W 17275
   Othniel, Cont. & Cont., wid. Sarah .... W 21660
   Richard, Conn. & Cont .... S 40740
      (78 in 1840.)
   Seth, Cont. (Conn.) wid. Christian .... W 17266
      (Is it Christiana, who was 85 in 1840?)
BELDING, Abraham, Conn. & Cont., wid. Mary .... W 17285
   Othniel. (See BELDEN.)
   Simeon, BLWt. 142–200, Lieut. issued Sept. 1, 1789. No papers.
BELKNAP, Francis, Conn. & Vt .... S 31548
   Simeon, wid. Miriam or Miniam, BLWt. 4093–160–55 .... R 717
   (See also BELNAP.)
BELL, Abraham or Abram .... S 12195
   Andrew, Conn. & Cont .... S 12993
   Benjamin .... S 38538
   James (Conn. Men, 1818) .... S 37735
   Jesse .... S 22639
   Jonathan, wid. Agnes .... W 1362
      (Fairfield Co. 1832; 85 in 1840.)
   Oliver, Conn. & Vt .... S 23123
   Stephen .... S 16636
      (Fairfield Co. in 1832.)
   Thaddeus .... S 17274
      (Fairfield Co. in 1832; 81 in 1840.)
BELLAMY, Asa .... S 42086
      (Ohio in 1818.)
   Justus .... S 17838
   Matthew .... S 23117
BELLOWS, Isaac, wid. Mary, BLWt. 2354–160–55 .... W 18591
   Thomas, Conn., N. Y. & Vt., wid. Delia .... W 17284
BELNAP, Jesse, Cont. (Conn.) .... S 2068
BEMAN, BEMENT and BEMONT. (See BEAMAN.)
BENEDICT, Aaron (95 in 1840) .... S 12133
   Abraham .... S 10363
   Amos, Conn. & Mass., wid. Mary .... W 23568
   Darius (83 in 1840) .... S 37744
   Ebenezer (Fairfield Co. in 1832) .... S 12202
   Elisha, Conn. & N. Y .... S 12183
   Ezra .... S 12144
   Gamaliel (Fairfield Co. in 1832) .... S 12983
   Isaac (Fairfield Co. in 1832) .... S 17276
      (89 in 1840.)
   James (Fairfield Co. in 1832) .... S 17273
   John, wid. Reunah .... W 17287
   John, Conn. & Cont., wid. Chloe .... W 23599
   Jonah, wid. Elizabeth .... W 18587
   Jonathan, wid. Huldah, BLWt. 26709–160–55 .... W 23579
   Joshua .... S 23116
   Levi, wid. Elizabeth .... W 18589
      (N. Y. in 1818.)
   Nathaniel (Fairfield Co. in 1832) .... S 17272
   Nimrod (Fairfield Co. in 1832) .... S 15316
   Noah .... S 12987
   Noble .... BLWt. 1256–300
   Samuel .... S 6625
   Thomas .... S 21064
   William, wid. Ruth .... W 18578
BENHAM, Ebenezer, wid. Elizabeth .... W 25230
      (Hartford Co. in 1832.)
   Elihu (New Haven Co. in 1832) .... S 15748
   Isaac, Conn. & Cont .... S 15320
   James .... S 45247
   Jared, wid. Elizabeth .... W 17267
   John, wid. Elizabeth .... W 16636
   Joseph (New Haven Co. in 1832) .... S 17268
   Lemuel, wid. Margaret .... W 21666
   Lyman, wid. Lois .... W 25325
      (Lois was 85 in 1840.)
   Samuel .... S 45269
   Silas .... BLWt. 1295–200
   Thomas .... S 8068
BENJAMIN, Aaron, Conn. & U. S. A., wid. Dorothy .... W 25223
   BLWt. 149–200, Lieut., issued May 16, 1796. No papers. His pension was paid in D. C.
   and then transferred to Conn. (Fairfield).
      (Wid. was 72 in 1840.)
   Asa (of Preston, New London Co., 1832), wid. Mary, BLWt. 9489–160–55 .... W 23586
   Asa (Fairfield Co., 1832) .... S 12207
   Barzillai, Cont. (Conn.) & Mass, wid. Mary (Vt. in 1818) .... W 17291
   James, former widow of Mary Crampton .... W 20935
   Jesse (N. Y. in 1818) .... S 45275
   Phineas or Phinehas (N. Y. in 1818) .... S 45259
   Samuel (Hartford Co. in 1832) .... S 31546
      (83 in 1840.)
BENNET or BENNETT, Aaron .... S 19203
   Aaron .... R 748
   Ames or Amos, Conn. & Cont., wid. Wealthy .... W 3377
   Benjamin .... S 12187
   Benjamin .... S 22645

BENNET or BENNETT, Benjamin, wid. Mercy... W 10405
   Benjamin... S 38529
      Betty Bennet, wid. of above soldier, was pensioned as the former wid. of Wolcott, Patchen or Patchin, W 25326.
   Caleb, wid. Freelove... W 18579
   Cromwell... R 751
   Daniel.. S 37734
   Daniel, Conn., Navy & R. I., wid. Delight... W 24653
   David.. S 12201
   Ebenezer... S 23118
   Ebenezer... R 753
   Elias.. S 15319
   Elias, wid. Lydia.. W 2908
   Elijah, Conn. & Cont., wid. Rebecca.. W 20701
      (1818 in Vt.)
   Ezekiel, Cont. (Conn.).. S 45253
      (N. Y. in 1818.)
   Isaac (N. Y. in 1818).. S 45249
   Jabez, wid. Abigail... W 25328
   James, Conn. & N. Y., wid. Catharine.. W 16191
      BLWt. 150-200, Lieut., issued April 9, 1791. No papers.
      (N. Y. in 1818.)
   Jeremiah, Conn. & N. Y. wid. Lois... W 23591
   Jesse, Conn. & N. Y... S 12184
   Jesse, wid. Temperance.. W 17263
      (Wid. was 95 in 1840.)
   John.. S 23119
   John, Conn. & R. I.. S 23541
   John, Cont. (Conn.)... S 45252
   Joseph.. S 37742
   Joseph, Conn., N. Y. & Vt... S 21639
   Josiah.. S 12136
      Spelled his name BENNIT.
      (Fairfield Co. in 1832.)
      (74 in 1840.)
   Joshua, wid. Esther... W 17298
      (Conn. Men, pensioner, 1818.)
      (Wid. was 79 in 1840.)
   Miles... S 12166
   Nathan.. S 45258
   Oliver, wid. Catharine.. W 4886
   Rufus, wid. Martha.. W 3378
      (Penna. in 1818.)
   Samuel.. S 10368
   Samuel.. R 21769
   Samuel (also spelled BANNET).. S 15747
   Stephen... S 37760
   Stephen, wid. Hannah.. W 25236
   Stephen, wid. Mary.. W 2906
   Thaddeus, wid. Martha... W 17278
   Thomas.. S 12143
   William... S 23538
   William, wid. Elizabeth, BLWt. 26061-160-55.. W 25235
      (Elizabeth was 73 in 1840.)
   Wolcott, wid. Joanna.. W 17264
BENTLEY or BENTLY, Azel.. S 29007
   Charles, Conn. & Cont., wid. Hannah... W 14298
   Elisha, Conn., Mass. & R. I... R 783
   George, wid. Lucy... W 17272
   John.. S 45262
BENTON, Adoniram, Conn. & Cont., wid. Betsey... W 1360
   (New Hamp. in 1818.)
   BLWt. 19808-160-55.
   Chandler... BLWt. 2430-100
   Elijah or Elisha, Conn. & Cont., wid. Sarah... R 787
      He was living in 1818 in N. H. and was a Rev. pensioner. Signed his name Elijah. She called him Elisha; her claim was rejected.
   Jacob (Tolland Co. in 1832), wid. Sarah... W 17276
      (80 in 1840.)
   Joel, Conn. & Vt., wid. Elizabeth... W 20711
   Jonathan.. S 29004
   Nathaniel W., wid. Susannah... W 16186
      (N. Y. in 1818.)
   Noah, wid. Phebe.. W 18574
   BLWt. 29037-160-55.
   (New Haven Co. in 1832.)
   Samuel, Conn. & Mass., wid. Mary.. W 5807
   Selah, BLWt. 137-300, Capt., issued Nov. 19, 1792. No papers.
   Zadock, wid. Lydia.. W 3926
   Zebulon, Conn. & Cont... S 34007
BERIS. (See BEARS.)
BERNARD, Phares, wid. Huldah... W 25229
BERRAY. (See BERRY.) (See also BARNARD.)
BERRY, Asahel, wid. Abigail.. W 25225
   Barnabas.. S 12186
   Kellog (called Dr Kellog)... S 17279
      (Litchfield Co. in 1832; 77 in 1840.)
   Lemuel (Litchfield Co. in 1832)... S 10360
   Seth, wid. Anna, BLWt. 30610-160-55... W 24646

BETTS, Daniel (Fairfield Co. in 1832)... S 17275
    (84 in 1840.)
  David (Conn. Men, in 1818).. S 37737
  Hezekiah, wid. Grace... W 29929
    Dau. Juliette obtained the pension.
    (He was pensioner in 1818.)
    (Fairfield Co. in 1832.)
  Isaiah.. S 17277
  Isaiah, wid. Hannah.. W 23592
  Peter, wid. Bathsheba, BLWt. 26569-160-55.. W 25222
  Peter, wid. Phebe, Conn. & Cont.. W 20700
  Reuben... S 14947
  Silas.. R 810
  Stephen, Conn. & Cont.. S 37749
    BLWt. 139-200 Capt. issued Mch. 18, 1789. No papers.
    (Conn. Men, 1818.)
  Uriah, wid. Lucy, BLWt. 27619-160-55... W 476
  William Maltby, Cont. (Conn.)... R 811
BEVANS or BEVINS, Ebenezer, Conn. & Cont. Dis. No papers.
  Henry, Cont. & Conn... S 37754
    (Conn. Men, 1818.)
BEWEL, Matthew, wid. Mary (see also BUEL)... W 20810
BIBBENS or BIBBINS, Benjamin, Cont. (Conn.) & War of 1812, BLWt. 44801-160-55.......... R 819
BICKNELL, Josiah... S 37777
  (Conn. Men, 1818.)
BIDLACK, Benjamin, Cont. (Conn.) & N. J... S 39991
  Philemon, Conn. & Penna., wid. Sarah, BLWt. 26086-160-55.. W 4895
BIDLOCK. (See BIDLACK.)
BIDWELL, Allen, Cont. (Conn.), wid. Anna.. W 18600
  (New Hamp. in 1818.)
  Eleazer (88 in 1840)... S 14955
  Elisha.. S 12221
  John, Conn. & Cont., Sarah Potter, former wid. of... W 16684
  Ozias (Conn. Men in 1818).. S 37766
  Phineas... S 12220
  Samuel, Cont. (Conn.) & Mass.. R 826
  Thomas, Conn. & Cont., wid. Elizabeth... W 21672
    (Wid. was 83 in 1840.)
BIERCE. (See BASS and also BEARS.)
BIGELOW or BIGLOW, Eli, Cont. & Conn... S 37768
  Frederick.. S 37767
  Joel, wid. Lucretia.. W 1535
  Josiah, wid. Lucy.. W 20716
  Sarah, former wid. of Avery, Simeon, Cont. (Conn.).. W 23615
    BLWt. 5210-160-55.
  Timothy.. S 2074
BIGLOW. (See BIGELOW.)
BIGSBY. (See BIXBY.)
BILL, Abiel (New London Co. in 1832)... S 22643
  Azariah, Conn. & N. Y... S 17283
    (New London Co. in 1832.)
  Benajah, Conn. & Privateer, wid. Content.. W 1730
    (New London Co. in 1832.)
  Daniel (Hartford Co. in 1832)... S 15751
  Eleazer (New London Co. in 1832).. S 18316
    (81 in 1840.)
  Elijah, Conn., Cont. & Privateer.. S 12218
BILL, Jonathan (N. Y. in 1818)... S 12222
  Jonathan, wid. Hannah... R 834
  Joshua, Conn. & Privateer... S 17282
    (New London Co. in 1832, 78 in 1840.)
  Phineas, wid. Mary.. W 16844
  Roswell or Rozzell... S 37771
  (See also BILLS.)
BILLINGS, Benjamin, wid. Wealthy, BLWt. 541-160-55.. W 1702
  Elisha, wid. Lucretia.. W 17392
    (Wid. was 91 in 1840.)
  Ezekiel, Conn., Cont. & Navy, Privateer & R. I.. R 837
  James, Conn. & Cont... S 45285
    (N. Y. in 1818.)
  John, Conn. & Cont., wid. Olive... W 23601
  Joseph, Conn. & Cont.. S 12210
    (Vt. in 1818.)
  Matthew, Conn. & Cont... S 45282
    (N. Y. in 1818.)
  Stephen, BLWt. 135-300, Capt., issued Oct. 26, 1795, to Joseph Emerson, Assignee. No papers.
    Anna Dennis, former wid. of... W 25523
BILLS, Sylvanus, wid. Lydia.. W 10414
  BLWt. 36611-160-55.
  (New Haven Co. in 1832, 74 in 1840.)
  (See also BILL.)
BINGHAM, Aaron (N. Y. in 1818).. S 45280
  Abel (Conn. Men, 1818)... S 37772
  Alvan, Conn. & N. H., wid. Elizabeth... W 5220
  Chester, Conn. & Mass... S 37765
    (Conn. Men, 1818.)
  Elias, Conn. & Cont... S 38543
    (Vt. in 1818.)
  Gurdon (Conn. Men, 1818).. S 37762

BINGHAM, Ithamar, wid. Hannah... W 17301
    Jeremiah.. S 12211
    Johnson, wid. Anna, BLWt. 26556-160-55... W 18595
    Maltiah, wid. Marcy... W 21667
        (Mercy was 97 in 1840.)
    Ozias... S 22120
    Samuel... S 12230
    Silas, Conn. & Vt.. S 2076
    Thomas... S 38550
BINNS, Thomas, BLWt. 466-100.
BIRCH. (See BIRGE, BURCH, and BURGE.)
BIRCHARD, Daniel, wid. Anna, BLWt. 26920-160-55... W 1379
    (Fairfield Co. in 1832; 80 in 1840.)
    Elias... S 12216
    (See also BURCHARD.)
BIRDSEYE and BIRDSLEY, Ezra.. S 14954
    (Fairfield Co. in 1832.)
    Thaddeus, wid. Helen, BLWt. 10242-160-55.. W 25247
    (See also BEARDSLEY.)
BIRGE, David, Conn. & Cont. (Vt. in 1818).. S 38549
    Hosea, Cont. (Conn.) (N. Y. in 1818).. S 12224
    James (Litchfield Co. in 1832).. S 10364
        (82 in 1840.)
    John, wid. Lucy, BLWt. 26631-160-55... W 8362
    John, wid. Ruhama, BLWt. 9471-160-55.. W 17309
    (See also BURGE.)
BISBY. (See BIXBY.)
BISHOP, Abraham, wid. Charity, BLWt. 26563-160-55.. W 5822
    Austin, wid. Annah.. W 17306
        (Hartford Co. in 1832.)
    David... S 6652
    Hezekiah, wid. Polly, BLWt. 50857-160-55.. W 2587
    Jacob (Fairfield Co. in 1832)... S 17280
        (85 in 1840.)
    James... S 16641
    James, wid. Elizabeth... W 25241
        (Wid. 71 in 1840.)
    Jared... R 860
    Jared, Sarah Foot or Foote, former wid. of.. W 17915
    Jesse, Conn. & Mass... S 41437
        (Vt. in 1818.)
    Joel, d. Oct. 23, 1843.. R 862
    Joel, wid. Phebe.. R 864
    John (N. Y. in 1818).. S 45281
        BLWt. 1667-100.
    John (New Haven Co. in 1832).. S 12219
    John, wid. Sarah (pensioner, 1818).. W 17303
    Joseph, wid. Ruth BLWt. 10229-160-55.. W 25245
    Josiah... S 29633
    Moses, wid. Jerusha... W 20714
    Nathaniel, BLWt. 231-200, Lieut. issued Dec. 31, 1795; also recorded as above under BLWt.
        269-2659. No papers.
    Newman (Mass. in 1818), BLWt. 24614-160-55.. S 29634
    Richard, wid. Mercy, BLWt. 815-160-55... W 23613
        (N. Y. in 1818.)
    Seth (New London Co. in 1818)... S 12212
        (82 in 1840.)
    Simeon, Conn. & Cont... S 19910
        (Conn. Men, p. 648.)
    Stephen.. S 37769
    Thalmeno, BLWt. 40-100.
    Thomas, d. 1801, wid. Amy... W 17305
    Thomas F.. S 14953
        (1818, & Hartford Co. in 1832; 76 in 1840.)
    Timothy.. S 28646
BISSEL or BISSELL, Benjamin.. S 12214
    Benjamin... S 37774
    Benjamin, wid. Elizabeth.. W 5825
    Calvin (Litchfield Co. in 1832)... S 14956
    Daniel, wid. Theoda... W 23604
        (N. Y. in 1818.)
    Daniel, Conn. & U. S. A. until 1821, wid. Deborah....................................... W 9735
    Eben Fitch... S 18315
        (Eben F. in Conn. Men.)
    Elisha, wid. Rhoda.. W 17304
    Ezekiel (Litchfield Co. in 1832).. S 31553
    George... S 12227
    George, wid. Lois... R 871
    Jerijah (Hartford in 1832).. S 24064
    John, wid. Huldah... R 870
    Lemuel, wid. Sally, BLWt. 26639-160-55.. W 520
        (Hartford Co. in 1832.)
BISSELL, Leverett, Conn. & Cont., wid. Sarah, BLWt. 28540-160-55........................... W 25248
    Noadiah.. S 22647
    Ozias, Cont. & Conn... S 37764
        (Conn. Men, 1818.)
    Return (Litchfield Co. 1832).. S 15257
    Thomas, wid. Eleanor, BLWt. 57522-160-55.. W 12295
        (Hartford Co. in 1832; 82 in 1840.)

BIXBEE, BIXBEY, BIXBY and BISBY, and BIGSBY.
  Aaron, wid. Mary .... R 877
     (Windham Co. in 1832; 79 in 1840.)
  Benjamin, Conn. Cont. & Mass .... S 42618
     (In Ohio in 1818.)
  Elias, wid. Grace .... W 20718
     (N. Y. in 1818.)
  Jacob (New Hampshire in 1818) .... S 49305
  Joseph .... S 45284
  Moses, wid. Mary or Molly .... W 25240
     (Windham Co. in 1832; wid. was 72 in 1840.)
  Solomon, wid. Lucy, BLWt. 56972-160-55 .... W 23607
BLACK, Benjamin, wid. Patty .... W 24974
  also known as SIMMONS.
BLACKISTON OR BLACKSTONE, John .... S 14963
  (New Haven Co. in 1832.)
BLACKLEACH, John .... S 37786
  BLWt. 156-200 issued Nov. 19, 1792. No papers.
BLACKMAN, BLOCKMAN, BLAKEMAN, BLECKMAN, BLEEKMAN.
  Chloe, former wid. of Hill, David .... R 15052
  Dan (N. Y. in 1818) .... S 45286
  Daniel, wid. Mary .... W 16848
  David, Conn. & Cont .... S 37791
  Edward, wid. Hannah .... W 25249
  Elijah, Cont. (Conn.) .... S 42622
  Elisha .... S 2084
  Enoch, wid. Lydia .... W 2059
  James, wid. Ann .... W 17312
     (Fairfield Co. in 1832.)
  Jonathan (Mass. in 1818) .... S 34038
  Nehemiah, wid. Hannah was pensioned as former wid. of Terrill, Asahel, Conn. & N. Y.... W 17311
  Phoebe, former wid. of Northrop, Joshua .... W 10419
  Sampson (Conn. Men in 1818) .... S 37787
  Samuel, Conn. & Cont .... S 37793
     (Conn. Men, 1818.)
  Zachariah (N. Y. in 1818) .... S 45295
  Zachariah, Conn. & Cont., wid. Sarah .... W 20729
     (Wid. was 83 in 1840.)
BLACKMARR or BLACKMORE, John, Conn. & Navy. wid. Silence .... W 23637
BLACKSLE, BLACKSLEE, BLAKELEY, BLAKELY, BLAKESLEE, BLAKSLEY.
  Abel, wid. Mary D., BLWt. 26691-160-55 .... W 8369
  Ambrose .... R 907
  Caleb (Mass. in 1818) .... S 34034
  Eber, Conn. Sea Service .... S 23129
  Enos (Conn. Men, p 649). Dis. No papers.
  James .... S 2085
  Jared, wid. Rhoda .... W 20722
     (N. Y. in 1818.)
  Jesse .... S 37792
  Moses, Conn. & Cont .... S 12232
  Obed, Conn. Cont. & Mass .... S 44629
  Philip .... S 38610
  Rebecca, former wid. of Hull, Henry .... W 3332
     BLWt. 2470-100.
  Samuel .... S 45293
  Samuel, Conn. & Vt .... S 16052
     (Litchfield Co. in 1832.)
  Zealous (Conn. Men, 1818) .... S 37789
BLAKE, Christopher (N. H. in 1818) .... S 45598
  David .... S 23128
  Elijah (Litchfield Co. in 1832) .... S 14964
  Reuben, wid. Eunice, BLWt. 2184-160-55 .... W 25250
  William, Sarah Miller, former wid. of .... W 10502
BLAKEMAN, BLECKMAN and BLEEKMAN. (See BLACKMAN.)
BLAKSLEE, or BLAKESLEY. (See BLACKSLEE.)
BLANCHAR, Jedediah (see also BLANCHARD) .... S 14961
BLANCHARD, Elias, Conn. & Cont .... S 12247
  (Windham Co. in 1832.)
  Jacob (Conn. Men, 1818) .... S 37784
  William, wid. Sarah .... W 17320
     (Conn. Men, p 649.)
     (See also BLANCHAR.)
BLANDIN, Jonathan, wid. Submit .... W 1704
BLANDIN or BLANDEN, Samuel, Conn. & Mass .... S 10339
BLATCHFORD, John C. (Va. in 1818) .... S 37788
BLIN or BLINN, Justus (Conn. Men, 1818) .... S 37790
  Simeon, Conn. & N. Y .... S 45202
  William .... S 41444
BLISH, Azuba, former wid. of Ransom, Joseph .... W 25255
  BLWt. 47614-160-55.
  Ezra (Conn. Men, 1818.) .... S 37785
     (72 in 1840.)
BLISS, Dan, wid. Eunice .... W 23626
  (New London Co. in 1832.)
  David, wid. Jane .... W 5829
  Eli, Conn. & Cont .... S 34046
  James, wid. Mehitable, BLWt. 814-160-55 .... W 9728
  John, Mary Freeman, former wid. of .... R 3781
  John, wid. Reliance .... W 18609

BLISS, Samuel	S 18329
Samuel, wid. Elizabeth	W 17314
(Wid. was 75 in 1840.)	
William, Conn. & R. I.	S 4953
BLODGET and BLODGETT, Artemas or Artomes	S 45287
(N. Y. in 1818.)	
Abisha, Conn. & U. S. A.	S 15752
Benjamin	S 16050
Samuel, wid. Abigail	W 17316
(Wid. was 87 in 1840.)	
Silas, Conn. & Mass	S 44631
(Lieut. in N. Y. in 1818.)	
BLOGGETT. (See BLODGETT.)	
BLOSS, Joseph	S 21071
Zadok, Conn. & N. H.	R 960
BLOUNT or BLUNT, Asher	S 29016
Elisha, wid. Sally	W 16850
BLUSH, Joseph	R 969
BOARDMAN or BORDMAN, Amos	S 21077
Elijah, wid. Mercy	W 10433
Elijah, wid. Nancy	W 15754
Elijah, Cont. (Conn.), wid. Mary Ann	W 25262
Jonas, wid. Elizabeth	W 23549
Jonathan (N. Y. in 1818)	S 46204
Josiah, wid. Susannah	W 16854
Moses. Discharged. No papers.	
Samuel Allen, wid. Catherine	R 12576
Seth (Conn. Men, 1818)	S 36419
Timothy	S 22128
BOGUE or BOOGE, Jeffrey A., wid. Freedom	W 18638
(See also BOGE.)	
BOLLES, BOLLS or BOWLES, James	S 36420
Joseph, wid. Betsey	W 17327
BOND, Jacob, Conn., N. J. & N. Y.	S 12273
BONFOY or BONFY, Benanuel, wid. Concurrence	W 17330
(Pensioner in 1818; wid. 78 in 1840.)	
Henry, Conn. & Cont.	S 12266
(N. Y. in 1818.)	
BOOGE or BOUGE, Samuel Cook, wid. Tryphena	R 1013
(See also BOGUE.)	
BOONE, Deidamia, former wid. of Davison, Ezra	W 25260
BOOTH, David, wid. Betsey, BLWt. 26719-160-55	W 1370
Erastus (N. Y. in 1818)	S 44644
Gideon, former wid. Hannah Lewis, BLWt. 5378-160-55	W 26206
Isaac	S 14983
Isaiah, Conn. & Cont. wid. Polly, BLWt. 8174-160-55	W 1809
John, wid. Sarah	R 1022
(New Haven Co. in 1832.)	
Lucretia, former wid. of Chapin, Frederick	W 18626
Nathaniel	S 10381
Ruth, former wid. of Jones, Isaac	W 20741
Samuel	S 12272
Silas	S 14969
Thomas (Hartford Co. in 1832)	S 14970
Walter, Conn. & Cont.	S 36422
(Conn. Men, 1818.)	
BORCE. (See BARCE.)	
BORDEN, Benjamin, Conn. & R. I., wid. Sarah	R 1028
Joshua, wid. Betsey	W 16855
BORRES or BURROUS, John Proctor, wid. Lydia	W 18636
(In Conn. Men, Barres.)	
BOSSET or BOSSETT, Isaac (Conn. Men, 1818)	S 36426
(Under name of BUSSETT; 82 in 1840.)	
BOSTWICK, Amos, Cont. (Conn.)	S 45312
(Ensign, N. Y. in 1818.)	
Andrew, Cont. (Conn.)	S 36915
(Conn. Men. 1818.)	
David	S 36418
BLWt. 2193-160-55.	
Doctor	S 2384
Ebenezer, BLWt. 32-100	S 42090
(Ohio in 1818.)	
Elisha, Conn. & Cont.	S 10376
(Litchfield Co. in 1832.)	
Elizur or Eliezer	S 4269
Jonathan	S 14978
(Litchfield Co. in 1832.)	
Levi, wid. Anne or Anna	W 21699
(Wid. was 84 in 1840.)	
Medad, wid. Mary M., BLWt. 34591-160-55	R 1042
Nathan	S 40009
(Ensign in 1818.)	
Oliver. Discharged. No papers.	
Reuben	S 19551
BOSWORTH, Allen, wid. Sarah, BLWt. 50856-160-55	R 1048
Daniel, Conn. & Cont., wid. Rachel	W 447
Jacob, BLWt. 1625-100	S
(79 in 1840.)	
Nathaniel, Conn., Cont. & Vt.	S 38561

BOTSFORD or BOTCHFORD, Aaron, wid. Comfort.. W 23654
    Clement, wid. Mary.. W 20742
        (Wid. was 82 in 1840.)
    Eli, wid. Polly... W 25264
    Samuel (New Haven Co. in 1832)... S 31560
    Simeon, wid. Esther.. R 1051
BOTTOM or BOTTUM, Abel.. S 45305
    Amaziah, wid. Wealthy... W 17322
    Asahel or Asel (New London Co. 1832).. S 15341
    Darius (New Haven Co. in 1832).. S 14982
    Jabez L.. S 14868
    John, BLWt. 1396-100.. S 46459
BOUGE. (See BOOGE.)
BOUGHTON, BOUTON, BOWTON, Azor Cont. (Conn.), BLWt. 5537 issued in 1798......... S 45310
        (N. Y. in 1818.)
    David, wid. Dinah... W 15755
        (In N. Y. in 1818.)
    Eleazer.. S 32130
    Joseph, wid. Zeruah... W 21698
    Matthew, Conn., Cont. & N. Y... S 10378
    Samuel, wid. Elizabeth, BLWt. 36512-100-55.. W 25271
        (Fairfield Co. in 1832.)
    Seth (86 in 1840).. S 12262
    William, wid. Sarah... W 17324
        (Wid. was 88 in 1840.)
BOURN, Shubael... S 22055
    (See also BOWEN.)
BOUTELL or BOUTTELL, James, wid. Chloe... W 20740
    Joseph, wid. Molly, BLWt. 36609-160-55.. W 893
        (New Hamp. in 1818.)
BOUTON. (See BOUGHTON.)
BOW, Edward, wid. Ruth... W 24776
    Samuel, wid. Mary... W 25209
BOWEN, Benjamin, Conn. & R. I... S 15340
    Christopher, Cont. (Conn.), wid. Betsey, BLWt. 26803-160-55................................ W 1802
        (Mass. in 1818.)
    Eleazer (Windham Co. in 1832)... S 17290
        (86 in 1840.)
    John, wid. Catharine.. W 20747
        (Wid. was 79 in 1840.)
    Shubael (also spelled BOURN).. S 22055
BOWER or BOWERS, Alpheus.. S 14977
        (Windham Co. in 1832; 85 in 1840.)
    Benajah or Banaiah... S 36424
    Ephraim (Conn. Men in 1818).. S 36423
    Joab, wid. Elizabeth, BLWt. 30-60-55.. W 8231
    John, wid. Sarah.. R 1073
    Jonathan, wid. Rebecca, BLWt. 27666-160-55... W 25265
        (Conn. Men, p. 648; wid. was 82 in 1840.)
    Olive, former wid. of Kelly, John... W 393
    Zephaniah or Zepheniah (N. Y., 1818)... S 45306
BOYD, Joseph (N. Y. in 1818)... S 45299
BOYNTON, Bela (Tolland Co. in 1832)... S 18322
        (87 in 1840.)
    Eunice, former wid. of Rogers, Chester... W 20744
BRACE, Charles, wid. Perses... R 1363
    David... S 16658
    Elijah, wid. Catherine... W 17339
    Jeffery, called also, Stiles, Jeff.. S 41461
    Joseph, wid. Lois, BLWt. 34525-160-55... W 25298
BRACKET, BRACKETT or BROCKETT, Benajah..................................... BLWt. 962-100
    Hezekiah, wid. Asenath, BLWt. 29-60-55... W 8167
    (See also BROCKETT.)
BRADFORD, Elisha, wid. Lucy.. W 24676
        (N. Y. in 1818.)
    Hannah, former wid. of Lyon, Ephraim.. W 17366
    Thomas, Conn. & Cont., wid. Philena.. W 17351
        (She was 70 in 1840.)
BRADLEY, Aaron, Conn. & Cont... S 17302
    Alexander, wid. Lydia... W 17336
        (She was 87 in 1840.)
    Alling... S 36447
        (Conn. Men, 1818.)
    Aner, wid. Anna... W 17335
        (Conn. Men, p. 648.)
        (Wid. was 82 in 1840.)
    Ashbel, wid. Chloe, BLWt. 8172-160-55.. W 25295
    Daniel, Conn. & U. S. A. until 1802.. S 36442
        BLWt. 148-200, Lieut. issued Mch. 13, 1790. No papers.
    Daniel, BLWt. 2478-100... S 36443
    David... S 34099
    Dimon, wid. Beulah... W 14380
        (Mass. in 1818.)
    Elihu, wid. Sybel.. W 16864
    Elijah... S 15343
    Elijah, Conn. & Privateer, wid. Esther... W 18664
    Elisha, Conn. & Vt.. S 12310
    Elisha, wid. Ann S... R 1129

BRADLEY, Gilead, Conn. & Cont... S 17293
   (New Haven Co. in 1832; 83 in 1840.)
  Joseph, Conn. & Vt.. S 12347
  Lemuel.. S 14990
   (New Haven Co. in 1832.)
  Moses... S 23138
  Nathan.. S 12301
   (Fairfield Co. in 1832.)
  Nathaniel... R 1138
  Philip, Burr, wid. Ruth... W 21702
   BLWt. 131-500, Lieut. Col., issued May 14, 1796. No papers.
  Reuben, Conn. & Mass... R 1139
  Stephen, wid. Mehitable... W 25301
   (New Haven Co. in 1832.)
  Sturgis... R 1140
  Thaddeus or Thaddeus, wid. Parnal, BLWt. 6394-160-55.......................... W 5942
  Thomas.. R 1141
BRADSHAW, James... S 29023
BRAINARD, BRAINERD, BRANARD or BRAYNARD.
  Amos, wid. Jerusha, BLWt. 27572-160-55.. W 5234
  Ansel, Conn. & War of 1812, wid. Mary... W 8168
   BLWt. 83430-120-55; & BLWt. 70805-40-55.
  Bezaleel, wid. Lydia.. W 23671
   (Wid. was 82 in 1840.)
  Church, Conn. & N. H... S 29032
  Daniel.. S 3099
  Elijah.. S 10105
  Jabez... S 4968
  Othniel (N. Y. in 1818)... S 44683
  Seba, wid. Anna... R 1146
  Simon (Middlesex Co. in 1832)... S 17296
  Stephen, wid. Rachel.. W 20794
  Timothy, wid. Sarah... W 14392
BRAMAN or BRAYMAN, Daniel (Conn. Men, 1818).................................... S 46777
  Daniel (New London Co. in 1832)... S 12276
  James... S 18746
  Sylvanus, Conn. & Mass.. S 18743
BRAMBLE, Robert, wid. Hannah.. W 25297
  (New London Co. in 1832; 78 in 1840. Only Robert Bramble in files from any State.)
BRANARD. (See BRAINARD.)
BRANCH, Samuel, wid. Ruth, BLWt. 26155-160-55................................... W 2717
  Walter, Eunice Snow, former wid. of... W 4076
  William, wid. Lucretia, BLWt. 73-60-55.. W 1544
   (N. Y. in 1818.)
BRASHER, John, Conn. & N. Y.. S 1605
BRATTLE, Dick, Conn. & Mass... R 1167
BRAY, Sampson... S 28659
BRAYNARD. (See BRAINARD.)
BREED, Jabez Sally Wheeler, former wid. of, BLWt. 1911-160-55................... W 19621
  Joseph, Conn., Navy & R. I., wid. Mercy....................................... W 2751
  Oliver.. S 12298
  Stephen, wid. Esther.. W 16511
BREWER, Daniel, Conn. & Cont.. S 36435
  (Conn. Men, 1818.)
  Daniel, wid. Molly.. W 25302
  Lois, former wid. of Ebenezer Drake... W 20791
BREWSTER, Darius, Conn. Sea Service... S 30900
  Elias (New London Co. in 1832).. S 15765
  Elisha, Cont. (Conn.), wid. Sarah H... W 14394
   (Conn. Men, 1818. Mass.)
  Frederick... S 15346
   (New London Co. in 1832; 77 in 1840.)
  Hezekiah (Conn. Men, 1818).. S 36439
  Joseph, Conn., Cont., Mass. & R. I.. S 12286
  Justus, Conn. & Cont., wid. Joanna, BLWt. 7099-160-55......................... W 14354
  Morgan.. R 1189
  Nathaniel (see claim of Anna, wid. of Isaac Holmes)........................... W 7769
  Zadoc, Conn. Sea Service, wid. Lucy... W 23685
BRIANT or BRYANT, Jacob, Conn. & Vt.. R
  (See also BRYANT.)
BRIDGEMAN, Gideon, Conn., Green Mt. Boys & N. H................................ S 15002
BRIDGES, Samuel, wid. Content, BLWt. 31306-160-55............................... W 10299
BRIGGS, Abial or Joseph, Conn. & R. I., wid. Jane............................... W 20764
  Ephraim, Cont. (Conn.), wid. Dilla.. R 1199
  Ephraom, Cont. (Conn.) & Vt., wid. Rhoda...................................... W 23710
  Ezra (Conn. Men, 1818).. S 46788
  Isaac, wid. Lucy Ann.. W 23664
   (Conn. Men, 1818.)
  James (N. Y. in 1818)... S 44676
  John.. S 12331
  Joseph. (See Abial.)
  Joshua, wid. Tryphena... W 20753
   (N. Y. in 1818.)
  Joshua, Conn. & N. Y.. R 1203
  Owen, Conn. & Mass., wid. Margery... W 18644
  Polly, former wid. of Seth Holcomb.. R 1206
  Stephen, wid. Deborah... W 17337
  William... S 12281
  Zephaniah (Fairfield Co. in 1832)... S 12336

BRIGHAM, Don C., wid. Polly .... W 17350
    (Hartford Co. in 1832, as Dow C. 77 in 1840.)
  Elnathan (Tolland Co. in 1832) .... S 14987
  Jonathan .... S 22665
  Mary, former wid. of Elisha Johnson .... W 17348
  Paul, wid. Lydia .... W 23695
BRIGHTMAN, Henry, wid. Mary .... W 25293
  (wid. was 74 in 1840.)
BRINSMADE, Cyrus, wid. Sally, BLWt. 26611-160-55 .... W 2559
  (Fairfield Co. in 1832.)
BRISCO OR BRISCOE, Nathaniel .... S 12313
BRISTALL or BRISTOL, John .... R 1217
BRISTER or BRISTEE, John, wid. Lilly, BLWt. 5461 issued 1790 .... W 20772
  (Candes Lilly was 83 in 1840.)
  (See also BRISTOR.)
BRISTOL, Austin .... R 1218
  Bezaleel, wid. Mary .... W 20781
  David (New Haven Co. in 1832) .... S 17300
    (76 in 1840. Only David in files from any State.)
  Eli (also given BRISTOLL) .... S 22664
  Gideon (New Haven Co. in 1832) .... S 12323
    (Only Gideon Bristol in files from any State.)
  John. (See BRISTALL.)
  Jonathan (New Haven Co. in 1832) .... S 12288
    (Only Jonathan from any State.)
  Nathaniel, Conn. & Cont. .... S 12341
  Reuben, Conn. & Cont. .... S 12316
BRISTOR, Stephen .... S 36437
  (Given Brister in Conn. Men, 1818.)
  (See also BRISTEE or BRISTER.)
BROCK or BROCKE, John, wid. Hannah .... W 20767
  (Vt. in 1818.)
BROCKET, BROCKETT, BROCKIT, or BROCKITT.
  Enoch .... S 12337
  Giles (New Haven Co. in 1832) .... S 16661
    (79 in 1840. Only Giles Brockett from any State.)
  Hezekiah, wid. Asenath. (See BRACKETT.)
  Isaac (Conn. Men, 1818) .... S 36441
  Joel, wid. Elizabeth .... W 10452
    (New Haven Co. in 1832; 80 in 1840.)
  (See also BRACKETT.)
BROCKWAY, Asa (Litchfield Co. in 1832) .... S 15350
  Benjamin (Conn. Men in 1818) .... S 36428
  Ephraim .... S 12278
  Gideon, wid. Tryphena .... W 20786
  John, wid. Irene, BLWt. 19716-160-55 .... W 25280
    (New London Co. in 1832; 85 in 1840. Only John Brockway in files from any State.)
  Pardon, BLWt. 40907-160-55 .... W 12340
  Sarah, former wid. of Isaac Sill .... W 17358
  Semilius, Bridget Ely, former wid. of. This soldier was the first husband of Bridget Ely, and
    died in service. (See claim of Ely, Abner, Conn. W 21056.)
  Zebulon (New London Co. in 1832) .... S 31565
BROGA, Andrew (Mass. in 1818) .... S 34086
BROMLEY. (See BRUMBLEY.)
BRONSON, BROWNSON, or BRUNSON, Asa .... S 36433
  (Conn. Men, 1818.)
  Asahel (80 in 1840) .... S 12289
  Ashbel .... R 1359
  Elijah, wid. Delia or Deliverance .... W 17363
  Isaac .... S 40027
  Isaac, wid. Thankful .... W 10470
    (New Haven Co. in 1832; 78 in 1840.)
  Isaac, Cont. (Conn.), wid. Anne .... W 5932
    Soldier received no pension, but BLWt. 152-300 was issued to Isaac Brunson, Surg's.
    Mate, Col. Sheldon's reg't. of Cavalry, July 28, 1789, per Richard Smith, Assignee. No
    papers. Wid. was resident of N. Y. when she obtained her pension.
  Jabez, wid. Marilla .... W 25303
    (Tolland Co. in 1832; wid. was 71 in 1840.)
  Joel (Hartford Co. in 1832) .... S 15006
  Joseph (N. Y. in 1818) .... S 44685
  Joseph .... S 12295
  Levi .... S 2100
  Luman (Vt. in 1818) .... S 49297
  Michael, wid. Eunice .... W 20773
  Pheneas or Phinehas .... S 32137
  Reuben, wid. Huldah .... W 25300
    (Litchfield Co. in 1832.)
  Samuel (Hartford Co. in 1832) .... S 16055
  Selah, wid. Anna, BLWt. 61329-160-55 .... W 9367
    (New Haven Co. in 1832.)
    (Soldier was 77 in 1840.)
  Silas, wid. Sally .... W 17365
  Titus, wid. Hannah .... W 17356
    (Wid. was 85 in 1840.)
BROOKER, Isaac .... S 29653
  Samuel, wid. Polly, BLWt. 8151-160-55 .... W 5945
BROOKS, Ahira, BLWt. 26700-160-55 .... S 29037
  Asa (N. Y. in 1818), wid. Betsey .... W 16193
  Caleb E., wid. Jane E. .... R 1244
  David, wid. Jane .... W 4148

BROOKS, Jabez-(Mass. in 1818), wid. Rhoda.. W 15601
    James.. R 1249
    James, Conn. & Cont., wid. Lydia.. W 3929
        (Washington's Guards, Conn. Men, p. 632. Soldier pensioned in 1818.)
    John.. S 15003
    John, BLWt. 26157-160-55... S 23557
    Joseph B... R 1254
    Josiah (Hartford Co. in 1832), wid. Abigail... W 20766
    Lemuel, wid. Hannah... R 1248
    Reuben.. S 30294
    Samuel, wid. Elizabeth.. R 1246
    Samuel Lewis, Conn. & Cont... S 44671
    Silas (N. Y. in 1818).. S 17861
    Thomas, BLWt. 30-100; wid. Esther.. W 16871
    Thomas, wid. Surviah or Zurviah.. W 23701
BROTHWELL or BROTHWILL, Benjamin (81 in 1840).................................... S 14991
    Joseph F (Litchfield Co. in 1832).. S 15008
    Thomas, wid. Nancy BLWt. 26802-160-55 (Fairfield Co. in 1832)................. W 5928
        (Soldier was 74 in 1840. Only Thomas Brothwell in files.)
BROUGHTON, Ebenezer (Vt. in 1818), wid. Lois.. W 18650
    John, wid. Hannah.. W 20769
    Michael, wid. Sarah... W 18666
BROWN or BROWNE, Aaron.. S 6733
    Aaron.. S 36434
    Amasa, wid. Mary... R 1326
    Amasa, Conn. & Cont., wid. Jerusha.. W 17344
        (Wid. was 76 in 1840).
    Asher, wid. Mary... W 25277
    Austin (N. Y. in 1818), wid. Anne.. W 23697
    Bridgham, wid. Mary.. W 17364
    Charles... S 18745
    Charles... R 1283
    Charles F., Lucretia Hilliard, former wid. of... R 1321
    Christopher, Conn. & Privateer.. S 10411
    Christopher, Cont. (Conn.), wid. Eunice, BLWt. 35844-160-55................... W 12339
    Cyrus, Conn. & N. Y... S 6579
    Daniel... S 10408
    Daniel, Conn. & Navy, wid. Lydia... W 20787
    Daniel, Conn. Sea Service... R 1286
    Daniel, Cont. (Conn.), wid. Anna..
    David.. S 22136
    David.. S 28353
    David, wid. Lydia.. W 10453
    David..BLWt. 461-100
    Ebenezer.. S 36446
    Ebebezer.. S 44650
    Ebenezer, wid. Abigail.. R 1270
    Eleazer (Vt. in 1818)... S 39231
    Eli... S 23548
    Eli... S 44659
    Elias, Conn. & Cont. (N. Y. in 1818)... S 12332
        (An Elias Brown was 81 in 1840; above was only Elias with Conn. service, but an Elias
        with R. I. service was pensioned from Conn.).
    Elijah (N. Y. in 1818)... S 44661
    Elkanah.. S 44647
    Ephraim... R 1297
        (Is he the one who called himself a pensioner, and was 68 in 1840.)
    Ezekiel, wid. Ruhannah... W 16868
    Ezra.. S 2391
    Gershom, wid. Eunice, Conn. & Cont... W 14389
    Humphrey.. R 1302
    Humphrey, wid. Olive, BLWt. 29010-160-55... W 18648
    Ichabod.. S 28657
    Isaac, Conn. & Cont., wid. Hannah... W 17343
    Isaac, Conn., N. Y. & R. I... S 6745
    Jabez, wid. Annis... R 1278
    Jacob (Vt. in 1818)... S 39235
    James, wid. Deborah.. W 21701
    James, wid. Silence, BLWt. 347-100.. W 3219
    Jedediah, wid. Mary... W 20763
    Jedediah, Conn. & Cont... S 36432
        (Pensioned in 1818 as Washington's Life Guards.)
    Jepthah (New London Co. in 1832)... S 12340
        (Given Jeptha, and 82 in 1840; only Jeptha or ah in files.)
    Jeremiah, wid. Anna, BLWt. 6423-160-55 (Tolland Co. in 1832)................ W 25283
    Jerusha H., daughter of Hayward, Samuel... W 29934
    John.. S 22660
    John.. S 40749
    John, born Aug., 1757, in Eng.. R 1314
    John, wid. Elizabeth... W 5871
    John, wid. Rebacca.. W 17357
    John, Conn. & N. Y.. S 12339
    John, Cont. (Conn.), wid. Phebe.. W 25284
    Jonathan.. S 3058
    Jonathan.. S 17294
    Jonathan.. S 17295
    Jonathan.. S 40751
    Jonathan, wid. Esther, BLWt. 12826-160-55... W 5229
    Josiah, Conn. & Cont... S 45164
    Jude (Vt. in 1818).. S 40029

BROWN or BROWNE, Libbeus or Lebbeus, Cont. (Conn.) .... S 36445
   (Conn. Men, 1818; 83 in 1840 as Lebius; only man of the name in the files.)
  Marcy, former wid. of Oliver Babcock... W 16865
  Mary, former wid. of John Flint.. W 20785
  Nathan... S 23136
  Nathan, wid. Philadelphia, BLWt. 36613-160-55... W 15603
  Nathaniel, wid. Abigail.. W 20757
  Nathaniel, Conn. & Cont.. S 36427
  Nathaniel..BLWt. 1772-100
  Nehemiah, Conn. & N. Y... S 17299
   (Fairfield Co. in 1832.)
  Obediah or Obadiah (N. Y; in 1818)... S 44649
  Oliver (Ohio in 1818), Hannah Winslow, former wid. of, BLWt. 5446-160-55....................... W 1118
  Peter, Mercy Gallup, former wid. of.. W 25615
   Mercy's last husband, Nehemiah Gallup, was also a pensioner, Conn............................ S 13110
  Reuben, wid. Matilda... W 20775
  Reuben, wid. Ruth, Cont. (Conn.)... W 17359
  Robert, wid. Lorinda, BLWt. 9211-160-55.. W 1374
  Robert, wid. Mary.. W 20771
  Samuel... S 10413
  Samuel... S 12283
  Samuel... S 44653
  Samuel, wid. Anna.. W 16866
  Samuel, Conn., Mass. & Vt.. S 8108
  Solomon, wid. Betty.. W 5901
  Stephen, wid. Lydia.. R 1323
  Thaddeus... S 44657
  Thomas... S 29022
  Waldo, wid. Abigail.. W 25286
   (Windham Co. in 1832.)
  William, Conn, & Cont., wid. Sarah... W 10469
  William.. S 10406
  William, Conn. or Mass., wid. Miriam... R 1331
  William, Cont. (Conn.), Elizabeth Tryon, former wid. of.. W 18164
  Zebedee, Conn. & Cont., wid. Rosamund (1818 in R. I.).. W 23698
BROWNING, Daniel... R 1354
BRUMBLEY, BRUMBLY, or BROMLEY, Alas, wid. Esther, BLWt. 34206-160-55.............................. W 9748
  (New London Co. in 1832; & 75 in 1840.)
  William, Mary Hilliard, former wid. of... W 21324
BRUSH, Benjamin, wid. Semantha... W 10455
  (Fairfield Co. in 1832.)
  Eli.. R 1375
  John Cicero.. S 35789
  Jonas, wid. Tamar.. W 5924
BRYAN, Benajah, wid. Lucy.. W 17342
  (Litchfield Co. in 1832.)
  Elijah, BLWt. 5519 issued Apr. 9, 1791; no papers to Elijah Bryon.............................. S 17860
   (N. Y. in 1818.)
  Jehiel, wid. Polly... W 10450
   (New Haven Co. in 1832.)
  John... S 12280
  Oliver, wid. Esther.. W 20762
   (New Haven Co. in 1832.)
BRYANT, Daniel D., wid. Bethiah.. W 18652
  Ebenezer (Hartford Co. in 1832).. S 17849
  Fowler... R 1335
  Jacob. (See also BRIANT.)
  Reuben (Conn. Men, 1818)... S 36444
   (Given as Briant, 77 in 1840.)
BRYDIA, David, Conn. & N. H.. S 39234
BUBE. (See BEEBE.)
BUCHER. (See BEECHER.)
BUCK, Abner (N. Y. in 1818).. S 44694
  Amasa.. S 17869
  Asaph, wid. Phebe.. W 2534
   BLWt. 26597-160-55.
  Benton... S 15330
  Elijah, Conn. & Mass... S 12387
  George, wid. Agnes... W 23737
  Hepsibeth T., former wid. of John Swift, BLWt. 2505-100.. W 8172
   Swift served from Conn., N. Y. & in 1812.
  Joel... S 44693
  Jonathan... S 3108
  Josiah... R 1397
  Thomas... S 22666
  Zebediah (Windham in 1832)... S 17316
BUCKINGHAM, Reuben... S 44708
  Stephen, wid. Polly, BLWt. 87018-160-55.. W 25306
  Thomas... R 1403
BUCKLAND, Alexander, Conn. & Mass., wid. Lois.. R 1404
  George (Hartford Co. in 1832).. S 23561
   (82 in 1840.)
  Jonathan, wid. Laura, BLWt. 32240-160-55... W 25315
   (Hartford Co. in 1832; 76 in 1840.)
  Joshua (Hartford Co. in 1832).. S 15332
BUCKLEY. (See BULKLEY.)
BUCKMAN, Stephen, wid. Abigail... W 17366
BUDD, Bristol, wid. Phebe, BLWt. 24772-160-55.. W 25304
  Also known as Sampson, Bristol.

BUDLONG, Benjamin, Conn., N. Y. & R. I.	S 15011
BUEL, BUELL or BEWEL, Asa, wid. Mercy	W 21735
(N. Y. in 1818.)	
Daniel	S 22149
David	S 12348
David	S 31584
Deborah, former wid. of William Kircum or Kirkum, Conn. & Cont.	W 20795
Gideon (Vt. in 1818), wid. Lucy	W 2520
Isaac, Cont. (Conn.)	S 10395
(N. Y. in 1818.)	
James (Middlesex Co. in 1832)	S 17305
Job, wid. Ruth	W 17375
John	S 12363
John H. BLWt. 136-300, Capt. issued Jan. 25, 1791. No papers.	
Joseph, wid. Lucy, Cont. (Conn.)	W 14408
(Mass. in 1818.)	
Josiah	S 44707
Levi, Conn. & Vt.	S 18313
Martin, wid. Sybil	R 1413
(He was pensioned from New Haven Co. in 1832. Her claim was rejected.)	
(Is he the one who is given in Conn. Men as Marlin, 81 in 1840?)	
Matthew. (See BEWEL.)	
Nathan	S 23558
Oliver, wid. Elizabeth	W 20801
Orange	R 1412
Phebe, former wid. of Benjamin Thacher or Thatcher, BLWt. 26736-160-55	W 2521
Solomon	S 17318
Solomon, wid. Sophia	W 18670
Timothy. (See also BEWEL)	S 15013
BUFFUM, Samuel, Conn. Sea Service & Mass. Sea Service	S 12352
BUGBEE, BUGBEY or BUGBY, Amos, wid. Martha	W 17388
(She was 82 in 1840.)	
Benjamin (Conn. Men, 1818)	S 36461
Benjamin (Vt. in 1818), wid. Mehitable	W 23722
Edward. BLWt. 312-200, Lieut. in Hazen's Reg't. issued Jan. 5, 1797 to Benjamin Dana, assignee. No papers.	
Elijah, wid. Sarah	W 20802
(Wid. was 88 in 1840.)	
James, wid. Thirza, BLWt. 28576-160-55	W 479
(Conn. Men, 1818.)	
John, Conn. & Cont., wid. Hannah	W 17378
(Wid. was 77 in 1840.)	
Pelatiah or Peletiah	S 44698
(Given as Patrick in Conn. Men.)	
Peter, wid. Isabel, BLWt. 7066-160-55	W 21720
Rufus	S 18751
BULKLEY, BULKLY, BUKELY, BUCKLEY, BULKELEY.	
Abraham or Abram, Conn. & Conn. Sea Service	S 15331
(Fairfield Co. in 1832.)	
Charles, Navy (Conn.)	S 12349
(Lieut. Ship *Alfred*, pensioner, 1818, & New London Co. in 1832; & 87 in 1840.)	
Daniel, wid. Rhoda	R 1407
Edward, wid. Prudence	W 21727
BLWt. 138-300, Capt. issued Apr. 22, 1796 to Prudence Bulkley, adx. No papers.	
Eleazer, Conn. & Conn. Sea Service	S 18336
(Fairfield Co. in 1832; 77 in 1840.)	
Francis, wid. Elizabeth, BLWt. 951-160-55	W 1221
Gershom, wid. Amelia	W 17367
(Wid. as Buckley, was 86 in 1840.)	
John, Conn. & Cont.	S 17314
(1818, and 1832, New London Co.)	
Joseph	S 23141
Joseph, wid. Grizzel	W 20799
Nathan, wid. Jerusha, BLWt. 24773-160-55	W 25318
(Fairfield Co. in 1832.)	
Seth, Mary Dayton, former wid. of	W 20956
Solomon (Hartford Co. in 1832)	S 31583
Turney, wid. Esther	W 17371
BULL, Aaron Cont. (Conn.) BLWt. 151-200, Lieut. in Sheldon's reg't, was issued June 25, 1789. No papers.	
Henry (pensioner, 1818; d Mch. 30, 1819)	S 36459
Jeremiah, wid. Anne	W 17374
John, wid. Martha	W 17377
(Litchfield Co. in 1832.)	
(Wid. was 76 in 1840.)	
Reuben (Middlesex Co. in 1832)	S 17307
BUMFRIES, BUMPHRIES or BUMPHREY.	
Stephen, Conn. & N. Y. wid. Sarah, BLWt. 30623-160-55	W 8182
(Mass. in 1818.)	
BUMP, John, wid. Rebecca	W 2590
(Conn. Men in 1818.)	
BUMPUS, Edward (Mass. in 1818)	S 34112
BURNAP or BUNAP, John, wid. Abigail.	
BUNCE, Asa, wid. Sarah	W 24695
Rory, wid. Elizabeth	W 18673
Timothy	R 1428
BUNDY, Joshua, wid. Elizabeth	W 20817

BUNEL, BUNNEL, BUNNELL, Amos.. S 36460
    (Conn. Men, 1818.)
    Daniel... R 1432
    Enos, wid. Naomi.. W 17385
      (New Haven Co. in 1832.)
    Frederick (N. Y. in 1818).. S 44716
    Jehiel, wid. Stetira... R 1434
    Joel (Hartford Co. in 1832).. S 15334
    John.. S 12382
    John, wid. Pure.. W 20825
      (Pure was 85 in 1840.)
    Joseph... S 10403
    Joseph... S 36448
    Patience, former wid. of Giles Andrews....................................... R 1493
    William (New Haven Co. in 1832)... S 17317
    (See also BURNELL.)
BURBANK, Joel, wid. Eunice... W 21717
BURCH or BIRCH, Ebenezer, wid. Phebe....................................... W 16204
BURCHARD, or BIRCHARD, Joseph.. R 844
    Sabra, former wid. of Hosea Gridley.. W 15992
    (See also BIRCHARD.)
BURDEN. (See BORDEN.)
    Nathaniel, Conn. & Mass... S 17313
BURDWIN, Samuel, wid. Lois... W 20814
BURGE, Lothrop... S 12392
    Lott, Conn. & Mass., wid. Hannah... W 20804
    (See also BIRGE.)
BURGESS, Asa, Conn. & Cont., wid. Sarah..................................... W 20798
    (Windham Co. in 1832.)
    Ephraim... S 34114
BURKMAR, Nathan.. S 36947
BURLEY, Jacob (Conn. Men, 1818)... S 36451
BURNAM. (See BURNHAM.)
BURNAP, Jeriah, wid. Abigail; BLWt. 26311-160-55........................... W 10472
    (Tolland Co. in 1832.)
    John, wid. Abigail; BLWt. 24331-160-55...................................... W 25313
    (Windham Co. in 1832.)
    Also given as BUNAP and BURNETT.
BURNELL, Samuel, wid. Sophia... W 17390
    (See also BUNNELL.)
BURNET or BURNETT, James, wid. Phebe...................................... W 25317
    (Windham Co. in 1832.)
    John. (See BURNAP.)
BURNHAM or BURNAM, Abner... S 12390
    Asa, Conn. & Cont.. S 12371
    Asahel, BLWt. 447-100... S 44712
    Eben or Ebenezer... S 15766
    Gurdin, Conn., Cont. & Navy.. S 31585
    Isaac (N. Y. in 1818)... S 42638
    James, wid. Mehetabel... W 20823
      (Windham Co. in 1832; wid. was living in 1840.)
    James, wid. Tamma.. W 17380
      (Wid. given BARNHAM, was 74 in 1840.)
    James, Cont. (Conn.), wid. Eunice.. W 14428
    Jedediah... R 1479
    John, wid. Bridget.. W 1548
    John, Conn. & Cont.. S 18339
    John, Cont. (Conn.).. S 46822
    Joseph.. S 12381
    Joseph, Conn. & Cont.. S 17315
    Joshua... R 1480
    Josiah (Windham Co. in 1832)... S 12386
    Nathan... S 36457
    Nathan... S 36452
    Oliver, Conn. & Cont... S 15333
      (Conn. Men, p. 647.)
      (79 in 1840. Only Oliver Burnham in files from any State.)
    Orrin... S 28664
    Roger (Hartford Co. in 1832; 79 in 1840)..................................... S 23563
    Stephen, Conn. & Cont.. S 36450
      (Conn. Men, 1818.)
    Sylvester, wid. Caroline.. W 21728
      (New London Co. in 1832.)
    William, wid. Marcy.. W 23742
      (N. Y. in 1818.)
    Wolcott, wid. Sarah B., BLWt. 16259-160-55................................. W 1220
BURNS, Daniel, wid. Martha.. W 16519
    William (Conn. Men, 1818).. S 36462
BURR, Asa, wid. Malinda.. W 16202
    David, wid. Sarah Anna.. W 17373
      (Sarah A. was 78 in 1840.)
    David, Jane Sherwood, former wid. of.. R 9502
    Edmund, Conn. & Navy.. S 37810
    Hezekiah, wid. Mary.. W 17382
      (Fairfield Co. in 1832.)
    Jabez, wid. Mary.. R 1490
    Joel... S 12385
    Nathaniel (Middlesex Co. in 1832)... S 16667
    Roger, wid. Jane.. W 20806

BURR, William, wid. Sarah, BLWt. 15421-160-55... W 25375
 (New Haven Co. in 1832.)
 (Wm. was 78 in 1840.)
 Zabina or Zebina (88 in 1840).. S 16064
BURRALL, or BURRILL, Ebenezer.. S 12395
 Jonathan... S 29046
 (See also BURWELL.)
BURRETT or BURRITT, Andrew... R 1496
 Anthony, wid. Abigail, BLWt. 34807-160-55...................................... W 2996
  (Surgeon, New Haven Co. in 1832.)
 Charles, wid. Hannah.. W 23747
  (Lieut. in N. Y. in 1818.)
 Eben, wid. Sarah, BLWt. 82008-160-55.. W 17384
  (Litchfield Co. in 1832.)
 Elihu, wid. Elizabeth... R 1497
 Israel, Conn. & Vt.. S 19229
 Josiah, Mabel Curtis, former wid. of.. W 25463
 Joseph, wid. Sally.. W 21627
  (Wid. was 79 in 1840.)
  (Also given as BARRETT.)
 Nathan (Fairfield Co. in 1832).. S 17306
  (77 in 1840.)
 Wakeman... S 12942
  (Spelled BARRETT in Conn. Men.)
 Zalmon.. S 16331
BURROUGHS, BURROWS, or BURRUS.
 Caleb, wid. Judith, BLWt. 11076-160-55.. W 25311
 Elisha.. S 28406
 Hubbard, wid. Mary.. W 25316
 Joseph, Conn. & Cont., wid Mary... W 5237
  (N. Y. in 1818.)
 Josiah, wid. Sarah.. W 16518
 Nathan, former wid. of, Anna Cunningham... W 17674
 Paul, wid. Catharine.. W 21724
  (New London Co. in 1832.)
  (Catharine was 82 in 1840.)
 Robert, BLWt. 26363-160-55.. S 28663
 Stephen... S 3110
 Stephen... R 1032
 Thomas, wid. Esther, BLWt. 57751-160-55... W 8402
  (Conn. Men, 1818.)
  (Also BARRUS.)
 William... S 19927
 William, Conn. & Navy, wid. Sarah... R 1505
 William, Conn. & Vt... S 12396
 Zebulon, wid. Hannah.. W 23751
 (See also BARRUS and BORRES.)
BURROUS. (See BORRES.)
BURT, John, wid. Eunice... W 3653
BURTIS, Elizabeth, former wid. of Robert Eldredy.................................... W 1513
BURTON, Daniel, Conn. & Cont.. S 12377
 Elijah, Conn., Cont., & Vt.. S 18335
 Isaac, Conn. & N. Y., wid. Abigail, BLWt. 26393-160-55.......................... W 2719
 James, wid. Naoma... W 24682
  (Naomi was 92 in 1840.)
 Lewis (Fairfield Co. in 1832)... S 17310
  (78 in 1840.)
 Nathan (Litchfield Co. in 1832)... S 17311
 Seeley or Selah, or Othaniel Selah.. S 12394
BURWELL or BURWILL, Daniel, wid. Abigail.. W 17386
 (Litchfield Co. in 1832.)
 Jere, wid. Lucy... W 17381
  (Conn. Men, 1818.)
 (See also BURRALL and BURRELL.)
BURZETT, or BURZETTE, Charles, Cont. (Conn.).. S 44356
 (N. Y. in 1818.)
BUSH, George (Middlesex Co. in 1832; 83 in 1840).................................... S 15768
 Rufus, Conn. & Cont... S 12374
  (Hartford Co. in 1832.)
 Samuel (Conn. Men, 1818).. S 36450
 Stephens, Conn. & Mass.. S 12357
BUSHNELL, Daniel (Middlesex Co. in 1832).. S 17319
 (Prob. also Conn. Men, p. 647.)
 David, BLWt. 141-300, Capt., issued Feb. 3, 1800. No papers.
 David, Conn. & Privateer.. S 18752
 Elisha, wid. Lydia.. W 17368
  (Middlesex Co. in 1832.)
 Ephraim... S 12368
 Jason... S 2104
 Nathan, wid. Esther... W 17372
BUTLER, Benjamin, Conn. & Cont., wid. Lydia... W 17376
 David... S 10397
 Eleazer... R 1543
 Ezekiel, wid. Lydia... W 17392
 Ezra, wid. Mehitable.. W 17370
 George, Conn. & Mass.. S 12375
 Isaac (Vt. in 1818)... S 39257
 Israel (N. Y. in 1818).. S 44329

BUTLER, Joel, Conn., Conn. Sea Service & Privateer	R 1546
John	S 44328
John, wid. Patty	W 20821
Joseph (Vt. in 1818)	S 40775
Josiah, wid. Hannah	W 16517
Matthew (New Haven Co. in 1832)	S 16673
Peter	S 37811
Solomon	S 21095
Stephen	S 12350
Stephen	S 37796
Stephen, wid. Cata	W 23724
Stephen, Conn. & Cont., wid. Phebe	W 4908
Walter	W 16520
William (Middlesex Co. in 1832)	S 12360
Zebulon, wid. Phebe	W 5955
BLWt. 132-500, Col., issued Sept. 15, 1791. No papers.	
BUTTEN. (See BUTTON.)	
BUTTOLPH, George or Georg	S 37809
(Conn. Men, 1818.)	
BUTTON or BUTTEN, Benjamin	S 44352
Daniel, Conn. & R. I.	R 1562
Elijah	S 17312
Isaiah, Conn. & R. I.	S 21096
Jonathan (Tolland Co. in 1832)	S 17870
Mary, former wid. of Jonathan Hale	W 17387
Newbury	R 1563
Samuel	S 38587
BUTTS, Esaias	S 37803
(Is the one who is given as Isaac, 80 in 1840, the same as this?)	
John, former wid. of, Susanna Kirkland	W 26724
Josiah, wid. Eunice	W 20800
Josiah, wid. Lydia	W 14414
Sherebiah	S 29674
BUXTON, Peter, wid. Susanna	W 17383
BYINGTON, Ebenezer	S 37814
Isaac, wid. Elizabeth, BLWt. 6413-160-55	W 1380
(N. Y. in 1818.)	
John (Conn. Men, 1818.)	S 29051
Justus, wid. Lucy	W 23754
Samuel, wid. Olive	W 15625
Zuba or Zuby, former wid. of William Pratt	R 1570
BYRNE, Abigail, former wid. of Rogers, Stephen or Steven, BLWt. 2851-160-55	W 25319

MEN WHO WERE PENSIONED FROM CONN. FOR THE MOST PART, AND ARE MENTIONED IN CONN. MEN AMONG THE CONN. PENSIONERS, BUT ARE NOT SO CONSIDERED BY THE AUTHORITIES AT THE PENSION OFFICE IN WASHINGTON; ALSO NAMES MISPRINTED IN CONN. MEN.

BABCOCK, Ichabod (R. I. in 1832), R. I. not Conn. service. (This man was living in Conn. in 1840, and was 82 vrs. of age, his name being spelled BADCOCK.)
    Simon (82 in 1840), R. I. not Conn. Service.
    William, East Haddam, 54 in 1840. Not a Rev. pen.
BADLAM or BADLUM, Sylvanus (Conn. Men, 1818), Cont. and Mass. service, not Conn., widow Hannah, lived in Conn. .... W 25188
BAILEY, John, Jr. (C. Men, p. 649). No papers in files.
    Michael (Kent, 96 in 1840), as BARLEE in Pension Roll of 1835, but Mass. not Conn. service also Navy. (Conn. Men, 1818, as BARLEE.)
    William, Jr. (Conn. Men, p. 649). No papers on file.
BAKER, Windsor (Conn. Men, 1818), Mass. not Conn. Service.
BARBER, Timothy. Misprint in Conn. Men. This man was Timothy BARKER, and died before his pension was granted, and his wid., Irene, obtained the money due him to the date of his death.
BARDEEN, Aaron (Conn. Men, 1818), Mass. Service.
BARDWIN, Samuel. This is a misprint. It is either BURDWIN or BARDEN, both of whom were pensioners.
BARNES, Jonas. Misprint for Jonah.
BARRES, John Proctor (Conn. Men, 1818). Misprint for BORRES.
BARRETT, Wakeman, pensioned as BURRITT.
BARRON, Joseph (Conn. Men, 1818 in Vt.). He lived in Vt. in 1818, and N. Y. in 1820, where his wid. Magdelaine lived when she obtained her pension. But he only claimed Cont. and N. H. service, not Conn.
BATES, Asa (1832, pensioner), R. I. not Conn. service.
BASSETT, Howard or Hayward (Conn. Men, 1818), but he had Cont. (Mass.) not Conn. service. S 38521
BEDWELL, Eleazer, misprint for BIDWELL .... S 14955
BEEBE, Alexander (N. Y. in 1818). His service was Cont., Mass. & Navy, not Conn.
    William C. (68 in 1840). Not in files, and probably not Revolutionary; too young.
BELLOWS, Elihu (Mass. in 1818). He is pensioned for Cont. (Mass.) service; had a wid. Sarah, who was also a pensioner. W 14296. .... BLWt. 488-100
BENJAMIN, Judah (N. Y. in 1818), Cont. (N. H. & N. Y.) not Conn. service .... S 39981
BENSON, Barak (Windham Co. in 1832), Cont. (Mass.), not Conn. service; had a wid. Sarah, also a pensioner who was 88 in 1840. .... W 25329
BENTLEY, Ezekiel (New London Co. in 1832), R. I. not Conn. Service; had a wid. Anna, a pensioner, who was 83 in 1840. .... W 10407
BETTS, Aaron or Aron (Fairfield Co. in 1832), Mass. not Conn. service. .... S 16634
BIGELOW, Abijah (Windham in 1832), Mass. not Conn. service, although he lived in Brooklyn after the Revolution.
BILL, Benjamin (Conn. Men, p. 649); no such name on files; is it Bell, Benjamin .... S 38538
    Bozzell (Conn. Men, 1818); no such name on file, probably Rozzle or Roswell .... S 37771
BILLINGS, John S.; he was pensioned from Conn. but his service was N. J. and Privateer; he was 77 in 1840, and had a wid. Phebe, who got a Bounty Warrant, 30943 .... S 19909

BINGHAM, Ralph. No papers in files. (Conn. Men, p. 649.)
BIRDSEY, Ellen (79 in 1840). Probably Helen, wid. of Thaddeus BIRDSEYE (q. v.).
BITGOOD, John (Windham Co. in 1832), R. I. not Conn. service.
BLACKMAN or BLACKMAR, Jacob (Windham Co. in 1832), R. I. not Conn. service; had a wid. Zeruiah. (Jacob was 80 in 1840.)
BLISS, Isaac (Hartford Co. in 1832), Mass. not Conn. service (80 in 1840)......................... S 12246
   Moses (87 in 1840), Mass. not Conn. service.
BOUTON, Daniel (Conn. Men, p. 647). Not in files.
BOWERS, Michael (New Haven Co. in 1832), N. J. service not Conn. He did not move to Conn. until about 1790. Had a wid. Electa, also a pensioner, W 9360 and BLWt. 51880-160-55.
BOWMAN, Albert (Conn. Men, p. 649). No papers in files.
BRISTOL, Thomas (Conn. Men, p. 649). No papers in files.
BROWN, Ambrose (Conn. Men, 1818), Mass. not Conn. service; had a wid. Susannah, also a pensioner.. W 25285
   BLWt. 13421-160-55. (He was 73 in 1840.)
   Edward (Conn. Men, p. 649); none from Conn. in files; one each from Mass., N. H., and Va. but none seem to have been residents of Conn.
   Joseph (Conn. Men, 1818), Mass. not Conn. service; had a wid. Sarah, also pensioned........ W 20777
   Othniel, Navy & R. I. not Conn. service; had a wid. Nancy, also pensioned................. W 1135
   BLWt. 27620-160-55. (As Othaniel he was 81 in 1840.)
BRUSH, Gilbert (N. Y. in 1818). N. Y. not Conn. service.
BUCK, Aaron (Conn. Men, 1818). R. I. not Conn. service.
(He was 86 in 1840.)
BUD, Solomon (Hartford Co. in 1832). In the printed report of 1835 the name appears BUEL, not BUD. That is a misprint in Conn. Men.
BUELL, Salmon (Conn. Men, p. 649). No papers on file.
BUGBEE, Patrick (N. Y. in 1818). Misprint in Conn. Men. Should be Peletiah, as given in U. S. Report.
BUKER, Windsor (82 in 1840). Mass. not Conn. service.
BUMFRIES, Edward (Mass. 1818). Misprint in Conn. Men, as shown by U. S. Report. Should be BUMPUS.
BURBECK, Henry (Conn. Men, 1818). Cont. & Mass. service not Conn.; had a wid. Lucy E., who also was pensioned W 10480, BLWt. 122-300, Capt. issued to him Dec. 3, 1789. No papers. He was 85 in 1840.
BURDICK, Walter (Conn. Men, p. 648). R. I. not Conn. service................................ S 19925
BURKMAR, Thomas (Maine, in 1818). Not Conn. service.
BURTCH, Billings (New London Co. in 1832), R. I. not Conn. service; had a wid. Jane, also pensioned... W 20797

C.

CABLE, Abner (Conn. in 1818: Fairfield Co. in 1832).. S 10438
CADWELL, Aaron, wid. Mary.. W 17595
   John, Fabius, N. Y., 1832... S 12442
   John, Schaghticoke, N. Y., in 1818... S 44365
   Phineas, Cont. (Conn.).. S 37822
      (N. Y. in 1818, as Corporal.)
      BLWt. 16127-160-55.
   Reuben, wid. Rebecca.. W 18875
   Theodore, wid. Lucy, BLWt. 27637-160-55... W 22738
CADY, Abijah (Conn. 1818, d. May 16, 1819)... S 37818
   Abner, wid. Molly... W 17589
      (Tolland Co. 1832.)
   Elijah.. S 31591
   Elisha.. S 10433
      (Windham Co. 1832: 91 in 1840, Pomfret.)
   Elizabeth, former wid. of Obadiah Daley, Cont. (Conn.)..................................... W 23757
   Ezra (Windham Co. 1832)... S 18434
   Jonathan, pensioned from R. I... S 17323
   Jonathan, Brooklyn, Conn. 1832.. S 18344
   Luther, Conn. & N. Y... S 28670
   Manasseh, Conn. & Navy, wid. Elizabeth... W 20838
   Nedabiah, Conn. & Cont... S 12436
   Reuben (N. Y. in 1818)... S 44729
   Richard, wid. Alice.. W 10571
      BLWt. 26991-160-55.
      (Soldier was in Windham Co. in 1832: and 78 in 1840, at Canterbury.)
CADY, Squire or Squier, wid. Abiah.. W 1553
   BLWt. 26991-160-55.
   (Soldier was in Conn. 1818, as Serg't.; Windham Co. in 1832; 88 in 1840 at Plainfield.)
   William... S 39276
   Zadok, wid. Lucy... W 1714
CALDER, William, Conn. & Cont... S 44725
CALKIN, CALKINS, CAULKINS, CAULKINGS.
   Daniel.. S 44374
   Darius (Penna. 1818), wid. Abigail.. W 6648
   Durkee.. S 22156
   Frederick, Navy (Conn.), wid. Annis... W 5056
   James, wid. Esther... W 23778
   Joel.. S 23567
   Moses, Conn. & N. Y.. S 12426
   Nathaniel, wid. Lois... W 16884
   Nathaniel Skiff, Conn. & Conn. Sea Service... S 15034
   Roswell, wid. Eunice... W 4915
   Solomon, Conn., N. H. & Vt... S 23563
CALL, John, d. Jan. 25, 1813: BLWt. 1727-100.
   or McCALL, John, wid. Loruhamah.. R 6599

CAMP, Abel, Conn. & Cont............	S 12435
Chauncy............	R 1613
Elias (New Haven Co. in 1832)............	S 17326
Ephraim............	S 12432
Ezra (Litchfield Co. in 1832)............	S 15033
Israel............	S 16689
James, wid. Elizabeth............	R 1615
John, Litchfield Co., Conn., in 1832............	S 37819
John............	R 1616
John, New Milford, Conn., in 1832............	W 23762
Wid. Annis. BLWt. 31457-160-55.	
Manoah, wid. Clarissa............	W 1818
(Middlesex Co. 1832; 79 in 1840 at Durham.)	
Mial. (See BEACH, Thaddeus.)	
Rejoice............	S 16066
(Middlesex Co. 1832; 81 in 1840 at Durham.)	
Samuel, N. Y. in 1818, as Serg't............	S 23148
Samuel, Conn. in 1818 as private............	S 33590
Sharp (Conn. 1919)............	S 37821
CAMPBELL, Archibald, N. Y. in 1832............	S 12448
(NOTE.—There was another pensioner by name of Archibald Campbell, who was born at Voluntown, Conn., May 11, 1873, and applied for pension in 1832 from Salisbury, Conn. He was living in Berkshire Co., Mass., in 1781 and enlisted in the N. Y. State Line. Both he and his wid. were pensioned. N. Y. Campbell, Archibald, wid. Eliza or Elizabeth, W 1138; BLWt. 13434-160-55.)	
Betsey or Betsy, former wid. of Seelye, John............	W 4419
Isaac............	S 12406
John, Windham Co. in 1832............	S 17321
Noble, wid. Janet............	W 16888
Robert (N. Y. in 1818 as Serg't)............	S 44373
CANADA, David (Conn. 1818), wid. Lucy, BLWt. 26313-160-55............	W 25388
CANDE or CANDEE, or CANDER, Job (New Haven Co. in 1832; 80 in 1840 in Oxford)............	S 13036
Nehemiah............	R 1656
Samuel (New Haven Co. in 1832; 87 in 1840 in Oxford)............	S 17327
Zacheus or Zaccheus............	S 29062
CANFIELD, Andrew, wid. Eunice............	R 1658
Daniel, Cont. (Conn.)............	S 29696
Elijah (Ohio in 1818)............	S 2106
Isaiah, Conn. & Service on Lake Champlain, wid. Anne............	W 16883
Ithamar, wid. Betsey............	R 1657
Oliver............	S 23566
Philo, wid. Mary P............	R 1659
Samuel, Conn. & Cont............	S 15772
CANNON, Mary, former wid. of John Heminger............	W 23769
BLWt. 67542-160-55.	
CAPEN, Purchase, wid. Theodosia............	R 1670
Timothy............	S 30313
CAPRON, Jeremiah, wid. Jerusha............	R 1674
BLWt. 2453-100.	
NOTE.—The soldier obtained a BLWt. It was the widow's claim that was rejected.	
CARD, Elisha............	R 1676
CAREL, John (New London Co. in 1832; 79 in 1840 at New London)............	S 12416
CAREY or CARY, Anson............	S 9148
Hezekiah, Conn. & Cont............	S 39279
(Vt. in 1818. (BLWt. 33561-160-55.	
Jabez, wid. Mary, BLWt. 18952-160-55............	W 25399
CAREY or CARY, John; BLWt. 578-100.	
Joseph, wid. Sarah............	W 18865
Levi, Conn. & Cont............	S 8157
Oliver, Conn., Cont., & Mass............	S 23149
CARLTON, Richard (Vt. in 1818 as Serg't)............	S 39280
CARMAN, John............	S 12409
CARPENTER, Allen (Vt. in 1818)............	S 44367
Comfort, Tolland Co. in 1832............	S 12422
Comfort, Conn. in 1818............	S 37823
Daniel............	S 42116
David, Mass in 1832............	S 29063
David, New Haven Co. in 1832; wid. Azubah............	W 16892
Elias............	S 21683
Elijah, former wid. Sarah Sargeant............	R 9204
Eliphalet (Vt. in 1818)............	S 23151
Ephraim............	S 12670
Esther, former wid. of Clement Stoddard, Conn. & War of 1812............	R 10202
Isaiah............	S 23672
Israel............	S 30315
John............	S 15371
Joseph............	S 12411
Joshua A., Cont. (Conn.)............	S 45319
(N. Y. in 1818.)	
Nathaniel, wid. Elfrida............	W 20839
Phebe, former wid. of Solomon Eaton............	W 8591
BLWt. 30597-160-55.	
Simeon............	R 1718
Timothy, BLWt. 26546-160-55............	S 12675
(77 in 1840, at Ellington, Windham Co.)	
Uriah, wid. Elithal............	W 25379
(72 in 1840 at Ashford; is prob. this wid.)	
William, Cont. (Conn.)............	S 37820
(Conn. in 1818.)	

CARR, Clement (Conn. 1818)	S 38597
Ebenezer (N. Y. in 1818)	S 45318
Robert	S 44724
William	S 39289

NOTE.—Margaret Carr, wid. of above soldier, received pension as former wid. of William Brown, Cont. (Penna.), W 73.
(See also KERR.)

CARRIER, David, wid. Rebecca	R 1727
Hannah, former wid. of Guy Dodd	W 10573
John	S 12429

(See also CURRIER.)

CARRINGTON, Jesse, former wid. Elizabeth Lewes or Lewis	W 20429
Lemuel, former wid. Abigail Rice	W 17538
Reverius, former wid. Loly Merrick	W 9959
BLWt. 17577-160-55.	
CARTER, Aaron, wid. Rachel	W 22726
Benjamin, wid. Phebe	W 1715
Elihu, Cont. (Conn.)	S 12420
(Hartford Co. in 1832.)	
Heman (N. Y. in 1818)	S 44358
Ithiel, Conn. & Cont., wid. Lois	W 17591
(Conn. 1818, as Serg't.)	
Jirah	S 23147
John, Vt. in 1818, wid. Lucinda	W 20840
John, N. Y. in 1818 as Serg't., wid. Susanna	W 10565
Jonah, former wid. Tempa Barlow, BLWt. 113036-160-55	W 10383
Ned or Chappel, Edward Carter, wid. Eunice (Conn. 1818, as Carter, Edward)	W 20850
Reuben, former wid. of Elizabeth Moss, BLWt. 571-100.	
Rufus	S 9208
Samuel (Windham Co. in 1832)	S 10437
Solomon	S 18340
Stephen (New Haven Co. in 1832)	S 12407
CARTRIGHT or CARTWRIGHT, Cyrus, wid. Mary	W 6627
(N. Y. in 1819.)	
CARTY, or McCARTY, Clark, wid. Mabel	W 20248
CARVER, Aldric, Cont. service, but Conn. Agency	S 38596
Asa	S 23150
Joseph, wid. Tabitha	W 20829
Nathaniel, wid. Lydia	R 1763
CASE, Aaron, wid. Abigail	R 1764
Abel, Hartford Co. 1832	S 12668
Abel, Cont. (Conn.), N. Y. in 1818	S 44362
Abner, wid. Hannah	W 17588
Asahel (Litchfield Co. in 1832)	S 16068
Ashbel, wid. Azubah	R 1765
Fithen, wid. Amarilla or Amrilles	W 17586
George	S 3115
Giles, wid. Dorcas	W 17585
Hosea, wid. Sarah	W 17584
(Hartford Co. in 1832.)	
Ichabod	S 31602
James, wid. Lydia	R 1767
John M., wid. Abigail	W 23770
(Hartford Co. in 1832; BLWt. 26725-160-55; 77 in 1840 at Hartland.)	
Lemuel, wid. Mary, BLWt. 93530-160-55	W 9766
Micah, Conn. & Mass	S 17328
(Hartford Co. in 1832.)	
Nathan, Conn. & Cont	S 22159
Oliver, wid. Amy	W 17587
(Hartford Co. in 1832.)	
Reuben	R 1769
Richard, wid. Mary	W 20833
(Conn. in 1818.) BLWt. 264-100.	
Roswell (Conn. 1818)	S 38593
Rufus, wid. Rachel, BLWt. 9062-160-55	W 3655
William, Conn. & Cont	S 44361
CASEY, John, Conn., R. I. & Vt., BLWt. 85507-160-55	W 25378
CASH, Lois, former wid. of Zenas Goodrich	R 1780
CASHMAN. (See CUSHMAN.)	
CASS, Moses, former wid. Abia Judd	W 20223
CASTLE, Joel	S 8143
CASWELL, Ezra (Mass. in 1818)	S 34177
Julius	R 1802
Samuel	R 1803
CATLIN, Abel, Conn., Navy & Privateer	S 3
David (Litchfield Co. in 1832)	S 12430
Eli, Conn. & Cont	S 40812
(Penna. in 1818 as Capt.)	
Elisha, wid. Roxanna	R 1812
Elizabeth, former wid. of Simeon Curtiss, BLWt. 14667-160-55	W 10569
Hezekiah, wid. Sarah	W 18851
Isaac (Litchfield Co. in 1832)	S 12433
Lewis, Conn. & Cont	S 17320
Nathan, wid. Abigail	W 20827
Phineas, Cont. (Conn.) wid. Sarah, BLWt. 545-100	W 18872
Putnam, wid. Mary or Polly	R 1810
Roswell (Vt. in 1818)	S 39278
Simeon, Conn. & Cont	S 10432
CAULKINGS or CAULKINS. (See CALKINS.)	

CAVARLY, John, wid. Caroline... W 17593
CAWDERY or CAWDRY. (See COWDERY.)
CHACE. (See CHASE.)
CHADWICK, James... BLWt. 1458-100
 Nathan, Conn. & Vt... S 16709
 Richard (New London Co. in 1832).. S 12690
CHAFE. (See CHAFFEE.)
CHAFE, CHAFEE, CHAFFE, or CHAFFEE.
 Abiel, wid. Hannah.. W 25401
  (Conn. in 1818; 79 in 1840 at Woodstock.)
 Calvin, wid. Ruth... W 16208
 Chester, wid. Caroline.. W 17599
  (85 in 1840 at Thompson; Windham Co. in 1832.)
 Frederick (Hartford Co. in 1832).. S 17881
 Joel, wid. Eleanor, BLWt. 26046-160-55.. W 6909
  (Litchfield Co. in 1832; and 81 in 1840 at Sharon.)
 Jonathan, Conn. & Mass., wid. Olive... W 2271
 Joseph.. R 1829
 Josiah, wid. Joanna, BLWt. 3531-160-55.. W 1887
 Serrill, Conn. & Mass... S 18346
 Thomas (Conn. in 1818).. S 37833
 William, wid. Mary.. W 17619
  (Conn. in 1818.)
CHALKER, Jabez, wid. Hannah.. W 20852
  (Middlesex Co. in 1832; and 83 in 1840 at Durham.)
 Jesse, wid. Elizabeth... W 17596
 Moses (Middlesex Co. in 1832; 81 in 1840, at Saybrook)............................ S 31604
 Oliver (Middlesex Co. in 1832; 80 in 1840 at Saybrook)............................ S 17329
 Samuel, wid. Damaras.. W 23802
CHAMBERLAIN, CHAMBERLIN or CHAMBERLINE.
 Aaron, wid. Wealthy... W 27394
 Ephraim, BLWt. 372-300, Captain, was issued Feb. 6, 1797. No papers.
 Isaac, Conn. & Cont... S 45836
 Jeremiah, wid. Sarah.. W 23790
  (Maine in 1818.) BLWt. 3516-160-55.
 Jireh... S 22170
 Joseph S.. S 37826
  (Conn. in 1818, where the name is incorrectly given as Joseph H.)
 Leander (Vt. in 1818)... S 40826
 Nathaniel, wid. Rhoda... W 14474
 Pliney or Pliny, wid. Martha, BLWt. 17724-160-55.................................. S 29708
 Samuel (Conn. in 1818).. S 37841
 Swift, wid. Mary, BLWt. 30694-160-55.. W 1555
 Theodore or Theodorus, wid. Fanny... W 1226
  (Conn. in 1818.) BLWt. 31893-160-55.
 William... S 44733
 Wyatt or Wayatt, wid. Dinah... W 17612
CHAMBERS, William (Ohio in 1818)... S 42644
CHAMPION, Elisha, wid. Phebe... W 25406
  (Wid. was 75 in 1840 at Lyme.)
 Epaphroditus (Ass't. Deputy Commissary, Middlesex Co. in 1832).................... S 16711
 Ezra (Conn. in 1818) wid. Lucy.. W 6662
  BLWt. 110-60-55.
 Henry, Conn. & Cont... S 12463
  (New London Co. in 1832.)
 Reuben, Lyme, 1818 & 1840... S 38600
 Reuben, wid. Rhoda H.. W 9783
  NOTE.—This pension was granted after both soldier and widow were dead, by special act of Congress to son, Reuben J., in Hillsdale, Mich. Soldier was son of Israel and grandson of Henry Champion, Commissary General.
 Salmon.. R 1839
 Samuel, Conn. & Cont.. S 38604
CHAMPLIN, Caleb (New London Co. in 1832)... S 15043
 Charles (Windham Co. in 1832), wid. Mary.. W 17614
 Silas, Conn. & Cont... S 18347
  (Conn. 1818; New London Co. in 1832; Lyme, in 1840.)
 Stephen... S 15040
  (New London Co. in 1832; 77 in 1840, at Lebanon.)
 William, Conn., Privateer & R. I.. S 12473
CHANCE, Evans or Evens, Conn. & Vt... S 10441
CHANDLER, Daniel... S 13035
 Jacob, Conn. Sea service & Navy, wid. Anna.. W 14462
 Jonathan, Conn , Conn. Sea Service & Privateer.................................... R 21842
 Joseph (Ohio in 1818)... S 35206
 Josiah.. S 22167
 Robert (also given SHANDLER).. S 40399
 Simeon.. S 15774
CHAPEL, CHAPPEL, CHAPELL, CHAPPAL or CHAPPLE.
 Amaziah (N. Y. in 1818)... S 44749
 Curtis (N. Y. in 1818), wid. Sarah.. W 17603
 Dan, wid. Experience.. W 20843
 Daniel, wid. Anna... W 17606
 Daniel, wid. Mary... W 2527
  BLWt. 6193-160-55.
 Edward Carter. (See CARTER, Ned.)
 Guy, wid. Delight... W 25407
  (New London Co. in 1832; and 81 in 1840 at Montville.)
 Hiram, Cont. (Conn.).. S 12474
 Jedediah, wid. Lucy, BLWt. 6287-160-55.. W 17597
 Noah (N. Y. in 1818).. S 40825

CHAPEL, CHAPPEL, CHAPELL, CHAPPAL or CHAPPLE—Continued.
Noah (N. Y. in 1818), wid. Lydia	W 16530
Samuel, wid. Abigail, BLWt. 26525-160-55	W 23385
Stephen, wid. Lucy, BLWt. 26012-160-55	W 18880
Stephen, wid. Lydia	W 16533
William	S 22677
William, wid. Lydia	W 4154

CHAPIN, Asa (Tolland Co. in 1832) ... S 15775
David (N. Y. in 1818), wid. Ruth, BLWt. 2490-160-55 ... W 22768
Elias, wid. Dimmis, BLWt. 27621-160-55 ... W 2528
Frederick, former wid. of Lucretia Booth ... W 18626
Ichabod ... S 15372
John, Conn. & Mass., wid. Elizabeth, BLWt. 31438-160-55 ... W 10601
CHAPIN, Oliver wid. Elizabeth ... W 25408
 (Tolland Co. in 1832; and 82 in 1840 at Somers.)
Phinehas, Conn., Cont. & N. H ... S 12701
Timothy, Cont. (Conn.), wid. Tacy ... W 18890
 (N. Y. in 1818.)
CHAPLIN, Ebenezer (Hartford Co. in 1832; and 90 in 1840 at Suffield) ... S 16075
CHAPMAN or CHOPMAN, Abner, Conn. & Cont ... S 12461
 (Conn. in 1818, as Serg't. Middlesex Co. in 1832.)
Albert, Cont. service, N. Y. Agency, Conn. residence ... S 27612
Albert, BLWt. 367-400, Major, was issued June 6, 1797, to Nathaniel Satterlee, Assignee. No papers.
Asa, wid. Elizabeth ... W 17621
Ashbel, wid. Lydia ... W 25404
Caleb, Stephenson, N. Y. in 1832 ... S 15309
 Conn. & Privateer.
Caleb, Steuben Co. N. Y. in 1832: wid. Lydia ... W 16209
Collins (Conn. in 1818), wid Mary ... W 17600
Comfort ... S 44377
Constant, wid. Jemima ... W 6652
 (N. Y. in 1818.)
Dan, N. Y. in 1818 ... S 23571
Daniel, New London Co. in 1832 ... S 12682
David ... S 22161
Ebenezer, wid. Mary ... W 17618
 (Conn. in 1818.)
Edward, Conn. in 1818 ... S 38606
Edward, Conn. & N. Y. service; N. Y. in 1832, wid. Rebecca, BLWt. 30612-160-55 ... W 14466
Eliakim (Tolland Co. in 1832) ... S 31603
Elijah (Conn. 1818, as Capt.) ... S 37848
 BLWt. 375-300, Captain, was issued May 19, 1797, to Elijah Chapman. No papers.
Elijah (Cairo, N. Y. in 1818) ... S 44739
 BLWt. 627-100.
Elijah, d. 1804; Conn. & Cont., wid. Esther ... W 17605
Elizabeth, former wid. of Joseph Smith ... R 1865
Frederick or Frederik ... S 24107
 (Hartford Co. in 1832; and 79 in 1840 at Windsor.)
Israel, Conn. & Navy ... R 1870
James, New London Co. in 1818 ... S 37835
 (89 in 1840 in New London.)
James, Fairfield Co. in 1818 ... S 37831
 Mrs. Ellen Turney, former wid. of James Chapman, was pensioned as former wid. of her first husband, Samuel Squires, Conn., W 22458.
Jason, wid. Mary ... R 1877
 (Soldier was pensioned and living in New London Co. in 1832, and 78 in 1840 at Waterford.)
Jedediah (Conn. 1818; Middlesex Co. in 1832; and 81 at Westbrook in 1840) ... S 12691
John ... S 24108
Joseph, Preston, Conn. in 1832 ... S 10445
Joseph, Conn. & Cont. Penna. in 1818, as Lieut ... S 40821
 BLWt. 377-200, Lieut. issued Sept. 24, 1790, to Peleg Sanford, assignee. No papers.
Joshua, wid. Lucy ... R 1874
Lebbeus ... S 37842
 (Conn. 1818, as Libbeus, Lieut.)
Lydia, former wid. of William Cochran, BLWt. 27597-160-55 ... W 23793
Michael ... S 42645
Nahum ... S 44376
Oliver, wid. Eunice ... R 1868
Richard ... S 22168
Robert, wid. Judith, BLWt. 27625-160-55 ... W 24844
 (Litchfield Co. in 1832.)
Salathiel, wid. Amy, BLWt. 26440-160-55 ... W 4920
 (Hartford Co. in 1832; and 80 in 1840, at Simsbury, as Salathel.)
Samuel ... S 12472
Samuel ... BLWt. 1954-100
Silas (Conn. in 1818) ... S 37847
Simeon ... R 1879
Stephen ... BLWt. 186-100
Taylor ... S 28675
Thomas, Conn. Cont. & Mass., wid. Phebe, BLWt. 1903-160-55 ... W 25405
Timothy, wid. Avis ... W 15881
Zachariah ... S 28677
CHACE or CHASE, Isaac ... S 37849
 (Conn. in 1818, and d. Oct. 20, 1818.)
Lot, wid. Rhoda ... W 20846
 (Litchfield Co. in 1832.)
Mary, former wid. of Ziba Roberts ... W 22759
Samuel, BLWt. 103392-160-55 ... S 19240

CHATFIELD, Dan.. S 37830
    (79 in Huntington, in 1840.)
  Isaac, Cont. (Conn.)... S 12475
    (Conn. in 1818.)
  John.. S 38605
CHATFIELD, Jonathan, wid. Dinah... R 1894
  Josiah (Conn. in 1818)... S 37837
  Levi (Conn. in 1818.)... S 37843
CHATTERTON, Wait, Conn. & Privateer, wid. Melinda or Millinda, BLWt. 11096-160-55.... W 529
CHAUNCEY, Nathaniel W.. S 15044
    (Middlesex Co. in 1832.)
CHEADEL or CHEADLE, Elijah.. S 11994
CHEESEBROUGH, CHEESEBROUGH or CHESEBRO, or CHESEBRA.
  Asa.. R 1899
  Christopher.. R 1900
  Elijah, wid. Thankful, BLWt. 26591-160-55... W 22748
  James... S 38607
  Lois, former wid. of Joseph Hilliard... W 16901
  Nathaniel, Conn. & Cont... S 37845
  Perez... S 15042
    (New London Co. in 1832; and 78 in 1840 at Bozrah.)
CHEEVER or CHEVER, Ebenezer, Conn. & Privateer................................. S 12452
CHENEY or CHENY, Elijah.. S 37839
    (Conn. in 1818.)
  Joseph, Auburn, N. Y. in 1818.. S 44754
  Joseph, d. 1790, wid. Rebecca.. W 20847
  Waldo, wid. Priscilla... W 20854
  William, wid. Sarah.. R 1905
CHESEBRA, CHESEBRO, or CHESEBROUGH. (See CHEESEBROUGH.)
CHESTER, Christopher Conn. & Cont... S 40043
    (R. I. in 1818.)
  Giles, Navy (Conn.), wid. Mary... W 17611
    (Conn. in 1818, as Seaman on Brig *Calvert*.)
  John, Conn. & Navy... S 38603
CHEVER. (See CHEEVER.)
CHICHESTER, David, wid. Mary.. W 17610
  Henry.. S 17330
    (Fairfield Co. in 1832; 77 in Norwalk in 1840.)
  Nathan, wid. Theodosia.. W 17607
    (Fairfield Co. in 1832.)
CHIDESTER, William, wid. Martha... W 4918
CHIDSEY, Ephraim, wid. Hannah.. W 17620
    (New London Co. in 1832.)
  Isaac, wid. Lydia... W 17601
CHILD or CHILDS, Cephas, Conn. & Cont... S 12469
  Elias (Windham Co. in 1832).. S 31605
  Jesse.. R 1919
  Lyman... S 21690
  Obadiah (Conn. 1818, as Ensign).. S 37832
  Penuel, Rutland Co. Vt. in 1832, wid. Sabra... W 716
  Penuel, d. 1813; wid. Sarah.. W 20842
  Stephen, wid. Zilpha... W 18886
    (Vt. in 1818.)
  Timothy, wid. Anna.. W 20859
  Willard.. S 10444
    (Windham Co. in 1832; and 82 in 1840 at Woodstock.)
CHIPMAN, John, Cont. (Conn.).. S 46351
    BLWt. 376-300, Capt. issued March 3, 1797, to Samuel Fitch, assignee. No papers.
  Nathaniel (Vt. in 1818 as Lieut.).. S 18780
  Thomas, Conn. & Cont.. S 44741
    (N. Y. in 1818 as Serg't.)
  Timothy (Conn. in 1818)... S 37834
CHITTENDEN, CHITTENDON, CHITTINGTON, or CRITTENDEN.
  Abraham... S 16703
    (New Haven Co. in 1832; and 89 in 1840 at Guilford.)
  Asahel, former wid. of, Anna or Anne McFariand; BLWt. 28539-160-55..... W 25688
  Benjamin (Conn. 1818, as Ensign)... S 37836
  Calvin.. S 17334
  Cornelius, BLWt. 11279-160-55.. S 17880
    (Middlesex Co. in 1832; and 77 in 1840 at Westbrook.)
  Gideon... S 42660
  James (Vt. in 1818)... S 23570
  Jared or Jerard, Conn. & Cont... S 44742
  John, Conn. & Cont.. S 17332
    (Conn. in 1818; and Middlesex Co. in 1832; and 83 in 1840 at Westbrook.)
  Levi, wid. Hannah.. W 17622
    (New Haven Co. in 1832.)
  Nathan (New Haven Co. in 1832; and 82 in 1840 at Guilford)................... S 17331
  Reuben.. S 44743
  Solomon, wid. Susanna... R 1934
  William... S 34197
CHOPMAN. (See CHAPMAN.)
CHURB, Joseph (N. Y. in 1818 as Serg't.)... S 44747
  William, Cont. service, but Conn. residence of daughter, who obtained BLWt. 917-100.
CHURBUCK, Ebenezer, wid. Lucina or Lusina... W 2919
CHURCH, Amasa, Conn. & Cont.. S 12688
  Daniel.. S 23155
  Ebenezer, wid. Eunice.. W 3130
  Elihu (N. Y. in 1818)... S 44379
  Fairbanks, Conn. & Cont.. S 12470
  Gideon, wid. Abigail... W 2755

CHURCH, James Cady	S	44380
(Given James E. in N. Y. in 1818.)		
Joel W., Cont. (Conn.)	S	28674
John Jonathan, John J., or Jonathan or Jonathan Ellis, wid. Abigail, BLWt. 39497-160-55	W	1143
John, Conn., Green Mt. Boys & Mass.	S	15373
(Litchfield Co. in 1832.)		
Joseph, Conn. & Cont., wid. Priscilla	W	23806
(Conn. in 1818; and 80 in 1840 at Montville.)		
Nathaniel	S	19933
Parly	R	1951
Philemon (N. Y. in 1818)	S	42122
Samuel, pensioned as Samuel 1st, at Dorset, Vt., in 1818	S	40830
Samuel, pensioned from Oneida Co., N. Y., in 1832; wid. Lydia	R	1950
Samuel, Cont. (Conn.), pensioned as Samuel 2nd, Fletcher, Vt., 1818	S	39309
Simeon, Conn., Mass. & N. H	S	12471
Uriah, Mass., 1818, as Serg't	S	34185
Uriah, Conn., in 1818 as Lieut	S	37844
Willard (N. Y. in 1818)	S	44750
CHURCHILL, Jacob, wid. Lillis	W	14471
John	R	1952
Nathaniel, wid. Lydia	W	22770
Oliver, wid. Lydia, BLWt. 9433-160-55	W	2560
Samuel	R	1953
Stephen, wid. Mary	W	1225
CLAP or CLAPP		
Abigail, former wid. of Benjamin Barnes or Barns	R	1957
Oliver (Hartford Co. in 1832; 80 in 1840)	S	16718
Samuel, Conn., Cont. & N. H	S	39321
CLARK or CLARKE.		
Abel Farmington, Conn., in 1832; wid. Lois	W	1561
Abel, d. 1788; former wid. Hannah Murray	W	21770
Abel, wid. Sarah	R	13178
Abraham or Abram (N. Y. in 1818)	S	44776
Adna	S	8209
Amasa (Windham Co. in 1832; 76 in 1840 at Hampton)	S	17348
Amos, Chatham, Conn., in 1832 as Sergeant and 83 in 1840	S	23574
Amos, Dryden, N. Y., in 1818, as 2nd	S	44774
Amos, New Haven Co. as Amos, Jr	S	37872
Amos, Chaplin, Conn., in 1832; and 78 in 1840; wid. Hannah	W	25419
BLWt. 26492-160-55.		
Andrew, Middlebury, Conn., in 1832; wid. Anna	W	17633
Andrew, Norwich, Conn., in 1832; wid. Vashti, BLWt. 31890-160-55	W	480
Andrew, Conn., N. Y. & Vt.; res. N. Y. in 1832	S	28687
Asa, N. Y. in 1832	S	12504
Asa, Vt., in 1818	S	38611
Augustus, wid. Anna	W	16211
(N. Y. in 1818.)		
Barnabas	BLWt.	1451-100
Benjamin, Columbia Co., N. Y., in 1832	S	10455
Benjamin, Tioga Co., N. Y., in 1832	S	12502
Benjamin, Conn. & Penna	S	41487
Penna. in 1818.		
Benoni or Bennoni, Conn. & Mass.	S	12491
Beriah	S	34209
Caesar, Negro	S	37871
Champion	S	16082
(Litchfield Co. in 1832; and 79 in 1840 at Bethlehem.)		
Chipman	S	9181
Comfort, wid. Esther	R	1973
Cyrenus (Conn. in 1818)	S	37868
Daniel, Litchfield Co. in 1832	S	12695
Daniel, New Haven Co. in 1832	S	17341
Daniel, Windsor Co., Vt., in 1832	S	18354
Daniel, Conn. & Cont., Windham Co., Conn., in 1832	S	10457
Daniel, Cont. (Conn.), Bennington Co., Vt., in 1818	S	23161
David, Middlesex Co., Conn., in 1832	S	17349
David, N. Y., in 1832; wid. Jane	W	25424
David, wid. Sarah	R	2015
Elias, Hartford Co., Conn., in 1832	S	15046
Elias, Conn. & N. Y	R	1970
Elijah (Conn. in 1818)	S	37867
Eliphalet, or Eliphlael, Berkshire Co., Mass., in 1832	S	44767
Eliphalet, N. Y. in 1818	S	12477
Elisha, Milford, Conn., in 1832; wid. Srarh	W	17630
Elisha, Conn. in 1818; Cont. (Conn.); wid. Martha, BLWt. 8159-160-55	W	718
Ezra, Conn., N. Y., R. I. & Vt	S	18353
Vt. in 1832.		
Ezra, Cont. (Conn.), pensioned in 1818, as artificer, in Conn.; wid. Eunice	W	18911
Flavel (Conn. in 1818)	S	12481
Francis (Windham Co., Conn., 1832)	S	23165
George, Conn. & Cont., Litchfield Co., Conn., in 1832	S	12489
George, Onondaga Co., N. Y., in 1832	S	28683
George, Middletown, Conn., in 1818	S	37873
Gershom, N. Y. in 1832	S	23575
Gershom, d. 1815; wid. Lavina	W	20890
Gideon, wid. Jemima	W	17627
(Tolland Co. in 1832.)		
Giles, wid. Polly	W	2592
(Conn. in 1818.)		
Hezekiah, wid. Lucy	W	6688
(N. Y. in 1818, as Surgeon's mate.)		

CLARK or CLARKE—Continued.

Ira (Conn., in 1818)	S 37854
Isaac, Milford, Conn., in 1832	S 16714
Israel, Conn. & Cont (Ohio in 1818.)	S 42129
Jabez (Windham Co., Conn., in 1832)	S 12495
Jacob (New London Co. in 1832; 81 in 1840 at Lebanon)	S 10453
James	BLWt. 2045-200
James, Conn. & Cont., N. Y. City, 1832	S 12514
James, Conn. & Cont., in 1818	S 44768
James, d. 1816, Conn. & Cont.; wid. Jerusha	W 20874
James W., wid. Betsey (New Haven Co. in 1832.)	W 20873
Jerome, Conn., Cont. & Privateer (N. Y. in 1818); wid. Nancy, BLWt. 14510-160-55	W 4156
Jesse, wid. Olive	W 17632
Joel, wid. Susannah, BLWt. 1515-100 (N. Y. 1818, Musician, as Clarke).	W 22799
John, Suffolk Co., N. Y., in 1832, BLWt. 32223-160-55	S 12500
John, b. 1754, res. Washington, Conn.	S 37857
John, enl. Windham, Conn., d. 1818; wid. Phebe	W 17629
John, Conn. & Conn., Sea Service b. 1746 in N. J.; claimed to have enlisted from New Haven, Conn.; res. N. Y.	R 1986
John, Conn. & Cont., b. 1763, d. 1831; enl. from Lebanon, wid. Amy	W 14482
John, Conn. & Cont., b. 1752, d. 1841; enl. from Hampton & Mansfield; wid. Lucy	W 25423
John, Cont. (Conn.), b. 1753, enlisted fr. Mansfield, res. Ashford, d. 1833	S 44386
John, styled John Clarke, 2nd, of Middletown, N. H. Co., in 1818	S 37859
Jonas, Conn., Cont. & Mass., wid. Sarah	R 2016
Jonathan	R 1992
Jonathan	R 1993
Jonathan, wid. Martha	R 2001
Jonathan, wid. Polly	W 9387
Joseph, Middlebury, Conn., in 1832	S 17347
Joseph, Windham Co. in 1818	S 37855
Joseph, Hartford Co. in 1818	S 37858
Joseph, former wid. Jemimah Spelman	R 9969
Joseph, Middlesex Co., Conn., in 1832; wid. Sarah	W 20871
Joseph, d. 1814, Conn. & Mass., wid. Judith, res. Mass.	W 14479
Joseph, former wid. Rozina King	R 19377
Joseph, BLWt. 383-200 Lieut. issued Jan. 29, 1790, to Joseph Clarke. No papers.	
Joseph C., wid. Sally	R 2018
Lamberton or Lambert, wid. Martha (Vt. in 1818.)	W 18919
Levi, Conn., 1818, as Corporal	S 37852
Levi, wid. Anna	W 1146
Lydia, former wid. of Joseph Judson	W 22782
Lyman (Conn. in 1818; and 89 in 1840 at Harwinton)	S 37851
Moses, Suffolk Co., N. Y., in 1832	S 10454
Moses, Musician, Niagara Co., N. Y., in 1832; wid. Patty	W 6684
Nathan, d. 1840, New London Co., wid. Miriam	W 17635
Nathan, Mansfield, Conn., 1832, d. 1839; wid. Ruth	W 25420
Nathaniel, wid. Sarah (Conn. in 1818.)	W 20879
Noah	R 2008
Oliver, d. N. Y. 1825, wid. Betsey	W 23816
Oliver, Brookfield, Conn., 1832; wid. Huldah, BLWt. 33758-160-55	W 717
Phebe, former wid. of Samuel Husted	W 16909
Reuben, New London Co. 1832	S 12506
Reuben, d. Conn. 1812; wid. Prudence, BLWt. 8171-160-55	W 10624
Reuben, d. Mass. 1813; wid. Zeruiah	W 14483
Robert (Conn. in 1818)	S 37864
Roger (Conn. in 1818)	S 44773
Roswell, Hebron, Conn., 1832; wid. Dolly, BLWt. 8167-160-55	W 6686
Roswell, Vt. 1832; wid. Susannah, BLWt. 26590-160-55	W 6681
Rufus, wid. Lydia (Middlesex Co. 1832; and 75 in 1840 at Saybrook.)	W 10621
Samuel, Watertown, N. Y., in 1818	S 44771
Samuel, Lewis Co., N. Y., in 1832	S 12484
Samuel, Milford, Conn., in 1832	S 18350
Samuel, wid. Hannah	R 1976
Samuel, d. 1813; wid. Susannah	W 17626
Sarah, former wid. of Miles Dickson	W 20881
Silvanus or Sylvanus (New Haven Co. 1832 as Sylvanus.)	S 17342
Smith, wid. Jane	R 1981
Solomon, wid. Mahitable	W 16536
Stephen (Middlesex Co. in 1832; 83 in 1840 at Chatham)	S 17886
Thomas	S 19247
Waters or Watrous, Cont. (Conn.)	S 38612
William, Columbia Co., N. Y., in 1818	S 44758
William, Hampshire Co., Mass., in 1832	5009
William, Chaplin, Conn., in 1832	S 10458
William, Milford, Conn., in 1832	S 16713
William, Middletown, Conn., in 1818	S 37863
William, Fabius, N. Y., in 1818	S 44760
William, Rensselaer Co., N. Y., in 1832; and d. in 1839; wid. Anner	W 22791
William, Chenengo Co., N. Y., in 1832; and d. in 1840; wid. Eunice Ford, BLWt. 7082-160-55	W 18906
Zelotes	S 3161
CLARY, Daniel (N. Y. in 1818)	S 23576
James, Conn., Cont. & N. Y.	S 44785
Samuel	S 44791

CLASON, Isaac, wid. Rachel, BLWt. 50859-160-55.. W 10619
CLEAVELAND, CLEAVLAND, CLEVELAND or CLEVLAND.
  Chester, wid. Elizabeth.. W 20865
  Cyrus, wid. Mary.. W 20877
  Frederick, wid. Susannah.. W 20884
  Gardner, wid. Huldah, BLWt. 12715-160-55.. W 25425
  Isaac, wid. Mamre.. W 22796
  Jacob (Windham Co., Conn., 1818).. S 37860
  John, Conn. & Mass., Whitehall, N. Y., in 1818.. S 44780
  John, d. 1824, N. Y.; wid. Sarah, BLWt. 2334-160-55..................................... W 16535
  John, wid. Thankful.. W 20869
  Johnson (Conn. 1818)... S 37862
  Joseph, Conn. & Cont... S 10447
  Josiah, Conn. & Mass.; N. Y. 1818.. S 44782
  Josiah, Conn. in 1818.. S 37850
  Samuel, Windham Co. in 1818; wid. Lucy, BLWt. 6040-160-55.............................. W 720
  Samuel, Vt. in 1832.. S 15378
  Silas, Conn. & Navy.. S 12486
    (Windham Co. in 1832; 84 in 1840 in Hampton.)
  Solomon, Vt. in 1818; wid. Martha.. W 6699
  Solomon, d. 1823; wid. Hannah.. W 10617
  Squier, wid. Pamelia, Conn. & Cont... W 22798
    (Vt. in 1818.)
  Stephen, wid. Hannah... W 23815
  Timothy; BLWt. 442-200, Lieut. was issued Dec. 31, 1795; also recorded as BLWt. 2658. No
    papers.
  Tracy.. S 2124
  William, N. Y. in 1818... S 12494
  William, d. 1799, former wid. Sarah Converse... W 23836
CLIFT, Lemuel; BLWt. 373-300, Capt. was issued Sept. 2, 1790. No papers.
  Wills, Conn. & Cont., wid. Mary.. W 22788
    BLWt. 368-400, Major, issued June 6, 1797, to Nathaniel Satterlee, Assignee. No papers.
CLINTON, Allen (Fairfield Co. in 1832), BLWt. 34501-160-55.................................... S 12510
  Henry.. R 2052
  Isaac.. S 12498
  Joseph B., Conn. & Cont., former wid. Margaret More or Moore........................... W 6832
    (N. Y. in 1818.) BLWt. 1873-100 and BLWt. 313-60-55.
CLOCK, John, wid. Sarah... W 17623
    (Litchfield Co. in 1832.)
CLOSE, Abraham, wid. Mary... W 25414
    (Fairfield Co. in 1832.)
  Benjamin... S 27645
  Solomon (Fairfield Co. in 1832).. S 15377
CLOUD, DeForest or Forest, wid. Anna.. W 25415
CLOUGH or CLUFF.
  Isaac (Conn. in 1818).. S 37870
  Jonathan... R 2058
CLUXTON, Samuel (Conn. in 1818)... S 37866
COAN. (See CONE.)
COATES, COATS, or COTES.
  Amos, wid. Anna.. W 10643
    (Windham Co. in 1832.)
  Edward (New London Co. in 1832).. S 15780
  John... S 10474
  Robert, Conn. & Cont... S 12599
  Thomas, former wid. Lois Delano.. W 22925
COBANN. (See CORBIN.)
COBB, Benjamin, wid. Azubah... W 10661
  BLWt. 26248-160-55. (79 in 1840 at Chatham.)
  Henry S.. R 2073
  John, wid. Mary.. R 2076
  John, Conn. & Mass.; in 1818 he was living in Vt., pensioned as Corporal, in Conn. Line.... S 38618
    BLWt. 537-100.
  Simeon (Conn. in 1818)... S 38629
COBORN or COBURN.
  Daniel, Piermont, N. H., 1818.. S 34242
  Hezekiah... S 15054
  James, Ovid, N. Y., in 1818.. S 43401
  Lemuel, Vt. in 1818, d. 1839; wid. Sarah, who moved to Mass., BLWt. 34961-160-55........ W 18946
    (See also COLBURN.)
COCHRAN, William, former wid. Lydia Chapman, BLWt. 27597-160-55............................... W 23793
COE, Abner.. S 18364
  Asher, wid. Huldah... W 17639
  Ebenezer... S 2448
  Jedediah... S 21141
  John, wid. Lois.. W 23852
  Samuel (N. Y. in 1818)... S 43404
  Seth (Litchfield Co. in 1832).. S 18363
  Thomas... S 38630
  Timothy, wid. Abigail.. W 5250
    (Hartford Co. in 1832; and 79 in 1840 at Hartland.)
  Zachariah.. S 9195
COFFIN or COFFING, Isaac, former wid. Sarah Stiles.. W 17876
COGER, Enoch, Cont. (Conn.), wid. Avis.. W 1054
  Joseph Cont. (Conn.)... BLWt. 1889-100
COGGESHALL, William, Conn. & Conn. Sea Service, wid. Eunice................................... W 17658
COGGSWELL or COGSWELL.
  Amos (Tolland Co. in 1832)... S 24127
  Benjamin, wid. Mercy... W 14523

COGGSWELL or COGSWELL—Continued.
- Jesse .... S 12565
- John .... S 12613
- William .... S 17360

COHOON, John .... S 12705
COIT, Benjamin, Conn. & Conn. Sea Service, wid. Sarah, BLWt. 26047-160-55 .... W 10639
   Farwell, wid. Anna .... W 17669
     (Conn. 1818, as Serg't.)
   Isaac, wid. Ruamy .... W 14517
     (Mass. in 1818, as Serg't.)
   Richard (Litchfield Co. in 1832) .... S 12521
COLBURN, Daniel, wid. Elizabeth .... W 17655
   Josiah .... S 10475
     (See also COBURN and CORBIN.)

COLE or COLL.
- Abner, Conn. & Cont .... S 38631
     BLWt. 382-150, Ensign, issued April 15, 1800. No papers.
     (Conn. in 1818, as Ensign.)
- Amos .... S 12594
- Benjamin, wid. Jemima .... W 1236
     BLWt. 17701-160-55. (Vt. in 1818.)
- Benjamin, Cont. (Conn.), former wid. Rachel McMurphy .... R 6797
- Daniel, Conn. & Cont., wid. Edith .... W 22848
     (Conn. in 1818.)
- David .... S 38626
- Elisha, wid. Asenath, BLWt. 12578-160-55 .... W 18932
- Hendrick, wid. Phebe .... W 17644
     (Middlesex Co. in 1832.)
- Jabez .... S 15053
- James .... S 23171
- John, wid. Mary, BLWt. 30595-160-55 .... W 2068
- Jonathan, wid. Lois .... W 17643
- Levi .... S 28694
- Nathaniel .... S 15048
- Samuel .... S 23167
- Samuel, Cont. (Conn.) .... S 10478
- Sands .... S 31619
- Solomon, wid. Lydia, BLWt. 26797-160-55 .... W 1827
     (Conn. in 1818.)
- Thankful, former wid. of William Fancher .... W 22811
- Thomas, wid. Mary .... W 17637
COLEMAN or COLMAN, John (Tolland Co. in 1832) (87 in 1840 at Bolton) .... S 17350
   Nathan, wid. Deborah .... W 17652
     (Conn. in 1818.)
   Noah, BLWt. 369-100, Surgeon, issued March 1, 1797. No papers.
COLES. (See COWLES.)
COLFAX, Jonathan, wid. Elizabeth .... W 262
   Robert .... S 34219
   William, Conn. & Cont., wid. Esther .... R 2174
     BLWt. 378-300, Capt., issued Dec. 9, 1796. No papers.
COLL. (See COLE.)
COLLAR or COLLER.
- John, Cont. service, Conn. res. in 1818 .... S 38623
- Norris or Narris, Conn. & Cont .... S 12576
COLLARD or COLLERD, Thomas T .... R 13363
COLLENS. (See COLLINS.)
COLLEY, George (New Haven Co. in 1832) .... S 18361
COLLIER, Joseph (N. Y. in 1818) .... S 43399
   Oliver .... S 12555
COLLINS, COLLINGS, or COLLENS.
- Ambrose (Litchfield Co. in 1832) .... S 17892
- Daniel, Conn. & Cont., wid. Anna .... W 20899
- Daniel, wid. Eunice, BLWt. 16104-160-55 .... W 17648
- Elisha, Conn. & Mass., wid. Roxa, BLWt. 96060-160-55 .... W 10305
- Jabez .... S 16088
- Jonathan .... S 23577
- Lois, former wid. of Nathaniel Wood, Conn., Green Mt. Boys & Vt .... W 16925
- Nathaniel, Cont. (Conn.) .... S 12585
     (Hartford Co. in 1832.)
- Samuel, wid. Betsey .... W 17645
     (N. Y. in 1818.) BLWt. 41-100 and BLWt. 17622-160-55.
- Sarah, former wid. of Thomas H. Hooker .... W 24442
- Stephen or Stephens .... S 10484
- William, Ill. in 1832 .... S 32184
- William, N. Y. in 1818 .... S 43350
- William Lock .... S 36472
COLMAN. (See COLEMAN.)
COLENEY or COLONY, Isaac, BLWt. 26464-160-55 .... S 12564
COLT, Jabez or Jabish .... S 9321
     (N. Y. in 1818 as Jabez.)
   John, Conn. & Conn. Sea service .... S 18769
   Peter, wid. Sarah .... W 5880
COLTON, Mehitable D., former wid. of Pownal Deming, BLWt. 8403-160-55 .... W 20894
   Samuel, Conn. & Cont., wid. Lois .... W 17663
COLVER. (See CULVER.)
COMBS, John, Conn. & Cont .... R 2185
COMES, Ebenezer .... R 2188
COMINS, COMMINGS or COMMINS. (See CUMMINGS.)
COMSTOCK, Aaron, wid. Ann .... W 17647
     (Fairfield Co. in 1832.)
   Abner .... S 12575

COMSTOCK, Achilles, wid. Sarah	W 20900
Ansel, wid. Betsey	W 18950
BLWt. 32222-160-55.	
Anson	S 1253
Caleb, wid. Lucy	W 67252
David	S 12589
Elisha	S 12570
James, wid. Amy	W 17651
(New London Co. in 1832; and 90 in 1840 at Montville.)	
Jason, wid. Sarah	W 17646
(New London Co. in 1832.)	
John, wid. Charlotte	W 25434
(New London Co. in 1832.)	
Martin L.	S 19260
Nathan	R 2194
Oliver, wid. Amy, Conn., Cont. & Navy (Conn. in 1818)	W 17660
Samuel, N. H. in 1832	S 22693
Samuel, Wilton, Conn. in 1818	S 36471
BLWt. 374-300, Capt., issued Jan. 16, 1797. No papers.	
(Conn. in 1818, as Brevet Major.)	
Samuel, Saybrook, Conn. in 1818	S 36475
Samuel, former wid. Else Scofield	W 22163
BLWt. 10029-160-55.	
(Soldier was from Fairfield Co. Conn., but d. in 1788 and never received a pension.)	
Serajah or Sarajah, former wid. Clemina Austin	W 16170
(Pensioned in 1818 in N. Y. as Saragah.)	
Simeon (Conn. in 1818 as Corporal; 86 in 1840 at Groton)	S 36463
Stephen	S 12573
Theophilus	S 43379
(N. Y. in 1818 as Serg't.)	
CONANT, Ebenezer	S 29095
Josiah, former wid. of, Ruth Barton	W 17260
Silvanus or Sylvanus, Conn. & Cont	S 16737
CONE or COAN, Beriah	S 9237
Daniel (Mass. in 1818)	S 17352
Daniel, H. (Conn. in 1818; 87 in 1840 at Winchester)	S 36473
Henry, wid. Waitstill	W 25432
(Wid. was 79 in 1840 at Lyme.)	
Israel (Conn. in 1818, as Serg't)	S 36477
Jesse (Conn. in 1818 as Corporal)	S 36478
John (New Haven Co. in 1832 as Coan; 77 in 1840 at Guilford)	S 31628
Joseph, Conn. & Cont	S 12569
(N. Y. in 1818.)	
Joshua, East Haddam in 1832, wid. Sarah, BLWt. 81566-160-55	W 25428
Joshua, Conn. & Cont. d. 1807, wid. Mehitable	W 18933
Nathaniel, Cont. (Conn.)	S 36476
(Conn. in 1818.)	
Noadiah, wid. Polly	W 1030
BLWt. 30696-160-55. (Middlesex Co. 1832; 80 in 1840, Haddam.)	
Oliver	S 12525
Ozias (N. Y. in 1818), BLWt. 1317-100	S 4334
Reuben, Cont. (Conn.), former wid. of, Esther Edwards	R 3256
Robert, wid. Sarah	W 18961
(Mass. in 1818.)	
Samuel, Maine in 1818	S 36988
Samuel, Conn. & Cont., wid. Betsey	W 16538
(N. Y. in 1818.)	
Timothy	S 9197
William, Conn. & Cont	S 38635
CONGAR or CONGER.	
Elijah (Fairfield Co. in 1832)	S 12544
Joseph	S 9223
CONGDON, John (N. Y. in 1818)	S 43388
CONNELL, Benoni, Conn. & Cont., wid. Sarah	W 20914
(See also CORNWELL.)	
CONNELY, CONNOLY, or CONNOLLY, James	S 34229
CONVERS or CONVERSE.	
Benjamin (Windham Co. in 1832)	S 12549
Demon Read	R 2241
Dyer (Conn. in 1818, and d, Sept. 11, 1818)	S 36479
Elisha, Conn. & Cont	S 12517
Jeremiah, Conn. & Mass	R 2242
Jonathan, wid. Zurnah or Zuruah	W 722
(Windham Co. in 1832; and 80 in 1840 at Thompson.)	
Nathaniel, wid. Abigail	R 2240
Sarah, former wid. of William Cleaveland	W 23836
Solvin, wid. Sarah	W 25436
Stephen, Conn. & Mass., wid. Sarah	W 22847
Thomas, BLWt. 371-300, Capt., issued Feb. 14, 1791. No papers.	
CONWAY, Elizabeth, former wid. of Stephen Hill, Cont. service, Conn. res. & Agency	W 18885
COOK or COOKE, Abial or Abiel, Conn. & N. Y., wid. Julia Anna, BLWt. 24761-160-55	W 6704
Abraham. wid. Elizabeth	W 3224
Archibald (Vt. in 1818)	S 15781
Atwater, wid. Mary	W 16914
Ebenezer or Ebenezer H., wid. Jemima, BLWt. 24330-160-55	W 6929
Elisha, wid. Lois	W 2066
Elijah	S 29085
Ezekiel	S 12526
George	R 2254

COOK or COOKE, George.. BLWt. 665-100
   Gideon, wid. Huldah... W 20924
   Jesse, BLWt. 385-300, Capt. issued April 23, 1798, to Jesse Cook. No papers.
   Joel, Penna. 1818 and 1832... S 3182
   Joel, Ohio in 1818... S 43392
   Johnson, Serg't. Ohio 1818.. S 10461
   Johnson, Fairfield Co., Ohio.. S 42141
   Johnson, Serg't. BLWt. 5572 issued in 1791.
   Jonah... S 19948
   Joseph, wid. Mercy... R 2269
   Lemuel (N. Y. in 1818)... S 23173
   Lucy, former wid. of John Priest... W 16539
      BLWt. 2227-100.
   Merriman or Marimon, BLWt. 26126-160-55... S 2453
   Miles (N. Y. in 1818)... S 43366
   Moses, Windsor, Conn., in 1832... S 15056
   Moses.. R 2270
   Nathan (Conn. in 1818)... S 36482
   Nathaniel, wid. Anise.. W 17642
   Oliver, wid. Submit.. W 16929
   Richard, Utica, N. Y., in 1832.. S 12545
   Richard, Oneida Co., N. Y., in 1818.. S 43368
   Samuel, Vt. in 1832... S 22187
   Samuel, Conn. & Cont., wid. Mary.. W 15829
      N. Y in 1818.
   Serad... S 12533
   Shubael, wid. Sarah.. R 2274
   Trueworthy... S 43395
   Urijah.. R 2279
   Warren, Conn. & Cont., wid. Lois, BLWt. 49466-160-55..................................... W 18926
   William, Middletown, Conn., 1818.. S 36467
   William, Vt. in 1818.. S 38641
   William, Green Co., N. Y., in 1818, BLWt. 1415-100.. S 43381
   William, Pompey, N. Y., in 1818, wid. Asenath, BLWt. 11421-160-55......................... W 1723
   William, Mexico, N. Y., in 1818, wid. Keziah... W 23871
COOLEY, or COOLY, Reuben (Conn. in 1818).. S 36469
   Thomas, wid. Elizabeth... R 2282
COOLIDGE, Persis, former wid. of John Allen, Conn. & N. Y.................................... W 23429
COON, Daniel... S 12568
   James, Cont. (Warren's reg't.), BLWt. 381-200 Lieut., issued March 18, 1790, to Deborah
      Beach (late Coon), Adx. Also recorded BLWt. 2548. No papers.
   Joseph, Conn. & R. I... S 12583
      (New London Co. in 1832.)
COOPER, Abner.. S 22178
   Abraham (Conn. in 1818).. S 36468
   Isaac, wid. Lydia... W 3946
   Price... S 43349
COPELAND, COPELIN or COPLAND.
   Amasa, Conn. & Cont... S 36464
      (Conn. in 1818 & 82 in 1840 at Pomfret.)
   Asa, wid. Abilene.. W 2594
   Jonathan (Windham Co. in 1832)... S 31616
COPLEY, Daniel, Conn. & Cont.. S 12518
      (Litchfield Co. in 1832 & Milford in 1840.)
   Samuel... S 18362
COPP, Ebenezer, wid. Deborah... W 20911
      (Conn. in 1818.)
   Joseph (N. Y. in 1818, as Drum Major)... S 43398
      BLWt. 569-100.
CORBIN or COBANN, Clement, wid. Sabra... W 3661
      (N. H. in 1818.) BLWt. 9418-160-55.
   Joseph... S 34601
   Joseph, Conn. & Mass... S 9323
   Peter, wid. Villette, BLWt. 13412-160-55.. W 24836
   (See also COBORN and COBURN.)
CORBITT, Joseph, wid. Hannah... W 17661
COREY or CORY, Benedick, Conn. & R. I.. R 2317
   Jerusha, former wid. of Eliphaz Parrish.. W 1563
CORLISS, Bliss, wid. Phebe... W 17650
CORNELIUS, John, Conn. res. in 1821.. R 2324
CORNING or CORNNING.
   Allen (Conn. in 1818).. S 36480
   Bliss... S 22684
   Uriah, Conn. & Navy.. S 15262
      (New London Co. in 1832; Preston, 1840.)
CORNISH, George (Hartford Co. in 1832; 79 in 1840 at Simsbury).............................. S 15058
   Joel.. S 12561
CORNWALL or CORNWELL.
   Amos.. R 2334
   Ashbel, Conn. & Privateer, wid. Roxana, BLWt. 15192-160-55................................. W 27665
   Benjamin (N. Y. in 1818).. S 43393
   Daniel, wid. Rachel, BLWt. 7061-160-55... W 25427
   Isaac... S 23584
   John (Middlesex Co. in 1832; 80 in Middletown in 1840)...................................... S 10485
   Nathaniel, wid. Anna.. W 17653
   Richard.. BLWt. 1586-100
   Samuel, wid. Sarah.. W 23844
      (See also CONNELL.)

CORTIS or CORTTIS. (See CURTIS.)
CORWIN, Amaziah... S 12582
   Selah, wid. Joanna... W 22805
     (N. Y. in 1818.)
CORY. (See COREY.)
COSSIT, Timothy... S 23170
COTES. (See COATES.)
COTTEN or COTTON.
   Bibye, L... S 12571
   George, BLWt. 380-150, Ensign, was issued Feb. 15, 1799. No papers.
   Rowland, Conn., Cont. & War of 1812... S 11170
   Samuel, Conn. & Navy... R 2356
   Ward, wid. Nabby... W 22826
   William (Vt. in 1818)... S 34244
COUCH, Abraham... S 36481
     (Conn. in 1818 and 73 in 1840 at Reading.)
   Amos, wid. Phebe (Conn. in 1818)... W 20901
   Daniel... S 29086
   Ebenezer (Conn. in 1818)... S 36483
   Ebenezer, wid. Asenath, BLWt. 27599-160-55... W 23839
   John, wid. Lois... W 17640
   John, wid. Prudence... R 2360
   Joshua, wid. Patty, Conn. & Conn. Sea Service... W 17656
   Samuel, Conn., Cont. & Mass... S 29717
   Stephen, Poliphena... W 14508
   Thomas, wid. Sarah... W 20906
   William, or FREEMAN, William, colored... R 2358
CONNEY, Michael, Cont. (Conn.), wid. Mehitable... W 16919
COVEL, or COVELL or COVIL or COVILL.
   Abraham, wid. Mehitable... R 2378
   David, wid. Sarah (N. Y. in 1818)... W 18952
   Ebenezer (N. Y. in 1818)... S 31625
   Ebenezer, Conn. & Cont... S 15261
     (Windham Co. in 1832 as Covel; 81 in 1840 as Covill.)
   Eliphalet, Conn., Mass. & Privateer... S 10477
   Ephraim... S 12597
   Henry Conn. & Mass... S 30954
   James, wid. Lucy... R 2377
   James, Cont. (Conn.), wid. Margaret, BLWt. 6256-160-55... W 5251
COVERT, Jeremiah... S 10466
COWDERY, COWDRY, CAWDERY or CAWDRY.
   Ambrose (Hartford Co. in 1832)... S 15050
   Asa (Hartford Co. in 1832; and 82 at Hartland in 1840)... S 10479
   Edward, wid. Submit... W 23863
     (Vt. in 1818.)
   Samuel, Cont. (Conn.)... BLWt. 132-100
   William... R 2392
COWEL or COWELL, Samuel... S 10476
COWLES, COWLS or COLES.
   Asa (Conn. in 1818)... S 36466
   Cynthia, former wid. of Ezekiel N. Root... W 4027
   Ezekiel (Hartford Co. in 1832)... S 12614
   Isaac (Hartford Co. in 1832)... S 16089
   Jabez (84 in 1840, Hartford Co.)... S 15057
   Noah... R 2394
   Phineas... S 23197
   Samuel... R 2395
   Solomon, Conn., Cont. & N. Y... S 15049
     (Hartford Co. in 1832.)
   Thomas, wid. Tamer, BLWt. 9202-160-55... W 23851
COX, Robert, Vermont in 1818... S 43400
COY or COYE.
   David (N. Y. in 1818)... S 43364
   David... R 2413
   Edee, Cont. (Conn.)... S 43376
     (Mass. in 1818 as Corporal.)
   Ephraim, wid. Rebekah... W 17638
     (Windham Co. in 1832.)
   Joseph, Conn. & Cont... S 43371
     (N. Y. in 1818 as Serg't.)
   Nehemiah, wid. Anne... W 20909
     (N. Y. in 1818.)
   Vine... S 10262
CRAFT or CRAFTS.
   Benjamin, wid. Jane, BLWt. 202-60-55... W 5258
     (N. Y. in 1818.)
   Joseph, Cont. (Conn.), BLWt. 51-100... S 46352
   Samuel, wid. Lucy... BLWt. 56948-160-55
CRAIN. (See CRANE.)
CRAMER, CRAMMER or CREAMER.
   Henry, Conn. & Cont., wid. Jemima... R 2436
CRAMPTON or CRAMTON.
   Elon (Litchfield Co. in 1832)... S 10502
   Jonathan, wid. Elizabeth, BLWt. 8453-160-55... W 1725
     (New Haven Co. in 1832.)
   Mary, former wid. of James Benjamin... W 20935

CRANDAL, CRANDALL, CRANDEL, CRANDELL, CRANDOL or CRANDOLL.
Amariah or Ammariah, BLWt. 26081-160-55	S	16090
Azel	S	12633
Christopher, Conn. & R. I	S	15269
Edward, Conn. & Cont	S	43410
(N. Y. in 1818.)		
Ezra	S	12618
Gideon, Conn. & R. I	S	15272
Isaiah, Conn. & R. I	S	12636
Jeremiah, Conn., N. Y. & R. I	S	10506
John	R	2438
Richmond, Conn. & Conn. Sea Service	W	20930
Wid. Lucretia. BLWt. 34962-160-55.		
CRANE or CRAIN, Amariah, wid. Tryphena	W	17688
(N. Y. in 1818 as fifer.)		
Curtis, wid. Elizabeth	W	16547
Daniel, Conn. & Cont	S	12713
(Tolland Co. in 1832 as Crain.)		
Ebenezer, Conn. & Mass	R-	
Elihu	S	24134
Elijah, wid. Susannah	W	16223
Elisha	S	15256
Elizabeth, former wid. of Ozins Hanford	W	25449
Enos, former wid. of Sophia Williams, BLWt. 101838-160-55	W	11832
(N. Y. in 1818.)		
James	S	23588
John, N. Y. in 1818	S	43415
John, Cortland Co., N. Y., in 1832, wid. Phillis, BLWt. 26324-160-55	W	8192
Jonathan, wid. Sybil	W	23882
Nathaniel (Conn. in 1818 as Serg't.)	S	36484
Roger, Conn. & Mass., wid. Sarah	W	18981
Rufus, wid. Rachel	W	23877
Silas, wid. Clarissa, BLWt. 85080-160-55	R	13483
Simeon, Conn. & Mass., wid. Anne	W	18977
(New London Co. in 1832.)		
CRARY, Joseph, Conn., Privateer & R. I., wid. Lucy	W	23867
Nathan, Conn. & Vt., wid. Lydia	R	2456
CRAW. (See CROW.)		
CRAWFORD, James, wid. Hannah	W	17685
Jason, former wid. of, Bethsheba Strobridge or Strowbridge	W	19110
(N. Y. in 1818.)		
NOTE.—Bethsheba's other husband, George Strobridge or Strowbridge, was also a Revolutionary soldier.		
CREAMER. (See CRAMER.)		
CRESEY, CRESSEY or CRISSEY.		
Gould, wid. Eunice	R	2483
John	S	12965
Jonathan, Cont. (Conn.)	S	34262
(Mass. in 1818.)		
CRIPPEN, Silas, Conn. & N. Y., wid. Elizabeth	W	20929
CRITTENDEN, Gideon (also given CHITTENDEN)	S	42660
CROCKER, David, Conn. & Navy	S	42146
Dyer	S	22710
James, wid. Mary	R	24921
John (Conn. in 1818)	S	36485
Peter	R	2493
Zebulon, wid. Sarah	W	25453
BLWt. 26682-160-55.		
CROFOOT or CROFUT.		
Elizabeth, former wid. of Lewis Hunt	W	17686
Ephraim, Cont. (Conn.), wid. Lois	W	20927
(Conn. in 1818.)		
John	R	2497
Seth, wid. Sarah	W	22859
BLWt. 26319-160-55.		
CROOK, Joseph	S	15271
CROSBY, David (Ohio in 1818 as Corporal)	S	43413
Ebenezer	BLWt.	7759-400
Obed, wid. Jerusha	W	25446
Sawney, or YORK, Sawney	S	36862
Simon (N. Y. in 1818)	S	43420
Thomas, Conn. & N. Y., wid. Diantha	W	3516
CROSLEY, Prince, wid. Caroline	W	24833
CROSMAN. (See CROSSMAN.)		
CROSS, Eunice, former wid. of Isaac Tubbs	W	16937
Joseph, Vt. residence	S	39385
Joseph, N. Y. in 1818, wid. Serviah	W	16940
Nero (Vt. in 1818.)	S	39370
Solomon	S	21148
Stephen, wid. Sarah	W	23892
Uriah, Conn., Cont. & Green Mt. Boys	S	10499
CROSSMAN, Trobridge, wid. Phebe	W	25448
CROSWELL, John	S	22703
CROUCH, Christopher (Tolland Co. in 1832)	S	17904
David, former wid. of, Eleanor Wiley	W	18354
Conn. & N. Y. BLWt. 33553-160-55.		

CROW or CRAW, David, N. Y. in 1832	S 12622
Elias	R 2458
Jacob	S 12631
Reuben, Conn. & Cont	S 38643
(Vt. in 1818 as Craw.)	
Shubael, Cont. (Conn.), wid. Huldah	W 25447
(Wid. was 74 in 1840 at New Hartford.)	
CROWELL, Edward, wid. Rachel	W 17684
(Middlesex Co. in 1832.)	
Samuel, d. 1811, Bedford Co., Penna., wid. Jerusha	W 4931
Samuel, Middletown, Conn., in 1832, wid. Sarah. BLWt. 27631-160-55	W 25451
Solomon	S 23587
CRUMB, Joseph, former wid. of, Oliviet Tuthill. BLWt. 99761-160-55	W 11675
CRUMBIE, Aaron or Aron, Conn. & Mass	S 34716
(Vt. in 1818 as Corporal.)	
CUFF, Cato (Conn. in 1818; 83 in 1840 in Stonington)	S 36487
Samson or Sampson	S 34616
CULVER or COLVER.	
Aaron, wid. Phebe	R 2569
Abel	BLWt. 2128-100
Christopher	S 12660
(New London Co. in 1832; 87 in 1840 in New London.)	
David, Conn. & Cont., wid. Mary, BLWt. 14514-160-55	W 4933
Eliakim	S 23184
Enoch, wid. Lucy	W 25464
James, wid. Hannah	W 23900
John	S 45713
Nathaniel, wid. Catharine, BLWt. 92083-160-55	W 10697
(Also given, COLVER, Nathan.)	
Reuben	R 2572
Sarah, former wid. of Josiah Atkins	W 17673
Thomas	S 23185
Timothy, Conn. & Cont	S 40871
(Penna. in 1818 as Serg't.)	
CUMMINGS, CUMMINS, COMINS or COMMINGS.	
Asa, wid. Cathelina	W 18992
(N. Y. in 1818.) BLWt	31442-160-55
John	S 23582
Simeon, former wid. of, Naomi Lilly	W 26217
Stephen (N. Y. in 1818)	S 43342
William, Vt. in 1818	S 39389
William, Mansfield, Conn., in 1832, wid. Rhoda	W 17671
William	BLWt. 13-100
CUNE, or McEWEN, John	S 11056
CUNNINGHAM, Anna, former wid. of Nathan Burrows	W 17674
John	S 18367
Peter, Conn. & Mass. sea service, wid. Elizabeth	W 17672
Robert, wid. Hannah	R 2584
CURRIER, Joseph	S 43426
(See also CARRIER.)	
CURTICE, CURTIS, CURTISS, CORTIS, or CORTISS.	
Agur, 1760-1844, wid. Huldah, BLWt. 26316-160-55	W 25456
Agur, 1755-1838, wid. Mercy	W 25465
NOTE.—Both of the above soldiers lived in Fairfield Co., Conn.	
Amos	S 36488
Andrew, Conn. & N. Y., wid. Eunice	R 2597
Benjamin, wid. Amelia, BLWt. 9206-160-55	W 6900
Caleb, wid. Catharine	W 17682
Chauncey or Chauncy, Conn. & Cont	W 6746
Wid. Mary Ann. BLWt. 1986-100.	
Daniel, Conn. & Cont., wid. Mary	R 2605
Davis, wid. Lois	R 2603
Ebenezer	S 18789
Eli (Conn. 1818 as Ensign)	S 37001
Elijah	S 12641
Everard	S 17368
Felix (N. Y. in 1818)	S 43429
Frederick, wid. Persis	W 17676
(N. Y. in 1818.)	
Gideon, wid. Hannah	W 9400
(Vt. in 1818.) BLWt. 5440-160-55.	
Giles, wid. Hannah, BLWt. 26794-160-55	W 22874
Giles, wid. Lucy	W 637
BLWt. 379-200, Lieut. was issued Nov. 10, 1789. No papers.	
Hull, Conn. & Cont	S 18787
Isaac (Ohio in 1832)	S 16094
NOTE.—The Isaac Curtis who lived in Conn. after the Revolution served from R. I.	
Jacob	S 12657
James, Conn. & Mass. Sea service	S 12659
James, d, 1811, wid. Sarah	W 17679
Japheth, wid. Mary	W 17649
Joel, Ohio in 1818, wid. Sally, BLWt. 26318-160-55	W 25460
Joel, N. Y. in 1818	S 43428½
Joseph, wid. Lydia	W 25457
Jotham, wid. Elizabeth, BLWt. 33760-160-55	W 6745
Lysander	S 17367
Mabel, former wid. of Josiah Burrit	W 25463

CURTICE, CURTIS, CURTISS, CORTIS, or CORTISS—Continued.
 Martin.. S 22711
 Philip.. S 12658
 Robert, wid. Clara, BLWt. 40943-160-55... W 25466
 Robert W... S 28698
 Samuel, Conn. Sea service & Navy, wid. Zipporah................................... W 3956
 Samuel... R 2608
 Sarah, former wid. of Robert Lewis.. W 20939
 Silas, Cont. (Conn.) & War of 1812.. S 43436
 Simeon, former wid. of, Elizabeth Catlin, BLWt. 14667-160-55...................... W 10569
 Solomon, Conn. & Mass., wid. Hannah... W 23895
 Thomas, Conn. or Mass., wid. Eunice... R 2598
 Timothy, wid. Rebecca... W 20943
 William, Conn., Cont., N. H. & Vt., wid. Charry................................... W 23902
 Zadock, wid. Rosy... W 17681
 Zerah or Zarah, wid. Abigail.. W 282
  (Ohio in 1818.) BLWt. 205-60-55.
  This woman's claim for BL on acc't. of her former husband (Elias Edward or Edwards, War 1812) was rejected. See papers in this file.
CUSHMAN, CUSHMON or CASHMAN.
 Benjamin, Conn. & Cont., wid. Elizabeth... W 22883
 Charles, former wid. of, Desire Gates... W 17003
 Daniel, Cont. (Conn.)... S 23183
 Eliphalet (N. Y. in 1818)... S 44389
 Frederick, Conn. & Vt... S 10512
 Joab, wid. Hannah... W 17683
 Jonah, wid. Rachel.. W 14557
 Joseph, wid. Tabitha, BLWt. 14501-160-55.. W 20593
 Joshua.. S 43437
 Nathaniel, Vt, in 1818.. S 38648
 Nathaniel, wid. Hannah.. W 25459
CUTLER, Jonathan... S 15794
 Joseph.. S 43432
 Joseph, Conn. & R. I.. S 12643
 Seth.. S 28700
CUTTING, Bille, BLWt. 26077-160-55... S 16355
 Zebedee... S 12645
CYRUS, Exeter (Conn. in 1818).. S 36491

D.

DABALL or DABOLL, Benjamin, wid. Prudence.. W 6991
 NOTE.—This woman was also pensioned on account of the service of her former husband, Joseph Moxley, Conn., who received a pension for disability and died Nov. 10, 1815. No papers in his claim. See her papers within.
 John, act of 1816, Conn. Agency... S 19950
 John, Groton, Conn., 1818, d. 1830, N. Y. from which State wid. Anstiss (or Austiss) was pensioned, Conn. & Cont. service.. W 24033
DAGGETT, Henry, wid. Anna.. W 17709
 BLWt. 539-200, Lieut. was issued Aug. 21, 1789. No papers.
 John, Conn. & Vt.. S 23595
 Nathan, Conn. Sea service & Mass. Sea service..................................... R 21987
 Silas, Conn. Sea service & Mass. & Mass. Sea service; wid. Deborah................ W 22899
DAILEY or DAILY or DALEY.
 David... S 43445
 Giles... S 36500
 James... S 43465
 Johnson or William Johnson, wid. Lydia, W 1393, and BLWt. 7212-160-55.
 Obadiah, Cont. (Conn.) former wid. Elizabeth Cady................................. W 23757
 Samuel.. S 44128
DAINS, Asa, Conn. & Privateer, wid. Jane... W 6960
 Ephraim Cont. (Conn.), wid. Irene, BLWt. 15128-160-55............................. W 4937
 Jesse, wid. Chloe... R 2624
DALIBA, DALLABY or DALLIBA, George, Conn. & Cont., BLWt. 943-100..................... S 43461
DAMAN. (See DEMING.)
DAN or DANN, Squire, wid. Rhoda, BLWt. 50901-160-55.................................. W 2439
DANA, David.. S 22194
 Joseph.. S 28705
DANIELS, Daniel.. S 43471
 David, wid. Lucina.. W 3959
 Ezekiel, Conn. 1818... S 36498
 Ezekiel, N. Y. in 1818.. S 43454
 Job, wid. Jane.. W 4662
 John.. S 38653
 Jonathan.. R 2652
 Nathan.. S 12730
 Nehemiah, wid. Elizabeth.. W 2074
 Peletiah, wid. Huldah... W 25513
 Reuben.. S 36499
 Samuel, New Haven Co., Conn., in 1832... S 16753
 Samuel, N. Y. in 1832; wid. Lydia, BLWt. 11179-160-55............................. W 25510
DANN. (See DAN.)
DARBE, or DARBEE or DARBY.
 Asa... S 15396
 Jedediah, Conn. & Cont.. S 43455
 Moses, wid. Dorothy... W 3339
 (See also DERBY.)
DARLING, Benjamin, Jaffrey, N. H., 1818, then N. Y. & Vt.............................. S 43452
 Benjamin, d. 1820, Conn., wid. Mary... W 17705

DARRANCE. (See DORRANCE.)
DARRIN, Daniel, Conn. & N. Y., wid. Martha, BLWt. 26924-60-55................................. W 19141
DARROW, Benjamin, Tenn. 1828, BLWt. 1945-100... S 46229
  Benjamin, Conn. Sea service & Navy, Conn. 1818; d. 1827; wid. Grace.......................... W 24850
  Christopher, Conn. & Cont., wid. Bridget... W 16554
  Daniel... S 36492
  Ebenezer, Waterford, Conn., 1832.. S 18369
  Ebenezer, Cont. (Conn.), Litchfield, Conn., in 1818, as Corporal............................. S 15072
  James, wid. Sarah... W 1394
  Nathan.. S 15075
  Samuel.. S 23186
  William, wid. Sally... R 2670
DART or DEART, Caleb, wid. Margaret.. W 16943
  David... S 18368
  Dolphin... S 36496
  Ebenezer, Cont. (Conn.), wid. Hannah, BLWt. 10305-160-55................................... W 1243
  Elias, wid. Ruth.. R 2673
  Jonathan.. S 17922
  Levi, wid. Elizabeth.. W 24046
  Thomas, Conn. & N. H... R 2674
DASKAM, John... S 43453
  William... S 36495
DAUD. (See DOWD.)
DAVENPORT, or DEAVENPORT, or DEVENPORT, Benjamin, former wid. of, Elizabeth
    Judson.. W 7948
  Charles, wid. Mabel... W 17706
  David, wid. Patience.. R 2682
  Eliphalet, wid. Elizabeth.. W 16233
  Hezekiah... BLWt. 2329-200
  Humphrey, Conn. & Cont., wid. Jerusha... W 20952
  John, d. 1830, not pensioned; wid. Mary S., from Fairfield.................................. W 17711
  John, N. Y. 1818; d. 1830, wid. Polly, from Wayne Co., N. Y................................ W 24031
  Noah, wid. Lydia.. W 22911
  Phebe, former wid. of Yale Todd, Cont. (Conn.), q. v.
  Squire.. S 44148
DAVIDSON, DAVISON or DAVISSON.
  Benjamin, Conn. & Cont. (Mass.), wid. Roxy.. W 16946
  Douglas or Douglass, wid. Asenath, BLWt. 31287-160-55...................................... W 19145
  Ezra, former wid. of, Deidamia Boone.. W 25260
  Hezekiah.. R 2689
  John, N. Y. in 1832... S 32209
  John, Conn. & N. Y. serv.. BL Rej.
  Joseph, wid. Lydia.. W 25517
  Paul, wid. Sally.. W 20962
  Peter... S 15063
  Thomas.. S 15066
  Zachariah, wid. Hannah... W 17712
DAVIS, Abel, Conn., Green Mt. Boys & Vt.. S 12902
  Cornelius, wid. Ruth, BLWt. 31897-160-55... W 10716
  Daniel, Fairfield Co., Conn., 1851, aged 87.. S 17915
  Daniel, Groton, Conn., 1818, wid. Deborah... W 20947
  David... S 23592
  Ebenezer.. S 34292
  Elijah.. S 10548
  Elisha, wid. Elizabeth, BLWt. 29736-160-55.. W 1730
  George, Northumberland Co., Penna., 1832.. S 22193
  George, never pensioned; wid. Deborah, Fulton Co., N. Y................................... R 2712
  Hannah, former wid. of Stephen Palmer, q. v.
  Jacob, wid. Catherine, BLWt. 2-60-55.. W 19136
  James, Harwinton, Conn., 1832.. S 17378
  James, New Haven Co., Conn., 1832; d. 1852; son of James, also Rev. sol., wid. Ruth, BLWt.
    10239-160-55... W 10706
  Jesse, former wid. of, Mary Ginnings.. R 3971
  John, N. Y. in 1832... S 12720
  John, Fairfield Co., Conn., 1832; d. 1840; wid. Eunice....................................... W 17699
  John, Cont. & Conn., Vt. in 1818.. S 39402
  John, Conn. & Cont., Warner, N. H., in 1818, BLWt. 765-100................................ S 45716
  Jonathan.. S 36494
  Joseph, Conn. & Cont., Conn. in 1832... S 17373
  Joseph, Conn., Mass. & Vt., Franklin Co., Mass., 1832, & died Dec., 1832; wid. Azubah...... W 14581
  Josiah, wid. Annis F., BLWt. 26658-160-55.. W 20961
  Kitteridge, Conn. & Mass.. S 10537
  Lathrop, wid. Mary... W 20958
  Lois, former wid. of Elihu Judd, q. v.
  Micajah, wid. Betsey.. R 2703
  Nancy, former wid. of Abner Lee, q. v.
  Nathan, Cont. (Conn.), wid. Betsa... W 19142
  Nathaniel... R 2751
  Samuel, Ohio in 1832.. S 9380
  Samuel, not pensioned; wid. lived Mich.. R 2752
  Samuel, Conn. & R. I., d. 1826; wid. Lucy, New London Co., Conn., 1838, BLWt. 30700-160-55. W 17701
  Silas, Conn. & Cont., wid. Matilda.. W 10709
  Solomon, wid. Mary... R 2765
  Stephen B... S 36497
  Thomas.. R 2769
  Thomas, d. Fairfield Co., Conn., 1827; wid. Abigail, applied from N. Y...................... W 19152
  Thomas, Windham Co., Conn., 1832, & died there Nov., 1832; wid. Rebecca................. W 17703
  Willard.. BLWt. 67513-160-55
  William... S 42668

DAVISON or DAVISSON. (See DAVIDSON.)
DAWSON, Titus .... S 15070
DAY, Comfort, wid. Esther .... W 16232
    Isaac, Cont. (Conn.), wid. Sarah, BLWt. 11-60-55 .... W 6954
    John, wid. Annis .... W 17694
    Noah .... S 23591
    Russell, wid. Anna .... R 2780
    Samuel .... S 10530
    Solomon .... S 22725
    Thomas, wid. Susannah .... S 17695
    Westbrook .... S 39405
DAYTON, Andrew, wid. Jerusha .... W 17708
    Benjamin .... S 17369
    David, wid. Elizabeth .... R 2793
    Ephraim, wid. Mary, BLWt. 91508-160-55 .... W 10707
    Jonah .... S 13691
    Mary, former wid. of Seth Bulkley, q. v..
    Nathaniel .... S 10527
    Samuel, wid. Naomi .... W 20955
DEAN, DEANE or DEANS, or DEIANS, or DEEN.
    Aaron, BLWt. 28523-160-55 .... S 9384
    Benjamin. NOTE.—BLWt. 1988-100 was given his daughter, who resided in Conn., for Cont. service of her father.
    David, Vt. in 1818 .... S 39424
    David, Tolland Co. Conn. in 1832; wid. Mary, BLWt. 26489-160-55 .... W 1246
    Ebenezer .... S 31647
    Elijah, wid. Anna, BLWt. 3766-160-55 .... W 19162
    Enos, Conn. & Vt .... S 15400
    Hopestill or Hoptill, former wid. of Ephraim Johnson, q. v.
    James L., BLWt. 56505-160-55 .... S 22200
    Joel, Conn. & Mass .... S 15083
    John, wid. Martha .... W 17714
    Phineas or Phinehas, Conn. & Cont., wid. Ruth, BLWt. 17576-160-55 .... W 25527
    Reuben, Litchfield Co., Conn., in 1818; died in 1821; wid. Lucretia .... W 25524
    Reuben, Norfolk, Conn. in 1832; died in 1836; wid. Roxalana .... W 17713
    Samuel, Conn. & N. Y., wid. Hannah, BLWt. 71027-160-55 .... W 25520
    William, Cont. services but Conn. res. after Rev.; N. Y. when pensioned; wid. Anna .... W 20977
DE ANGELIS, Paschal Charles Joseph, Conn., Conn. Sea Service & Privateer; wid. Elizabeth .... W 17715
DEAR, Jonathan .... S 34740
DEART. (See DART.)
DEAVENPORT. (See DAVENPORT.)
DEEN. (See DEAN.)
DE FOREST, Abel .... S 15086
    Ebenezer .... S 31643
    Gideon, N. Y. in 1832; wid. Hannah .... R 2842
    Mary, former wid. of Thomas U. Ruland, q. v.
    Mills .... S 13046
    Reuben, Conn. & N. Y. (also given DEFREES) .... S 17380
    Samuel, BLWt. 538-200, Lieut. was issued June 3, 1789. No papers.
    Samuel, wid. Mary .... W 16559
DE FREES, Reuben. (See DE FOREST.)
DEIANS. (See DEAN.)
DELANO, Aaron, Conn., Cont. & Mass., wid. Anna .... W 19171
    Jonathan .... S 39429
    Lois, former wid. of Thomas Coats, q. v.
    Thomas .... S 23194
DELANOY, Ellen, former wid. of Abraham Resseguie, Conn. W 24054; also former wid. of Richard Hill, Mass .... R 2853
DELLEBER. (See DILLEBER.)
DEMING or DEMMING or DENING, or DAMAN.
    David, wid. Ann, BLWt. 14961-160-55 .... W 2599
    Davis, wid. Elizabeth Ann .... W 17716
    Edmund or Edmond, wid. Bethiah .... W 10313
        Given also DAMAN.
    Elijah, wid. Lucy .... W 17717
    Gideon, Conn. & Mass .... S 10552
    James .... R 2866
    John, b. 1749, wid. Elizabeth .... W 14606
    Jonathan, BLWt. 745-100 .... S 39428
    Julius .... S 17381
    Pownal, Conn. & Cont., former wid. of Mehitable D. Colton .... W 20894
        BLWt. 8463-160-55 and BLWt. 537-200, Lieut. was issued Apr. 22, 1796 to Mehitable Deming, Adx., marked "Entered Feb. 22, 1816." No papers.
    Stephen .... S 37883
    Theron .... S 31648
    Wait, former wid. of, Ruth Morey .... W 17135
DEMMON, Thomas .... R 2880
    Also given DENNISON.
DENING. (See DEMING.)
DENISON or DENNISON, Abigail, former wid. of Asa Gillet, q. v.
    Amos .... S 39438
    Avery, wid. Prudence .... W 20984
    Bebee or Bebee .... S 9328
    Chauncy, wid. Sarah .... W 24055
    Daniel, wid. Lucy .... W 17718
    David, Conn. & Vt .... S 5335
    George, Madison Co., N. Y., in 1832 .... S 10551
    George, Conn. in 1832 .... S 12768
    Gilbert .... S 15805
    Henry, Conn., Cont. & Navy, wid. Mary .... W 15890

DENISON or DENNISON, James	S	37881
James P.	S	15079
Jedediah	S	15084
Joseph, Cont. (Conn.)	S	10564
Nathan	S	22203
Samuel	R	2878
Thomas	R	2880
Also given DEMMON.		
DENMARK, Burnardus or Barnardus	S	43482
DENNIS or DENNISS.		
Anna, former wid. of Stephen Billings, q. v.		
Russell	S	15804
Samuel, Navy service, Conn. res.	S	37884
DENNY, Absalom, wid. Bethia	W	20969
DENSLOW, Benjamin	S	27671
Eli, wid. Polly, BLWt. 104-60-55	W	25528
Elijah	S	15087
Martin, former wid. of, Roxarene Wright	W	6593
BLWt. 3191-160-55 and BLWt. 540-200, Lieut. issued (no month) 26, 1790. No papers.		
DENSMORE, Thomas, wid. Hannah	W	2601
DENTON, Daniel, BLWt. 1747-100	S	43486
DERBY, Benjamin, d 1830, never pensioned; wid. Constant, Albany, N. Y., 1838	W	20979
Benjamin, fifer, never pensioned; died 1829; wid. Esther, pensioned from Vt	W	26207
(See also DARBE.)		
DEVENPORT. (See DAVENPORT.)		
DE WITT, Garret or Garrit, wid. Elizabeth	W	25522
Jacob, wid. Martha	W	20970
DE WOLF, DE WOLFE, DEWOOLF or D'WOLF.		
Benjamin, Conn. & Navy	S	43490
Daniel, Michigan in 1832	S	29117
Daniel, Conn. in 1832, died 1834; wid. Hannah, BLWt. 14507-160-55	W	1245
Edward, Conn. & Privateer	S	15089
Elisha, Cont. (Conn.)	S	29756
Joseph	S	3280
Levi or Levy, wid. Huldah, BLWt. 3519-160-55	W	25521
Peter	S	18377
Samuel, wid. Susannah	W	20978
Seth, wid. Hannah, BLWt. 26504-160-55	S	2562
Stephen, wid. Abigail	W	2600
DEXTER, Abigail, former wid. of Aaron French, q. v.		
John	S	23192
Nathan	S	37889
Warham	R	
DIBBLE, DIBLE or DIBOL.		
Abraham	R	2928
Benjamin	S	15098
Daniel, wid. Susannah	W	17723
Israel	S	20337
John, Darian, Conn., in 1832	S	15097
John, N. Y. in 1818	S	39445
Moses, wid. Elizabeth	W	27931
DICKENSON or DICKERSON. (See DICKINSON.)		
DICKEY, Peter	S	23600
DICKINSON, DICKENSON or DICKERSON.		
Asahel, wid. Lucy	W	19179
Benjamin	S	27691
David, wid. Sybil	W	17725
Friend	S	44147
Ichabod, Conn. & N. Y	S	17385
Jesse	S	42157
Josiah, wid. Lucy	W	24062
Levi, Conn. & Privateer, wid. Bethiah	W	14619
Nathaniel, wid. Lucy	W	25540
Oliver, wid. Anna	W	17726
Ozias, wid. Mary W	W	17721
Samuel, wid. Hannah	W	16955
Silvanus, Cont. (Conn.), wid. Mary	W	17724
Simeon, Conn. & Privateer	S	17386
Solomon, wid. Elizabeth	W	1736
Waitstill, Conn. & Cont	S	17928
DICKS, David	S	43500
(See also DIX.)		
DICKSON or DIXON, or DIXSON.		
Amos	S	23602
BLWt. 26588-160-55.		
David	S	43499
Jared	S	39441
John, Cont. & Conn., Dutchess Co., N. Y., in 1821 as Drummer, BLWt. 1021-100.		
John, Monroe Co., N. Y., in 1832, as private; wid. Jane	W	25544
Joseph, wid. Mercy	W	22939
Miles, former wid. of, Sarah Clark	W	20881
Robert	S	10571
Thomas, wid. Lydia	W	1397
DIGGINS, Martin, wid. Lydia P., BLWt. 9187-160-55	W	540
DIKE, William	S	10572
DIKEMAN, Daniel	S	15408
Eliphalet, wid. Huldah, BLWt. 7056-160-55	W	25542
Frederick or Frederic	S	39447
Hezekiah, wid. Esther	W	25545
Levi, wid. Rebecca	W	24857

DILLEBER or DELLEBER, John	S 12747
DILLINGHAM, Benjamin, Conn. residence in 1819	R-
DIMICK, DIMMICK, or DIMOCK.	
Amasa, wid. Matilda	W 3396
Benjamin, N. Y. in 1818	S 43501
BLWt. 541-200, Lieut. was issued Sept. 11, 1789. No papers.	
Benjamin, former wid. of, Miriam Raymond, soldier d. 1797, Vt., BLWt. 27575-160-55	W 18787
David, Conn., Cont. & Vt	S 5347
Edward, wid. Esther	W 4427
Elias	S 21737
Jeduthan	S 37890
John	S 12775
Joseph, Vt. in 1818	S 39448
Joseph, N. Y. in 1832, died in 1845; wid. Fanny	W 22942
Peter	S 23197
Shubael, Conn. & Mass	R 2962
Simeon, wid. Priscilla	W 4942
DINER, James	S 37891
DISBRO, DISBROW, or DESBRO, Asa	S 9335
Henry, wid. Hannah, BLWt. 11260-160-55	W 9408
Joshua	S 37882
Justus	S 37885
Simon, wid. Philama, BLWt. 821-160-55	W 17722
DIX, Benjamin	S 39446
Samuel, former wid. of, Sarah Willson	W 18414
(See also DICKS.)	
DOAN or DOANE or DONE.	
Joel, wid. Jemima; BLWt. 6108-160-55	W 3525
Josiah, wid. Lois	W 16239
Oliver, Conn. Sea service & Mass	S 20339
Richard	S 43510
DODD, Bishop	S 37894
Guy, former wid. of, Hannah Currier	W 10573
John, wid. Anna, Conn. residence in 1843	R 2989
John, former wid. of, Hannah Mansfield	W 17092
Timothy, wid. Susannah	W 20991
DODGE, Benjamin, wid. Tabitha	W 16956
Daniel, former wid. of, Irena Hubbs	W 9963
Elihu, wid. Lucretia	W 17730
Ira	S 8335
Joel	S 15099
Reuben, wid. Dolly or Dorothy	W 20994
William	S 43512
DOLE, James, Conn., Cont. & N. Y	S 43518
BLWt. 542-200, Lieut. was issued Dec. 1, 1789. No papers.	
DOLPH, Stephen	S 35897
DOND. (See DOWD.)	
DONE. (See DOANE.)	
DONNELLY, Robert	R 3008
DOOLITTLE, Benjamin, wid. Sarah	R 3015
Charles	S 12796
David, Conn. & N. Y., wid. Ann Elizabeth; BLWt. 35832-160-55	W 25537
Eber, former wid. of, Mary Doolittle; BLWt. 26686-160-55	W 26974
Mary's second husband was also pensioned. (See Doolittle, Obed, S 16766.)	
Ezra, wid. Sarah	R 3016
George, wid. Grace	R 3014
John, wid. Hannah	W 19194
Joseph	S 37893
Obed	S 16766
Thomas	R 3017
Uri	S 10577
DORCHESTER or DORCKESTER.	
Alexander, Cont. (Conn.), wid. Anna	W 19190
Reuben	S 10576
Stephen, wid. Abigail	W 19192
DORMAN, David, wid. Mabel	R 3021
DORR, Elisha	R 3023
Samuel, Cont. (Conn.), wid. Abigail	W 14632
DORRANCE, David, Conn. & Cont	S 45331
BLWt. 535-300, Captain was issued March 5, 1793, to Samuel Dorrance, Assignee. This warrant was issued under DARRANCE.	
DOTA, John, Conn. & N. Y	S 12791
DOTEY or DOTY, Benjamin	S 45327
Danforth, wid. Sarah	W 19193
Daniel, wid. Talitha or Talatha	W 22952
John	S 12781
Joseph, wid. Mary	R 3034
Samuel	S 45326
William	S 10584
DOUBLEDAY, Ammi, N. Y. in 1832; wid. Lois	R 3037
Asahel	S 18903
Jacob	R 3036
Joseph, Sharon, Vt., in 1818	S 39453
Joseph, Mass. in 1818 & 1832; wid. Lucy	W 14625
Seth	S 10580
DOUD. (See DOWD.)	
DOUGAL or DUGAL, Thomas, former wid. of, Ann Page or Paige	W 17417
DOUGLAS or DOUGLASS, David	S 10579
James, Rockland, N. Y., in 1832	S 46033
James, d. 1817, not pensioned; wid. Elizabeth	R 3045

DOUGLAS or DOUGLASS, Joseph, wid. Hannah	R 3046
Nathaniel	S 45333
Richard, wid. Lucy	W 730
BLWt. 536-300, Capt., was issued Jan. 25, 1790. No papers. Sarah, former wid. of Lebbeus Harris, q. v.	
Skeen or Sacket, Skene Douglas, wid. Lorrilla	W 4619
BLWt. 18019-160-55.	
DOW, Nathan	S 23202
DOW'D, or DAUD, or DOND, or DOUD.	
Benjamin	S 21739
Daniel, Conn. & R. I.	S 12789
Moses, former wid. of, Abigail Smith. See papers in claim of Elijah Smith, R 9676, Navy (Mass.) and Sea Service.	
Richard, Cont. (Conn.), former wid. of, Rebecca Wilcox	W 22641
Samuel	R 3038
Solomon, BLWt. 419-100	S 38663
William, wid. Hannah	W 19183
DOWER. (See DOWNER.)	
DOWN or DOWNS, David	S 17392
Elijah, wid. Ruth	W 10755
Jabez	S 45643
James	S 38664
Joseph	S 12785
Nathaniel	S 15813
DOWNER, Avery, Conn. residence	R 3063
Elisha, Conn. & Cont	S 12786
James (also given DOWER)	S 21741
Jason, Conn. & Vt	S 16769
Zaccheus or Zacheus, Conn. & Vt	S 12782
DOWNING, Daniel	S 15414
John	S 39451
Jonathan, Conn. & Cont., wid. Huldah	W 24868
Phineas	S 31651
Stephen	S 29122
DOWSETT, Amos, wid. Mary	W 17728
(See also DUSETT.)	
DRAKE, Abial, wid. Anna, applied from N. Y	R 3071
Abiel, Conn. 1818	S 38674
Ebenezer, former wid. of, Lois Brewer	W 20791
Elihu	S 38673
Gideon, wid. Annah	W 14643
Lemuel	S 31655
Lory or Lowry, not pensioned; wid. Sarah applied from Penna., BLWt. 43879-160-55	R 3078
Moses, wid. Abigail	W 17731
Noah	S 12802
Phinehas	S 31657
DREW, Samuel, Conn., Green Mt. Boys, Mass., N. H. & N. Y	S 45238
DUCIT. (See DUSETT.)	
DUDLEY or DUDLY, Benajah	S 12824
Eber or Ebor, wid. Hannah	W 21016
Harman	S 27737
Isaac, wid. Anne	R 3101
Jared, wid. Anna	W 17737
Medad	R 3104
Roswell	S 10592
Samuel, Conn. & Privateer	S 6806
Thomas	S 22222
DUGAL. (See DOUGAL.)	
DUGLASS. (See DOUGLASS.)	
DUMMER, Stephen	R 3116
DUNBAR, Joel	S 43525
Miles, wid. Tryphosa	W 16962
Robert	S 39463
Thomas, Conn. Sea Service & R. I., wid. Eunice, BLWt. 29039-160-55	W 24081
DUNCAN, Jared, pensioned for disability in 1810; wid. Dolly R	R 3122
DUNCOMB or DUNCOMBE, Edward, wid. Anna	W 25553
DUNHAM, Cornelius	S 12828
Daniel, BLWt. 10235-160-55	S 43523
Elisha, wid. Mehitable	W 25546
Gershom, wid. Mary	W 21013
Gideon, wid. Anna	W 16565
Hannah, former wid. of John Lawrence	W 26662
James	S 31658
Salathiel, wid. Lucy	W 19202
Samuel, Ontario Co., N. Y., 1832; former wid. of, Asenath Turner, BLWt. 114388-160-55	W 27795
Samuel, Cont. (Conn.), Stillwater, N. Y., 1818	S 45346
Stephen	S 12804
DUNING. (See DUNNING.)	
DUNMORE, Jane, former wid. of James Merrill, q. v.	
DUNN, Samuel, Conn. & N. J., wid. Barbara, BLWt. 26927-160-55	W 7048
Timothy, wid. Mehitable, BLWt. 11176-160-55	W 1249
DUNNING or DUNING, David	S 15103
Edmund	S 15819
James, Conn., Cont., & N. Y	S 12830
Josiah, Conn., N. Y., & Vt	S 23207
Luther	R 3151
DUNWELL, Stephen	S 2188
William	S 34772
DUNWORTH, George, wid. Abigail W., BLWt. 26314-160-55	W 9416
DUPLEX, Prince, wid. Lement	W 16963

DURAND, Alexander, wid. Elizabeth	W 21014
Andrew	S 2528
Ebenezer, wid. Polly, BLWt. 13202-160-55	W 25547
Eleazer	S 45354
Fisk or Fish	S 12807
Isaac	S 19961
John, Derby, Conn., in 1818	S 37898
John, Service in Navy; Conn. residence; Milford, Conn., in 1818	S 37900
Joseph, Conn. & N. Y.	S 12829
Lemuel, wid. Catharine	W 1248
Samuel, wid. Susanna	W 17734
William, Conn. & Sea Service, wid. Mary	W 25552
DURFEE, DURFEY, or DURPHEY.	
Ebenezer, wid. Abigail, BLWt. 13187-160-55	W 2080
Elijah, wid. Elizabeth, applied from Knox Co., Ohio	R 3156
John, Conn. & Privateer, wid. Mary	W 21011
Joseph, wid. Experience, BLWt. 6415-160-55	W 1839
DURHAM, Simeon	S 10595
DURKEE, Asahel or Asel, wid. Sarah, BLWt. 9453-160-55	W 19201
Benjamin, Conn. & Cont., BLWt. 420-300	S 39473
Daniel	S 22742
Ebe.	S 2524
John, wid. Jemina; BLWt. 100834-160-55, soldier, a private, died in 1838.	
John, Conn. & Cont.; BLWt. 580-500, Colonel; Soldier died May 30, 1782.	
John, Conn. & Cont.; BLWt. 533-300, Captain, was issued July 7, 1791, to John Durkee, Captain, and son of Col. John Durkee.	
Nathaniel, wid. Melinda, BLWt. 19729-160-55	W 25548
Phineas	BLWt. 606-100
Robert	BLWt. 432-300
Sally (Sarah), former wid. of Walter Tiffany, q. v.	
Solomon, Cont. (Conn.)	S 42682
William	S 18385
DURPHY. (See DURFEE.)	
DUSETT or DUCIT, John	S 45351
(See also DOWSETT.)	
DUTTON, Amasa, wid Elizabeth	W 1399
Asa	S 39464
Joseph, wid. Mary	W 25551
Oliver, Serg't, Bristol, Conn., 1818, & died 1826 in N. Y., from which State wid. Ruth was pensioned	W 24861
Oliver, Conn., Cont., & Mass., Hampden, Mass., in 1832, wid. Phebe, BLWt. 9437-160-55	S 18383
This woman's former husband was also pensioned for service in the Revolution. See Mass. Powers, Stephen, W 25550.	
Thomas	R 3170
Titus, Conn. & Cont	S 45344
DWIGHT, Alpheus, wid. Fanny, BLWt. 29738-160-55	W 25554
Timothy, Cont. (Conn.), wid. Mary	W 21025
D'WOLF. (See DE WOLF.)	
DYAR or DYER, Benjamin, former wid. of, Ann Mills	W 18520
Ebenezer	R 3177
Joseph, wid. Charlotte, BLWt. 9203-160-55	W 25555
DYGART, Orpha, former wid. of Solomon Welch, q. v.	
ESTABROOK. (See ESTABROOK.)	
EASTEN. (See EASTON.)	
EASTMAN, Asahel, wid. Mary	W 19210
Clark, wid. Betsey, BLWt. 36638-160-55	W 9421
Deliverance	S 8389
Eli, Conn. & Vt	S 18810
Joseph, wid. Elizabeth, BLWt. 26434-160-55	W 7101
Nathaniel, Conn. & N. H., wid. Ruth	W 22992
EASTON, Giles, Cont. (Conn.), wid. Anna	W 22997
Julian, BLWt. 1209-100	S 37902
Obadiah	S 21171
EATON, Abigail, former wid. of Ashbel Merrell, q. v.	
Benjamin, Conn., Cont., & N. J., also War of 1812	S 45359
Cyril or Cyrel	S 32227
Daniel, wid. Mary	W 19211
Ebenezer, Conn., Mass., & R. I.; in 1832 was in Chenango Co., N. Y.; wid. Polly Ann	W 7067
Ebenezer, never pensioned; wid. Lois, Windham Co., Conn	W 21038
Eunice, former wid. of Joseph Walker, q. v.	
James, d. 1814; wid. Anna, from Conn	W 25556
James, d. 1807, Mass., wid. Eleanor	W 21037
Josiah, Conn. & Cont	S 12839
Luther, wid. Sally	W 21034
Maverick	S 18809
Nathan	S 15821
Samuel	S 12837
Solomon, former wid. of, Phebe Carpenter	W 8591
BLWt. 30597-160-55.	
Stephen	S 23209
ECCLESTON or ECCLESTONE, David, wid. Catharine	W 19217
(See also EGGLESTON.)	
EDDY, Asa, wid. Rebecca	W 25561
BLWt. 26789-160-55.	
Gilbert, Conn. & Privateer, wid. Prudence; also in War of 1812	W 25560
BLWt. 15046-160-55 for service of above soldier as Brig. General N. Y. Militia from Sept. 1 to Sept. 19, 1814.	
Levi, wid. Rhoda	W 21046
Sarah, former wid. of Samuel Waterous, q. v.	
Seth	S 39483

EDER, Anthony, or NEEDAR, Toney, Conn. & Cont., wid. Phillis, BLWt. 19813-160-55...... W 7073
EDGAR, Thomas, Navy (Conn.)... S 37905
EDGECOMB or EDGECOMBE.
  Jabez... S 37906
  Roger, Conn., Cont. & Navy.. S 10615
  Samuel, Conn. & Privateer.. S 20743
EDGERTON or EGERTON.
  Abel, Conn. & Cont... S 10613
  Ariel, Conn., Cont. & Privateer... S 18816
  David, Conn., Conn. Sea service & Privateer.. S 15110
  Ebenezer, pensioned as Jr. in Conn. in 1818, and transferred to Mass......... S 34793
  Ebenezer, pensioned as Senr.—Granby, Conn. in 1818................................ S 37904
  James, Conn. & Privateer.. S 18391
  Jediah, Richford, N. Y., in 1832 as Serg't., wid. Sarah............................. R 3235
  Jedediah, Vt. in 1832.. S 21743
  Lydia, former wid. of John Babcock, q. v.
  Roger, Cont. (Conn.), wid. Betsey.. W 19219
EDMOND, EDMONDS, EDMUND or EDMUNDS.
  Andrew, Capt. & Lieut. Train Band, wid. Esther.................................... R 3247
  Andrew, wid. Elizabeth... R 3248
    Pension applications of both soldier and widow were rejected.
  Esther, former wid. of Peter Rose, q. v.
  George, Cont. (Conn.), wid. Abigail... W 17744
  William.. S 20472
EDSON, Benjamin, wid. Anne, BLWt. 39494-160-55.................................... W 19220
  Eliab... S 15419
  Josiah.. S 39486
  Lydia, former wid. of Timothy Harrington, q. v.
  Nathan.. S 39482
  Seth, Conn. & Cont... S 10614
EDWARDS, ABEL, wid. Sarah... W 17745
  Clark, Conn. & R. I., wid. Catharine... W 14671
  Daniel, Conn. & Privateer; Tomkins, N. Y., in 1832.............................. S 8395
  Daniel, Delaware Co., N. Y., in 1832, & died in 1836; wid. Hannah........ W 17743
  Esther, former wid. of Reuben Cone, q. v.
  Hezekiah... S 16780
  Isaac, wid. Mary, BLWt. 26586-160-55... W 25558
  Jabez.. S 10607
  Jonathan... S 42696
  Mercy or Marcy, former wid. of Joel Judd, q. v.
  Nathaniel.. S 44797
    BLWt. 659-200, Lieut. was issued Dec. 14, 1792, to Nathaniel Edwards. No papers.
  Samuel.. S 12855
EELLS, ELLES or ELLS.
  Daniel... R 3267
  Edward, wid. Abigail.. BLWt. 102-300
  Jeremiah... S 44798
  John.. S 29132
  John.. R 3268
  Samuel, Conn. & Cont... S 37912
EGERTON. (See EDGERTON.)
EGGELSTON, EGGLESTON or EGLESTON.
  Benedict, BLWt. 6381-160-55... S 38694
  Gershom or Garshom, wid. Avis... W 1739
  James, Conn. & Cont., wid. Jemima... W 17747
  Joseph, Conn. & R. I., wid. Elizabeth.. W 17748
  Samuel.. R 3270
  Timothy, Conn. & Cont... S 42698
ELDERKIN, Elisha, Conn. & Conn. Sea service, wid. Mary........................ W 17758
ELDRED or ELDRID, John, Conn. & Cont.. S 42705
  Judah.. S 6817
ELDREDG, ELDREDGE, ELDRIDG, ELDRIDGE or ELDRIGE.
  Elisha, wid. Cynthia.. W 23007
  Henry, Conn. & R. I., wid. Elizabeth... W 23004
  James.. S 22231
  John.. S 37911
  Jonathan... S 39487
  Joseph, Cortland, N. Y., in 1832.. S 23213
  Joseph, not pensioned, d. 1830, Hartford, Conn., wid. Rhoda................. W 17756
  Robert, former wid. of, Elizabeth Burtis... R 1513
  Zoeth, wid. Bethiah.. R 3280
ELEY. (See ELY.)
ELITHORP, ELLITHORP, ELITHROP or ELLITHROP.
  Azariah... S 10618
  Samuel, Conn. & Cont. wid. Amy... W 21064
ELLES. (See EELLS.)
ELLIOT or ELLIOTT.
  George, wid. Percy.. W 25612
  Henry.. R 3296
  Richard, Cont. (Conn.).. S 12864
  Thomas... S 31664
ELLIS, Asa... S 29138
  Nathan, wid. Phebe.. W 17752
  Phenix Carpenter, Conn. & Cont... S 17941
  Stephen, wid. Rebekah... W 6716
  William, Conn. & Conn. Sea service.. S 28720
ELLITHORP or ELLITHROP. (See ELITHORP.)

ELLSWORTH or ELSWORTH.
  Benjamin .... S 37910
  Eliphalet, Cont. (Conn.), wid. Jemima .... R 3332
    Also War of 1812.
  Job, wid. Huldah, BLWt. 9078-160-55 .... W 7103
  John, liv. Farmington, Conn. in 1832, & moved to Pittsburgh, Ohio .... S 2196
  John, Conn., N. H. & R. I. serv., liv. Montgomery Co., N. Y., in 1832 ..... S 9854
  Mary, former wid. of William Gillespie, q. v.
  Moses .... S 37909
ELLWOOD. (See ELWOOD.)
ELMER, Elijah .... R 3328
  Joel, wid. Zillah .... W 24112
  Joseph, wid. Ruth .... W 19224
  Samuel .... S 31665
  Stephen .... S 23617
ELMORE, Daniel, wid. Elizabeth .... W 21060
  Joel .... S 30399
ELSWORTH. (See ELLSWORTH.)
ELTON, Bradley, wid. Grace .... W 17751
ELWELL, Ebenezer .... S 43527
ELWOOD or ELLWOOD.
  Abijah .... W 25562
  Abram .... S 44803
  Isaac .... S 44804
  Joseph, wid. Naomi .... W 21058
  Nathan, wid. Abigail .... W 15765
  Stephen, wid. Betty .... W 17757
  Thomas, Navy serv. Conn. res .... S 37907
ELY or ELEY, Abner, Conn. & Conn. Sea service, wid. Bridget .... W 21056
    Bridget's first husband, Semilius Brockway, died in service.
  Andrew, Cont. (Conn.) .... S 44801
  Daniel .... S 31663
  Gabriel, wid. Eunice .... W 2775
  Gurdon .... S 17404
  Jabez .... S 44802
  Jacob .... S 15111
  John .... S 3329
  Wells .... S 44800
  William .... S 42706
EMERSON or EMMERSON.
  Catharine, former wid. of John Skinner, q. v.
  Joseph .... R 3343
  Nathaniel, wid. Mary .... W 21068
  Stephen .... S 22754
EMES, Joseph, wid. Hannah; also given AMES.
EMMONS or EMONS, Arthur .... S 29140
  Daniel Spencer, wid. Luna .... W 17760
  Jonathan .... S 22755
  Phineas or Phinehas, Conn. & N. Y., wid. Keziah .... W 21071
  Samuel, wid. Sarah, BLWt. 26995-160-55 .... W 7106
  Solomon .... S 22753
ENO, Isaac, Conn. & Vt .... R 3356
  Levi .... S 31667
  Reuben, wid. Lois .... W 25564
ENOS, Alexander .... S 15113
  David, Hartford Co. in 1818 .... S 37914
  David, N. Y. in 1818, moved to Vt .... S 39497
  Elisha, wid. Sarah .... W 16252
  Erasmus, not pensioned; wid. Anna .... R 3358
  Matthias or Mathias, Conn. Sea service & R. I., wid. Anna .... W 16251
  Olive, former wid. of Joseph Holcomb, q. v.
  Roger, wid. Jerusha .... W 24127
ENSIGN, Daniel, wid. Elizabeth .... W 10957
  Eliphalet .... S 12874
  James .... S 37913
  Otis, wid. Hannah, BLWt. 6421-160-55 .... W 9428
ENSWORTH, Jesse .... S 15114
  John, wid. Mary .... W 17761
ESTABROOK, ESTBROOK or EASTABROOK, Nehemiah .... S 44809
ETTICK, George J., Conn. & N. Y .... S 10635
EVANS or EVENS, or EVINS.
  Abiathar or Abiather, wid. Mary .... W 21080
  Allen .... S 37916
  Benjamin Stacy, wid. Sybil, BLWt. 6268-160-55 .... S 22759
  Benoni .... S 43535
  Cotton Daniel .... S 23623
  Daniel, wid. Sarah .... W 17766
  David .... S 12887
  Isaac .... S 44813
  Josiah .... S 43533
  Moses, wid. Thirza .... W 7121
  Randall or Randol, Conn. & N. H .... S 12879
  William, Conn. & N. Y .... S 12880
EVARTS or EVERTS.
  Daniel, Conn. & N. Y .... S 10637
  Eber, Conn., Cont. & Green Mt. Boys .... S 12881
  Ezra, wid. Lorrain .... W 21078
  Nathaniel, wid. Mary .... W 21077
  Reuben .... S 23624

EVARTS or EVERTS, Solomon.. S 12888
  Stephen, Bergen, N. Y., in 1818.. S 44811
  Stephen, Cont. (Conn.).. S 21768
    Conn. in 1816, N. Y. in 1827.
EVENS. (See EVANS.);
EVEREST, Daniel, wid. Eunice.. W 21082
  Elisha.. S 43534
EVERETT, EVERIT, EVERITT or EVRIT.
  Abner.. S 15827
  Andrew.. S 12884
  Daniel... S 22758
  Ebe... S 15417
  Eliphalet, wid. Rhoda... W 19234
  Jeremiah, Navy (Conn.), wid. Maria, BLWt. 26585-160-55........................ W 21081
  Oliver, wid. Mary, BLWt. 265-60-55... W 1583
EVENS. (See EVANS.)
EVERTS. (See EVARTS.)
EVRIT. (See EVERETT.)

F.

FAIRBANKS, Samuel... S 16788
FAIRCHILD, Abel... S 12892
  Clement, wid. Jerusha.. W 1741
  Ephraim, wid. Mary.. W 2929
  Gilbert... S 15116
  James, wid. Mary... W 21093
  John, Conn. & N. Y.. S 10641
  Joseph... S 43542
  Nathan, wid. Sarah... W 25568
  Peter, Newtown, Conn., 1818... S 38688
    Also given FAIRFIELD.
  Peter, Fairfield, Conn., as Corporal in 1818; wid. Rachel......................... W 7248
FAIRFIELD. (See FAIRCHILD.)
FAIRMAN, Daniel.. S 12894
  Roswell or Roswill, wid. Anna, BLWt. 26372-160-55............................... W 645
FAIRWEATHER or FAYERWEATHER, Samuel.. S 37917
FANCHER, Rufus... S 43540
  William, former wid. of, Thankful Cole.. W 22811
FANNING, Asa, wid. Jerusha, BLWt. 34996-160-55.................................. W 19247
  Charles.. S 13001
    BLWt. 723-200, Lieut.; was issued Dec. 24, 1799, to William Wells, Assignee. No papers.
  John, wid. Abigail.. W 1585
  Jonathan, Conn. Sea Service & Navy.. S 23214
  Thomas, wid. Susannah... W 17891
FARGO or FERGO, Ezekiel... S 10650
  Samuel, wid. Hannah... W 24178
  Thomas.. S 29152
  Timothy, wid. Betsey... W 25569
  William, wid. Polly... W 19240
FARLOW, Hulaah, former wid. of Joseph Moger, q. v............................... S 43546
FARMER, Thomas.. S 43546
  BLWt. 722-200, Lieut., was issued Oct. 7, 1789. No papers.
FARNAM or FARNAN or FARNHAM or FARNUM.
  Abial, wid. Chloe... W 21089
  Benjamin, Conn. & Cont., former wid. of, Ann Griffin............................ R 4305
  Bezaleel or Barzaleel... S 40058
  Elijah.. S 10643
  Eliphalet, wid. Hannah... W 24175
  John, wid. Mary.. W 5273
  Joseph... S 13003
  Levi, former wid. of, Dorcas Taylor... W 16752
    Dorcas' second husband, Ebenezer Perry, Conn. or Mass., also served in the Revolution. Her third and last husband, Taylor, Thomas, S 46202, was a Rev. pensioner....
  Peter, Newtown, Conn. in 1832.. S 17405
  Peter, d. 1817, Hebron, Conn., wid. Sylvia... W 25571
  Rufus, Conn. & Navy, wid. Priscilla, BLWt. 26181-160-55....................... W 10973
  Thomas, Conn. & Cont.. S 17408
  Zedediah... S 38689
FARRAND, Joseph, Conn. & Vt.. S 18396
FARWELL, Isaac.. S 12893
  Thomas.. S 34831
FASSET or FASSETT, Adonijah.. R 3459
FAULKNER or FAULKNOR.
  Caleb, wid. Martha... W 19239
  Thomas.. R 3467
FAY, John... S 43543
  Moses, Conn. & Cont., wid. Mary.. W 21086
  Nathan, Conn. & Vt., wid. Mary.. R 3471
  Sherebiah, Conn. & Mass.. W 10647
  Timothy, Conn., Cont. & Mass., former wid. of Sarah How..................... W 13469
  William.. S 43538
FAYERWEATHER. (See FAIRWEATHER.)
FEERO, Peter... S 16792
FELLOWS, Abial, Conn. & N. Y., wid. Dorcas, BLWt. 92023-160-55............ W 25576
  Isaac, Conn. & Cont.. S 13006
  Rosel, wid. Molly... W 17899
  Samuel.. S 34840
  Sarah, former wid. of Benjamin Fenn.. q. v.
  Varney, wid. Anna.. W 23027

FENN, Benjamin, Middlebury, Conn., in 1832... S 13011
  Benjamin, Lieut. not pensioned; former wid. of, Sarah Fellows............................. W 17898
  Daniel... S 37918
  David... R 3490
  Edward, Conn. & Cont.. S 13012
  John.. S 2545
  Thomas... S 13010
  Titus.. R 3491
FENTON, Adonijah... S 23217
  Asa.. S 31674
  Elijah.. S 10662
  Gamaliel, wid. Elizabeth, BLWt. 26989-160-55... W 4951
  John, former wid. of, Lucy Scott.. W 26957
  Jonathan, Conn. Sea service, wid. Rosalinda... R 3496
    Both soldier and widow were rejected.
  Jotham... S 37919
  Nathaniel, Chataqua Co., N. Y., in 1832.. S 13014
  Nathaniel, Mass., in 1832... S 18398
  Solomon, Willington, Conn., in 1818... S 13007
  Solomon, Conn. & Cont., Unadilla, N. Y., in 1818, d. 1831, & arrears of pension were given
    his children—Polly McFarland, Solomon & Washington Fenton, & Fanny Johnson—in 1832 W 17120
FERGO. (See FARGO.)
FERGUSON, FORGASON, or FURGESON.
  Daniel... R 3500
  Samuel.. S 29151
FERIN or FERRIN, Zebulon... S 21752
FERRE. (See FERRY.)
FERRIS, Gould... S 28726
  Jeremiah, wid. Nancy.. W 17897
  Jonah, wid. Anne... W 25572
  Oliver, Conn. & Conn. Sea service, wid. Abigail... W 16254
FERRIS, Rainford A., or Ramford A.. S 20751
  (See also FORRIS.)
FERRY or FERRE, Eliphalet, wid. Mercy.. W 21104
  Moses, Conn. & Cont., wid. Jerusha.. W 19255
FIDDIS, Hugh E., Conn. Sea service & Navy, BLWt. 75105-160-55.................. R 3525
FIELD or FIELDS.
  David... R 3526
  Edmond... S 37920
  George... S 43556
  Ichabod... S 16800
  James, wid. Anna or Anna Hurd... W 25582
  Joarab.. R 3528
  John.. S 13018
  Pardon... S 43555
  Samuel, wid. Huldah... W 17907
FILER, Orris... S 23632
  (See also FISLER and FYLER.)
FILLEY, FILLY, & PHILLEY.
  Mark, wid. Elinor.. W 17901
  Moses... S 13016
  Remembrance, Conn. & Cont., wid. Hannah... W 17903
    BLWt. 193-60-55 & BLWt. 5817-100, issued April 21, 1791. No papers.
  Sylvanus, wid. Jemima.. W 17906
FILIMORE or FILMORE.
  Cyrus, Conn. & N. Y., wid. Jemima.. R 3539
  Henry... S 28538
FILLOW, Adams. (See PHILO.)
  Isaac... S 17416
FILLY. (See FILLEY.)
FILMORE. (See FILLMORE.)
FINCH or FINCHE.
  Abraham or Abram... S 28727
  Ezra.. R 3541
  Jeremiah, Serg't., Fairfield Co., Conn. 1818... S 37923
  Jeremiah, N. Y., in 1818, as private... S 43560
  Jonathan, Conn. & N. Y. service... S 37924
  Samuel, pensioned as priv., Corp. & Serg't., N. Y., in 1832; wid. Polly......... R 3543
  Stephen, wid. Mindwell.. W 24187
  Timithy... R 3544
  William, Ohio, in 1832, as priv.. S 3359
  William, Conn. & N. Y., pensioned in Penna., in 1832 as priv. & Serg't....... S 22768
FINCHLEY, George, wid. Sarah... S 43557 & W 19261
FINNEY, FINNY, or PHINNEY.
  Eleazer... S 17415
  Jonathan, Conn., Cont. & Mass., wid. Sarah, BLWt. 34594-160-55............... W 19262
  Joseph, wid. Mary... W 16988
  Josiah... S 15280
  Sylvester, Conn. & N. Y... S 16114
FISH, Aaron, Conn. & Navy... S 10673
  Aurelia. (See FISK.)
  David... S 13019
  Esther, former wid. of John Ladd... q. v.
  John, wid. Eunice; also given FISK.
  Moses... S 13029
FISHER, Asahel, wid. Anna.. W 19236
  Jeremiah, wid. Sabra, BLWt. 11424-160-55.. W 7270
  John.. S 13020
  Timothy.. S 38695

FISK or FISKE.
  Abijah, Conn., Conn. Sea service & Mass... S 5394
  Aurelia, former wid. of Nathaniel Stowell.. q. v.
  James, Conn. & Mass.. S 21199
  John, wid. Eunice.. W 17900
  Jonathan, pensioned in Otsego Co. N. Y., in 1818; wid. Mehitable.............. R 3578
  Samuel.. R 3580
FISLER, Jacob... S 2551
  (See also FILER and FYLER.)
FITCH, Andrew, wid. Abigail... W 2116
  BLWt. 721-300, Capt. was issued August 7, 1789. No papers.
  Cordilla, former wid. of, Joanna Walker, BLWt. 31740-160-55..................... W 18263
  Daniel, BLWt. 38-60-55... S 37922
  Darius, wid. Lydia, BLWt. 17587-160-55.. W 1162
  Elnathan.. S 45134
  Giles... S 13408
  Hannah, former wid. of Robert Williams.. q. v.
  James, wid. Esther... W 17905
  James, Conn. & Vt.. R 3582
  Jesse.. S 10668
  John, N. Y., in 1832 as Serg't... S 13028
  John, Vt., in 1832 as priv... S 13030
  John, Chittenden Co., Vt., in 1832, as priv. of Dragoons & infantry............. S 10664
  Luther, Conn. & Privateer.. S 16794
  Nathaniel, N. Y., in 1832, d. 1837; wid. Caty..................................... W 23035
  Nathaniel, Serg't, Artificers, d. 1814; "Cont. service but Conn. residence," wid. Abigail..... W 21122
  Prentice... S 44818
  Rufus, Conn. & Cont.. S 44817
  William, N. Y., in 1832 as priv., wid. Mary....................................... W 19265
  William, Surgeon, Conn. & Conn. Sea service, not pensioned; wid. Elizabeth..... W 16990
FLAGG, Abijah, wid. Thankful... W 17909
  Jonathan, wid. Christiana... W 14726
FLEMING or FLEMMING, Benoni, wid. Louisa.. W 19288
FLETCHER, Jonathan... S 22771
FLING, Abel, wid. Susanna.. W 24214
  Lemuel, pensioned in N. H. as Ensign, moved to N. Y., wid. Sarah............... R 3611
FLINT, Aaron... S 15124
  Asel or Asael, Conn. & Conn., Sea service, wid. Sally, BLWt. 3823-160-55..... W 25507
  Daniel.. S 38703
  Davis, wid. Lucy... W 16991
  Jabez.. S 10681
  James.. R 3613
  James or James L., wid. Jerusha.. W 17911
  John, Conn. & Cont., former wid. of, Mary Brown................................. W 20785
  Jonathan... S 15834
  Joshua, Cont. (Conn.), wid. Sarah... W 17910
  Luke... S 42195
  Nathaniel.. S 38702
  Zacheus, wid. Sarah.. W 16260
FLOWER, Abdiel.. S 46361
  Zephon, Conn. & Cont., BLWt. 3-60-55.. S 6856
FLYNN, Michael, wid. Fanny.. W 24212
FOARD. (See FORD.)
FOBES, Nathaniel.. S 2218
  Simon, Cont. & Mass.. S 161/9
FOLKER, Chloe, former wid. of William Russell, q. v.
  Ebenezer... S 37938
FOLLET, Robert.. S 8509
FOORD. (See FORD.)
FOOT or FOOTE.
  Abraham, wid. Abby... R 14246
  Ambrose... S 13059
  Amos... S 13069
  Beeri.. S 13074
  Bronson, wid. Thankful... W 21144
  Darius, Conn. & N. Y.. S 17957
  Ebenezer or Ebenezer E., N. Y. in 1818, as priv.................................. S 44841
  Ebenezer, Serg't, Capt. & Inspector of Cattle; d. N. Y. in 1829; wid. Matilda, BLWt. 34276-160-55... W 25583
  Elihu, Conn. & Sea service... S 15838
  Ezra, former wid. of, Mercy Parson or Parsons.................................... W 19962
  Hannah, former wid. of Robert Kimberley, q. v.
  Heli, Conn. & Conn. Sea service, wid. Ruth....................................... W 21142
  Isaac, Cont. (Conn.).. S 44839
  Jacob, wid. Lucy.. R 3641
  Jesse, Cont. (Conn.).. S 29157
  John... R 3640
  Prudence, former wid. of James Knowles, q. v.
  Sarah, former wid. of Jared Bishop, q. v.
  Stephen, wid. Hannah... W 17912
  Susannah, former wid. of Benjamin Johnson, q. v.
  Timothy.. S 17958
FORBES or FORBS.
  Eli... S 15837
  Elisha... S 27801
  James.. S 37928
  John, Vt. in 1832... S 15427
  John, Conn. & Cont., d. 1786; daughter, Mary Blinn, got BLWt. 1298-100. Wid. was Mary Adams.
  Levi, wid. Sarah.. W 21133

FORCE, Ebenezer... S 34873
FORD, or FOARD or FOORD.
  Amos, Windham Co., Conn., in 1832 as Jr.. S 15428
  Amos, Hampton, Conn., in 1818.. S 37936
  Amos, Milford, Conn., in 1832, d. in 1835; wid. Eunice, BLWt. 26167-160-55............... W 25585
  Benjamin.. S 44842
  Hezekiah.. S 45538
  John, wid. Anna.. W 14743
  John Morrison, Privateer (Conn.)... R 3656
  Jonathan, Genesee Co., N. Y., in 1832.. S 23222
  Jonathan, Rensselaer Co., N. Y., in 1818... S 44844
  Jonathan, d. 1829; son Eliakim got BLWt. 1498-100.
  Martin.. S 37932
  Nathan.. S 2557
  Nathaniel... S 13049
  Phinehas.. S 37929
  Stephen... S 16807
FORDHAM, Nathan, Conn., Sea service & N. Y.. S 6848
FORGASON. (See FERGUSON.)
FORRIS, Peter, wid. Mary or Mony, BLWt. 1331-100 & 53-60-55...................................... W 19281
FORSTER. (See FOSTER.)
FORSYTH, Latham, wid. Abigail, BLWt. 26049-160-55.. W 2442
  William, wid. Prudence... W 11007
FORTUNE, Richard... S 37933
FOSDICK, James... S 38707
  Thomas U., Cont. (Conn.) BLWt. 1239-150.
  William... R 3678
FOSTER or FORSTER.
  Alpheus, wid. Esther... W 21129
  Asa, wid. Sarah.. W 5277
  Benjamin... S 37931
  Chauncey, wid. Charlotte... W 17917
  David... S 44835
  Edward... S 37935
  Faith, former wid. of John O. Waterman, q. v.
  Giles... S 13051
  Isaac, wid. Esther... R 3683
  Jacob, wid. Susanna.. W 24219
  Jesse... S 37934
  John, b. Mass., enl. from Conn. & liv. Conn. 1832.. S 13047
  John, Conn. & N. Y. serv., Lieut. liv. N. Y. in 1832... S 17902
  John, Fairfield Co., Conn., in 1818; wid. Pruella.. R 3692
  Jonathan.. S 22247
  Joseph, Conn. & Mass. service, liv. Conn. in 1832, pensioned as priv. & fifer............... S 16802
  Joseph, Conn. & Vt. service, liv. Vt. in 1832; wid. Dolly, BLWt. 9043-160-55................ W 736
  Peter, d. 1805, Mass., wid. Tammy.. W 14745
  Peter, Conn. & Conn., Sea service.. R 3691
  Samuel, Catskill, N. Y., in 1832... S 13043
  Samuel, S., Conn., Sea service & Privateer... S 13071
  Saul.. S 16808
  Timothy, wid. Desire... W 16577
  Wareham, Conn. & Cont., wid. Lucretia.. R 3688
FOWLER, Abiathar, wid. Asenath.. W 14746
  Amos, Warren, Conn., in 1832 as Serg't... S 15839
  Amos, priv., Corp. & serg't under Capt. Cook in Lebanon, Conn., in 1832; d. 1837; wid. Rebecca. W 17914
  Caleb, former wid. of, Olive Pratt... W 4057
  Daniel.. S 10685
  Ebenezer.. S 10689
  Eli... R 3702
  Elisha A., Serg't in Bethel, Vt., in 1818; wid. Mary... R 3710
  John, wid. Anna.. W 17919
  Jonathan, Conn. & Cont... S 41542
  Nathaniel, wid. Ruth... R 3713
  Reuben.. S 44851
  Samuel, Conn. Sea service.. R 3715
  Silas... S 13072
  Theophilus, wid. Sarah... W 17916
FOX, Aaron, wid. Lydia.. W 4437
  Allen, wid. Chloe, BLWt. 1315-100.. W 19275
  Amon.. R 3722
  Amos, d. 1794, wid. Jemima or Jamima... W 11009
  Amos, Conn. in 1818; wid. Mary... W 25390
  Appleton.. R 3723
  David, Ohio in 1832.. S 2217
  David, N. Y. in 1832 as drummer.. S 23223
  Ebenezer, Washington, Vt., in 1832, as priv. & teamster, moved to N. Y....................... S 13066
  Ebenezer, Milton, Vt., in 1818... S 39539
  Elijah, Cont. (Conn.).. S 22774
  Elisha, Penna. in 1832 as priv... S 22777
  Elisha, Conn. & Cont., N. H. in 1832... S 10693
  Eunice, former wid. of Marshall Palmer, q. v.
  Ezekiel, wid. Susan.. W 25592
  Isaac... S 37937
  Israel.. S 4288
  Jabez... S 13053
  Jacob, Conn, in 1832 as priv... S 17956
  Jacob, N. Y. in 1818 as Lieut.. S 44829
    BLWt. 725-200, Lieut. was issued April 5, 1793, to Reuben Murray, Assignee. No papers.
  Jedediah.. S 44830
  Jesse, New London Co., Conn., in 1832; wid. Ruth... R 3732

FOX, Joel, wid. Mercy.. W 4673
   John, N. Y. in 1818 as priv., wid. Louisa, BLWt. 7203-160-55......................... W 2091
   John, Conn. in 1832 as priv. & Serg't. Conn. & Cont. service........................ S 15426
   Lemuel, wid. Prudence.. W 11018
   Peter.. S 22245
   Reuben... S 32225
   Robert.. BLWt. 2177-100
   Roswell, former wid. of, Martha Hall... W 17051
   Samuel, Dryden, N. Y., as Corp. in 1818.. S 44832
   Samuel, Sherburne, N. Y., in 1818, as priv. "Samuel 2nd"......................... S 44834
   Simeon... S 44831
   Stephen, wid. Mary... W 10031
     Soldier also in Harmar's Indian War, 1790.
   Thomas, b. Glastonbury, Conn., son of David & Sarah, Hartford Co., Conn., in 1846......... S 13048
   Thomas, Penna. in 1832 as priv., d. 1834; wid. Cloe.............................. W 3673
   Vaniah or Vernia, Conn. & Cont... S 9335
   William, Conn. & Cont.. S 9334
FRANCES or FRANCIS.
   David, wid. Anna... W 21148
   Elijah, wid. Jane.. W 25610
   James, wid. Mary... R 3743
   James, wid. Sarah.. R 3747
   James, Killingworth, Conn., in 1832.. S 15841
   James, Cont. (Conn.) Litchfield Co., Conn., in 1818 as Corp...................... S 37942
FRANCES, FRANCIS or FRANSSESS.
   Job, BLWt. 26395-160-55.. S 13084
   Justus, former wid. of, Abi North.. W 10822
   Robert, wid. Lydia Deming.. W 25606
     BLWt. 2496-160-55.
   Titus.. S 16813
   William.. S 37944
FRANCOIS, Anthony. (See O'CAIN, Anthony Francis.)
FRANK, Joshua... S 37945
FRANKLIN, Abel.. S 37948
   Ezra... S 16812
   Jehiel or Jeile.. S 44863
   Samuel... S 37940
FRANKS, John, Conn. & Mass.. S 34884
FRANSEWAY. (See O'CAIN, Anthony F.)
FRANSSES. (See FRANCIS.)*
FRANSWOI. (See O'CAIN, Anthony F.)
FRARY or FRERY, Seth.. S 29517
FREEDOM, Cato... S 44849
   Dick.. BLWt. 590-100
   Ned.. S 37946
FREEMAN, Andrew, wid. Elizabeth... W 21149
   Call... S 36513
   Caser or Caesar.. S 43567
   Chatham.. S 36524
   Cuff, Conn. in 1818.. S 36522
   Cuff, d. 1800, Litchfield, Conn.; not pensioned, wid. Amelia..................... W 19298
   Daniel... S 44543
   David.. S 36511
   Devonshire... S 36519
   Enoch, wid. Sarah.. W 21157
   Jack. (See ROWLAND, Jack.)
   James, New London Co. in 1818, as priv... S 36518
   James, Washington Co., R. I., in 1818, as priv................................... S 38708
   Jethro... S 36520
   John... S 36517
   Joseph, Conn. & Cont., BLWt. 1540-100.. S 39548
   Mary, former wid. of John Bliss, q. v.
   Peleg, Conn. & Privateer... R 3782
   Peter, Hartford Co. in 1818.. S 36516
   Peter, New London Co. in 1818, as priv... S 36521
   Philemon... S 36523
   Phoebe, former wid. of London Wallace or Wallis, q. v.
   Plymouth or Plymmouth.. S 44852
   Prince... S 39549
   Providence, wid. Azuba, BLWt. 31307-160-55....................................... W 739
   Roger.. S 43574
   Samuel, wid. Jemima, BLWt. 1413-100.. W 17926
   William.. S 13085
   William. (See COUCH, William (colored).)
FRENCH, Aaron, former wid. of, Abigail Dexter..................................... W 22937
   Abel, Cont. (Conn.).. S 13087
   Comewell or Cromwell, wid. Elizabeth... R 3790
   Ebenezer, Conn., Mass. & N. Y.. S 13090
   Francis, wid. Sylvia... W 17928
   James.. S 1200
   James R.. S 15844
   Jonathan, Conn. Sea service.. S 38737
   Levi, Cont. (Conn.), BLWt. 5826, issued 1792.
   Nathaniel H.. S 18827
   Samuel, Trumbull, Conn., in 1832 as Serg't....................................... S 16814
   Samuel, priv. in Fairfield Co. in 1818... S 36515
   Truman... S 36512
   William, former wid. of, Lucy Smith.. W 3609
     BLWt. 1200-100.

FRERY. (See FRARY.)
FRINK, Isaac .... S 10705
    Jabish or Jabesh or Jabez .... S 28736
    Nathan, wid. Clarissa .... W 24251
    Nathaniel Lothrop, former wid. of, Rebecca Gilbert .... W 25623
    Thomas .... BLWt. 506-100
FRISBE, FRISBEE or FRISBIE.
    Abraham, wid. Olive .... W 3341
    Asahel .... S 10708
    David .... R 3807
FRISBE, FRISBEE or FRISBIE, or FRISBY.
    Ichabod C .... S 15842
    Israel, wid. Esther .... R 3808
        Heirs allowed claim by special act.
    John, wid. Rachel .... W 17921
    Josiah, Conn. & Conn. Sea service .... S 17425
    Joseph, wid. Diantha .... R 3806
        His commission as Serg't. is on file in the Dep't. He never applied for a pension. The
        wid. was rejected.
    Luther, Cont. (Conn.) .... S 4273
        Sally Frisby, wid. of above soldier, was pensioned on account of service of her first hus-
        band, Elizur or Eleazer Talcott, Conn. W 27522.
    Noah .... S 23227
    Philemon, wid. Rhoda .... R 3809
    Reuben .... S 36514
FRISSELL or FRIZZLE, John, wid. Martha .... W 19293
    BLWt. 11268-160-55.
FROST, Amos, BLWt. 5790 issued 1796.
    Joseph .... S 29164
    Solomon .... R 3816
FROTHINGHAM, Ebenezer, Cont. service, but Conn. residence of heirs in 1827 when they ob-
    tained BLWt. 1229-200.
    Samuel .... S 46253
FRY, Peleg, Conn. & R. I., wid. Barbara .... W 17924
FULLER, Abijah, Conn. & Cont., wid. Abigail .... W 17928
    Abraham .... R 14329
    Asa, wid. Abigail .... W 24258
    Benajah, wid. Catharine .... W 4675
    Benjamin, Hampton, Conn., in 1832, brother of John, who d. in 1807; soldier d. in 1840; wid.
        Clarissa, BLWt. 26625-160-55 .... W 1746
    Benjamin, Rome, N. Y., in 1832; wid. Polly .... W 21163
    Daniel, wid. Sarah .... W 19302
    Darius .... S 22782
    David, wid. Eunice .... W 17931
    Dayton .... S 29136
    Ebenezer, wid. Juan Fernandis .... W 21162
    Edward .... S 36528
    Eleazer, Litchfield Co., Conn., in 1818, moved to Mass .... S 32707
    Eleazer, Conn. & Mass. service; d. 1819, Hampden, Mass., was priv. & corp., wid. Rachel ... W 14762
    Eli .... S 36527
    Ezra .... S 36526
    Isaac, wid. Elizabeth, BLWt. 24155-160-55 .... W 11029
    James .... S 36525
    John, Litchfield Co. in 1832 as serg't .... S 13115
    John, Tolland Co. in 1832 as priv .... S 31684
    John .... R 3834
    John, d. 1813, New London Co., wid. Wealthy .... W 17929
    John, Conn. & Cont., N. Y. in 1818 .... S 43580
    Joseph .... S 17428
    Joshua .... S 43579
    Josiah .... S 16815
    Lemuel, wid. Polly, BLWt. 26490-160-55 .... W 648
    Luther, Conn. & Mass .... R 3837
    Nathan, Windham Co., Conn., in 1832 .... S 17427
    Nathan, N. Y. in 1832, d. 1840; wid. Hannah .... W 19301
    Noah, wid. Lucy .... W 23073
    Samuel, d. 1821, priv. under Capt. Millard, Otsego Co., N. Y., in 1820; wid. Lydia .... W 17932
    Samuel, d. 1826, Herkimer Co., N. Y.; priv. under Capt. Holmes; wid. Mary .... W 25603
    Samuel, Cont. (Conn.) & N. H., pensioned in 1818, as res. of Burlington,Vt., moved later to
        N. Y. State .... S 44869
    Shubael .... R 3841
    Timothy, former wid. of, Hannah Hayes or Hays .... W 17974
        This woman's second husband, Benjamin Hays, also served in the Revolution.
FURBECK, John, Cont. (Conn.) .... S 13108
FURGESON. (See FERGUSON.)
FYLER, John. Colebrook, Conn. in 1832; wid. Asenath; BLWt. 26014-160-55 .... W 2379
    John, d. 1810, Guilford, Conn., wid. Ruth (given also as TYLER) .... W 17936
    (See also FILER and FISLER.)

G.

GAGE, Moses .... R 3861
    Thaddeus, Livingston Co., N. Y., 1832; wid. Judith .... R 3860
GAGER, Samuel R., wid. Lucretia, BLWt. 26045-160-55 .... W 7495
GAINS, Jude, wid. Anner .... W 17004
GALLOP, John .... S 10721
GALLUP, Amos .... S 13116
    Andrew .... S 17430
    Benadam, wid. Mary, BLWt. 24441-160-55.
    Ezra .... S 29168
    George, former wid., Freelove Kinne .... W 21532

GALLUP, Isaac, Conn. & Cont., former wid., Anna Williams................................. W 26032
 Joseph.. S 15137
 Levi.. S 8544
 Nehemiah.. S 13110
  Mercy, wid. of above soldier, was pensioned as former wid. of Peter Brown (q.v.).
 Robert, BLWt. 28531-160-55... S 23651
 William... S 15581
GALPIN, Amos, Conn. & Cont... S 13129
 Daniel, Cont. (Conn.), BLWt. 253-100.. S 13113
 Jehiel, former wid., Lucy Morgan.. W 17161
 Samuel.. S 15132
GALUSHA, Abiram... S 43583
 Jacob, wid. Dinah... W 24270
 Thomas.. S 23648
GANSEY, Seth, BLWt. 897-100... S 39565
 (See also GARNSEY and GUERNSEY.)
GANTT, Erasmus... S 10727
GARDENER, GARDINER, GARDINIER or GARDNER.
 Abijah.. S 44154
 David, New London Co., Conn., in 1818... S 36532
 David, New Haven Co., Conn., in 1818; wid. Fanny, BLWt. 31909-160-55.................... W 1850
 Elizabeth, former wid. of Ezekiel Tinker (q. v.).
 Isaac, wid. Esther.. W 7499
  BLWt. 26788-160-55.
 John, Conn. & N. Y.. R 3903
 Jonathan.. S 17429
 Phebe, former wid. of Joel Beers (q. v.).
 Sherman... S 5176
 Thomas, wid. Esther... W 16020
 William, Conn. 1818, d. 1826, N. Y. Co., N. Y.; wid. Hannah............................. W 25618
 William, Elmira, N. Y., in 1818; d. 1823; wid. Margaret. BLWt. 8387-160-55.............. W 1750
GAREY or GEAREY or GARY.
 Eneas... S 13128
 Gilbert, wid. Nancy or Anna... R 3961
 Josiah, Cont. (Conn.)... S 37003
GARNSEY, Chauncey... S 13120
 David... S 22785
 Joel.. S 15136
 Samuel.. S 13111
 (See also GANSEY and GUERNSEY.)
GARRET, GARRETT, GARRIT.
 Abigail, former wid. of Gideon Scofield (q. v.).
 Francis... S 16124
 John, Oneida Co., N. Y., 1832... S 43581
 John, Litchfield Co., Conn., in 1818.. S 44159
GATES, Asa, Conn. & R. I.. S 21214
 Cyrus, Conn. & R. I... S 22262
 Daniel.. R 3871
 Desire, former wid. of Charles Cushman (q. v.).
 Ezra, Conn. & N. Y.. S 10726
 Freeman... S 42735
 James, wid. Polly... W 23083
 Jehiel.. S 44875
 Joseph, wid. Mary... W 4203
 Luther, wid. Ann.. W 21168
 Marvin.. S 15138
 Nathan.. S 21764
 Nathaniel, Navy (Conn.)... S 41562
 Nehemiah, wid. Ruth... W 25614
 Oliver, Conn. & Sea Service, Bradford, Penna., 1832; wid. Jemima........................ R 3941
 Samuel.. S 18833
 Thomas, wid. Rachel... W 11040
 William... S 43594
 Zebulon Waterman, wid. Alice.. R 3939
GAY, Asahel, wid. Temperance.. W 17940
 Edward.. S 13172
 Jason... S 44871
 Richard... S 16817
GAYLARD or GAYLORD.
 Ambrose, wid. Eleanor, BLWt. 290-100.. W 4677
 Chauncy... S 13112
 Deodate... S 17433
 Eleazer, wid. Sylvia.. W 17941
 Elijah, BLWt. 9465-160-55... S 15139
 Jedediah or Jedidiah.. S 22784
 Joel, Conn. & Mass., BLWt. 374-100.. S 46357
 John, wid. Charlotte.. W 17005
 Jonathan.. S 44876
 Jonathan, Conn. & Navy.. S 42736
 Joseph.. S 15848
 Josiah, wid. Mary Ann... W 19483
 Justus, wid. Lucretia... W 3342
 Lemuel.. R 3958
 Levi, Conn. & Cont.. S 4293
GEAR, George... S 36534
GEAREY. (See GAREY.)
GEDDINS, John, wid. Achsah.. W 25624
 (Also given GIDDINGS.)

GEER or GEERE.
Allyn, Conn. & Mass.	S	17972
Amos	S	23230
Asa	S	41571
Benajah	S	43588
David	R	3965
Ebenezer Steel, wid. Catherine, BLWt. 31910-160-55	W	1265
Elihu, wid. Eleanor	W	21180
George	S	17434
Gurdon, Cont. (Conn.)	S	42738
Jedediah	S	42741
John, wid. Onnah	W	14782
Nathan	S	16126
Nathaniel	S	15849
Richard	S	13132
Robert	S	13131
Roger	S	8552

GENNINGS, Mary, former wid. of Jesse Davis (q. v.).
GEORGE, Amos	S	43593
Prince	S	43594
GEORGIA, Simon	BLWt.	1289-100
GERALD, GERALDS, GERRALD or JERALDS, Thomas, Cont. (Conn.)	BLWt.	1034-100
GERMAN or JARMAN, Charles, wid. Betsey	W	20169
GHADEN or GLADING, Joseph	S	36548
GIBBS, David	S	13141
Eldad	S	29176
Gershom, Conn. & Cont.	S	15144
Ithamar	S	44161
Moore, Conn. & Cont., wid. Patience	W	25628
(Consolidated with S 36546.)		
Philo, wid. Lois, BLWt. 19524-160-55	W	7518
Samuel, private, Berkshire Co., Mass., in 1818; wid. Caty, BLWt. 29731-160-55	W	689
Samuel, Capt. Conn. in 1818; wid. Julia F	W	7519
BLWt. 822-200, Lieut. was issued July 27, 1789. No papers.		
Simeon, wid. Esther	W	17008
Solomon	S	17439
Spencer	S	36542
Stephen, Hartford Co., in 1818; wid. Ruth	R	3989
Sylvanus, wid. Betsey	W	24276
William	S	13145
GIBSON, Roger	S	29827
GIDDINGS, Benjamin, wid. Apphiah	W	17946
John, wid. Achsah. (Given also GEDDINS (q. v.).)		
Joseph, Norwich, Conn., in 1818, d. 1832; wid. Mary	W	25625
Joseph, Conn., Cont. & N. Y. service; Litchfield Co., Conn., in 1832, living in 1836	S	10736
Joshua	S	3396
Niles	S	10738
Thomas, wid. Anna, BLWt. 29021-160-55	W	1410
GIFFEN, Ezra, Conn. & N. J.	S	16136
(Also given GRIFFIN.)		
GIFFIN, Simon, Cont. & Conn	S	36543
GIFFORD, Absalom	S	13134
Jeremiah, wid. Sally	W	1411
William, Conn. & R. I.	S	2236

GILBERT, or GILBUT.
Allen	S	44162
Asa, Conn. & Cont., wid. Mary	W	17944
Asahel, Cont. (Conn.)	S	32268
Benjamin, Conn. & Cont	S	13139
Burr, former wid., Clarissa Turney	W	18165
Butler	S	43607
David, wid. Molly	W	25621
Ebenezer, Brooklyn, Conn., 1818	S	36539
Ebenezer, d. 1798, wid. in Fairfield Co., wid. Ruth	W	17945
Ebenezer, Navy (Conn.) service; surgeon, Revenue Cutter; son Joseph M	S	27
Gardner, Conn. & Cont., wid. Mary, BLWt. 91126-160-55	W	13265
Gershom	S	10743
Heber, wid. Lucina	W	4966
Hooker	S	13136
Isaac	S	13137
Jesse	S	36544
John, Grafton Co., N. H., in 1832	S	15585
John, d. 1816, Westchester Co. N. Y.; wid. Elizabeth	W	16268
Joseph, Bloomfield, N. Y. in 1818	S	43605
Joseph, Corp. & Serg't. Conn. & Cont. service; d. 1812, Livingston Co., N. Y.; wid. Miriam	W	23112
Lemuel, wid. Amorillis	W	21185
Lewis	S	22265
Moses	S	15145
Nathan	S	17440
Obadiah	S	39579
Rebecca, former wid. of Nathaniel Lothrop Frink (q. v.).		
Samuel	S	16127
Solomon, wid. Thankful	W	17009
Thaddeus	S	43596
Theodore, Conn. & Mass. service; Madison Co., N. Y., in 1818	S	10739
Theodore, Volney, N. Y., in 1818	S	43601
Thomas	S	31689
Truman	S	18417
William, wid. Hope	W	24275

GILES, Thomas.. S 15141
GILL, John.. S 39576
   Samuel.. R 4025
GILLBERT. (See GILBERT.)
GILLESPIE, William, Cont. (Conn.); former wid., Mary Ellsworth.............. W 16249
GILLET, GILLETT, GILLETTE or GILLIT.
   Adna... R 4033
   Alpheus or Alphius, Cont. (Conn.).. S 41577
   Asa, former wid., Abigail Denison.. R 4032
   Asa, Cont. (Conn.), Mich. res. & Agency.. S 34898
   Benjamin, Conn. & Privateer.. S 15143
   Benjamin, Cont. service, Conn. res. & Agency; ch. David W., Polly Gillett, & Sally Derrick
     (Mrs. John) obtained... BLWt. 437-100
   Benoni, 62 yrs. New Haven, Conn., in 1819, d. June, 1844, wid. Phebe......... W 25630
   Benoni, Granby, Conn. in 1832, d. April, 1844; wid. Polly, BLWt. 29022-160-55.. W 2607
   Elijah.. S 17436
   Ephraim.. S 36538
   Isaac... S 17978
   Jabez, Conn. & N. Y., wid. Hannah.. W 19501
   Jeremiah, Burlington, Conn. in 1818.. S 36535
   Jeremiah, N. H. in 1818... S 45554
   Joel.. S 36540
   John, wid. Mary.. S 36537
   John, d. 1810, Cortland, N. Y.; former wid., Mercy Hoar...................... W 18035
   Jonathan, Mus. & Corp. 1832.. S 15851
   Joseph, Lyme, Conn. in 1832.. S 15850
   Joseph, Del. Co. Ohio in 1832; wid. Parcey, BLWt. 9546-160-55................ W 7524
   Luther... S 6890
   Nathan or Nathaniel... S 42744
   Othniel.. S 36536
   Reuben... S 21228
   Reuben, Conn. & Cont.. R 20374
   Rufus, wid. Ellen... W 17948
   Samuel... S 22789
   Stephen, Conn. & Cont.. S 13143
   William, Conn. & Mass. service, wid. Abigail................................. W 2930
GILMAN, Calvin, wid. Hannah.. W 19506
GILSON, Eleazer.. S 17973
   Jacob... S 39584
GLADDEN, Azariah, Conn. & Navy service.. S 29828
GLADDING, Jedediah, wid. Elizabeth... W 25634
GLADING, Joseph. (See GHADEN.)
GLASS, Alexander, wid. Jemima.. W 15770
GLAZIER, Eliphalet, wid. Rachel.. R 4060
   John, wid. Hannah.. W 4208
GLEASON or GLESON, Benjamin, Conn. & Cont. service, BLWt. 642-100........... S 39589
   James, wid. Lovina... W 24280
   John... S 31694
   Joseph, Conn. & N. Y., wid. Elizabeth.. W 17949
GLENNEY, GLENNY or GLINNEY.
   Isaac, Cont. (Conn.) & Mass., wid. Sarah..................................... W 17015
   William, wid. Polly or Mary... W 17950
     BLWt. 815-200, Lieut. was issued Aug. 5, 1789. No papers.
GLESEN. (See GLEASON.)
GLINNEY. (See GLENNEY.)
GODARD or GODDARD.
   Ebenezer, priv. & Serg't. Hartford, Conn., in 1832........................... S 15153
   Ebenezer, Conn. & Navy service; Hartford, Conn., Serg't. Marines, in 1832.... S 15857
   Edward... S 44166
   Isaac, Granby, Conn. in 1832; wid. Rosanna................................... R 4079
   John... S 15148
   Levi, wid. Mary... W 19521
   Rufus, wid. Mindwell.. W 17958
     (Given also as GOSSARD.)
   Tilley... R 4080
GODFREY, Isaac... S 17444
   Jonathan... S 16834
   Reuben, Conn. Sea service & Navy... S 15152
   Stephen.. S 13071
GOFF, Charles, Conn. & Cont... S 13178
   Comfort.. S 28744
   David, wid. Elizabeth... W 690
   Ezekiel, Conn. & Cont... S 15149
   Gideon... S 36558
   Hezekiah, Conn., Conn. Sea service, Mass. & 1812; Vt. in 1818; wid. Rebecca.. R 4087
   James, wid. Mary.. W 7539
   Richard, Conn., Navy & Privateer; wid. Polly................................. W 24287
   Samuel... S 36551
   Samuel D... S 39598
   Solomon.. S 42749
GOLD. (See GOULD.)
GOLDSMITH, James.. S 22794
GOODALE, Chester, wid. Asenath.. W 19522
   BLWt. 26983-160-55.
   Ebenezer, wid. Jerusha.. W 4967
     (Also given GOODALL.)

GOODALL, GOODELL or GOODDELL.
Alvan or Alvin, Conn. & Cont., former wid. Alice Potter .... W 18769
Asa .... S 15865
Ezra .... S 43608
Jabez, wid. Peninah .... W 14800
Jacob .... S 45562
Silas, Conn. & Cont .... S 36559
    BLWt. 813-200, Lieut.
    (See also GOODALE.)
GOODFAITH, David .... S 36553
GOODHARD, David .... R 4106
  (Also given GOODFAITH.)
GOODMAN, Moses, Cont. (Conn.) .... S 36550
Richard .... S 13165
GOODRICH, Abel .... S 13181
Abner, Conn. & Cont .... S 42754
Allen .... S 18418
Bethuel .... S 38740
    BLWt. 5833-100 was issued April 19, 1790. No papers.
Crafts .... R 4115
David, former wid. Penelope Hillyer .... R 5026
    NOTE.—Widow's second husband, Elijah Hubbard, and her third husband, James Hillyer, also served in the Revolutionary War. David died in service at Fort Lee, N. J., in 1776, and her pension was rejected because she was unable to prove that he had served six months before he was killed.
David, Conn. & Cont .... S 10760
Elisha .... S 43612
George .... S 32755
Gideon .... S 10753
Ichabod .... S 36556
Isaac, d. 1847, not pensioned; wid. Electa; BLWt. 21835-160-55 .... R 4116
Isaac, d. Del. Co., N. Y., in 1834; wid. Sarah .... W 17016
James, Conn., Conn. Sea service & Privateer .... S 15864
Jared, Conn., & Cont., wid. Deborah .... W 17954
John, Conn. & Cont .... BLWt. 1607-100
  (Also given GOODRICK.)
John, Conn. & Cont., wid. Mabel .... W 24292
John H., wid. Mary .... W 4682
Levi, Conn. & Cont., wid. Julia Ann .... R 4118
Micah .... S 15858
Michael .... S 43628
Nathan .... S 32276
  (Given also GUTRICH.)
Ozias, BLWt. as Ensign, 821-150.
  (Given also GOODRIDGE.)
Roswel or Roswell, Glastonbury, Conn., 1832, as musician .... S 31696
Roswell, Conn. & Cont., N. Y. in 1818, as artificer .... S 13182
Simeon, Vt. 1832, Serg't. Artificers .... S 21772
Simeon .... R 4119
Solomon P., wid. Anna .... W 2095
Stephen, Conn. & Cont .... S 38735
William, wid. Phebe .... W 17019
Zenas, former wid. Lois Cash .... R 1780
GOODRICK. (See GOODRICH.)
GOODRIDGE. (See GOODRICH.)
GOODSEL, Ephraim, Conn. & Navy .... S 29182
Isaac, former wid. Elizabeth Webster BLWt. 40502-160-55.
John, wid. Abigail .... W 17952
Rachel, former wid. of William Bailey (q. v.).
Samuel, wid. Abigail .... W 21192
Thomas .... S 10756
GOODSPEED, Nathaniel, Conn., Mass. & N. H., wid. Abigail .... W 23117
GOODWIN, Hezekiah, wid. Polly .... W 27873
Joseph .... S 29180
Levi .... S 17442
Moses .... S 13157
Nathaniel .... R 4130
Seth, wid. Mahitable, BLWt. 28557-160-55 .... W 1412
Solomon, wid. Anna .... W 24283
Zebedee, Cont. (Conn.), wid. Caroline .... W 21198
GOODYEAR, Edward .... S 43623
Stephen .... S 16832
GOOKINS, Samuel, wid. Polly .... W 10064
GOOLD. (See GOULD.)
GORDON, Alexander, Conn. & Privateer .... R 4137
George, Conn. & Cont .... S 39599
Samuel .... S 43614
GORE, Obadiah .... S 39601
    BLWt. 817-200, Lieut. was issued Feb. 22, 1791. No papers.
GORHAM, Daniel, Conn. & Cont .... S 13159
George, Cont. (Conn.) .... S 13161
Joseph, Cont. (Conn.), wid. Elizabeth Baldwin .... W 17247
Nathan, Conn. & Conn. Sea service .... S 15150
Nehemiah .... S 36552
    BLWt. 814-200, Lieut., issued Feb. 25, 1800 to Jones Stansbury, Assignee. No papers.
Seth, Castleton, Vt. in 1832; private under Capt. Hubbell, Col. Silliman .... S 15587
Seth, Rutland, Vt. in 1832; private under Capt. Godding, Col. Beardsley; wid. Lovisa, BLWt. 26199-160-55 .... W 9467
GORTON, Benjamin, Cont. (Conn.) .... S 13154
Joseph .... S 31698

```
GOSLEE, or GOSLEY, Solomon.....................................................................   S  31697
    Consolidated with S  36554.
GOSS, Andrew..........................................................................................   S  32747
GOSSARD, Rufus.  (See GODARD.)
GOUGE, Phebe, former wid. of Eli Smith (q. v.).
GOULD, GOLD and GOOLD.
    James, wid. Mary..................................................................................   W  17022
    John, Conn., & R. I...............................................................................   S  16128
    John, Windsor Co. Vt. in 1818;  private Capt. Durkee.....................................   S  39605
    Nathan, Conn. & Navy, wid. Patience.........................................................   W  17957
    Noah M...............................................................................................   S  37013
    Samuel, wid. Sarah...............................................................................   W  21201
    Silas....................................................................................................   S  37023
    Thomas, Cont. (Conn.)...........................................................................   S  22271
    Willard, Conn., Cont. & Mass..................................................................   S  13180
    William, Conn., Cont. & Mass..................................................................   S  42752
GOWDY, Alexander.................................................................................   S  10750
    Hill, wid. Roxana..................................................................................   W  17951
    John....................................................................................................   S  31066
    Samuel................................................................................................   S  15151
GRAHAM, Jesse, wid. Elizabeth.................................................................   W  25663
    John....................................................................................................   S  42755
    Oliver..................................................................................................   S  22797
    William................................................................................................   S  13222
GRANGER, Bildad....................................................................................   S  36561
    Ebenezer, wid. Patience.........................................................................   W  1169
    Ithamar, wid. Jemima............................................................................   W  14812
    Jacob, Cont. (Conn.), wid Esther..............................................................   R  4189
        Soldier was a pensioner in Galen, N. Y., in 1818.
    Moses, wid. Lucy..................................................................................   W  15907
    Moses, Conn. & Vt................................................................................   R  4190
GRANNES or GRANNIS or GRANNISS.
    David, wid. Clarissa..............................................................................   W  24302
    Elle......................................................................................................   S  17449
    Enos, Conn. & Cont...............................................................................   S  39613
        BLWt. 818-200, Lieut. of Art. Artificers was issued Mar. 10, 1796, under name of Eneas
        Grannis, and also recorded as above BLWt. 2663.  No papers.
    Jared, Conn. & Privateer........................................................................   S  31704
    Robert.................................................................................................   R  4192
    Samuel, Cont. service, former wid. Charity Irion or Trion or Tryon, res. Conn......   W  26154
GRANT, Aaron, wid. Lucy.........................................................................   W  17967
    Andrew...............................................................................................   S  18847
    Azariah...............................................................................................   S  38775.
    David..................................................................................................   S  15870
    Elihu...................................................................................................   R  4194
    Elnathan..............................................................................................   S  13193
    Gideon.................................................................................................   S  36565
    Gustavus, wid. Phebe, BLWt. 9204-160-55.................................................   W  2101
    Hamilton, wid. Lucy, BLWt. 2521-160-55..................................................   W  1417
    Hezekiah.............................................................................................   S  30446
    Isaac...................................................................................................   R  4195
    James..................................................................................................   S  38759
    Jehu....................................................................................................   R  4197
    Jesse, BLWt. 823-300, Capt. was issued Feb. 18, 1793.  No papers.
    Oliver, wid. Hannah..............................................................................   W  25126
    Reuben, wid. Anna................................................................................   W  21228
    Roswell, b. Aug. 18, 1762, priv................................................................   S  15161
    Roswell, b. Mch. 20, 1746, Capt. & Paymaster..........................................   S  31710
    Thomas................................................................................................   S  8605
    William, Conn. & Mass. Sea service, wid. Polly.........................................   W  19531
GRAVE or GRAVES.
    Amos, Conn. & Mass., wid. Hannah.........................................................   W  7579
    Asahel.................................................................................................   R  4205
    Bela.....................................................................................................   S  9344
    Benjamin, Conn. & Cont., wid. Sarah, BLWt. 157-60-55............................   W  4972
    Elijah, Herkimer Co., N. Y., in 1832 as Serg't............................................   S  8596
    Elijah, N. Y. in 1818, as private..............................................................   S  44173
    Gilbert, wid. Elizabeth...........................................................................   W  25649
    Hobart.................................................................................................   S  28746
    John, wid. Hannah................................................................................   W  25661
    Josiah..................................................................................................   S  29842
    Peter....................................................................................................   S  43640
    Seth, wid. Elizabeth..............................................................................   W  21222
    Simeon.................................................................................................   S  43641
    Thaddeus, Conn. & Mass.......................................................................   S  16134
    Timothy, private, Madison, Conn. in 1832................................................   S  31705
    Timothy, priv. & Serg't, Hoosick, N. Y., in 1832........................................   S  15162
    Whitney...............................................................................................   S  15159
GRAW.  (See GROW.)
GRAY, Daniel..........................................................................................   R  4219
    Ebenezer, BLWt. 812-450 Lt. Col.  No papers.  No date of issue.
    Eliphalet, wid. Lydia.............................................................................   R  4223
    Jabesh.................................................................................................   S  43643
    James, Conn., Cont. & N. Y....................................................................   S  2245
    Joseph, Weston, Conn., priv. Militia, d. 1840, Fairfield Co., wid. Eunice.......   W  21226
    Joseph, Conn. & Mass. service; priv. & Corp., d. 1833, Ridgefield, Conn., wid. Lydia.........   W  21225
    Samuel, former wid. Abigail Hadley (soldier never pensioned).....................   R  4415
        Abigail Hadley's second husband, Joseph Hadley, also served in the Revolution, and
        Abigail was pensioned for his service, so was rejected for her first husband's service.
    Samuel, Conn., Cont. & N. Y. private, 1818..............................................   S  43638
    Samuel, Cont. (Conn.), Deputy Commissary General...................................   S  13188
```

GREEN or GREENE.
- Abel... S 43642
- Abner... S 17448
- Amasa, Cont. (Conn.), wid. Lurena... W 4684
- Amos, wid. Lavina... W 25646
- Asahel, wid. Grace... W 17962
- Benjamin, Conn. & R. I... S 21783
- Caleb, wid. Rebecca... W 21206
- Dorastus... S 30564
- Ebenezer... S 13217
- Eleazer or Elezer... S 44885
- Ezra, wid. Amy... W 17965
- Gideon... R 4255
- Henry, Conn. & Cont... S 13187
- Jabez, Conn. & R. I... S 13189
- Jack... S 43631
- Jacob... S 44176
- James, Conn., in 1832... S 10770
- James, Orange Co., N. Y., in 1832; wid. Sarah, BLWt. 36502-160-55... W 25644
- Joel... R 4257
- John, N. Y., in 1832, as private... S 23659
- John, wid. Esther... R 4251
  (Soldier not pensioned.)
- Joseph, Conn., Cont. & Mass. & Vt., former wid. Jerusha Morey... W 17148
- Josiah, former wid. Susanna Holbrook... W 21395
- Noah... S 29840
- Obadiah... S 18422
- Roswell, BLWt. 9403-160-55... S 28749
- Samuel, Madison Co., N. Y., in 1832; priv... S 13196
- Samuel, Milford, Conn., d. 1843, wid. Polly, BLWt. 8179-160-55... W 25662
- Samuel, Elmira, N. Y., in 1818, private, Col. Chandler, wid. Tamazen... W 21223
- Sebra, former wid. of Stephen Harrington (q. v.).
- Timothy, wid. Jane... W 21207
- Willard... S 13198
- Zachariah, Conn. & Cont., BLWt. 13732-160-55... S 28747
- GREENFIELD, Enos... S 44177
- James... S 13192
- William, Conn., Cont. & Green Mt. Boys (soldier not pensioner), wid. Prudence... R 4283
- GREENOLD. (See GRINNELL.)
- GREENSLET or GREENSLIT.
- Benjamin, wid. Martha... W 25659
- Joel, Conn. & Cont... S 10765
- John, Cont. service, Conn. residence in 1820... S 36563
- John, private under Durkee; Washington, Vt., in 1832; wid. Saloma, BLWt. 34327-160-55... W 9465
- GREGG, David, Conn. & Mass. & N. H... S 15590
- GREGGS or GRIGGS, Ephraim, wid. Hannah... W 16024
- GREGORY, Daniel... S 17453
- Elias, wid. Elizabeth... W 17960
- Elnathan... S 29841
- Ezra, wid. Huldah, BLWt. 15197-160-55... W 4971
- Jabez, wid. Mercy... W 21213
- James... S 17445
- John, wid. Jerusha... W 1419
- Joseph, wid. Deborah... W 1596
- Josiah, wid. Ellen... W 24308
- Matthew... S 46360
  BLWT. 819-200, Lieut, was issued Dec. 5, 1799. No papers.
- Moses, wid. Abigail... W 25055
- Nathan... S 13214
- Nathaniel... R 4296
- Nehemiah... S 22803
- Samuel, wid. Charity... W 17970
- Silas, wid. Sarah... W 25053
- Stephen, Bradford Co., Penna., in 1832, private... S 22274
- Stephen, Conn. & Cont., N. Y. in 1832... S 13191
- Uriah, Conn. & N. Y... S 15157
- William... S 29191
- GRENELL or GRENNELL. (See GRINNELL.)
- GRIDLEY, Asahel, wid. Chloe... W 15771
- Ashbel, wid. Jemima... W 17961
- Elijah, wid. Abigail Eliza... W 4908
  BLWt. 29725-160-55.
- Elisha, wid. Lois... W 19545
- Hosea, former wid. Sabra Burchard... W 15992
- Obediah, wid. Elizabeth... W 16274
- Seth... S 15588
- Silas... S 4304
- Theodore, wid. Amy... W 5287
  BLWt. 11281-160-55.
- Thomas... S 29186
- GRIFFEN, GRIFFIN or GRIFFING.
- Ann, former wid. of Benjamin Farnam (q. v.).
- Ezra, Conn. & N. J... S 16136
- Joel... R 4319
- John... S 37037
- Joseph, Conn. & Cont... S 8615
- Martin, wid. Anna... W 21210
- Samuel... S 23666
- Stephen, Conn. & N. Y., wid. Elizabeth... W 19549
- Thomas, wid. Polly, BLWt. 26598-160-55... W 19537

GRIFFETH or GRIFFITH.
  Eli, Conn. & N. Y .... R 4324
  George .... S 43648
  Jeremiah, Conn. & N. Y., wid. Mary .... W 19532
    Lucy, former wid. of Ebenezer Hitchcock (q. v.).
GRIGG, Henry, wid. Elizabeth .... W 11087
  (See also GREGG.)
GRIGGS, Joseph .... S 30445
  (See also GREGGS.)
GRIMES, Abraham, Conn. & Mass .... S 13200
  Joseph, wid. Jemima .... W 21234
GRINNEL, GRINNELL, GRINNIEL, GRENELL or GRENNELL.
  Amasa .... S 43650
  Michael, BLWt. 26451-160-55 .... S 2251
  William .... S 29843
    (Also given GREENOLD.)
  William B., wid. Sarah .... W 17968
  Wise .... S 45573
GRISWOLD, Aaron, wid. Polly .... W 747
  Abel .... S 17447
  Alexander .... R 4342
  Andrew, Conn. in 1818, d. 1825; wid. Anna, BLWt. 1068-200 .... W 17963
  Andrew, d. New London Co., Conn., never pensioned, 1813, wid. Eunice .... W 21205
  Asa .... S 37028
  Constant .... S 16133
  Daniel, Conn. & Mass., wid. Nancy, BLWt. 40938-160-55 .... W 11086
  Edmund, wid. Jane, BLWt. 508-160-55 .... W 7608
  Edward, wid. Asenath .... W 19553
  Elihu, Conn. & Sea Service .... R 1204
  Elijah, Windsor, Conn., in 1818 .... S 37032
  Elijah, Hartford Co., Conn., in 1832, d. 1846; Ensign, wid. Lydia .... W 25650
  Francis .... S 23245
  George, priv .... S 17456
  George, Serg't. Conn. Line, 1818 .... S 31703
  Janna, wid. Lucy .... W 21220
  Joel .... S 31708
  John .... R 4345
  John, Rome, N. Y. in 1818; wid. Vashta, BLWt. 2346-160-55 .... W 9466
  John, Fairfield, N. Y. in 1818; wid. Lydia, BLWt. 10237-160-55 .... W 25654
  Joseph, Ontario Co., N. Y., in 1818 .... S 43652
  Joseph, d. 1829, Hampden Co., Mass.; wid. Mehitable .... W 14811
  Midian, Cont. (Conn.), wid. Annis .... R 4343
  Nathaniel .... S 31706
  Samuel .... R 4348
  Samuel, wid Hannah .... W 21230
    BLWt. 336-100 and BLWt. 235-60-55.
  Selah, Conn. & Cont .... S 17454
  Simeon, Conn. & Cont .... S 13092
  Sylvanus, wid. Mary Maria .... W 25648
  Zenas .... S 15158
GROSE. (See GROSS.)
GROSS, John, wid. Susannah .... W 21212
  Josiah .... S 32774
  Samuel .... S 49283
  Thomas .... R 4356
GROSVENOR, Asa .... S 10762
  Joshua .... S 15156
  Lemuel .... S 15154
  Polly, former wid. of Elihu Mather (q. v.).
  Thomas .... R 4361
  Thomas, Conn. & Cont .... S 37033
    BLWt. 811-500, Lieut. Col. Commandant was issued Jan. 28, 1790. No papers.
GROVENOR. (See GROSVENOR.)
GROVER, Amasa .... S 38751
  Amaziah, Conn. & N. H., wid. Joanna, BLWt. 9520-160-55 .... W 746
  Daniel .... R 4369
  Ebenezer, Conn. & N. Y., wid. Mary .... W 17964
  Jabez, wid. Jerusha, BLWt. 27644-160-55 .... W 7604
  Jacob, BLWt. 748-100.
  Joseph, Conn. & Cont .... S 39631
  Luther .... S 21777
  Peter, resided in Conn. in 1789; wid. Diadama .... R 14578
  Phineas, BLWt. 816-200, Lieut. was issued April 18, 1796 to Thomas Lloyd, assignee to Jabin
    Strong & Ruth Strong, Administrators. No papers.
  Stephen, wid. Mary .... W 268
GROW, Ambrose, Conn. & Vt., wid. Amy, BLWt. 26560-160-55 .... W 1416
  David, wid. Martha, BLWt. 6285-160-55 .... W 2609
  Ebenezer, BLWt. 1426-100 .... S 36560
  John .... S 13211
GRUMON, Moses .... R 4373
GRUNDEY or GRUNDY, Edmund .... S 38772
GUERNSEY, Southmayd .... R 3921
  (See also GANSEY and GARNSEY.)
GUILD, Richard, wid. Eleanor Rice, BLWt. 15444-160-55 .... W 1420
GUILE or GUYLE, Abraham, wid. Deborah .... W 1421
GUNN, Abel .... S 44887
GURNEY, Asa, wid. Sarah, BLWt. 9416-160-55 .... W 7616
  Bazaleel .... S 44993

GUSTENE, GUSTINE or AUGUSTINE.
  Edward... S 13234
  Joel. (See AUGUSTINE.)
GUTHRIE, James, wid. Mehitable... S 20777
  Consolidated with.. W 25667
GUTRICH. (See GOODRICH.)
GUYANT, Luke, Conn. & Cont... S 17990
GUYLE. (See GUILE.)

H.

HADLOCK, Samuel, Conn., Cont. & Navy, wid. Sarah, BLWt. 860-100................. W 25757
  Thomas, wid. Lovina, BLWt. 28589-160-55.. W 487
HADSALL or HADSELL, Elijah, wid. Anna, BLWt. 5070-160-55......................... W 1859
HAIL. (See HALE.)
HAINES. (See HAYNES.)
HAIT. (See HOYT.)
HAKES, Caleb, Conn. & R. I.. S 23247
  George, Conn., Cont. & R. I... S 44911
  Jonathan, Conn. & R. I.. S 23255
HAIL or HALE, Aaron, Conn., Cont. & N. Y., wid. Hannah, BLWt. 1203-200........... W 17041
  Ebenezer, wid. Theda.. W 17896
  Gershom... S 22283
    (Also given Garshom HAIL.)
  Jonathan.. S 21257
  Jonathan, former wid. Mary Button... W 17387
  Matthew, wid. Ruth.. W 25749
  Reuben.. S 44898
  Thomas.. S 44899
HALL, Aaron, priv. Capt. Hall; in 1818 & 1832 Wallingford, Conn.................. S 13330
  Aaron, priv. Capt. Leavenworth; in 1832, in N. Y., wid. Em...................... W 16286
  Abner... S 13273
  Alpheus, wid. Marcy... W 19717
  Amos, Serg't. Col. Swift; Vt. in 1832... S 18015
  Amos, d. 1827; Serg't. Capt. Hall; wid. Phebe................................... W 16289
  Anan, wid. Comfort.. W 21250
  Andrew, priv. Conn. State troops; Norwich, Conn., in 1832....................... S 13258
  Andrew, priv. Militia; New Haven, Conn., in 1832................................ S 13335
  Asa, wid. Elizabeth... R 4460
    (Soldier never pensioned; wid. applied from Ohio.)
  Asa, Cont. (Conn.), N. Y., in 1818.. S 44892
  Asahel.. R 4455
  Benajah, wid. Ruth.. W 17980
  Caleb... S 13292
  Christopher, Conn. & N. Y... W 27521
    Former wid. Sarah Benedict. BLWt. 8155-160-55.
    Sarah's other husband, James Benedict, was a Rev. pensioner from Mass. but her application was refused. (See BENEDICT, James, Mass., R 742.)
  Clarissa, former wid. of Solomon PINTO.
  Daniel, priv. Mass., in 1832... S 30472
  Daniel, Conn. & Cont., Serg't., N. Y., in 1832.................................. S 10789
  David, priv. Capt. Leavenworth; Conn. in 1818, wid.............................. S 37084
  David, d. 1824, Sapper & priv., wid. Ann, was pensioned in 1840 & moved to N. Y. W 17053
  Ebenezer.. S 31721
  Elihu or Ellehu... S 29210
  Elisha.. S 13249
  Enoch, wid. Esther.. W 25762
  Enos.. S 10806
  Ephraim, Conn. & Mass... S 13238
  Gad... S 23679
  Hezekiah, Cont. (Conn.)... S 16138
  Hiland, Conn. & Cont.. W 23371
    Former wid. Hannah Hulbard or Hulburd.
  Hiram... BLWt. 2352-100
  James... S 10784
  Jesse, Conn. & Mass... S 5432
  John, priv. Litchfield, Conn., in 1832; wid. Damaris............................ W 24400
  John, priv. Col. Burrill, Rome, N. Y., in 1818, d. 1832; wid. Sarah............. W 16282
  John, Conn. & R. I. service; priv. & serg't. Ohio in 1832....................... S 2588
  John B.. S 10814
  Jonathan.. S 29866
  Joshua, wid. Rhoda.. W 17050
  Jotham.. S 44964
  Levi, Middletown, Conn., in 1832.. S 10818
  Levi, Conn., Cont. & Mass. & R. I. service; N. H. in 1832....................... S 16850
  Lyman or Lymon, wid. Charity.. W 17983
  Martha, former wid. of Roswell FOX.
  Martha, former wid. of Gamaliel PARKER.
  Moses, never pensioned, d. 1827, priv. Col. Meigs; wid. Lucy, in N. Y. in 1838.. W 23193
  Moses, priv. Col. Baldwin; Meriden, Conn., in 1832; wid. Rebecca................ R 4484
  Moses, R.. R 4480
  Nathaniel, Lieut. Capt. Brewster; N. Y. in 1818................................. S 44891
  Nathaniel, pensioned as Nathaniel, Jr., drummer, Capt. Eldridge; wid. Elizabeth; BLWt. 28606-160-55... W 7637
  Peter, Conn., Cont. & Vt.. S 13268
  Richard... S 45580
  Robert.. S 37079
  Samuel, N. Y. in 1832; d. 1836, Wayne Co., N. Y., wid. Esther................... W 21260
  Samuel, priv. Capt. Burwell; Vt. in 1832; d. 1849; wid. Lucy.................... W 19673
  Seth.. S 10812

HALL, Stephen, Serg't. Conn. in 1818.. S 37053
    Stephen, Capt. 7th reg't., dau. Rachel obtained BLWt. 1193-300.
        Talmage... BLWt. 1232-300
        Titus, Conn. & Cont., wid. Olive.. W 21283
        Wildman... S 13344
HALLADY or HALLIDAY.
    Eli... S 2605
    Roger.. S 31723
        (See also HOLLADAY.)
HALLAM, John... S 13283
    Robert, wid. Lydia.. W 19731
HALLET, Thomas, Conn. & Cont.. S 37064
HALLOCK, William, wid. Ruth.. W 25754
HALLOW, Richard. (See PENHALLOW.)
HALLSTED, HALSTEAD, HALSTED or HOLSTED.
    John... S 44908
    Joseph... S 10811
    Richard, BLWt. 205-100... S 44909
    Timothy.. S 2625
HALSEY, Philip, Conn. & N. Y.. S 16845
    Stephen, Conn. & N. Y., wid. Hamutal.. W 24413
HAMBLIN. (See HAMLIN.)
HAMES, Samuel, wid. Jemina.. W 24411
    (Also given HAWES.)
HAMILTON, David, Conn. & Cont.. S 23678
    James, wid. Jemina.. W 2111
        BLWt. 28597-160-55.
    Joshua, wid. Mary.. W 21263
    Samuel, wid. Wealthy... W 2794
HAMLEN. (See HAMLIN.)
HAMLIN, HAMLEN or HAMBLIN.
    Benjamin... S 10815
    Cornelius... S 37050
    Elisha... S 10816
    James.. S 29196
    John, Cont. (Conn.), priv. Rutland Co., Vt., in 1832................................... S 18428
    John, Conn. & Privateer; Middletown, Conn., in 1832; d. 1834; wid. Caroline........... W 17985
    John, Cont. (Conn.), priv. pensioned in 1818, d. 1825; wid. Lucy in Ill. in 1839......... W 23219
    Joseph, wid. Rhoda, BLWt. 26684-160-55.. W 9057
    Levi, priv. Col. Wyllys; Ohio in 1818.. S 41617
    Levi, Cont. (Conn.), priv. & corp., wid. Mary; BLWt. 13440-160-55................... W 23168
    Mark... S 23680
    William... S 37068
HAMMOND, David, wid. Phebe, BLWt. 67686-160-55..................................... W 11243
    Isaac, Conn. & Cont., Seneca, N. Y., in 1818; wid. Dorcas............................. R 4532
    Jason, wid. Mary... W 16287
    Robert, priv. Col. Starr, Essex Co., N. Y., in 1832; wid. Ruanah....................... R 4539
    Thomas.. S 18865
    Titus, wid. Charity, BLWt. 26058-160-55... W 7653
HANCHET, HANCHETT or HANCKETT.
    Ezra... S 13291
    Jonah.. S 9568
HANCOCK or HANCOX.
    Edward.. S 16843
    Elihu.. BLWt. 1760-100
    Nathan, wid. Phebe.. W 19706
HAND, Edmund, wid. Huldah.. W 27775
    Ichabod.. S 31722
HANDFORD. (See HANFORD.)
HANDY. Nathaniel, wid. Martha... R 4560
    William, Cont. (Conn.), wid. Martha.. W 23241
HANFORD or HANDFORD.
    Ebenezer... S 31720
    Levi.. S 23676
    Matthew, wid. Elizabeth... W 21288
    Ozias, former wid. Elizabeth Crane... W 25449
HANKS, Elijah, wid. Mary.. W 4688
HANNAH, James, Conn. & Cont.. S 43653
HANSON or HENSON, Christopher.. S 37059
    William, BLWt. 1446-100... S 43669
HARDIN or HARDING.
    Ephraim, wid. Susan... W 17054
    George, wid. Martha... R 4602
    Israel, wid. Lydia.. W 2791
    James.. S 44194
    Jeremiah... S 13286
HARDY or HARDEY, Nathaniel... S 41598
HARDYEAR or HARGER, Elijah... R 4605
HARMAN or HARMON, Jacques or Jaques. BLWt. 969 for 150 acres issued for Ensign, May 26, 1790. No papers.
    Jehiel, wid. Betsey E.. W 25759
        BLWt. 26615-160-55.
    Joseph... R 4622
HARPER, Godfrey... S 29202
HARRINGTON, HERINGTON, HERINTON, HERRINGTON.
    Anna, former wid. of Elijah PORTER.
    Andrew.. S 37051
    Benjamin.. S 32813
    Benjamin.. R 4638

HARRINGTON, HERINGTON, HERINTON, HERRINGTON—Continued.
 Eber, Conn. & R. I., wid. Susannah... W 23229
 John, Oxford, N. Y., in 1832.. S 28759
 Parley.. S 44183
 Samuel, BLWt. 953-100.. S 44195
 Stephen, Sebra Green, former wid. of, BLWt. 128-60-55....................................... W 19541
 Timothy, Lydia Edson, former wid. of... W 17742
 William, wid. Elizabeth, BLWt. 33741-160-55... W 19726
HARRIS, Andrew, wid. Elizabeth.. W 27423
 Asa, Conn., Navy & N. H., wid. Rachel.. W 19667
 Daniel.. S 10797
 David... S 37062
 Ebenezer... R 4651
 Fanny P., former wid. of Levi ARNOLD, BLWt. 67536-160-55............................... W 9050
 Jason. Elizabeth Annis, former wid. of... W 23443
 Jedediah or Jedidiah... S 16844
 John, b. Preston, Conn., 1766, son of Job & brother of Joshua; priv. & cook, Capt. Latham;
  Vermont in 1832.. S 10787
 John, priv. Capt. Warner: Conn. in 1818... S 37049
 John, Conn. & Cont., BLWt. 1608-200. Served under Lieut. Col. Webb & killed 1777 in N.
  J., wid. Irene, of New London Co.; granson Zebulon Lee obtained BLWt. in 1830.
 Joseph, wid. Anna... R 4647
 Lebbeus, Sarah Douglass, former wid. of... R 3049
 Paul.. S 31719
 Pearly, wid. Aby... W 21287
 Philip, Conn. & Cont., wid. Anna, BLWt. 26553-160-55...................................... W 25755
 Robert, wid. Lucretia... W 10076
 Thomas, Conn. & Cont., wid. Elizabeth.. W 21270
 Water, Cont. (Conn.), wid. Jane A., BLWt. 30787-160-55..................................... W 2106
 William.. S 38811
HARRISON, Daniel.. S 15165
 Hannah, former wid. of Joseph BEACH.
 Jairus... S 37081
 Justus, Conn. & Conn. Sea Service, wid. Sarah.. W 19742
 Lemuel, BLWt. 31644-160-55... R 4680
 Nathan... S 13343
 Silas, Conn. & Cont.. S 13281
 Solomon... S 16137
 Stephen, Conn., Mass., N. H. & Vt... S 18433
 Theodore, Conn. & Cont.. S 13251
HART, HARTT, HEART or HEARTT.
 Aaron, wid. Sarah... W 19707
 Ard, wid. Lucy... W 8894
  BLWt. 949-160-55.
 Benjamin.. S 37080
 Bliss, wid. Silva or Sylvia... W 7630
 Elias, Conn. & Cont.. S 17462
 Elisha.. S 44408
 Frederick A., wid. Sally; BLWt. 1912-100... W 1603
  (Also given John HART.)
 Gilbert, Conn. & N. H.. S 13304
 Hezekiah.. S 15167
 Hosea.. R 4696
 Ithurel... S 15872
 James.. S 10793
 Job... S 44196
 John, Fairfield, Maine, in 1818.. S 36011
 John, Cont. (Conn.), Saybrook, Conn., in 1818... S 37054
 John. (See Frederick A.)
 Jonathan, BLWt. 955 for 300 acres, Capt. was issued Sept. 7, 1790. No papers.
 Lent.. S 13257
 Lewis, Cont. service, Conn. residence in 1810; BLWt. 497-100.
 Martin... S 5438
 Munson.. S 13252
 Peleg, wid. Hannah... W 17990
 Pharaoh or Pharo or Pharoh.. S 34392
 Reuben.. S 41633
 Reuben, wid. Ruth.. W 1972
 Samuel, wid. Patience, BLWt. 9472-160-55.. W 1176
 Selah, Canaan, Conn. in 1832... S 17471
 Selah, wid. Ruth.. W 21286
 Stephen, BLWt. 2373-100.
 Thomas, Chenango Co., N. Y., in 1832.. S 13325
 Thomas, d. 1829; wid. Mary, Guilford, Conn., in 1838.. W 17982
 Titus... S 13282
HARTSHORN or HARTSON.
 Hezekiah, wid. Mary... W 19733
 Joshua, wid. Huldah.. W 21279
 Oliver, wid. Hannah.. W 21256
HARTWELL, Oliver... S 44187
 Samuel.. R 4705
HARVEY, Anna, former wid. of Joseph STEWART.
 Jonathan.. S 13270
 Nathan.. S 13272
 Robert, wid. Asenath... R 4706
  (Soldier was pensioned from Litchfield, Conn., in 1832 as private.)
 Thomas.. S 13288
 William, Conn. & Conn. Sea Service, wid. Jane... W 4225
HARVY, George, Conn., Mass. & R. I., wid. Philena... W 1037

HASKEL or HASKELL.
 David, Conn., Mass. & N. H., wid. Mary, BLWt. 16110-160-55........................... W 7650
 Jacob, wid. Diantha... W 21298
 John.. S 21809
 Stephen, Conn. & Mass.. S 29859
HASKIN or HASKINS.
 Abraham... S 44923
 Benjamin, Conn. & Mass., wid. Mary, BLWt. 31697-160-55.............................. R 21635
  (Did not serve long enough for a pension.)
HATCH, Asa, Conn. & N. H., wid. Ruhamah, BLWt. 26958-160-55............................ W 752
 Dan, Lucy Northrup, former wid. of.. W 19922
 Ede... S 44918
 Gilbert, wid. Martha, BLWt. 9521-160-55... W 225
 Heman... S 34393
 Ichabod... S 38813
 Isaac, wid. Polly, BLWt. 26194-160-55... W 17993
 John.. S 13250
 Joseph.. S 37057
 Josiah.. S 5437
 Moses, Conn. & Cont., wid. Abigail.. W 25745
 Oliver, Conn., Cont. & N. Y., wid. Phebe.. W 21137
 Timothy, Hartford, Conn., in 1818; wid. Lucinda..................................... W 2109
 Timothy, Chenango Co., N. Y., in 1832... S 13296
 William, Conn. & Mass... S 13237
HATHAWAY, HATHEWAY or HATHWAY.
 Ebenezer.. S 23675
 Guilford.. S 13287
 John, Conn., Cont., Mass. & N. Y.. S 13271
 Zenas or Zenus.. S 44905
HAUGHTON. (See HORTON.)
HAULEY. (See HAWLEY.)
HAVEN or HAVENS.
 Cornelius... S 37093
 John, wid. Mary, BLWt. 11258-160-55... W 25760
 Peleg, Conn. & R. I... S 9349
HAWES or HAWS, Benjamin, Conn. & Mass., wid. Sarah..................................... W 24410
 Samuel, wid. Jemima. (Also given HAMES.)
 Zenas... S 37053
  (Also given HOWES.)
HAWKINS, Amaziah... S 23254
 David, Conn., Conn. Sea service & R. I., wid. Sarah................................. W 21264
 Ebenezer.. S 29208
 Isaac, wid. Anna.. W 17987
 James, wid. Nancy... W 19746
 Job, wid. Hannah.. W 19714
 Joseph.. S 23689
 Moses... S 23683
 Rodolphus, wid. Tryphena.. W 11230
 Samuel, wid. Hannah... W 13387
 William, Conn. & N. Y... S 44900
HAWKS, William... R 4769
HAWLEY, Abel, N. Y. in 1832.. S 9346
 Abel, wid. Sarah.. W 11245
  Conn. in 1832; BLWt. 26992-160-55.
 Abraham... S 28753
 Daniel, Cont. (Conn.)... S 6970
 Ebenezer, wid. Lucy, BLWt. 26511-160-55... W 1760
 Ebenezer Rice, Conn. & Cont... S 9572
 Elijah.. S 16847
 Elisha, wid. Charity, BLWt. 26508-160-55.. W 11251
 Gad... S 10805
 Hezekiah, wid. Anne... W 17989
 Israel.. S 17470
 James, wid. Martha.. W 19705
 Joseph, wid. Phebe.. W 19686
 Joseph C.. S 44906
 Liverius, wid. Anne... W 19715
 Nathan, priv. & corp.; wounded, 1777; invalid pension, 1790......................... S 20779
 Nathan, Del. Co., N. Y., in 1832, d. 1835; wid. Ruamy............................... W 7656
 Nero.. S 20784
 Ozias, wid. Sarah... W 4484
 Robert, wid. Mary Elizabeth... W 17984
 Salmon. (See Solomon.)
 Samuel, Conn. sea service & Mass. sea service; wid. Lucy............................ W 21295
 Seth.. S 23277
 Solomon or Salmon... R 4471
 Thomas, Ridgefield, Conn., in 1832; d. in 1840; wid. Keziah......................... W 25761
 Thomas, Trumbull, Conn., in 1832; died in 1850, wid. Mary; BLWt. 26652-160-55....... W 7657
 Zadock or Zadok... S 44907
HAWS. (See HAWES.)
HAYDEN, HEYDON or HEYDEN.
 Allen or Allyn.. S 29220
 Charles, Conn. & Cont., wid. Molly.. W 23243
  (Given also HEATON.)
 Daniel, wid. Zerviah.. W 21262
 David... S 43668
 Ezra, wid. Olive.. R 4781
 Jacob... S 43654
 Samuel.. S 16144

HAYES or HAYS.
  Aaron... S 9345
  Amos... S 10810
  Asa.. S 37060
  Benajah, Conn. & Cont... S 9565
  Benjamin, wid. Alathea.. S 9565
  Benjamin, wid. Hannah.. W 21285
  Asa.. S 3706
  Benajah, Conn. & Cont... S 95650
  Benjamin, wid. Alathea..
  Benjamin, wid. Hannah.. W 21285
      Is found in case of Fuller, Timothy, widow's former husband.
  Dudley, wid. Beda, BLWt. 3815-160-55... W 17975
  Elijah... S 13280
  Enoch, wid. Louisa, BLWt. 28577-160-55.. W 11252
  Ezekiel.. S 31724
  Hezekiah... S 37055
  Jesse, Conn. & N. Y... S 15168
  Joseph, Conn., Cont. & Privateer.. S 13327
  Levi... S 4328
  Obadiah, wid. Ahinoana or Ahinoam... W 17973
  Oliver... S 2262
  Samuel, wid. Eunice... R 4784
  Seth, Conn., Cont. & Mass., wid. Mehetable.. W 23207
  Zenas, wid. Sarah, BLWt. 71154-160-55... W 25752
HAYFORD, Ira, wid. Sarah, BLWt. 31569-160-55.. W 660
HAYNES or HAINES, John.. S 13240
  Margere, former wid. of Lovell or Lovewell HURD.
HAYS. (See HAYES.)
HAYT. (See HOYT.)
HAYWARD, Ebenezer... S 13248
  Samuel, wid. Sarah, BLWt. 29061-160-55.. W 29934
      Samuel's daughter, Jerusha H. Brown, was pensioned for her father's services under
      Special Act of Congress. Later she was dropped from the rolls and pensioned by Special
      Act, as the wid. of Lt. Col. Edward M. Brown, 8th Vt. Vol. Inf. (See Civil War, Wid.
      Cert. 608657.) She had not been reported as dead Sept. 30, 1910.
  Simeon, wid. Hannah... W 14882
      (Also given as HOWARD.)
HAZARD or HAZZARD, Stewart, Conn. & N. Y... S 13262
HAZEN, Andrew, wid. Polly.. W 23170
  Jacob, Conn. & Cont... S 17459
HEADY, Daniel, wid. Mary.. W 25764
HEALY, George, wid. Bethia.. W 17065
  John... S 23691
HEARD. (See HURD.)
HEARICK. (See HERRICK.)
HEART or HEARTT. (See HART.)
HEATH, Aaron, Conn. & Mass., wid. Rhoda... W 13440
  John, Conn. & Cont.. S 23693
  Peleg, BLWt. 957 for 200 acres, Lieut. was issued Feb. 5, 1790. No papers.
  Samuel C., wid. Leah.. W 21311
  Thomas, priv. Col. Welles, Copiah Co., Miss., in 1832... S 46041
  Thomas, Sharon, Conn., in 1832; priv. Col. Allen; wid. Polly.................................... W 24423
  William, priv. Col. Sage; Berkshire Co., Mass., in 1832... S 29219
  William, d. 1794, wid. Mary, lived Groton, Conn., in 1833....................................... W 17997
HEATON, Charles. (See HAYDEN.)
HEBARD. (See HIBBARD.)
HECOCK and HECOX. (See HICKOX.)
HEDGES, Henry... R 4839
HELMAGE, John... S 43667
HEMINGER, John, Mary Cannon, former wid. of, BLWt. 67542-160-55................................... W 23769
HEMINGWAY, Enos... S 10827
  Jacob.. S 10677
HEMPSTEAD or HEMSTEAD.
  Nathaniel, wid. Elizabeth... W 14902
  Stephen... S 24612
HENDEE, Caleb, Conn. & Cont... S 13349
HENDER or HENDOR, Thomas, wid. Sally.. W 17994
HENDERSON, David.. S 43658
  Joseph.. S 43661
HENDRAKE, HENDRICK or HENDRIX.
  Andrew.. S 39667
  Coe... S 18441
  David... S 37098
  Nathaniel... S 38015
HENMAN or HENMON. (See HINMAN.)
HENRY, John, priv. Capt. Dunlap, Hamilton, N. Y., in 1832; wid. Esther............................ R 4890
  John, priv. Capt. Hotchkiss, Wallingford, Conn., in 1832; wid. Fanny............................ W 19763
HENSEY, Andrew, wid. Sarah.. W 8922
HENSHAW, Benjamin, wid. Elsa or Sarah... W 21307
  William, BLWt. 962-200.
HENSON. (See HANSON.)
HERICK. (See HERRICK.)
HERINGTON, HERINTON. (See HARRINGTON.)
HERRICK or HEARICK or HERICK.
  Abel.. R 4919
  Daniel, wid. Olive.. W 25765
  Ephraim, Conn. & Navy... S 13346
  Hezekiah, Conn. & Mass.. S 10828
  Israel, wid. Ruth... W 17061

HERRICK or HEARICK or HERICK—Continued.
  John, Avis Howe, former wid. of.. W 21387
  Joseph... S 13368
  Lemuel, wid. Lucy.. W 19756
  Libeus... S 41634
  Robert, wid. Alice, BLWt. 835-100.. W 11287
  Simeon... S 13375
  Stephen, Conn. & Cont., wid. Rebecca... W 27784
HERRINGTON or HERRINTON. (See HARRINGTON.)
HERRON, John... S 37099
HEWES, George R. T., Mass. & Privateer (Conn. & R. I.).............................. S 13367
  (See also HUGHES.)
HEWET, HEWETT, HEWIT or HEWITT.
  Alice Rogers, former wid. of Josiah Rodgers or Rogers.
  Andrew, wid. Julia... W 27860
  Daniel, Serg't under Capt. Buck, pensioned from Conn. & transferred to N. Y. in 1823; wid.
    Sarah.. R 4930
  Edmund or Edward, Conn. & N. Y., wid. Hannah....................................... W 15774
  Elisha Cont. (Conn.)... S 16151
  Elkanah, wid. Desire... W 1280
    BLWt. 26030-160-55.
  Gershom.. S 31735
  Henry.. S 29218
  Israel, wid. Sally... W 2796
  John... S 43660
  Joseph... S 43659
  Lewis, Conn. & Conn. Sea service, wid. Charlotte................................... W 17066
  Randal... S 43664
  Richard, BLWt. 26032-160-55.. S 23258
  Richard, wid. Experience... W 16599
  Robert, wid. Abigail, BLWt. 5251-160-55.. W 3683
  Simeon, wid. Mehala.. W 25766
  Sterry, Conn. & Cont... S 13354
  Thomas, Conn. & Conn. Sea service.. R 4939
HEWLET or HEWLETT. (See HULETT.)
HEYDON. (See HAYDEN.)
HIBBARD, HIBBERD, HEBARD, HEBBARD or HEBBERD.
  Aaron, wid. Sarah.. W 16602
  Andrew, in Col. Meigs' reg't., father of Gen. Daniel F. Hibbard, who in 1829 obtained BLWt.
    1488-100.
  Andrew, Serg't. under Col. Durkee; in 1790 was in Hampton, Conn.; wid. Ruth was in Vt.
    in 1838.. W 19774
  Asa.. S 32824
  Bushnell, wid. Rebecca or Rebekah.. W 21190
  David, Conn. & Cont.. S 10835
  Diah, wid. Zerviah or Zeviah... W 21306
  Ebenezer... S 15170
  Ebenezer... S 13412
  Jabez.. S 18442
  Jedediah... S 43666
  Joseph, wid. Lydin, BLWt. 26703-160-55... W 23260
  Ozias, wid. Mary, BLWt. 26783-160-55... W 7722
  Rufus.. S 10840
  Timothy, under Col. Bradley, Bath, N. H., in 1818.................................. S 44422
  Timothy, d. 1804, Rutland, Vt., under Col. Swift; Abigail Noble, former wid. of.... W 19931
  Uriah.. S 43686
  Vine Timothy, wid. Dorcas, BLWt. 24755-160-55...................................... W 662
  William.. S 13400
    Arminda Hebard or Hibbard, wid. of above soldier, was pensioned as former wid. of
    Obadiah Phelps, Cont., W 4985.
HICKCOX. (See HICHOX.)
HICKMAN, Michael... R 20514
KICKOX, HICOCK, HICOK, HECOCX, HECOX, HICKCOX or HICKOK.
  Aaron.. S 16867
  Amos... R 4957
  Asa, wid. Esther... W 2798
  Asher.. S 46884
  Daniel... S 13402
  Darius, Lucinda Miles, former wid. of.. W 18521
  David.. S 41637
  Ebenezer, under Capt. Brown, Col. Waterbury, Amherst Co., Va., in 1832............. S 5541
  Ebenezer, under Capt. Dayton, Col. Baldwin; Ravenna, Ohio, 1832.................... S 2617
  James, wid. Hannah... W 18011
  Nathaniel.. S 2316
  Samuel... S 43673
  Samuel, Cont. (Conn.), wid. Lucena, BLWt. 51754-160-55............................. W 1036
  Truman... S 2304
HICKS, John.. S 13406
  Samuel, Conn. & Cont... S 18446
HIDE. (See HYDE.)
HIGBY, Nathaniel, wid. Nancy... R 4972
  Both soldier and wid. were rejected.
    (Also given HIGLEY.)
  Samuel, wid. Hannah.. W 11301
HIGGINS, Benjamin, wid. Jane... W 16600
  Cornelius, Conn. & Cont., wid. Esther.. W 21325
  Ebenezer, wid. Mary.. W 21320
  Hawes.. S 16873
  Isaac, Conn. & N. Y., wid. Hannah.. W 19773
    BLWt. 35839-160-55.

HIGGINS, Joseph, BLWt. 971-300, Surgeon's Mate, was issued Dec. 13, 1796. No papers.
 Timothy.. S 37109
 William, BLWt. 963-200, Lieut., was issued May 17, 1796, to Wm. Higgins. No papers.
HIGLEY, Brewster, Conn. & Vt., wid. Naomi.. W 7742
 Nathaniel, wid. Nancy. (See HIGBY.)
 Obed, Conn. & Cont.
 Roswell, Conn. & N. Y.. S 17481
 .... S 13411
HILL or HILLS, Abner... S 37100
 Asahel, Cont. (Conn.)... S 38829
 Abram, wid. Lydia... W 25770
  BLWt. 9429-160-55.
 Benajah.. S 23699
 Daniel, Conn. & Cont... S 10838
 David, Chloe Blackman or Blackmore, former wid. of................................... R 15052
  Soldier never pensioned; wid. rejected.
 Ebenezer, priv. Capt. Belcher; Conn. in 1818; BLWt. 1691-100....................... S 43691
 Ebenezer, BLWt. 974-300, Captain was issued June 14, 1790. No papers.
 Ebenezer, Jr., Conn. & N. Y. service; also in 1786; Albany, N. Y., in 1832; wid. Mary....... W 7735
 Ebenezer or Primus.. S 43677
 Elijah, wid. Esther.. W 13457
 Erastus... S 43675
 George, Elizabeth Conway, former wid. of, Cont. service but Conn. res. and Agency......... W 18885
 Grey.. S 13405
 Henry.. S 15455
 Ichabod, Cont. (Conn.), wid. Anna, BLWt. 2353-160-55.................................. W 2549
 Isaac... S 31747
 Jacob.. S 18447
 Jedediah, wid. Abigail, BLWt. 26491-160-55.. W 23274
 John, wid. Rhoda... W 11302
 Joseph, under Capt. Wells; East Hartford, Conn., in 1832............................. S 17477
 Joseph, Conn. Line: Farmington, Conn., in 1818... S 37107
 Josiah, Conn. & R. I., wid. Ellen.. W 13456
 Nathan.. R 5018
 Peleg, wid. Mary... W 23281
 Philemon, BLWt. 961-200, Lieut. was issued July 14, 1789, to himself. Warrant, via G. L.
  Office returned to ditto June 23, 1827. No papers.
 Primus, or Ebenezer, Colored, under Col. Hewett; Augusta, N. Y., in 1818.
 Reuben... R 5007
 Samuel... S 13407
 Seth, wid. Karine... W 19779
 Thomas.. S 43678
 Uri, Conn. & Mass.. S 19331
 Zimri... S 27996
 Zimry, wid. Mille.. W 3992
HILLARD. (See HILLIARD.)
HILLER, Timothy, Conn. & Mass... S 10833
HILLIARD, HILYARD, or HILLARD.
 Azariah.. S 13386
 Barnabas, wid. Martha, BLWt. 27669-160-55... W 7749
 Daniel, Conn., Conn. Sea service & Mass., wid. Rebecca, BLWt. 10230-160-55....... W 23294
 John... S 37102
 Joseph, Lois Cheesbrough, former wid. of.. W 16901
 Joshua, wid. Elizabeth, BLWt. 31273-160-55.. W 549
 Lucretia, former wid. of Charles F. BROWN.
 Mary, former wid. of William BRUMBLEY or BRUMLEY.
 Minor.. S 22302
 Sarah, former wid. of John STEELE.
 William, Cont. (Conn.), wid. Hannah.. W 18010
HILLYER or HILLER.
 Andrew, wid. Lucy... W 8933
  BLWt. 17720-160-55.
  (Also served in the British Army.)
 Asa... S 37105
 James, wid. Penelope.
  (See case of widow's former husband, Conn., GOODRICH, David, R 5026.)
 Pliny, wid. Jane... R 5025
  Soldier never applied; widow R.
 Seth, wid. Sibil.. W 4696
 Theodore.. S 37104
 Timothy, Conn. & Mass.. S 10833
HILYARD. (See HILLIARD.)
HINCHER, Isaac, wid. Marcy or Mary.. W 19780
HINCKLEY or HINKLEY.
 Benjamin, wid. Puanna.. W 18000
 David... S 13388
 Ebenezer.. S 13397
 Gershom, Conn. & N. Y., wid. Prudence... W 25771
 Gillet, wid. Tryphena or Typhena, BLWt. 14669-160-55................................ W 5297
 Ichabod, BLWt. 951-300, Capt. was issued Oct. 16, 1789 to Theodosius Fowler, Assignee. No
  papers.
 Jared.. S 19338
 John, wid. Rachel, BLWt. 17895-160-55.. W 691
 Wiat or Wiatt... S 13360
HINE, Benjamin.. S 28764
 Hezekiah, Cont. (Conn.).. S 37106
 Hollingsworth.. S 31741
 Newton, wid. Mary... R 5031
 Samuel... S 16874
 Titus (also given HINES)... S 37103

HINKLEY. (See HINCKLEY.)
HINMAN, HENMAN or HENMON.
Benjamin, Conn. & Cont., wid. Anna, BLWt. 21602-160-55.	W 23364
Enoch.	S 30486
Ephraim, wid. Sylvania.	W 17999
Husted, wid. Mercy.	W 17998
Isaac, wid. Martha, BLWt. 5452-160-55.	W 4986
Joel, wid. Sarah, BLWt. 30771-160-55.	W 21332
Jonas, wid. Caty.	R 5035
Soldier was pensioned from N. Y. in 1832.	
Lewis, Conn. & N. Y., wid. Lucy.	W 18001
Samuel, wid. Elizabeth.	W 21334
Timothy, wid. Phebe, BLWt. 14765-160-55.	W 1607
Wait or Weight, wid. Eunice. BLWt. 52615-160-55	S 13363

HINSDALE, Abel.
Elias.	R 5037
Elisha.	S 41640
Jacob, Litchfield Co., Conn., in 1832; wid. Sarah.	R 5038

HITCHCOCK, HITCHCOK or HITCHOCK.
Abel, wid. Mary.	W 21327
Ashbel.	S 13398
Daniel, wid. Lydia, BLWt. 15422-160-55.	W 1180
Ebenezer, Lucy Griffith, former wid. of.	W 7588
Ichabod, wid. Lucy, BLWt. 95681-160-55.	W 11293
Widow was also allowed pension as wid. of Charles TUTTLE, her former husband, who died in service in War of 1812.	
Ira, Cont. (Conn.), wid. Hannah.	W 23276
Jared, wid. Irene.	W 16601
John, Lucy Manley, former wid. of.	W 9929
John L., wid. Eunice.	R 5053
(Soldier never applied.)	
Jonathan.	S 7009
Lemuel.	S 43679
Levi, priv. Capt. Leavenworth; Oneida Co., N. Y., in 1832.	S 10837
Levi, priv. Col. Chandler; Colebrook, Conn., in 1818; wid. Mary.	W 8936
Samuel, under Capt. Stanley; Hartford Co., Conn., in 1832.	S 13404
Samuel, Cont. (Conn.), BLWt. 1185-100 was issued in 1826 for soldier's service in Sheldon's Dragoons, to brother Ambrose et al.	

HIXON, Sarah, former wid. of Joseph WOLCOTT or WOLCUTT; she was wid. of Elkanah HIXON, Mass. ... S 39614

HOADLEY or HOADLY.
Culpeper, BLWt. 11397-160-55.	S 17492
Ebenezer.	S 37122
Philo.	S 2624
Silas, Conn. & Privateer.	S 13355

HOBART, John, BLWt. 966 for 200 acres, Lieut. was issued July 6, 1795 to Eneas Munson Jr. No papers.
Mason.	S 17487

HOBBY, Hezekiah. ... S 17488
Thomas. ... BLWt. 1543-450

HOCKHISS. (See HOTCHKISS.)
HODGE, Asahel, Saratoga Co., N. Y., in 1818. ... S 43702
   BLWt. 954 for 300 acres, Captain was issued May 8, 1792 to Amos Muzzy, Assignee. No papers.
Asahel, wid. Martha, BLWt. 43876-160-55.	R 5080
Soldier was b. 1766, and son of Capt. Asahel H., under whom he enlisted; pensioned in 1832 from Portage Co., Ohio, wid. R.	
Benjamin, Conn. & Privateer.	R 5081
Benjamin, Conn. & R. I.	S 39720
David, Conn. & Cont.	S 44201
Levi.	S 33320
Philo, Conn. & Cont., wid. Lucy.	W 24447
(Also given HODG.)	
Thomas, Cont. (Conn.).	S 44426

HODGES, Job. ... S 37123
Leonard, wid. Sarah, BLWt. 11092-160-55. ... W 19815

HODGKIN, Ambrose. ... S 17493
HODGKINS, Nathaniel. ... S 23261
Thomas, Conn. & Cont., wid. Tryphena. ... W 23352

HOGAN, Benoni, Cont. (Conn.), wid. Anna. ... W 19802
HOIT. (See HOYT.)
HOLBROOK, Abel, wid. Hannah, BLWt. 31274-160-55. ... W 11343
Calvin.	S 10873
Ebenezer.	S 21820
Nathaniel, wid. Allice.	W 18061
Susannah, former wid. of Josiah Green.	

HOLBURTON or HULBERTON, William, wid. Eunice. ... W 21346

HOLCOMB or HOLCOMBE.
Abel, wid. Elizabeth.	W 18034
Abner.	S 13433
Abram.	S 17489
Asahel, priv., Capt. Hoagland; Hartford, Conn., in 1818.	S 37112
Asahel, priv. Capt. Phelps; Granby, Conn., in 1832; Hannah Holcomb, former wid. of.	W 7795
Hannah was allowed Bounty land for the services of her third husband, Jacob Holcomb (BLWt. 47422-160-55).	
Dose.	S 29910
Ebenezer, wid. Chloe.	W 25794
Elijah, priv. Capt. Phelps; Hampden Co., Mass., in 1830; Cont. (Conn.).	S 32853
Elijah, priv. in Sheldon's Dragoons; d. 1815; wid. Mary.	W 21353

77

HOLBCOMB or HOLBCOMBE, Ezekiel, wid. Susannah.. W 21358
   Increase, wid. Mary.. W 18017
   Jacob, wid. Hannah.. BLWt. 47422-160-55
   (See HOLCOMB, Asahel, wid. Hannah.)
   Joel, wid. Sarah... W 3685
   John.. S 31751
   John G.. S 37116
   Joseph, Berkshire Co., Mass., in 1832.. S 30489
   Joseph, Cont. (Conn.), d. 1797; Corp. in Sheldon's Dragoons; Olive Enos, former wid. of..... W 17762
   Levi... S 21818
   Luther, wid. Sally.. R 5134
   (Applications of both soldier & wid. R.)
   Nahum.. S 16879
   Noah.. R 5131
   Obed, Conn. & Indian Wars of 1783 & 1784; priv. Capt. Case; Essex Co., N. Y., in 1832; Elizabeth Worden or Wordin, former wid. of.. R 11866
   Peter... S 15175
   Phinehas... S 10862
   Roger, Conn. & Mass... R 5133
   Seth, Polly Briggs, former wid. of.. R 1206
   (Soldier never applied for pension.)
   Timothy... S 15892
HOLDEN or HOLDIN, Amos... S 32851
HOLDRIDGE, Hezekiah, BLWt. 947 for 450 acres, Lieut. Col. was issued Mch. 28, 1797. No papers.
   Robert, BLWt. 12720-160-55.. S 37124
   Rufus, wid. Hannah... W 18053
HOLISTER. (See HOLLISTER.)
HOLLADAY or HOLLIDAY, Amos.. S 10858
   (See also HALLADAY.)
HOLLAND, Joseph, priv. Col. Ledyard; Dutchess Co., N. Y., in 1832................................. S 5567
   Joseph, priv. Col. Burrall; Macomb Co., Mich. in 1832.. S 29240
HOLLENBACK, HOLLENBEAK, HOLLENBECK or HOLOMBACH, John, wid. Esther. W 23353
HOLLEY or HOLLY, Abraham, priv. Capt. Hoyt, Stamford, Conn., in 1818....................... S 37110
   Abraham, priv. Col. Chandler, Fairfield Co., Conn., in 1818.. S 37114
   Elijah, Conn., Mass. & R. I... S 32857
   John, priv. Capt. Watson, Fairfield Co., Conn., in 1818.. S 37111
   John, d. 1824, Fairfield Co., Conn., wid. Tammy.. W 21396
   Joseph, under Capt. Holley, Cortland Co., N. Y., in 1829... S 45386
   Joseph, under Capt. Spicer, d. 1813, Columbia Co., N. Y., wid. Dorothy....................... W 18037
   Robert, wid. Hannah... W 21391
   Stephen, under Col. Burrall; Addison Co., Vt., in 1832.. S 21819
   Stephen, under Capt. Hughes; d. 1833, Fairfield Co., Conn., wid. Deborah................. W 21354
HOLLIDAY. (See HOLLADAY.)
HOLLISTER or HOLISTER, Asahel, wid. Elizabeth... W 7803
   Ashbel, Conn. & Cont.. S 15461
   David, Tioga Co., N. Y., in 1832; d. 1836; wid. Hope, BLWt. 26704-160-55.................. W 21409
   David, under Capt. Hubbard, Delaware Co., N. Y., in 1832, d. 1843; wid. Sarah......... W 21347
   Elijah.. S 22315
   Innett, Conn. & Mass... S 10846
   Joseph, Conn. & Navy... S 16880
   Josiah, Conn. & Cont.. S 31748
   Josiah, Conn. & N. Y.. R 5158
   Lucy, former wid. of Gideon NOBLE.
   Nathan, Conn. & Cont.. S 4406
HOLLOW, Richard P. (See PENHALLOW, Richard.)
HOLMAN, Thomas, Conn. & Mass., wid. Mary, BLWt. 2695-160-55................................ W 7787
HOLMES or HOLMS, David... S 33309
   Ebenezer, wid. Abigail.. W 18058
   Edward, Conn. & Mass.. S 13423
   Eliphalet.. S 10859
   Elisha... S 15178
   Ezra, Conn., Cont. & Mass.. S 13421
   James, wid. Rhoda J., BLWt. 13386-160-55... W 25780
   John, Conn. & Cont., wid. Rachel... W 21386
   Joshua, wid. Lucretia... R 5176
   (Soldier did not apply.)
   Lemuel... S 13459
   Levi.. S 37117
   Nathaniel, Cont. (Conn.).. S 45380
   Samuel... S 45389
   Seth, wid. Rhoda, BLWt. 61310-160-55.. W 7770
   Silas, Cont. & Conn., Louisa Palmer, former wid. of.. W 8282
   Simeon... S 31754
   Thomas, Conn. & Cont.. S 13466
   Titus... S 18880
HOLOMBACH. (See HOLLENBACK.)
HOLSTED. (See HALLSTED.)
HOLT, Ebenezer, wid. Elizabeth.
   George.. W 25790
   Jesse... S 10875
   Jonathan, wid. Anna.. S 37121
   Samuel, Conn. & Navy, wid. Margaret.. W 21360
   Silas... W 3141
HOLTON, Elisha, wid. Lydia.. BLWt. 177-200
HOMISTON. (See HUMISTON.).. W 7801
HOOKER, Brainard, wid. Molly... W 16297
   Daniel... S 31360
   Gilbert, Conn., Mass. & N.Y.. S 9353
   Ira, Cont. (Conn.)... S 15180

HOOKER, James, Corp. Col. Chandler; Poultney, Vt., in 1818.	S 39735
James, Military Store-keeper, together with Horace Hooker in 1778-9; wid. Mary	W 25800
Martin	S 9919
Roger	S 37120
Thomas, wid. Mary, BLWt. 8169-160-55	W 19804
Thomas H., Sarah Collins, former wid. of	W 2442
William, Cont. (Conn.), wid. Hannah	W 21349
William, Conn & Vt	R 5199
HOPKINS, Charles	S 37119
Consider	S 13443
Elisha, BLWt. 956 for 300 acres, Capt. was issued August 9, 1798. No papers.	
Frederick, wid. Susan, BLWt 45961-160-55	R 5215
Soldier was pensioned by Special Act of Congress in 1847 for two years He was living then in Chenango Co., N. Y. This pension was not allowed his widow, but Bounty land was granted in 1855.	
George, Cont. (Conn.), wid. Rachel W	W 18068
John, Conn. & Mass.	S 13447
Rhoderick, Cont. (Conn.)	S 44929
Robert, Conn. & Penna., wid. Elizabeth	W 8946
Timothy, wid. Phebe	W 4238
HOPSON, Rew., wid. Sarah	R 5224
(Soldier never applied.)	
HORSAM or HORSOM, Ebenezer, BLWt. 886-100	S 22314
HORSKINS. (See HOSKINS.)	
HORTON, HOSTON, or HAUGHTON.	
Henry	S 41652
James, Cont. (Conn.)	S 44930
Lebbeus	S 37094
(Spelled also HAUGHTON.)	
Samuel, Conn. & Cont., wid. Adah, BLWt. 26931-160-55	W 4700
HOSKINS or HORSKINS.	
Asa, Hitty Adams, former wid. of	W 25366
Ashbel, wid. Rachel	W 5302
David	S 23708
Elijah	S 5568
John	S 21298
Timothy, wid. Rhoda	W 21344
Zebulon, wid. Kezia	W 18026
HOSMER, Ashbel, wid. Polly	R 5248
(Ashbel was an Invalid Pensioner; and as such recorded on the rolls of Conn.)	
David, wid. Sarah, BLWt. 30784-160-55	W 668
Graves, Conn & Navy	S 44938
John	S 45390
Prentice, BLWt. 959 for 200 acres, Lieut., was issued Dec. 12, 1789, to Theodosius Fowler, Assignee of Elizabeth Hosmer, Adx. No papers.	
Prosper, wid. Catharine	W 23339
Timothy, BLWt. 970 for 400 acres, Surgeon, was issued Feb. 15, 1799, to Timothy Hosmer. No papers.	
HOSTON. (See HORTON.)	
HOTCHKISS, HOCHKISS or HOTCHKIS.	
Abraham, wid. Rosetta	W 18057
Ambrose, wid. Lucretia	W 23321
Asahel, wid. Ruhamah, BLWt. 30770-160-55	W 25787
Eben	S 36582
Eldad, Conn. & Privateer	S 13432
Elihu, wid. Sally	W 21397
Elijah	S 10864
Ezekiel, Cont. (Conn.)	S 36585
Harris, Conn. & Navy	S 2632
Ira	S 36581
Isaac, priv. Col Swift; New Haven Co., Conn., in 1818; wid. Ann	W 18021
Isaac, Serg't. of Artillery; Conn. & Cont.; N. Y. in 1818; wid. Olive	W 18032
Jared, wid. Betsey	W 368
Jeremiah, wid. Mabel	W 24450
Rej. BLWt.	
(This woman was also pensioned as former wid. of Nathaniel TYLER, Conn. & Cont. W. 24450.)	
Joseph, wid. Temperance	W 18051
Josiah, wid. Asenath, BLWt. 30768-160-55	W 18030
Levi, wid. Susannah	W 18054
Lodowick or Lodwick	S 36583
Medad, Cont. (Conn.)	S 36586
Rueben, wid. Thankful	W 18062
Roswell	S 13453
Samuel, priv. Capt. Hooker, Col. Wolcott; Burlington, Conn., in 1832	S 10877
Samuel, priv. Capt. Watson, Col. Burrall; Steuben Co., N. Y., in 1832; wid. Chloe, BLWt. 8154-160-55	W 7811
Samuel, priv. Capt. Hand, Col. Walcott; Guilford, Conn., in 1832; d. 1835 in New Haven, Conn., wid. Chloe	W 18047
Simeon	S 10868
Stephen, wid. Tamar	W 18040
Thebus (also given HOTCHKIS)	R 5249
Titus, Conn. & Navy, wid. Rachel	W 18049
Trueman, wid. Ruth	W 18064
(Also given as Truman HOCHKISS.)	
HOUGH, Azel	R 5253
Bede, former wid. of Baldwin WOODRUFF.	
David, Conn. & N. Y., wid. Abigail	R 5252
(Soldier never pensioned.)	

HOUGH, Erastus.. S 13456
   Jabez, wid. Eunice... W 21357
   Joel... S 17495
   John, wid. Susannah... W 15685
   Samuel, Cont. (Conn.).. S 36580
   Walter, wid. Martha... W 3687
HOUGHTON, Ephraim, wid. Mary, BLWt. 26829-160-55................................ W 2550
HOUSE, Abner
   Benjamin.. R 5259
   Eleazer... S 18032
   Eleazer, Conn. & Cont... R 5262
   George, Cont. (Conn.), wid. Mary.. S 10847
   Joel, Conn. & Cont., wid. Lois, BLWt. 2482-100...................................... W 23317
   John, Cont. (Conn.), wid. Esther.. W 18023
HOVEY, Azel, wid. Lucy, BLWt. 39223-160-55.. W 18041
   Dudley.. W 1770
   Ivory, Conn. & Mass... S 18451
   Jacob... S 32842
   Nathaniel, Betsey Mason, former wid. of.. S 45394
   Roger, wid. Martha... W 21778
      (Soldier was pensioned from Orange Co., Vt., in 1832; wid. R.)
   Samuel... S 46641
   William, wid. Lucinda... W 4995
   Zaccheus.. S 18882
HOW. (See HOWE.)
HOWARD, Benjamin, wid. Freelove... W 18055
   Darius, Conn. & N. H., wid. Susan, BLWt. 26030-160-55......................... W 27713
   James, wid. Sarah.. W 18094
   Jeremiah, wid. Sally... W 18043
   John.. S 41658
   Simeon, wid. Hannah.
      (Also given HAYWARD.)
   Solomon, Conn., Cont. & Vt., wid. Anna.. W 7789
   William, priv. Windsor Co., Vt., in 1832.. S 15463
   William, Capt.; never pensioned; wid. Lucy, BLWt. 2027-160-55........... W 4699
HOWD, Benjamin.. S 20798
   Daniel, wid. Johannah.. W 11329
HOWE or HOW, Asa, wid. Priscilla, BLWt. 9526-160-55............................... W 2552
   Avis, former wid. of John HERRICK.
   David, wid. Phebe.. R 5290
      (Soldier never pensioned.)
   Israel, wid. Hannah.. W 25795
   Jazamiah, wid. Mary... W 21381
   Joseph.. S 45373
   Nathan.. S 15466
   Sarah, former wid. of Timothy FAY.
   Zadock or Zadok, Conn. & Cont.. S 32866
HOWEL or HOWELL, Nicholas, BLWt... 1517-100
   William, Conn. Sea service, Mass., Mass. Sea Service & Privateer...... S 18039
HOWES or HOWS, Benjamin.. S 30499
   John, wid. Lucy... R 5293
      (Soldier never pensioned.)
   Zenas.
      (Also given HAWES.)
HOWLAND, Joseph... S 39734
HOWS. (See HOWES.)
HOYT, HAIT, HAYT or HOIT.
   Daniel, priv., corp., fifer & serg't. Fairfield Co., Conn., in 1832............. S 16881
   Daniel, Serg't., d. 1777; former wid. Sarah Treadwell............................. W 18155
      Sarah was also pensioned as wid. of Daniel TREADWELL.
   David, Conn. & Vt., wid. Sarah... W 23301
   Ebenezer, Darien, Conn., in 1832.. S 16882
   Ebenezer, Norwich, Conn., in 1818.. S 36588
   Eleazer, Conn. & Cont., wid. Clarissa, BLWt. 24993-160-55.................. W 4990
   Ezekiel... S 13448
   James, wid. Sally, BLWt. 51755-160-55... W 11342
   Jared, Cont. (Conn.), wid. Mary, BLWt. 5991-100, issued 1789.............. R 5311
      (Soldier never pensioned.)
   Jesse, wid. Lydia.. W 21370
   Joel, Cont. (Conn.), wid. Abigail.. W 21378
   John, wid. Ruth... W 25786
   Jonathan, Artillery, Capt. Jackson; Sullivan Co., N. Y., in 1832........... S 10869
   Jonathan, under Capt. Benedict; New Haven, Conn., in 1832............... S 13428
   Joseph... S 36587
      BLWt. 946 for 450 acres, Lieut. Col., was issued Dec. 14, 1789. No papers.
      (Name recorded as HAIT.)
   Joseph, Hannah Weed, former wid. of... R 11273
      (Soldier not pensioned.)
   Mary, former wid. of
   Moses... S 10860
   Nathan.. R 5312
   Nathan.. S 13426
   Nathaniel... S 31750
   Samuel, fifer under Capts. Scofield & Lockwood; b. 1762, Stamford, Conn... S 17491
   Samuel, Conn. & Cont., wid. Hannah... W 11328
      BLWt. 953 for 300 acres, Capt., was issued June 27, 1789. No papers.
   Samuel... S 46004
      BLWt. 967 for 200 acres, Lieut., was issued June 27, 1789. No papers.
      (Also given HAIT.)

HOYT, HAIT, HAYT, or HOIT—Continued.
Stephen, wid. Hannah.. W 16290
Walter, wid. Grace.. W 18052
Warren, wid. Mary. BLWt. 10238-160-55... W 25782
   (Also given HOIT.)
William, priv. Artillery, Capt. Bean, d. 1828; wid. Anna.......................... W 11338
William, priv. Col. Mead; Greene Co., N. Y., in 1832; wid. Anna................ R 5309
William. Artificer, Col. Baldwin, Cont. (Conn.), Fairfield Co., 1832.............. S 15177
HUBBARD or HUBBART, Abijah, Cont. (Conn.)................................... S 44962
   BLWt. 5986-100, private, was issued Dec. 14, 1792. No papers.
Abner, wid. Esther... W 19846
Asa.. S 2333
Bathsheba, former wid. of Zebulon MYGATT.
David... S 17504
Elihu, wid. Martha... W 16610
Elijah, Penelope Hillyer, former wid. of.
   (See case of her former husband, David GOODRICH.)
Elijah, State Commissary, d. 1808, Middlesex Co., Conn., wid. Abigail......... W 21425
Elisha, Conn. & Cont.. S 18457
George, Corp. under Capt. Hinckley; New Hamp. in 1818........................ S 44451
George, priv. & serg't. under Col. Meigs; Granville, Mass., in 1832; wid. Emily; BLWt. 26536-160-55.. W 7828
Hezekiah, BLWt. 964-200, Lieut., was issued Nov. 19, 1789. No papers.
Jedediah... S 10897
Joel, Conn.. Cont. & Privateer.. S 10886
John, fifer, Capt. Abbott; Otsego Co., N. Y., in 1832.............................. S 5593
John, priv. under Capt. Church; Otsego Co., N. Y., in 1832....................... S 23715
Jonas.. S 38858
Josiah, wid. Mary.. W 19847
Lucretia, former wid. of John R. WATROUS.
Nehemiah, Conn. & Cont.. S 10882
Philip, wid. Ambrillis... W 19843
Robert, Poebe Skeel, former wid. of... R 9629
   (Soldier not pensioned.)
Thomas, wid. Silence... W 15916
Titus, Cont. (Conn.).. S 5572
HUBBEL or HUBBELL, Aaron, wid. Sarah... W 11360
Abijah.. S 10890
Amos, wid. Lucy.. W 18073
David, wid. Abiah... W 18075
   (Soldier died 1820, Fairfield Co., Conn.)
David, wid. Elizabeth... W 19849
   (Soldier pensioned in 1818 from Litchfield Co., Conn.; d. 1836.)
Ezbon.. S 44943
Gershom, wid. Sarah.. R 5316½
   (Neither soldier nor wid. applied for pension, but daughter Priscilla.)
Gideon... S 31763
Isaac, Conn. & N. Y... S 36601
Salmon... S 36604
   BLWt. 960 for 200 acres, Lieut., was issued June 16, 1789. No papers.
Samuel, wid. Mary.. W 18076
Seth, wid. Salome... W 2115
   BLWt. 1500-100 and BLWt. 67677-160-55.
Silliman, wid. Polly, BLWt. 26869-160-55... W 1774
Thaddeus.. S 13482
William, Conn. & Cont., wid. Margaret... W 8952
HUBBS, Irena, former wid. of Daniel DODGE.
HUDSON, Joshua, wid. Celia... R 5326
   (Soldier was pensioned from Cuyahoga Co., Ohio, in 1832, as priv. in State troops.)
Obadiah, Conn. & N. Y... R 5337
HUGG, Isaac... S 13492
HUGHES, William, Conn. & Cont... S 36599
   (See also HEWES.)
HULBARD or HULBURD, Hannah, former wid. of Hiland HALL.
HULBERT. (See HURLBERT.)
HULBERTON. (See HOLBURTON.)
HULBURT and HULBUT. (See HURLBERT.)
HULET, HULETT, HEWLET or HEWLETT.
Aaron, wid. Cynthia, BLWt. 18365-160-55... W 19831
Daniel, Conn. & Vt.. S 18864
Phinehas... S 34932
Seth... S 29249
HULL, Abner... S 2535
Asahel.. S 16159
Benjamin.. S 13510
Chester, Cont. (Conn.)... S 44965
David, priv.; called David 2d when pensioned in Otsego Co., N. Y., in 1832.... S 22843
David, First Lieut., Mass., in 1818... S 32871
David, priv. Conn. Line, Otsego Co., N. Y., in 1818; d. there 1842; wid. Abigail... W 19795
Eli... S 18041
   Priv. Col. Meigs; Monroe Co., N. Y., in 1832; applied, but pension not paid until 1850, when it was made payable to David Hull, his only surviving child.
Eli, priv. Col. Swift; N. Y., in 1818, d. 1828; wid. Sally, BLWt. 6114-160-55.... W 26663
Eliakim, wid. Rachel.. W 19840
Ezra, wid. Mary... W 8959
George.. S 44967
Henry, Rebecca Blakeslee, former wid. of, BLWt. 2470-100.................... W 3332
Jehiel, wid. Rachel, BLWt. 18022-160-55.. W 25813
Jeremiah, wid. Phebe... W 19718
Joseph, priv. Lampeter, N. H., in 1818.. S 23272

81

HUEL, Joseph, Conn. & Cont., wid. Freelove ... W 7815
    BLWt. 980 for 200 acres, Lieut., was issued Feb. 24, 1791. No papers.
  Josia or Josiah, wid. Mehitable ... W 16608
  Prince ... S 36596
  Samuel, priv. Capt. Morgan; Candor, N. Y., in 1832 ... S 13496
  Samuel, priv. Col. Webb; N. Y. in 1818 ... S 44966
  Samuel, priv. Col. Webb; Conn. in 1818, d. 1835; wid. Mabel ... W 21284
  Wakeman, wid. Esther ... W 7816
  Zalmon ... S 15472
  Zephaniah, Cont. (Conn.), wid. Rachel, BLWt. 521–100 ... W 25801
HULTS, Stephen, Conn. & N. Y ... S 10880
HUMASON, HUMASTON, HUMASTUN, HUMISTON, HUMMISTON or HOMASON.
  Abraham ... R 5369
  Daniel, Cont. (Conn.) ... BLWt. 305–100
  David ... S 17725
  Jesse, wid. Abi ... W 25809
  Joel, wid. Ann ... W 4244
HUMPHREY, HUMPHREYS, HUMPHRIES or HUMPHRY.
  Abraham ... S 23273
  Asahel, Cont. (Conn.), wid. Prudence ... W 21424
  David, BLWt. 948 for 450 acres, Lieut. Col., was issued Feb. 28, 1795. No papers.
  Elijah, Conn. & Cont., wid. Anna ... W 18092
    BLWt. 952 for 300 acres, Capt., was issued Feb. 5, 1800, to Anna Humphreys and John Humphreys, Adx., in trust for the heirs and legal representatives of Elijah Humphreys. No papers.
  Israel ... BLWt. 1600–100
  James, wid. Abiah ... W 19829
  Joel, wid. Amelia, BLWt. 13413–160–55 ... W 4245
  Levi, wid. Polly ... W 2619
  Lot ... S 31762
  Nathaniel, Conn. & Cont ... S 36594
  Noah, wid. Hannah Cyrene ... W 18099
  Roswell, wid. Elizabeth ... W 4998
  Samuel ... S 28771
  Solomon ... S 17498
  Timothy, Cont. (Conn.), wid. Rhoda ... W 18070
HUNGERFORD, Elijah ... S 13494
  Green ... S 46048
  James, priv. Capt. Fenn; Chanango Co., N. Y., in 1832 ... S 15182
  James, priv. Col. A. Ward; Jefferson Co., N. Y., in 1818 ... S 44946
  Jehiel ... S 13489
  Joseph ... S 13285
  Lemuel ... S 16160
  Mary, former wid. of Ashbel UPSON.
  Robert or Robart, wid. Olive ... W 19793
  Uriel, wid. Hannah ... W 18090
HUNN, Samuel ... S 13508
HUNT, Catharine, former wid. of Ezra ALLEN.
  Charles, Conn. & Conn. Sea service, BLWt. 6379–160–55 ... S 9920
  Daniel, Cont. (Conn.) ... S 39749
  Israel ... S 17499
  Joel ... S 36605
  Lewis, Elizabeth Crofut, former wid. of ... W 17686
  Russell, priv. Capt. Burrall; Litchfield Co., Conn., in 1832 ... S 13474
  Russell, Serg't., Litchfield Co., Conn., in 1818, d. 1831; wid. Hester ... W 25810
  Sampson R ... S 37125
  Walter ... S 44853
HUNTER, Daniel ... R 5400
  Elizabeth, former wid. of Seth JACKSON.
  Joseph ... S 32873
  Nathaniel, Conn. & N. Y., wid. Sarah, BLWt. 26031–160–55 ... W 19835
HUNTINGDON or HUNTINGTON.
  Andrew, priv. Capt. Baldwin, Col. Sheldon; Monroe Co., N. Y., in 1832 ... S 23716
  Andrew, Asst. Commissary of Purchases; d. 1824, New London, Conn.; wid. Hannah A ... W 21429
  Azariah ... S 10888
  Christopher, wid. Eunice ... W 7853
    BLWt. 57526–160–55.
  Ebenezer, Conn. & Cont ... S 36595
    BLWt. 949 for 450 acres, Lieut. Col., was issued Oct. 13, 1789. No papers.
  Hezekiah or Hesekiah, Conn. & Cont ... S 15475
  Hiram ... S 23722
  Jedediah, BLWt. 945 for 850 acres, Brigadier General, was issued Oct. 26, 1791. No papers.
  John, wid. Rebecca ... W 18081
  John S., wid. Keturah ... W 19844
  Joseph, wid. Susannah ... W 19839
  Roger, priv. infantry; Windham, Conn., in 1832 ... S 10901
  Roger, priv. Col. Durkee; Vt. in 1818, then moved to N. H ... S 44449
  Samuel ... S 23274
  Theophilus ... S 44960
  Thomas ... S 44961
  Wightman ... S 5411
  William ... S 13490
HUNTLEY or HUNTLY, Abner, Conn. & Cont ... S 13480
  Adriel, Lucy Stedman, former wid. of ... R 10092
    (Soldier never pensioned.)
  Andrew, wid. Zelinda ... R 5413
    BLWt. 85067–160–55.
    (Soldier's application rejected as he did not serve six months.)
  Dan ... R 5414

HUNTLEY or HUNTLY, Elihu, wid. Naomi .... W 19791
    Ezekiel .... S 13511
    Hoel .... S 18043
    Jabez .... S 36600
    Jehiel, Conn. & N. Y .... S 10894
    Jonathan .... S 18893
    Martin .... R 5415
    Moses .... S 21308
    Reuben, Cont. (Conn.) .... S 13501
    Reynold .... R 5416
    Rufus .... S 45404
    Solomon, wid. Abigail A., BLWt. 7438-160-55 .... W 27854
    Zadock .... S 23270
HURD or HEARD, Abijah .... S 44947
    Adam, Conn. & Vt .... S 18463
    Benjamin .... S 10885
    Cooley, wid. Sarah, BLWt. 26432-160-55 .... W 431
    Crippen or Crippin, wid. Elizabeth .... W 24458
    David .... S 20804
    Elijah, wid. Polly .... W 1773
    Elnathan, Conn. & Cont .... S 13505
    Graham, wid. Love .... W 23242
    Isaac, wid. Mary .... W 1184
        (Also given as HEARD.)
    Jacob, BLWt. 13021-160-55 .... S 17505
    Lewis .... S 18886
    Lovell or Lovewell, Margere Haynes, former wid. of .... W 25763
    Mead or Mede .... S 29250
    Philo .... S 36597
    Robert, Conn. & Cont., wid. Olive .... W 18095
    Roswell .... R 5431
    Wilson .... S 17506
HURLBERT, HURLBURT, HURLBUT, HURLBUTT, HULBERT, HULBUT.
    Abiram, Conn. & Cont .... S 10887
    Alfred, wid. Lydia .... W 25804
    Amos .... S 15896
    Bartholomew .... R 5424
    Daniel .... S 44454
    Daniel, wid. Esther .... W 18077
    David .... S 45401
    Elijah, wid. Ruth .... W 19845
    Eliphalet, wid. Mehitabel .... W 18093
    George, BLWt. 978- for 300 acres, Capt., was issued March 3, 1797, to Ann Welsh, Devisee;
        also recorded as above under BLWt. 2680. No papers. (Given also HURLBRETT.)
    Gideon .... S 36598
    Gideon, wid. Sarah .... W 18087
    John, priv. Col. Wyllys; Onondaga Co., N. Y., in 1818; wid. Judith .... W 16612
    John, wid. Sarah .... R 5426
        (Neither soldier nor wid. applied, but son Stephen, whose application was R.)
    Jubilee A., Cont. (Conn.), wid. Polly or Molly .... W 21423
    Matthias, wid. Clemence .... W 21426
    Seymour .... S 13500
    Shadrack, Conn. & Cont .... S 29915
    Silas, wid. Sarah .... W 18074
    Stephen .... R 5427
    Stephen, d. 1807; wid. Abigail .... W 25812
    Thomas, wid. Eunice .... W 21422
    Timothy, wid. Olive, BLWt. 2028-160-55 .... W 25807
    Wait .... S 39757
HURLEHOY or HURLEROY, or HURLEROI, John .... BLWt. 270-100
HUSTED, Nathaniel, wid. Ruth .... W 18089
    Samuel, Phebe Clark, former wid. of .... W 16909
    Thaddeus, Conn. & N. Y .... S 16158
HUSTON, William, wid. Elizabeth .... W 7847
HUTCHINS, Amasa, wid. Hannah .... W 19790
    John Church, wid. Irene .... R 5448
        (Soldier not pensioned.)
    Nathan, Conn. & Vt., wid. Lois, BLWt. 10236-160-55 .... W 1614
    Shubael, wid. Avis .... W 21428
    Zadoc .... S 13478
HUTCHINSON or HUTCHISON, Abijah, Conn. & Cont .... S 13491
    Amos, wid. Lucy .... W 18088
    Eleazer, wid. Huldah .... W 18079
    Job .... S 13493
    John, priv. Col. Durkee; d. 1804; Mary Adams, former wid. of .... W 20571
    John, wid. Tryphena .... R 5455
        (Soldier not pensioned.)
    John, priv. Col. Wyllys; Windsor Co., Vt., in 1818 and 1832 .... S 22321
    Jonathan .... S 17503
        (Also given as HUTCHISON.)
    Samuel .... R 5453
HUTINACK, Francis .... S 13488
HUXFORD, John .... S 13504
HYATT, Abraham, Conn., N. Y. & Privateer, wid. Anna .... W 16613
    Alvan .... S 18049
    Hezekiah .... R 5461
    Isaac, wid. Esther .... W 18098
    Samuel, Conn. & Cont., wid. Judy or Judia .... W 15776
    Stephen, wid. Eunice .... W 25818

HYDE or HIDE, Agur	S	36610
Alexander	S	36609
Andrew	S	15477
Azel, Corp. Col. Reed	S	46464
Azel, priv. Col. Wells; Lebanon, Conn., in 1832; wid. Arethusa	W	25817
Benjamin	S	13515
Clark	S	45407
Ebenezer	S	13516
Elihu, wid. Hannah	W	25814
Elijah, Conn. & Cont.	S	5597
Elisha, wid. Abigail	W	25815
Ichabod	S	15476
James, BLWt. 958-200, Lieut., was issued Oct. 22, 1789, to Theodosius Fowler, Assignee. No papers.		
James, priv. Col. Webb; Vt. in 1818; Conn. & Cont.; wid. Eunice BLWt. 258-60-55.	W	5000
Jedediah, Capt. under Col. Durkee; Grand Isle, Vt., in 1818	S	39759
Jedediah, Qr. Mr. Serg't. under Col. Parsons; d. 1824, Chittenden, Vt.; wid. Elizabeth	W	25816
Joel	S	13514
John	S	10902
Jonathan	S	23723
Joseph	R	5463
Joseph, Conn. Sea Service, wid. Betsey	W	1186
Moses, wid. Sarah (Soldier never pensioned.)	R	5465
Oliver	S	45406
Phineas, Navy (Conn.)	S	32

I.

IAMS, John Frederick, wid. Mary	W	434
INGALLS, Luther, BLWt. 26079-160-55	S	44972
INGERSOLL, Briggs, wid. Abigail BLWt. 9438-160-55.	W	1188
John	S	10904
Rosannah, former wid. of Abraham PARKER.		
INGHAM, Daniel	S	29255
David	S	35458
Holladay (Also given INGRAHAM.)	S	45409
Isaac, wid. Lucy	W	16305
Samuel, wid. Zillah, BLWt. 34285-160-55	W	297
Solomon, wid. Molly	W	13527
INGRAHAM, Amos	S	44971
Hezekiah, wid. Mary, BLWt. 6266-160-55	W	26152
Holladay. (See INGHAM.)		
James	S	17509
Jonathan	S	30505
Samuel	S	22325
Simeon	S	21835
IRION, Charity, former wid. of Samuel GRANNIS.		
ISAACS, Isaac, Chloe Wilcox, former wid. of	W	6541
ISBEL or ISBELL, Garner, wid. Mary	W	20160
Joel, wid. Mary Soldier pensioned as priv. in 1818, Wayne Co., Ohio, later Michigan.	R	5500
ISHAM, Daniel	S	15592
George I, or J	S	41682
Isaac, wid. Faith Soldier never applied for pension.	R	5491
Jehiel or Jehial	S	39766
Jirah	S	18466
John, wid. Lois	W	16304
Joshua, wid. Martha	W	26791
William	S	39765
IVES, Amos	S	15186
Charles	S	13319
Ichabod	S	18050
John, Conn. & Cont.	S	44974
Lent, priv. Col. Matthew Meade; N. Y. in 1822	S	28048
Lent, Conn. & Vt., priv. Capt. Kimball, Col. Chandler, Vt. 1818; d. 1838; wid. Mary	W	26812
Levi	S	15187
Phineas, wid. Martha	W	20161

J.

JACK, John, wid. Hannah	W	20167
JACKLIN, Ebenezer	S	32891
JACKSON, Archibald, Conn., Cont. & R. I.	S	13521
Benjamin, Cont. (Conn.), wid. Sabrina	W	26157
Daniel, priv. under Col. Webb; Stratford, Conn., in 1818	S	36615
Daniel, Conn. & Conn. Sea Service, Lieut. under Col. St. John; Fairfield, Conn., in 1832	S	17512
David, priv. under Capt. Betts; N. Y. in 1818	S	45412
David, priv. under Capt. Hawley; d. 1814, Sullivan Co., N. Y., in 1814; wid. Olive	W	20170
Elias, Conn. & R. I., wid. Agnes (or Nancy)	W	4002
John, priv. N. Y. in 1832 (Claim suspended.)	S	22851
John, priv. Capt. Davis, Col. Burrall; d. 1820, Litchfield, Conn.; wid. Delight, pensioned in 1836	W	21445
Joseph	S	10907
Matthew, Conn. & Mass., wid. Jane	W	10142

JACKSON, Michael, wid. Deborah	W 16033
Robert, Conn. & R. I.	S 9994
Samuel BLWt.	1167-100
Seth, former wid. Elizabeth Hunter, BLWt. 5447-160-55.	W 10131
JACKWAY. (See JAKAY.)	
JACKWAYS. (See JAKWAYS and also JAQUES.)	
JACOBS, Asa, Conn. & R. I., wid. Phebe, BLWt. 21819-160-55	W 9070
Asahel or Ashael	S 15478
Enoch wid. Lois	R 5532
(Soldier never applied for pension.)	
Ezekiel	S 10908
Gershom, wid. Mary	W 16309
(Also given as JACOCKS.)	
Nathaniel, Conn. & R. I.	S 13520
William	S 23278
JACOCKS. (See JACOBS and JACOX.)	
JACOX, JAYCOX or JACOCKS, Joshua.	S 45432
JACQUES or JACKWAYS, William, wid. Ann	W 2118
JAKWAY, JACKWAY or JAKWAYS, Daniel, wid. Olive.	W 20166
William	S 5612
JAMES, Amos, Conn., Mass. & R. I., wid. Phebe	W 1615
Jeffery	S 36616
Paul	S 44983
Rhoda, former wid. of Billy TROWBRIDGE.	
William, wid. Lovisa	W 20168
JAMESON, JAMESSON or JAMISON, Samuel, Cont. (Conn.), wid. Rosana	W 16032
JANES, Seth	S 28772
JAQUA, Gamaliel, wid. Eleanor, BLWt. 26826-160-55	W 7888
JAQUES. (See JACQUES.)	
JARMAN or GERMAN, Charles, Conn. & Cont., wid. Betsey	W 20169
JARRARD, Benjamin	R 5556
JARVIS, Henry	R 5559
JAYCOX. (See JACOX.)	
JEFFERS, George, wid. Martha	R 5562
JEFFERY, Charles	S 13539
JELLIFF, James	S 17514
JENCKS. (See JENKS.)	
JENINGS. (See JENNINGS.)	
JENKINS or JINKINS, Calvin	S 36624
John, wid. Bethiah, BLWt. 448-200	W 7895
Samuel, BLWt. 2203-100	S 44461
JENKS or JENCKS, John or John S., BLWt. 1821-100	S 39775
JENNINGS, Aaron	S 13535
Abijah, wid. Eleanor	W 26669
Abraham, wid. Charity	W 21455
Burritt, Navy (Conn.)	S 36625
Daniel	S 36628
Eliphalet	S 18468
Esbon, BLWt. 2208-100	S 41695
Jonathan, priv. under Capt. Benton; Dyberry, Pa., in 1818.	S 39778
Jonathan, Cont. (Conn.), in Sheldon's Dragoons six yrs., Addison Co., Vt. in 1818	S 38871
Joshua, wid. Sarah	W 20181
Justus	S 44987
Nathan	S 31775
Nathan B., wid. Ann or Nancy	R 5577
(Soldier was pensioned in Phila. in 1818, for service as Serg't. under Col. Meigs.)	
Noah	S 23727
Peter, wid. Sarah	W 24746
BLWt. 30766-160-55.	
William, private under Capt. Lacy; born 1765; Fairfield Co., Conn., 1835	S 13537
William, priv. under Col. Webb; 62 in 1820, Fairfield Co., Conn	S 36622
JERALDS. (See GERALD.)	
JEROME, David	S 36627
Thomas	S 17513
JESSUP or JESUP, Ebenezer, wid. Rebecca	R 5582
(Soldier was pensioned in Greenwich, Conn., in 1832 as priv. under Capt. Lockwood.)	
Jonathan, Continental service, resided in N. Y. in 1818, and Conn. in 1820	S 36626
Joseph, wid. Eunice	W 16310
JEWETT or JEWITT, Alpheus, Conn. & N. Y., wid. Abigail	W 24734
Joseph, wid. Rachael	W 21454
Joseph M.	S 4438
Nathan H.	S 13541
Zebulon, Conn., N. Y. & Vt.	S 18900
JINKINS. (See JENKINS.)	
JOHNSON, Abner, wid. Anna	W 21481
Abraham	S 36650
Amos, priv. Col. Canfield, d. 1828, Cayuga Co., N. Y., wid. Lucene or Luceny	W 21473
Amos, priv. Capt. Berry, Col. Enos; Oswego Co., N. Y., in 1832, BLWt. 26779-160-55	S 13575
Benjamin, former wid. Susannah Foot	W 7299
Benoni	S 13578
Bristol or Briston, wid. Vira, BLWt. 1592-160-55	W 20207
Caleb, wid. Naomi	W 26802
Calvin, wid. Sally, BLWt. 31283-160-55	W 20205
Constant, wid. Thankful	R 5668
(Soldier did not apply.)	
Daniel, priv. under Col. Wyllys; Lewis Co., N. Y., in 1818	S 45423
Daniel, priv. Capt. Meigs, Col. Hooker; Chenango Co., N. Y., in 1832	S 46051
Daniel, Cont. (Conn), priv. under Capt. Barton, Col. Flowers; Hartford, Conn., in 1828	S 36644
David, priv. under Col. Webb; d. 1827; Vt. in 1818; wid. Eunice	W 15779

JOHNSON, David, d. Tolland, Conn., in 1806; wid. Mary... W 21463
David, Conn. & Cont., priv. under Capt. Hubbard, Col. Huntington; Lexington Heights,
　N. Y., in 1832... S 13547
Ebenezer, teamster, Hartford, Conn., in 1837.. S 13570
Ebenezer, priv. Col. Whiting; Monroe, Conn., in 1832.. S 17519
Ebenezer, priv. under Capt. Collins; Greene Co., N. Y., in 1832; wid. Elizabeth, BLWt. 30765–
　160–55... W 1294
Edward... R 5609
Edward... S 13572
Elias... S 29263
Elijah.. S 44463
Eliphalet.. R 5611
Elisha, Northampton, Mass., in 1818, as priv. under Col. Wyllys...................................... S 29933
Elisha, priv. Col. Sage, died in 1813 at Tolland, Conn., former wid. Mary Brigham........ W 17438
Elisha, Conn. & Cont., priv. under Col. Lamb, enlisted from Litchfield, Conn., Tioga Co.,
　N. Y., in 1818.. S 45425
Ephraim, former wid. Hopstill Dean... W 16237
Fenn, wid. Rebecca.. W 20212
Gideon... S 17515
Henry, wid. Holdah... R 5619
　(Soldier was pensioned from N. Y. in 1818 as priv. under Col. Meigs.)
Hezekiah, Conn. & War of 1812... S 19353
Ichabod... S 10928
Isaac, priv. Col. Mead; Cayuga Co., N. Y., in 1832.. S 10920
Isaac, priv. Capt. Bull, Col. Meigs; Huron Co., Ohio, in 1829; wid. Lucy....................... W 20209
Isaac, priv. under Capt. Blackman, Col. Enoch; wid. Rebekah, Middlesex Co., Conn., in 1832. W 20211
Isaiah.. S 13581
Israel, priv. under Col. Wyllys; N. Y., in 1818.. S 43726
Israel, priv. under Capt. Hall, Col. Swift; d. 1820; wid. Huldah....................................... W 26681
Jacob, Cont. (Conn.) & Mass. Sea service.. R 5623
　(Also given as JONSON.)
James, priv. Capt. Dana, Col. Ward; Albany Co., N. Y., in 1832....................................... S 43720
James, priv. under Col. Wyllys; Bath, N. Y., in 1818... S 45417
James, priv. under Col. Webb; Norwich, Vt., in 1818; wid. Phebe, BLWt. 39212–160–55. W 26163
　(Also given as JONSON.)
James, Cont. (Conn.), Middletown, Conn., in 1832, as priv. under Capt. Sumner........ S 13557
Jedediah, wid. Lucy, BLWt. 27671–160–55... W 7943
John, priv. under Col. Wyllys; Greenup Co., Ky., in 1818... S 36027
John, priv. under Col. Swift; Highgate, Vt., in 1818.. S 38877
John, ensign; d. 1832, Middlesex Co., Conn., wid. Abigail... W 20198
John (1745–1834), priv. Serg't., Ensign, Lieut. & Capt. Broome Co., N. Y., in 1832; wid. Clarissa,
　BLWt. 7439–160–55... W 27621
John, priv. Col. Talcott; Middlesex Co., Conn. 1832; wid. Mary....................................... W 7933
Jonathan, BLWt. 1136–450, Lieut. Col., was issued Nov. 19, 1789. No papers.
Joseph.. R 5637
Joseph, Conn. & Cont. priv. under Col. Wyllys; Oswego Co., N. Y., in 1832................ S 13550
Joseph, Conn. & Cont.; priv. under Col. Webb; BLWt. 1277–100 granted in 1829 to daughter
　of deceased soldier, Elizabeth Fitch.
Josiah, priv. under Col. Talcott; Middletown, Conn., in 1832... S 16893
Josiah, Conn. & N. Y... R 5641
Justus.. S 13566
Lawrence, wid. Grace.. W 20202
Levi, wid. Ruth, BLWt. 9231–160–55.. W 1777
Miles... S 22855
Nathaniel, priv. under Col. Webb; Cazenovia, N. Y., in 1818.. S 45418
Nathaniel, priv. under Col. Penn; Derby, Conn., in 1832; wid. Rebekah......................... W 1979
Nathaniel, wid. Sarah.. R 5662
　(Soldier never applied.)
Phinehas.. S 36639
Reuben... S 16167
Reynolds, BLWt. 26472–160–55.. S 13544
Rufus, priv. under Col. Durkee; Canterbury, Conn., in 1832... S 13576
Rufus, Conn. & Mass., wid. Mary.. R 5647
　(Soldier did not apply.)
Samuel, BLWt. 1141–400, Major, was issued July 23, 1789 to Samuel Johnson. No papers.
Samuel, priv. under Capt. Belcher; Tioga Co., N. Y., in 1832.. S 13569
Samuel, priv. under Capt. Heath; Tolland Co., in 1832... S 15481
Samuel, priv. under Col. Huntington; Batavia, N. Y., in 1818... S 43710
Samuel... R 5659
Samuel, ensign under Col. Burrall; Delaware Co., N. Y., in 1818; wid. Rebecca.......... R 5655
Samuel, Cont. (Conn.), priv. in Hazen's reg't.; Batavia, N. Y., in 1818.......................... S 45420
Seth, wid. Abigail.. W 1295
　Abigail was also pensioned on account of the services of her former husband, Edmund
　　CARLETON, Mass.
(Seth, b. 1748, Middletown, Conn.; served under Capt. Hubbard, and died 1833 in N. H.)
Shadrach, wid. Hannah.. W 20201
Silas.. S 5636
Solomon, BLWt. 430–100.
Stephen, priv. Capt. Chapman, N. Y., in 1832... S 10919
Stephen, Conn. & Cont., Sheldon's Cavalry; d. 1831, Windha Co., Conn.; wid. Persis....... W 21487
Stephen W., Conn. Conn. Sea service & Navy... S 28776
Theodata, wid. Ruth... W 26672
Timothy, priv. Col. Durkee; Wayne Co., N. Y., in 1832.. S 22853
Timothy, priv. Col. Webb; New Haven Co., in 1818... S 36645
Turner... S 43724
Uzal, Conn. & R. I., wid. Mehetable... W 26161
William, priv. Capt. Meigs, Col. Spencer; Warren Co., Ohio, in 1832............................ S 8762
William, priv. under Capt. Brown; Stamford, Conn., in 1818... S 36635
William, priv. Capt. Wolcott; Windham Co., Conn., in 1818... S 36651
William, priv. Capt. Mills, Col. Webb; Cayuga Co., N. Y., in 1832; former wid. Anna White,
　BLWt. 102200–160–55... W 27500

JOHNSON, William, priv. under Col. Bradley; died in 1838; Harpersfield, N. Y., in 1818; wid.
  Hadassah, BLWt. 30762-160-55.. W 5305
  William, Navy (Conn.)... S 36634
JOHNSTON, Benjamin, Cont. (Conn.), wid Clarissa; BLWt. 25781-160-55............................... W 1435
  John, Navy (Conn.), wid. Ruth.. W 26673
JOINER, Hepsibah, former wid. of James SUTLIEF.
JOLIFF, Eunice, former wid. of John LOCKWOOD.
JOLLY, William, wid. Desire... W 20196
JONES, Amos, wid. Lydia... W 20183
  Asa, Serg't under Col. Durkee; in 1818 in Ohio; in 1832 in Tolland Co., Conn..................... S 13558
  Asa, Conn. & N. Y., priv. & Serg't under Col. Waterbury; Greene Co., N. Y., in 1832.............. S 13568
  Asaph, wid. Hannah, BLWt. 17704-160-55... W 1293
  Augustus... S 18059
  Benjamin, priv. under Capt. Edwards, Col. Waterbury; Preble, N. Y., in 1832...................... S 13565
  Benjamin, priv. under Capt. Brigham; Chenango Co., N. Y., in 1831............................... S 45428
  Crocker or Croker.. S 41702
  Daniel, Serg't under Col. Huntingdon; Morris Co., N. J., in 1832................................. S 2297
  Daniel, priv. Col. Huntingdon; Rensselaer Co., N. Y., in 1818.................................... S 45429
  David.. S 28777
  Deodate Pratt.. S 36649
  Eaton, Cont. (Conn.), wid. Mary.. W 20187
  Elkanah.. S 16170
  Epaphras... S 16889
  Ephraim, wid. Anna... W 2620
  Ethel.. S 22854
  Ezekiel.. S 28778
  Ezra... R 15464
  George, wid. Lucretia.. W 21484
  Harris... S 36655
  Isaac, priv. under Col. Wells; Hebron, Conn., in 1832.. S 18058
  Isaac, died 1793 in Fairfield, Conn.; priv. under Col. Whiting; Ruth Booth, former wid. of...... W 20741
  Issacher, wid. Eleanor... W 21472
  James, BLWt. 1141-100.
  Joel, Conn. & Mass... S 43730
  John, priv. under Capt. Sherwood, Col. Lewis; Delaware Co., N. Y., in 1832....................... S 13573
  John, priv. under Capt. Kirtland, Col. Ledyard; Saybrook, Conn., in 1832......................... S 31871
  Joseph... S 45845
  Moris or Morris, Conn. & Cont.. S 13571
  Oliver, wid. Hannah.. W 20185
  Philip... R 5734
  Phineas or Phinehas.. S 43707
  Reuben, priv. under Col. Swift; Plymouth, Penna., in 1832.. S 2292
  Reuben... R 5737
  Richard L., wid. Elizabeth, BLWt. 5439-160-55.. W 765
  Samuel, priv. in Col. Sheldon's Cavalry; Genesee Co., N. Y., in 1818; and Linklaen, N. Y.,
    in 1832.. S 28775
  Samuel, priv. under Col. Ely; died in 1827 in Saybrook, Conn.; wid. Mercy was living in
    Ulster Co., N. Y., in 1838... W 21485
  Samuel, priv. under Capt. Hutchinson, Col. Hofford; Pompey, N. Y., in 1832; wid. Tabitha........ W 26685
    BLWt. 6396-160-55.
  Samuel, Conn. & Cont., priv. under Capt. Smith, Col. Parsons; Rensselaer Co., N. Y., in 1832.... S 13559
  Samuel L., wid. Elizabeth.. R 5700
    (Soldier never applied.)
  Simeon... S 16894
  Solomon.. S 32903
  Squire, Cont. (Conn.) & N. Y., wid. Polly.. W 21471
  Stephen.. S 43728
  Thomas, Conn. & Cont... S 43716
  Timothy, wid. Lydia.. W 20186
  William, b. Jan. 18, 1764; priv. under Capt. Lathan; Madison Co., N. Y., in 1832................. S 13577
  William, Serg't under Col. Durkee; New Haven Co., Conn., in 1818................................. S 36640
  William, priv. under Col. Bradley; Middlebury, Vt., in 1818...................................... S 38875
  William, priv. under Capt. Chamberlin; Whitehall, N. Y., in 1818; pensioned as William 1st...... S 39784
  William, priv. under Col. Webb; pensioned as William 2d in 1818.................................. S 43715
  William C.. S 18473
JONSON. (See JOHNSON.)
JORDAN, John; also given KENEA, John Jordan.
  Stephen, wid. Mary... W 20220
JOSLEN, JOSLIN or JOSLYN, David.. S 13543
  Joseph, Conn. & R. I... S 17518
  Reuben, wid. Mary.. W 20219
JOSTIN. (See JUSTIN.)
JOY, Anna, former wid. of Clement MINOR.
  Benjamin... S 40888
  Ebenezer... S 22337
JOYCE, David, Conn. & N. Y... S 13548
  Abia, former wid. of Moses CASS.
  Anthony.. S 23282
  Calvin, wid. Mary.. W 26801
  Dan.. S 13590
  Demas.. S 10932
  Eben W., wid. Lydia.. W 26706
  Elias, Conn. & Cont.. S 17520
  Elihu, Lois Davis, former wid. of.. R 2743
    (Soldier never applied.)
  Freeman, Conn. & Cont., wid. Deborah... W 21500
  Isaac.. R 5781
  James, wid. Esther... W 20222
  Jehiel... S 20816
  John, wid. Mary, BLWt. 26116-160-55.. W 10160

JOYCE, Joel, Marcy or Mercy Edwards, former wid. of... W 17746
    John, Cont. (Conn.), wid. Hannah.. W 26707
    Levi... S 18067
    Nathan.. S 44467
    Reuben.. R 5782
    Samuel, Phebe Waters, former wid. of... R 11184
        (Soldier never applied.)
        It is alleged that Phebe's other husband, Oliver WATERS, also served in the Rev. War.
        See papers in this case.
    Solomon... S 23736
    Stephen, wid. Sarah... W 21499
    Thomas... S 31785
    Walter, wid., Margaret.. W 20221
    William, priv. under Capt. Edwards; Jefferson Co., N. Y., in 1832................................. S 19724
    William, BLWt. 1137-300, Capt., was issued July 1, 1790. No papers.
JUDSON, Aaron... S 17522
    Agur... S 15594
    David, wid. Elizabeth... W 21504
        BLWt. 1138-300, Capt., was injured October 7, 1789. No papers.
    Elizabeth, former wid. of Benjamin DAVENPORT.
    John B., wid. Hepsy... R 5784
        (Soldier never applied.)
    Joseph, Lydia Clark, former wid. of... W 22782
    Lemuel.. S 17521
    Nathaniel.. S 13592
    Nehemiah, Conn. & Cont... S 16899
    Phineas, Conn. & Cont... S 13591
    Solomon.. S 29266
    Stiles, wid. Naomi... W 21498
JUNE, Israel.. S 36670
    Joel... R 5787
    Reuben, wid. Mary.. W 2555
    Seth, wid. Hannah.. W 20224
JUSTIN or JOSTIN, Charles, BLWt. 1172-100... S 36869
    George, wid. Lucy... W 20226
    Gershom, Conn. & Navy, wid. Susannah.. R 5791
        (Soldier was pensioned as Mariner in Vt. in 1832.)
    Walcut or Walcot.. S 45433

K.

KALLAN, Luther, Conn. & R. I.. S 13594
KANNEDY. (See KENNEDY.)
KAPLE, John.. S 13593
KAULL, John, Cont. (Conn.)... R 5800
KEARN. (See KERN.)
KEATOR, Eunice, former wid. of Josiah PATCHEN or PATCHIN.
KEELER, Aaron, wid. Chloe.. R 5806
    (Soldier never applied.)
    Aaron, Cloriana Olmstead or Ollmstead, former wid. of... W 21867
        BLWt. 1191-150, Ensign Wm. Fisher; August 17, 1775. No papers.
    David, priv. under Col. Canfield; Brooklyn, Conn., in 1832.. S 16904
    David, priv. under Col. Chandler; Onondaga Co., N. Y., in 1818.................................. S 45442
    Ebenezer, wid. Lucy.. W 3261
    Henry, Conn. & R. I., Martha K. Miller, former wid. of.. W 7452
        BLWt. 355-60-55.
    Hezekiah, wid., Mercy... W 12005
    Isaac... S 45440
        BLWt. 1188-200, Lieut., was issued May 9, 1789. No papers.
    Isaac, matross, died 1814; wid. Deborah.. W 20314
    Isaac, Conn. & Cont., priv. & Corp. under Capt. Hoyt, Col. Webb; New Canaan, Conn., in
        1832; wid. Catherine... W 26178
    Jeremiah.. S 45441
        BLWt. 6052-100, private, was issued January 16, 1797. No papers.
    Levi, wid. Dorcas.. W 20294
    Lewis... S 4471
    Mathew, wid. Ruth... R 5809
        (Priv. under Col. Enos; Fairfield Co., Conn., in 1832; wid. only was rejected.)
    Nathan, wid. Huldah.. W 20302
    Nehemiah... S 15494
    Philip.. S 15493
    Samuel, BLWt. 201-300.
    Thaddeus, BLWt. 1187-200, Lieut., was issued January 16, 1797. No papers.
    Thomas, BLWt. 639-100.
    Uriah, wid. Lydia.. R 5810
        (Soldier was pensioned in Onondaga Co., N. Y., in 1818 as a priv. under Col. Chandler.)
KEENEY or KENEY, Ashbel, wid. Sarah.. W 20300
    Ethel... R 5813
    James, wid. Anne... W 20326
        (Also given as KINEY & KINNEY.)
    Richard... S 13620
    Thomas, Conn. & Penna... S 9366
    William... S 18072
KEITH, Barak.. S 13613
    John, Conn. & Mass.. S 44479
    Peter... S 45447
KELLEE, KELLEY or KELLY.
    Charles... S 45445
    Craig, wid. Sibbel... W 20304
    Jeremiah M... S 15911
    John, Olive Bowers, former wid. of.. W 393

KELLOGG, Daniel.. S 10944
   Eldad, Conn. & Mass., wid. Elizabeth.. W 7977
      BLWt. 523-160-55.
   Elijah, priv. under Capt. Mead, Col. Waterbury; Carlisle, N. Y., in 1832................. S 23738
   Elijah, Conn. & Mass., priv. under Capt. Swift, Col. Butler; Essex Co., N. Y., in 1832... S 13599
   Enoch.. S 45439
   Helmont... S 21847
   Horace or Horrace... S 45437
   Josiah... S 41722
   Martin... S 10940
   Medad, Conn. & Mass.. S 15492
   Noah... S 45436
   Phineas... S 42774
   Samuel.. S 39806
   Solomon... S 40896
   Stephen, wid. Lydia... W 21506
KELSEY or KELSY, Benjamin.. S 36676
   Ezra.. S 15491
   Heth or Heath... S 13611
   Joel... S 16432
      BLWt. 26777-160-55.
   John, wid. Lucy... W 20301
   Merry Seymour, Conn. or R. I., wid. Sarah.. R 5852
   Noah, wid. Margaret.. R 5851
      (Soldier never applied.)
   Reuben.. S 10937
   Samuel.. S 13622
   Seymour. (See Merry Seymour.)
   Stephen, wid. Lois.. W 26168
KENDAL, KENDALL, KINDAL or KINDALL.
   Ebenezer, wid. Elizabeth... R 5930
      (Neither soldier nor wid. applied.)
   Isaac, wid. Rachel.. W 12007
   John, Conn. & Cont... S 39812
   Joshua... S 13615
KENEA, John Jordan, Conn. & Cont., wid. Obedience...................................... W 26177
KENEDY. (See KENNEDY.)
KENEY. (See KEENEY.)
KENNEDY, KANEDY or KENEDY.)
   Hugh, Conn. & R. I.. S 42777
   Joseph, wid. Agnes.. W 13600
   Robert, Conn. & N. Y., wid. Eunice.. R 5868
      (Soldier never applied.)
   Seth, Conn., Cont., Mass. & Navy.. S 31789
   William, wid. Mary... W 15783
KENT, Bela, Cont. (Conn.), wid. Lucretia... W 7962
   Cato, wid. Beulah... W 26169
      (See also NEGRO.)
   Charles.. S 13618
   Darius... S 31791
   Elihu, wid. Elizabeth... W 26172
   Jacob.. R 20388
   John, wid. Mary... W 3559
      BLWt. 8384-160-55.
   Jonathan K... S 31792
   Joseph.. S 42764
   Samuel, wid. Mary.. W 5306
   Titus (colored), BLWt. 1665-100.
KENTNER, John P.. R 5876
KENYON, Payne... S 42767
   Zephrah, former wid. of William PRENTICE.
KERN or KEARN, Michael, Conn. & N. Y., wid. Mary...................................... W 7964
KERR, Robert.. S 31793
KETCHAM, Ezra.. S 42768
KEYES or KEYS, Daniel, wid. Abigail... W 20309
   David.. S 13623
   Ebenezer.. R 5897
   Elias, Conn. & N. H... S 15912
   John, Conn. & Cont... S 42766
   Marshal or Marshall... S 42771
   Sampson, Conn. & Mass... S 13606
KIBBE, KIBBEE, KIBBEY, & KIBBY.
   Elijah, wid. Hannah... W 26729
   Frederick or Fredrick... S 15499
   Israel, wid. Ruth.. W 20336
   Jedediah or Jedidiah.. S 15595
   Lemuel, wid. Love.. W 21530
   Philip or Phillip... S 13640
   Philip W.. S 44480
      (Also given as KILBEY.)
KILBORNE, KILBOURN or KILBOURNE, or KILBORN.
   Araunah or Arannah.. S 13649
   James, wid. Elizabeth.. W 20340
   Samuel.. S 36679
   Simon, wid. Eunice... W 20328
KILBY, Christopher A., Cont. (Conn.).. S 36678
   John.. S 31798
KIMBALL, Abraham T., wid. Sarah... W 26180
   Benjamin.. S 13631
   Charles, wid. Jerusha.. W 21527

KIMBALL, Isaac.. S 32954
    Jared.. S 41730
    Jedediah, wid. Eunice... W 26735
    Jesse.. R 5921
    Jesse, Conn. & Privateer... S 13639
    John... S 42792
    Joseph, Conn. & Mass., wid. Ede.. W 10176
    Lebeus or Libbeus.. S 16216
    Richard... S 39814
    Samuel, Conn. & R. I... S 21853
KIMBERLY, Ezra.. R 5924
    Robert, Hannah Foote, former wid. of.. R 3638
    (Soldier never applied.)
KINCH, William, wid. Ruth... W 21529
KINDAL or KINDALL. (See KENDALL.)
KINEY. (See KEENEY and KINNE.)
KING, Benjamin.. S 4767
    Eli, Chloe Strong, former wid. of.. W 16746
    Eliphalet, Cont. (Conn.), wid. Silence... W 20338
    Esau... S 23750
    Ichabod, Conn. & Cont.. S 40901
    James.. S 13654
    John, wid. Jane.. W 20349
    Jonah, Conn. & Mass.. S 16908
    Joseph... S 42786
    Joshua, Cont. service but Conn. residence.. S 13632
      BLWt. 1192-200, Lieut., was issued August 26, 1789. No papers.
    Lemuel, wid. Jane.. W 26179
      Rozina, former wid. of Joseph CLARK.
    Samuel, wid. Betsey.. W 21531
    Theodore, wid. Lydia... W 24854
KINGSBERY or KINGSBURY, Andrew, wid. Mary... W 20327
    Asa.. S 13644
    Daniel, wid. Martha.. W 20324
    Jabez.. S 17525
    Jacob, wid. Sally P.. W 1881
      BLWt. 1190-150, Ensign, was issued Sept. 12, 1789. No papers.
    Joseph, priv. under Capt. Clark; Coventry, Conn., in 1832... S 17524
    Joseph, fifer, under Col. Chandler; Ellington, Conn., in 1818..................................... S 36680
    Oliver, wid. Sally, BLWt. 6254-160-55... W 16038
    Sanford, Conn. & Vt.. S 2708
    Thomas, wid. Esther.. R 5967
      (Soldier was pensioned from Lawrence Co., N.Y., in 1832 as a priv. under Capt. Steadman.)
    Tilley, Conn. & Mass., Anne Seymour, former wid. of... W 19342
KINGSLEY, Aaron, wid. Sarah... W 1781
    Alpheus... R 5968
    Asahel.. R 5969
    Hezekiah, Cont. (Conn.), wid. Rhoda... W 26181
    Jabez... S 13651
    Jonathan.. S 13461
    Rufus... S 13659
    Wareham, Conn. & War of 1812... R 5971
    William, wid. Deborah, BLWt. 24994-160-55.. W 768
KINNE, KINEY, KINNEY or KINNY.
    Asa, Conn. & N. Y. & R. I., wid. Polly... W 26710
    Daniel, Cont. (Conn.)... S 42779
    Freelove, former wid. of George GALLUP.
    James, wid. Anne. (See KEENEY.)
    Jonas... R 5976
    Joseph.. S 22863
    Lawrence.. S 42787
    Paley... S 29943
    Samuel, wid. Dorothy... W 1197
    Seth, Conn. & Cont. and Vt., wid. Hannah... W 20330
    Stephen, Conn. & R. I.. S 2704
KIRCUM. (See KIRKHAM.)
KIRK, Thomas.. S 37130
KIRKHAM, KIRKUM, or KIRCUM.
    Philemon.. S 2703
    Samuel.. S 42780
    William, Conn. & Cont., Deborah Buell, former wid. of... W 20795
KIRKLAND, Jabez, wid. Eunice.. W 14997
    (Given also as KIRTLAND.)
    Joshua, Conn. & Privateer.. R 5991
    Susanna, former wid. of John BUTTS.)
KIRTLAND, Charles... S 13648
    Daniel, wid. Lovisa.. W 20348
    Elizur.. R 5994
    Jabez, wid. Eunice. (See KIRKLAND.)
    John.. S 23748
    Martin, priv. under Capt. Kirtland; Oneida Co., N.Y., in 1832..................................... S 10947
    Martin, captain, BLWt. 1085-300.
    Nathan.. S 17526
KNAP or KNAPP, Benjamin, wid. Hannah.. W 1296
    BLWt. 14761-160-55.
      Hannah also claimed a pension as the former wid. of Zebulon MOSES, Vt., R 6009.
    Charles, Cont. (Conn.)... S 37141
    Ebenezer.. S 37140
    Eleazar... S 40906
    Elijah.. S 27049

KNAP or KNAPP, Hezekiah, wid. Mary... W 20364
  Isaac, Conn. & Cont.. S 13673
  Jacob, wid. Mary.. W 20362
  James, BLWt. 1513-100.
  Jared, wid. Catharine.. W 1621
  John, priv. under Col. Waterbury; Fairfield Co., Conn., in 1832.. S 10958
  John, priv. Capt. Brown, Col. Waterbury; Putnam Co., N. Y., in 1832.................................... S 13665
  John, priv. Col. Davenport; Stamford, Conn., in Revolution, died 1832; wid. Sally or Sarah,
    BLWt. 28593-160-55... W 26189
    (Widow was pensioned from Orange Co., Vt., in 1853.)
  Joshua, wid. Lodema... W 5015
    BLWt. 1189-150, Ensign; was issued June 25, 1789.
  Lemuel... S 22865
  Nathan... S 10959
  Peter, wid. Sarah.. W 20366
  Samuel... S 42801
    Hannah, wid. of this soldier, was pensioned as the former wid. of John BURGER, Mass.,
    W. 16319.
  Solomon, wid. Rosanna... W 20355
  Titus.. S 16909
  Uzal... S 16182
    BLWt. 6066-100; Sergt., was issued June 27, 1789, to Uzal Knapp. No papers. And
    BLWt. 206-60-55.
  William.. S 16910
KNEELAND, Jesse... S 42802
  Jonathan, Mary Wood, former wid. of... W 18360
  Samuel... S 42798
  Seth R., Cont. service, but Conn. residence and Agency; wid. Eunice................................. W 20369
KNICKERBACOR or KNICKERBACKER, Samuel, BLWt. 43504-160-55... S 13662
KNIGHT, Artemas, Conn. & Mass... S 16438
  Charles.. R 6022
  Elijah... W 41732
  Jonathan, wid. Anna or Ann; BLWt. 56-300... W 3024
  Josiah... S 13664
  Phinehas... S 32959
KNOTT, Abraham. (See NOTT.)
KNOWLES, James, Conn. & Cont. priv. under Col. Baldwin (artificer); Ohio in 1818; wid. Martha W 4258
  James, Conn. & Navy; Serg't., Ensign, Lieut. & Midshipman; died in 1778; former wid. was
    pensioned from Berkshire Co., Mass., in 1832; Prudence Foot, former wid. of..................... W 14036
  John, Cont. (Conn.), wid. Heppy or Hepsibah... W 20356
  Seth... S 42799
  Walker... S 23294
KNOWLTON, Frederick, Conn., Cont. & Mass.. S 13670
  Nathaniel.. S 23291
  Stephen, wid. Deidamia; BLWt. 13426-160-55.. W 6261
  Thomas, BLWt. 1149-400; was issued to the heirs of Col. Thomas Knowlton, who was killed
    at the Battle of Harlem Heights.
  Thomas, priv., Corp. & Serg't. under Capt. and Col. Knowlton; Tolland Co., Conn., in 1832;
    BLWt. 3952-160-55... S 31803

L.

LACEY or LACY, Isaac L.. S 46501
  Zachariah, wid. Betty.. W 20405
LAD or LADD, Amasa, Elizabeth Miller, former wid. of.. W 26263
  Cyrus, wid. Amy.. W 20411
  Elisha... R 6076
  John, Esther Fish, former wid. of.. W 13162
  Oliver... S 21343
LAFLAN, LAFLEN or LAFLIN.
  Abraham.. S 40923
  Charles.. S 28785
  John... S 37601
  Samuel... S 42825
LAKE, Daniel, wid. Polly.. W 12071
  David.. R 6088
  Reuben, BLWt. 546-100.. S 35515
  Roger.. S 42809
  William, wid. Mary, BLWt. 11177-160-55... W 26191
LAM or LAMB, Asa, Conn. & Cont.. S 10970
  Benjamin... S 40915
  David, Conn. & Navy, wid. Anna... W 20410
  Silas, Cont. (Conn.), wid. Jane.. W 20399
LAMBERT, David, wid. Lois... W 20377
LAMBERTON, Obed... S 44493
LAMPHAER, LAMPHEAR, LAMBPHIER, LAMPHIER, LANPHERE, LANPHIR.
  Abel... S 16440
  Amos, Conn. & N. Y... S 13698
  Fitch, wid. Jerusha.. W 27145
    (Also given LANPHERE.)
  James, Conn. Sea Service & Navy, wid. Grace.. W 26197
  Jedediah, wid. Elizabeth or Betsey... W 20381
    (Also given LANPHERE.)
  Roswell, wid. Elizabeth.. W 21544
    (See also LANFAIR.)
LAMPSON or LAMSON, Benjamin, wid. Mary.. W 16323
  David, wid. Polly.. W 7163
  Ebenezer, wid. Martha, BLWt. 38518-160-55.. W 4262
LANDON, Ebenezer.. S 13706
  James.. S 15505
  Rufus, Conn. & Cont.. S 13682

LANE, Dan	S 31808
Jabez	S 31807
John	S 38129
Joseph	R 6126
Joseph, Conn. & N. Y.	S 4495
Nathaniel, wid. Melicent, BLWt. 3796-160-55	W 12060
LANFAIR, Roswell, Conn. & Conn., Sea service	S 30538
(See also LAMPHAER.)	
LANGDON, Philip, Cont. (Conn.)	S 35513
LANGTON, Daniel	S 32370
LAP, John	R 9200
(Also given as SAP.)	
LARABEE, LARABY, LARIBEE, LARRABEE.	
Lebbeus, wid. Mary	W 1882
Seth, wid. Sally	W 20404
Theophilus	S 40909
LARKIN, Joseph, Conn. & Vt., wid. Hannah	W 24497
Joshua	S 16914
Lorin, Conn., Mass. & Vt	S 13716
LARNED, Thomas, wid. Hannah, BLWt. 10219-160-55	W 13608
LASELL, Josiah, wid. Lydia	W 20380
LASHBROOK or LASHBROOKS, William, wid. Zeruah, BLWt. 1376-100; & BLWt. 330-60-55.	W 24466
LATHAM, Amos	S 36683
Christopher, wid. Sabra, BLWt. 12564-160-55	W 8031
Jesper	S 13707
John	S 32967
Joseph	S 16915
William	S 13688
LATHROP, Daniel	R 6179
David, wid. Anne	W 24509
Dixwell	S 17531
Elias, wid. Dorcas, BLWt. 53753-160-55	R 6180
(Soldier applied in 1832 from Orange Co., Vt., as teamster and also substitute in Militia for father ELIAS, but six months service was not proven.)	
Elisha	S 18925
Job. (See also PRIMUS, Job.)	
Joshua, wid. Betsey	W 15786
Oliver	S 18484
LATHROP, Samuel, wid. Lois	W 16134
LATIMER, Charles, wid. Mary	R 6177
(Soldier never applied.)	
George, wid. Louisa L., BLWt. 30755-160-55	W 12061
(Soldier was pensioned in Windsor, Conn., in 1832, as waggoner under Capt. Jones.)	
Solomon	S 31806
Witherell	S 31809
LATTIMER or LATTIMORE, George, ensign under Capt. Chapman; New London Co. in 1832.	S 13701
Jehiel	S 37600
LAW, John, wid. Lydia	W 16324
Joseph, Conn. & Cont., wid. Dulana	W 21549
Nathan, wid. Eunice	W 20385
Richard, Navy service, Conn. residence	S 13699
LAWRANCE, LAWRENCE or LORANCE.	
Abigail, former wid. of Edward Sutton.	
David, wid. Marven	W 26196
James	S 40921
John, priv. under Col. Meigs; Franklin Co., Vt., in 1818; former wid. Hannah Dunham	W 26662
John, Conn. & Cont., priv. under Col. Webb; Berkshire Co., Mass., in 1818; wid. Sarah, BLWt. 120-60-55	W 5017
Jonathan	S 10966
Richard, Cont. (Conn.)	S 42807
(Also given LORANCE.)	
LAWSON, David, wid. Sarah, BLWt. 1906-160-55	W 233
Ebenezer	S 15597
Samuel	S 13708
LAY, Asa, wid. Sarah	W 20412
BLWt. 1253-300, Capt., was issued July 7, 1792, to Jonas Prentice, Assigned. No papers.	
Edward, wid. Patty, BLWt. 27585-160-55	W 20383
John	S 37149
LEACH, Hezekiah, Conn. & Cont	S 49298
James, priv. under Capt. Humphrey; New Haven Co. in 1818	S 37606
James, priv. under Col. Barton; Rutland Co., Vt., in 1832; wid. Sibbel	W 24500
Jedediah, Conn. & Cont., wid. Phebe	W 20428
Lewis	S 38909
(See also LEECH.)	
LEAMING or LEMING, David, wid. Debby	R 6223
(Soldier was pensioned from N. Y. in 1818, as priv. under Col. Swift.)	
LEASON, Jesse	S 37608
Job, BLWt. 1272-100	S 37614
LEATHERS, Joseph	S 18077
LEAVENS, Hezekiah	S 13740
Jedediah, Conn. & Vt	S 16919
LEAVENWORTH, Edmund	R 6232
Eli, wid. Sarah	BLWt. 641-400
LEBARON, Solomon, wid. Zada, BLWt. 27673-160-55	W 9126
LEBRETT, Charles	S 32997
LEDYARD, Charles	S 21347
LEE, Abner, priv. in Third Conn. Reg't., Springfield, N. Y., in 1800	BLWt. 42-100
Abner, priv. under Col. Sherman; died in 1782, Pomfret, Conn.; Nancy Davis, former wid. of. Lived in Greene Co., N. Y., in 1841.	W 16947
Andrew	S 13748
Dan, Conn. & Cont	S 37157

LEE, David, priv. under Capt. Allen; Windham Co., Vt., in 1832... S 18940
    David, priv. under Capt. Betts, Col. Butler; Barkhamstead, Conn., in 1832; wid. Fanny;
      BLWt. 21816-160-55.. W 2449
    Ebenezer.. S 42829
    Eber, BLWt. 26107-160-55.. S 13729
    Elisha.. S 10977
    Ezra, Conn., & Cont... S 37613
    Israel, Conn. & N. Y... S 10981
    John, Conn. & 1812, wid. Bridget, BLWt. 6275-160-55.. W 674
    Jonathan, wid. Mindwell, BLWt. 6454-160-55.. W 20434
    Joseph... S 18078
    Levi.. S 37167
    Matthew.. S 37605
    Miles, wid. Fanny... R 6249
      (Both soldier and widow rejected.)
    Samuel, priv. under Capt. Mattox; Norwich, N. Y., in 1818....................................... S 42837
    Samuel, wid. Betsey.. R 6242
      (Soldier never applied.)
    Samuel, Lieut., died in Litchfield, Conn., in 1829; wid. Eliza, BLWt. 19714-160-55........ W 26203
    Thomas, wid. Theodocia... W 20437
    Timothy... S 15600
    William, priv. under Capt. Mason; Manchester, Conn., in 1832................................... S 31820
    William, Cont. (Conn.), Serg't. in Conn. Line; New Haven Co., in 1818; BLWt. 1748-100.... S 13735
    William H., wid. Phebe.. W 20445
LEECH, Stephen.. R 6261
    William... S 37616
      (See also LEACH.)
LEEDS, Abram... S 15191
LEET, Allen, priv. under Col. Swift; Vt. in 1818; wid. Asenath................................... R 6265
    Luther, wid. Sybil.. W 20467
    Miles... R 6266
    Richard, Navy (Conn.).. S 38908
LEMING. (See LEAMING.)
LEONARD, Asa, Conn. & Cont., wid. Olive.. W 24518
    Benajah, wid. Mary... W 20436
    Patrick, Conn. & Penna.. S 36038
    Silas, Conn. & Mass.. S 31818
    Solomon, Conn., Cont. & Mass., wid. Sarah... W 20466
LERAY or LEROY, John, wid. Bridget, BLWt. 27644-160-55..................................... W 12104
LESTER or LESTOR, Asa.. S 16921
    Ebenezer.. S 37615
    Elihu, Conn. & Cont... S 20041
    Jeremiah... S 13743
    Joshua.. S 17535
    Nathan... S 32991
LEWES or LEWIS, Abel, Serg't. under Capt. Burroughs; Danbury, Conn., in 1832..... S 16920
    Abel, priv. & serg't. under Capt. Belcher; Rutland Co., Vt., in 1832.......................... S 22358
    Abel, priv. in Conn. Line for six yrs. under Capt. Kimball; Hartford, Conn., in 1818..... S 37160
    Abel, Conn. Sea service... R 6306
    Abiah, former wid. of Reuben NICHOLS.
    Abijah... S 37161
    Abraham... S 29287
    Andrew, priv. under Capt. Curtis; Fairfield Co., Conn., in 1832................................. S 13724
    Andrew, priv. under Capt. Ely; Middlesex Co., Conn., in 1832.................................. S 17536
    Augustus, priv. under Cols. Parsons & Ely; Haddam, Conn., in 1832........................ S 17541
    Augustus, priv. under Capt. Smith; Albany Co., N. Y., in 1832................................. S 28789
    Basil or Bazzel... S 46230
    Benjamin, Conn. & Cont., wid. Polly, BLWt. 6291-160-55... W 675
    Chauncey, BLWt. 1278-100; BLWt. 13-60-55.. S 37168
    Ebenezer, priv. Conn. Line; Oneida Co., N. Y., in 1818. (Papers withdrawn before 1870.)
    Ebenezer.. R 6310
    Ebenezer.. R 6311
    Eleazer, wid. Catharine... W 20442
    Elijah, Conn. & Cont... S 13745
    Elisha, wid. Sarah... W 24525
    Elizabeth, former wid. of Jesse CARRINGTON.
    Francis, wid. Sarah... W 20435
    Isaac.. S 15922
    Jabez, priv. under Col. Swift; Lavonia, N. Y., in 1818... S 42838
    Jabez or Jabish, priv. under Col. Buell; Farmington, Conn., in 1818.......................... S 37169
    Jacob, wid. Eunice.. W 20453
    John, Conn. & Mass... S 10979
    Joseph, priv. under Col. Welch; Stratford, Conn., in 1832... S 13721
    Joseph, Conn. & Cont., priv. in Cavalry; died in 1825 in Berkshire Co., Mass.; wid. Esther. W 20455
    Justus, Cont. (Conn.), wid. Polly, BLWt. 14506-160-55.. W 1298
    Martin... S 28788
    Messenger... S 31207
    Naboth, Cont. (Conn.), wid. Phebe... W 27810
    Nathan, Conn. & Cont.. S 13737
    Nathaniel, ensign under Col. Norton; Wolcott, Conn., in 1832................................... S 17540
    Nathaniel, disability pension in 1816; priv. Col. Pettibone.. S 20844
    Nathaniel, priv. under Col. Waterbury; N. Y., in 1832; wid. Abigail........................ W 15022
    Oliver.. S 4530
    Peter, Conn. & Cont.; Patience Peat, former wid. of... W 17463
    Philo, Conn. Sea service, wid. Charity... W 20469
    Robert, Sarah Curtis, former wid. of... W 20939
    Roger.. S 37611
    Ruth, former wid. of Aaron PHELPS.
    Samuel, priv. under Col. Lewis; Newton, N. J.; in 1832... S 1047
    Samuel, Quartermaster Serg't. in Conn. Line; Plymouth, Conn., in 1818................... S 42839

LEWES or LEWIS, Sarah, former wid. of Stephen SEWARD.
    Seth, wid. Rhoda... R 6327
        (Soldier never applied; said to have been major in Revolution, and member of Cincinnati.)
        Wid. applied in 1853.
    Stephen... S 15506
    Valentine, priv. under Col. Bradley; New London Co., in 1818................................... S 37170
    Valentine, priv. under Capt. Stanton; died in 1819 in New London Co.; wid. Sally................ W 20431
    Wait... S 42858
    Walker, wid. Sarah.. R 6330
        Soldier never applied.
    William, priv. under Col. Webb; Poultney, Vt., in 1818.. S 40926
    William, Conn. & Cont., priv. under Col. Lewis; Fairfield Co., Conn., in 1832................. S 13725
LIBERTY, Pomp... BLWt. 1761-100
    Sharp (colored), Lucy Mix, former wid. of.. R 7286
        (Soldier never applied.)
LILLEY, LILLIE or LILLY.
    Abner, Sybil Upton, former wid. of.. W 15809
    Anna S., former wid. of Asa WATERMAN.
    Amariah... S 38914
    Benjamin, wid. Mary... W 20488
    Ebenezer, Conn. & Conn. Sea service, wid. Jerusha.. W 20474
    Elijah... S 22362
    Elisha... S 15509
    John... S 40092
    Jonathan.. R 6342
    Joseph.. S 42864
    Naomi, former wid. of Simeon CUMMINGS.
    Nathan, Conn. & Mass... S 13759
    Reuben.. S 42873
LINCOLN, Elijah, Conn. & Cont... BLWt. 2077-100
    Elisha, wid. Rhuama... W 20475
    Nathan, wid. Eunice... W 20494
    Simeon, Cont. (Conn.)... S 37626
        (See also LINKON.)
LINDSEY, David.. BLWt. 854-100
        (Given also as LINDSLEY.)
    Felix.. S 37627
    Solomon, wid. Lucy.. W 4266
        (Given also as LINSLEY and LINDSLEY.)
    Stephen... S 23771
LINDSLEY, LINDSLY, LINSLEY or LINSLY.
    Abiel, wid. Anna.. R 6366
        Soldier never applied.)
    Brainard.. S 13762
    Daniel, wid. Hannah... W 20486
    David. (See LINDSEY.)
    James, wid. Sarah... W 20479
    Obed, Conn. & Privateer... R 6358
    Simeon.. S 4553
    Solomon, wid. Lucy. (See LINDSEY.)
    Stephen, wid. Deborah, BLWt. 28571-160-55... W 677
LINES, Abel, wid. Arma.. W 12130
    Abraham, wid. Sarah... W 26214
    Benjamin.. S 13752
    Ebenezer, wid. Mercy.. W 2819
    John, priv. under Capt. Wilmot; Fairfield Co., Conn., in 1818................................. S 37622
    John, private under Col. Sherman; Brookfield, Vt., in 1818; wid. Judith....................... W 26775
        (Also given as LYNDE.)
    Rufus, Conn. & Cont., wid. Tamer.. W 2820
        (See also LYNDE and LYNES.)
LINKON, John, priv. under Col. Ward; Chittenden Co., Vt., in 1832; wid. Weightstill............ W 24555
    Nathaniel... S 17546
    Samuel.. S 40941
        (See also LINCOLN.)
LINN, James, Conn. & Vt., wid. Abigail.. R 6361
    (Soldier never applied.)
    (See also LYNN.)
LINUS, Robert.. S 13750
LISCOMB, Darius, wid. Sarah, BLWt. 26607-160-55... W 774
    Nehemiah.. S 18942
    Thomas.. S 18943
LITCHFIELD, Eleazer... S 13753
    James, wid. Lucretia, BLWt. 48-100.. W 16329
LITTEL, Ebenezer.. S
    Hannah, wid. of this soldier was pensioned as the former wid. of Jonathan BADGELEY, N.J. W 8047
LITTLE, James, wid. Rosetta, BLWt. 49049-160-55... W 8256
    John, wid. Sarah.. W 26216
    Nancy, former wid. of Nathaniel ABBE.
    Samuel.. R 6386
    William... S 37179
LIVINGSTON, Isaac... S 37625
LOBDELL, Josiah... S 17552
LOCHARY, William. (See LAUGHREY.)
LOCKWOOD, Betsey, dau. of Joseph & Sarah MATHER.
    Charles, wid. Betsey or Elizabeth... W 26225
    David, priv. under Capt. Granger; Stamford, Conn., in 1832.................................... S 16453
    David, priv. under Col. Bradley; pensioned as David 2d in Stamford, Conn., in 1818........... S 37642
    David, priv. under Capt. Brown, Col. Waterbury; d. in 1825, in Fairfield Co., Conn.; wid.
        Hannah... W 20491
    David, Cont. (Conn.) priv. under Col. Lamb; New Milford, Conn., in 1818; died in 1847 in
        Litchfield Co.; wid. Sarah.. W 26223

LOCKWOOD, Drake... S 17548
 Ebenezer, wid. Ann, BLWt. 34926-160-55................................... W 8262
 Enos, wid. Sarah.. W 20499
 George... R 6403
 Gideon, wid. Lydia... R 21786
  (Soldier never applied.)
 Henry.. S 23302
 Isaac, priv. under Capt. Bell; Stamford, Conn., in 1832................... S 17553
 Isaac, priv. under Capt. Billings, Col. Swift; Brookfield, Conn., in 1832; and died there in
  1838; wid. Ann.. W 20500
 James, priv. of infantry, and serg't. of cavalry; New Canaan, Conn., in 1832... S 17554
 James, wid. Anna... R 6402
  (Soldier never applied.)
 Jared, Conn. & Cont., wid. Betsey or Elizabeth............................ W 16639
 John, Eunice Joliff, former wid. of....................................... W 26166
 Lambert, wid. Elizabeth... W 20514
 Messenger, wid. Sarah.. W 8062
 Nathan, wid. Mary, BLWt. 26141-160-55..................................... W 776
 Noah... S 13778
 Reuben... R 6405
 Reuben, wid. Mary.. W 21856
 William, wid. Jemima... W 20521
LODER, Jacob.. S 31825
LOMBARD, Justin, wid. Elizabeth, BLWt. 26002-160-55............................ W 2556
 Solomon.. S 13769
LONG, Levi, wid. Martha, BLWt. 1965-160-55.................................... W 2138
 Stephen.. S 22370
 William, Conn. Sea service & Mass., BLWt. 26296-160-55................... S 29967
LONGWELL, Stephen, wid. Jane.. W 4268
LOOMIS LOOMISS or LUMIS.
 Abner, wid. Zilpha... W 13637
 Amasa, Cont. (Conn.), wid. Ruth.. W 24595
 Asa.. S 4568
 Benjamin... R 6441
 Benjamin, Cont. (Conn.), wid. Chloe...................................... W 20511
 Dan., wid. Sarah... S 20520
 Daniel... R 6442
 Eleazer, wid. Mary... W 15035
 Elijah, wid. Rachel.. W 26221
 Epaphras... S 13791
 Ezra... S 23772
 Gamaliel... R 6444
 George, wid. Deborah, BLWt. 26830-160-55................................. W 3701
 Hannah, former wid. of Charles WEBSTER.
 Hezekiah, wid. Else.. W 15042
 Isaiah, wid. Sarah, BWLt. 33745-160-55................................... W 8054
 Israel, priv. under Col. Chapman; Coventry, Conn., in 1832............... S 23777
 Israel, Conn. & Cont., priv. under Col. Crane; Chataqua Co., N. Y., in 1818; wid. Hannah.. W 9141
 Jacob, priv. under Col. Durkee; Windham Co., Conn., in 1820.............. S 46203
 Jacob, Hampden, Mass., in 1832; wid. Thankful............................ W 15037
 Jerome, Conn., N. H. & Vt., wid. Elizabeth, BLWt. 17727-160-55........... W 1627
 John, priv. under Col. Israel Loomis; Lebanon, Conn., in 1832; wid. Mary; BLWt. 26892-
  160-55... W 775
 John, Conn. & Mass., priv. under Col. Woodbridge; Erie Co., Penna., in 1832.... S 23774
 Joseph, Cont. (Conn.)... S 18947
  BLWt. 61312-100 was issued in 1790. No papers.
  BLWt. 76-60-55.
 Lebbeus or Libbeus, Conn. & Cont.. S 28796
  BLWt. 1256-200, Lieut., was issued April 20, 1790. No papers.
 Martin... R 6446
 Oliver, priv. under Col. Hoyt; Rutland Co., Vt., in 1832................. S 13770
 Oliver, Conn. & Cont... S 13781
  (Also given LUMIS.)
 Roswell.. S 23775
 Samuel, wid. Betsey.. W 20527
 Simon, priv. under Col. Ward; Tompkins Co., N. Y., in 1832, d. in 1842; wid. Molly.... W 20518
 Simon, Conn. & Cont., Corp. under Col. Ely; Hebron, Conn., in 1832....... S 17550
 Simon, Cont. (Conn.), priv. under Col. Sheldon; German Flats, N. Y., in 1818; wid. Martha.. W 15925
 Thaddeus... R 6447
 Thomas, Conn. & Cont... S -17551
LORANCE. (See LAWRENCE.)
LORD, Abner... S 37645
 Amey, former wid. of Edward MEAD.
 Asa, BLWt. 26412-160-55.. S 29298
 Daniel, wid. Anna, BLWt. 537-160-55...................................... W 26222
 David, wid. Hannah... R 6452
  (Soldier never applied.)
 Elijah... S 37188
 Eliphalet.. S 42890
 Frederick.. S 15599
 James, BLWt. 1257-200, Lieut., was issued April 23, 1800, to Damaris Lester and others. No
  papers.
 Jeremiah, priv. under Col. Webb; Saybrook, Conn., in 1818................ S 37644
 Jeremiah, priv. under Capt. Hezekiah Parsons as Jeremiah Jr.; died in 1812; wid. Tryphena.. W 20513
 John... S 15510
 Joseph, priv. under Capt. Wolcott; East Windsor, Conn., in 1832.......... S 18094
 Joseph, priv. under Col. Ely; Chenango Co., N. Y., in 1832; wid. Caroline; BLWt. 17872-160-55. W 20517
 Mercy, former wid. of Jonathan WHALEY.

LORD, Samuel, wid. Mary, BLWt. 15198-160-55... W 24572
    Theophilus... S 37187
    Timothy... S 42898
    William, priv. under Capt. Wadsworth; Oswego Co., N. Y., in 1832; died in 1849; wid. Anna.. W 20509
    William, wid. Chloe... W 20501
        BLWt. 1255-200, Lieut., was issued Jan. 29, 1793, to Jonas Prentice, Assignee. No papers.
LOUDEN or LOWDEN or LOUDON, William, wid. Eunice... W 4270
LOUNDSBERRY, LOUNDSBURY, LOUNSBERRY or LOWNSBURY or LOUNSBURY.
    David.. S 33005
    Jacob... R 6464
    Jarius or Jarias, wid. Amelia... W 20495
    Linus, wid. Prudence... W 20492
    Nathan Munn, Conn. & Cont., wid. Sarah W., BLWt. 510-160-55...................................... W 10204
    William.. R 6465
LOVEJOY, John, wid. Anna... R 6471
    (Soldier never applied.)
    Nathan, Conn. & N. Y... S 42885
LOVELAND, Abner... S 45876
    Amos, wid. Jemima... W 8090
    Charles, wid. Mary.. W 9146
        BLWt. 1194-100; BLWt. 294-60-55.
    Daniel, wid. Mehitabel.. W 20528
    Isaac, wid. Judah.. W 8059
    James, wid. Mary... W 20496
    John.. S 13776
    Levi, wid. Esther... W 9145
    Nathan.. S 42887
    Trueman, Navy service, Conn. residence... S 37189
LOVELL, Joshua... R 6477
LOVERIDGE, William, wid. Lucinda, BLWt. 38841-160-55.. R 6479
LOVETT, Joseph or Josephus, wid. Elizabeth... W 21584
    Samuel... S 40099
LOWDEN. (See LOUDON.)
LOWNDSBURY or LOWNSBURY. (See LOUNSBURY.)
LOWREY, James.. R 6494
LOYD, Samuel, Conn. & Cont... S 13788
LUCAS, Amaziah... S 13798
    Ichabod.. S 44203
    Israel, Conn. & N. Y., wid. Mabel, BLWt. 56943-160-55... W 10205
    Samuel, wid. Abigail, BLWt. 1539-100.. R 6502
    (Soldier never applied for pension.)
    Thomas, wid. Abigail.. W 26227
    William.. S 28798
LUCE, Jonathan, wid. Parnel.. W 20544
    Lucy, former wid. of David McCLURE.
    Luke... S 31827
    Nathaniel, wid. Hannah.. W 26226
    Timothy... S 37646
    Uriah... S 13802
LUCUS. (See LUCAS.)
LUDDINGTON or LUDINGTON, or LUDENTON.
    Eliphalet.. S 31828
    Jesse... S 18098
    Lemuel.. S 41785
    Stephen, wid. Betsey, BLWt. 26651-160-55.. W 1628
    William.. S 22885
LUMIS. (See LOOMIS.)
LUNG, Joseph.. S 42902
LUTHER, Cromwell... S 42903
    Elisha, Conn. & Cont., wid. Lucy, BLWt. 24903-160-55... W 12164
    Ellis, Cont. (Conn.)... S 30555
    Levi, Conn. & Cont... S 11009
    Martin, Conn. & Cont... S 42900
LYMAN, Asa, Conn. & Conn. Sea service, wid. Mary... W 26228
    Dan, wid. Hannah, BLWt. 24921-160-55... W 1792
    Elisha, wid. Abigail, BLWt. 17712-160-55... W 8267
    Ezekiel, Conn. & Cont., wid. Mabel... W 12169
    Francis... S 16456
    John, priv. under Col. Enos; Chittenden Co., Vt., in 1832.. S 13809
    John, priv. under Col. Butler; Pembroke, N. Y., in 1818... S 42904
    Jonathan, wid. Sarah... R 6545
    (Soldier never applied.)
    Richard, priv. under Col. Huntington; Salisbury, N. H., in 1818; died in 1838, at Washington
        Co., Vt., wid. Mehitable... W 2808
    Richard, priv. under Col. Starr; died in 1802 in Orange Co., Vt.; wid. Philomela.............. W 24616
    Samuel... S 11012
    Simeon, wid. Joannah.. W 20548
LYNDE, Cornelius, Conn. Green Mt. Boys & Mass., wid. Rebecca.................................... W 20489
    (See also LINES and LYNES.)
LYNE or LYNES, David.. S 11013
    John. (See LINES.)
LYNN, David... S 32388
    John, Conn. & Cont... S 11011
    Sarah, former wid. of John TURNER.
    William.. BLWt. 1763-200
    (See also LINN.)
LYON, Asa... BLWt. 1869-200
    Ebenezer, wid. Chloe... W 24615
    Ephraim, Hannah Bradford, former wid. of... W 17366
    Gideon... R 6555

LYON, Hezekiah	R 6557
Jesse. (See Jose.)	
Job	S 17557
Josse or Jesse, Lois Morris, former wid. of	W 26273
Joseph	S 22306
Joshua	S 13811
Nathan	S 13816
Nehemiah Web, BLWt. 26052-160-55	S 15928
Noah, wid. Mary	W 16640
Stephen, wid. Abigail	W 20547
Thomas, wid. Eunice	W 12172
William, wid. Sarah	W 21597
LYPORT, Jacob	S 13813

M.

MAAR. (See MEARA.)	
McCALL, John, wid. Loruhamah	R 6599
(Neither soldier nor widow applied.)	
(Also given CALL.)	
McCARTY, Clark, wid. Mabel	W 20248
(Also given CARTY.)	
Daniel	R 6612
McCLELLAN, Samuel, wid. Nancy	W 2224
McCLURE, David, Lucy Luce, former wid. of	W 12166
McCOY, Ephraim, wid. Sarah	W 4024
John, wid. Betsey, BLWt. 19731-160-55	W 2407
McCRACKIN, Philip, wid. Mary	R 6666
(Soldier never applied.)	
McCUFF, Pomp	S 36084
McCULLOUGH, Robert	S 41833
McDONALD, Charles	S 42963
James, Abigail Russell, former wid. of	R 9095
(Neither soldier not widow applied.)	
James, Conn. & N. Y	S 13902
William, Conn., Md. & Privateer & Navy (1813)	S 34978
McEWEN, John	S 11056
(Also given as CUNE.)	
McFARLAND, Anna, former wid. of Asahel CHITTENDEN.	
McGRAGORY or McGREGORY. (See MEGREGORY.)	
McGREGOR, John, Conn. & Cont	S 38937
BLWt. 1377-300, Capt., was issued Feb. 20, 1800; certified July 17, 1815. No papers.	
McGUIRE, Peter, wid. Ruth	R 6830
Also given as MAGIRA or MAGUIRA.	
(Under name of MAGUIRA, Peter was pensioned in 1818 at Chelsea Landing, Conn., as private under Col. Sherman, Conn. Line; died in 1827.)	
McINTOSH, Timothy	S 42936
McINTYRE or McINTIRE, Henry, wid. Jane Ann, BLWt. 1880-100	W 25684
MACK, Abner, wid. Anne or Anna	W 16641
Andrew	S 17569
Benjamin	S 40958
David	S 40967
Gurdon	S 23782
Hezekiah	S 13843
Jeremiah	S 42923
Joel, wid. Susanna	W 20234
Josiah, wid. Mary	W 17103
Nehemiah, wid. Caroline	R 6572
(Soldier never applied.)	
Ralph	S 29313
Richard, wid. Betty, BLWt. 1447-100	W 9910
Zebulon, wid. Mary	W 15691
McKEE, or MACKEE, Andrew, Conn. & Cont., wid. Diantha; BLWt. 38536-160-55	W 5364
Robert, wid. Elizabeth	W 20250
McKINLEY, John, Cont. (Conn. or N. H.), wid. Sarah	W 16644
McKINSTERY or McKINSTRY, Paul	S 42952
McKINZEY or McKINSEY, George, wid. Anna, BLWt. 1418-100	W 2226
McKNIGHT, Thomas	S 15500
McLEAN, Jacob	S 40993
James	S 31854
John	BLWt. 1942-100
McMANNERS, John, wid. Lucy, BLWt. 3963-160-55	W 306
McMURPHY, Rachel, former wid. of Benjamin COLE.	
McNARY, or McNEARY, Martin	S 42953
McNIEL, Henry, wid. Nancy	W 2143
McNULTY, John	S 28594
McQUEEN, William, Conn. & Conn. Sea service, Tryphena Palmer, former wid. of	W 17424
MAHAR. (See MEARA.)	
MAIN or MAINE, David	S 16037
Ezekiel	S 22893
Henry, Hannah Wells, former wid. of	W 22567
Peres	S 2720
Rufus, Conn. & R. I	S 17561
Stephen	S 13865
William, Conn. & R. I., BLWt. 8021-160-55	S 9392
MAKER. (See MEEKER.)	
MALARY. (See MALLERY.)	
MALETT. (See MALLETT.)	
MALLBIE, Benjamin	S 2752
(See also MALTBIE.)	

MALLERY, MALLORY, MALARY, MALORY.
 Aaron, wid. Huldah, BLWt. 26459-160-55 .... W 305
 Asa, Conn. & Conn. Sea service .... S 15515
 Benajah .... S 15930
 Dan, wid. Alice, BLWt. 57646-160-55 .... W 25678
 David, Conn. & Conn. Sea service .... R 6841
 David .... R 6840
 David, Cont. (Conn.), wid. Susannah, BLWt. 26375-160-55 .... W 4274
 Gideon .... S 5727
 Jacob, wid. Sarah, BLWt. 26623-160-55 .... W 555
 James, wid. Nancy .... W 18477
 Lemuel, wid. Rebecca .... W 6785
 Levi, Cont. service but Conn. residence .... R 6847
 Nathaniel, Serg't. 3rd Conn. regiment; Erie Co., Penna., in 1828; wid. Sarah ...... W 2650
  BLWt. 1389-100 & BLWt. 126-60-55.
   (Also given MALLONY.)
 Samuel .... R 6848
 Samuel .... S 23312
 Simeon .... R 6843
 Truman, wid. Olive .... W 2824
MALLESON or MALLISON, Benjamin .... S 37209
 Ezra .... S 19731
 Roswell. (See MATTISON.)
MALLETT, MALET or MALLET, John .... S 16936
 Lewis, wid. Anne .... W 21760
  (Also given as MULLETT.)
 Miles .... S 17560
MALLONY. (See MALLERY, Nathaniel.)
MALONE. (See MELONEY.)
MALORY. (See MALLERY.)
MALTBIE or MALTBY, Zacheus or Zaccheus, wid. Jerusha .... W 27448
 (Soldier and widow died, and children received the pension alleged to be due.)
  (See also MALLBIE.)
MANLEY, Lucy, former wid. of John HITCHCOCK.
MANN, Andrew .... S 16934
 Elisha, Conn., Cont. & N. J., wid. Sarah .... W 4544
 Jabez, wid. Ruhamah .... W 4540
 Joseph .... S 16932
MANNING, Andrew .... S 16935
 Cyrus, wid. Mary .... W 17082
 Dan, wid. Lydia .... W 17099
 Diah or Dyer, wid. Anna .... W 25673
 Increase .... S 13880
 Joseph .... S 15518
 Luther, wid. Sarah .... W 3573
 Nathaniel, wid. Matilda .... W 19864
 Rockwell, wid. Sarah .... W 25670
 Samuel .... BLWt. 1050-100
 Seabury .... S 13866
 Thomas .... S 2742
 William, priv. under Col. Webb; N. Y. in 1818, transferred to Vt .... S 40980
 William, Serg't. under Col. Starr; Franklin Co., Ohio, in 1818 .... S 41814
 William .... R—
MANROSE. (See MONROSE.)
MANROW, Joseph, Conn. & N. Y .... S 11024
 Noah .... R 6881
MANSFIELD, Charles, BLWt. 43-100 .... S 44539
 Ebenezer, Cont. (Conn.), wid. Polly .... W 18484
 Hannah, former wid. of John DODD.
 John .... S 37217
  BLWt. 1382-200, Lieut., was issued May 17, 1790. No papers.
 Jonathan, Conn. & Mass., wid. Martha .... W 18471
 Joseph (Capt.) .... S 37216
 Joseph .... R 6883
 Nathan, wid. Anna .... W 20240
 Richard .... S 37210
MANVIL or MANVILLE, David .... R 6888
 Simeon .... R 6889
MAPLES, Joshua .... S 13859
 Josiah .... S 11014
 William .... S 29317
MARBLE, Thomas .... R 6896
MARCHANT, Gurdon, Cont. (Conn.), wid. Hannah .... W 20239
  (Given also as MERCHANT.)
 Joel, wid. Molly, BLWt. 26724-160-55 .... W 9928
 John, Conn. & Cont., wid. Tabitha .... W 17088
 Joseph, wid. Mary, BLWt. 29040-160-55 .... W 25679
  (See also MERCHANT.)
MARCY, Alfred .... S 13869
 Alvan .... S 13860
MARK or MARKS, Joseph. (See claim of Silas BAILEY, R. I., R 390.)
MARKHAM, Dan .... R 6904
 Hannah, former wid. of Timothy ROGERS.
 Isaac, wid. Cynthia .... W 17073
 Jeremiah .... S 20860
 John .... S 11084
 Joseph .... S 44538
 Nathaniel, wid. Hannah .... R 6905
  (Soldier was priv. under Col. Wyllys; Chatham, Conn., in 1818.)

MARSH, Allen or Allyn, wid. Mabel	W 26245
Ashbel	R 6915
David	R 6917
(Also given as MASH.)	
Edmund	S 11019
Jasper, Conn. & Mass	S 42912
Job, wid. Salome	W 17096
John, priv. under Col. Swift; Barkhamstead, Conn., in 1832	S 11036
John, priv. under Col. Talcott; Wethersfield, Conn., in 1832	S 31836
John L	S 23309
Roswell, wid. Huldah, BLWt. 6279-160-55	W 4273
Silas, wid. Mary, BLWt. 26582-160-55	W 1977
MARSHALL, Eliakim, wid. Anna	W 17095
Elijah	S 36053
Elisha, wid. Mary	W 17109
Joel	R 6931
Joseph, Conn. & R. I	S 13819
Perez, wid. Dolly	W 19857
Preserved, wid. Ruth, BLWt. 34977-160-55	W 2313
Samuel B	S 36069
Sylvanus	S 3853
Thomas, Cont. (Conn.), wid. Freelove	W 25734
MARTENUS, Goddard	S 36062
MARTIN or MARTEN, Amasa, priv. under Col. Wyllys; Windham Co., Conn., in 1832	S 18494
Amasa, Conn. & N. Y., priv. under Col. Wells; Rensselaer Co., N. Y. in 1832; wid. Sarah; BLWt. 14964-160-55	W 1630
Andrew	S 18101
Asa	S 13858
Ashbel	S 18499
Charles, Conn., Privateer & R. I.; wid. Mary; BLWt. 26175-160-55	W 1778
David	S 22382
George	S 41794
Isaac	S 16186
John	S 42910
Joseph, priv. under Col. Hosford; Winfield, N. Y., in 1832	S 13863
Joseph, priv. under Col. A. Ward; Windham Co., Conn., in 1818	S 36061
Joseph, priv. under Col. Coe; St. Lawrence Co., N. Y., in 1832; wid. Anna	W 17101
Joseph, priv. under Col. Wyllys; died in 1829 in Wyoming Co., N. Y.; widow only pensioned; wid. Lovina	W 20241
Joseph, Cont. (Conn.), priv. under Col. Hazen; died in 1834 in Clinton Co., N. Y.; wid. May A. (Also known as POLLAND.)	W 27971
Joseph P., Conn. & Cont., wid. Lucy BLWt. 13410-100 was issued April 20, 1797, & BLWt. 209-60-55.	W 1629
Joshua, wid. Elizabeth, BLWt. 6255-160-55	W 18464
Luther	S 42932
Nathan, wid. Martha	W 26239
Nathaniel Ford, wid. Naomi, BLWt. 6028-160-55	W 2142
Reuben, wid. Sally, BLWt. 21838-160-55	W 1906
Samuel	S 22383
Stephen, wid. Bethiah	W 16337
Thomas	S 2730
MARVIN, Abraham, wid. Mary	R 6985
(Soldier never applied.)	
Benjamin, wid. Urania Pamela, BLWt. 26207-160-55	W 6786
David	S 15520
David	R 6984
John C., Navy (Conn.), wid. Clarissa, BLWt. 26026-160-55	W 18480
Jonathan	S 15601
Joseph	S 15516
Matthew	BLWt. 1061-100
Nathan, Rebecca Baker, former wid. of	W 18558
Ozias, wid. Althea, BLWt. 29054-160-55	W 1885
Samuel, Conn. & N. Y	R 6986
MASH. (See MARSH.)	
MASON, Ashbel, BLWt. 2251-100	S 42916
Betsey, former wid. of Nathaniel HOVEY.	
Elisha, Cont. (Conn.), BLWt. 7202-160-55	S 13882
Elnathan, wid. Mary	W 15842
Henry, wid. Anna	W 17097
Isaac, wid. Sarah	W 17084
James	S 42919
Jonathan, Conn., Cont., N. H. & Navy; wid. Deborah	W 21773
Joseph	S 36079
Luther, wid. Hepsibah or Hephsibeth	W 9172
Robert	R 7000
MASTERS, James, wid. Esther	W 23907
MATHER, Eleazer	S 2744
Elihu, Polly Grosvenor or Grovenor, former wid. of	R 4360
(Soldier was pensioned in Madison Co., Ill., in 1831 for services as priv. under Col. Webb.)	
Increase	S 31831
John, wid. Hepzibah	W 25674
Joseph, priv. & Serg't. under Capt. Bray; Berlin, Conn., in 1832	S 15929
Joseph, wid. Sarah	W 29696
(Soldier was priv., Serg't. & Ensign; Darien, Conn., in 1832. Betsey Lockwood, daughter, was pensioned by Special Act of Congress in August, 1888.)	
Joseph, Conn. & Navy; priv. under Col. Wolcott; Chenango Co., N. Y., in 1832	S 13878
Nathaniel	S 13872
Reuben	S 29306

MATHER, Samuel, Capt. & Surgeon in Conn. Militia; Lyme, Conn., in 1832	S 33
Samuel, priv. under Capt. Hooker; Hartford, Conn., in 1832	S 13871
Samuel, priv. under Capt. Bell; Fairfield Co., Conn., in 1832	S 17568
Silvanus or Sylvanus, wid. Caroline	W 21774
Stephen, wid. Elizabeth	W 16344
Timothy	BLWt. 1711-400
MATHEWS. (See MATTHEWS.)	
MATHEWSON, Elisha, wid. Elizabeth	W 3437
MATSON, John	S 18963
MATTESON or MATTISON, David	S 40129
Hezekiah, wid. Elizabeth	W 17090
Roswell, wid. Elizabeth	W 9913
(Also given as MALLISON.)	
William, BLWt. 3990-160-55	S 9395
MATTHEWS or MATHEWS, Amos V., wid. Delila, BLWt. 75006-160-55	W 9537
Gideon	R 7019
James, Conn. Sea service, wid. Desire	W 23909
Jesse	S 36075
John, Cont. (Conn.), BLWt. 321-100	S 36077
Moses	S 17558
Thomas	S 13857
William	S 33031
MAULEY. (See MORLEY.)	
MAXAM, Adonijah, wid. Catherine	W 5345
Rejected BL.	
MAXFIELD, Edward, wid. Mary	W 17070
MAXON, Silas	S 11028
MAY, Joseph, wid. Rebecca	W 21745
Stephen	S 40976
Thomas	S 40969
MAYHEW, Elisha, Cont. (Conn.), wid. Eunice	W 8421
MAYNARD, Christopher, wid. Lucretia; also given MINARD.	
Ebenezer	S 13874
Jabez	S 36072
James	S 17567
John	S 13829
Lebbeus ori Libbeus	S 13821
Zebediah, wid. Anna; also given MINARD.	
(See also MINARD and MYNARD.)	
MAYO, Isaac, Conn. & Mass., wid. Hannah	W 23900
MEACH. (See MEECH.)	
MEACHUM or MEACHAM, Elijah, wid. Frances, BLWt. 518-160-55	W 2318
Jeremiah, wid. Chloe (Conn. & Cont.)	W 23963
(See also MEECHUM.)	
MEAD or MEADE, Abraham, Captain, papers in case of WALL, John.	
Andrew, wid. Annah	W 25700
Calvin, Conn. & N. Y	S 17580
David, Conn. & N. Y., wid. Sarah	W 19875
Ebenezer, Conn. & N. Y	S 13919
Edward, Serg't.; died in Fairfield Co. Conn., in 1797; wid. Mary	W 25694
Edward, Amy Lord, former wid. of	R 6450
(Soldier never applied; died 1820.)	
Eli	R 7073
Enos, wid. Prudence	W 19874
Israel	S 13907
Jasper	R 7076
Jasper, wid. Elizabeth	W 9956
Jeremiah	S 36119
John, wid. Elizabeth	W 19872
Joseph	S 11066
Jotham	S 22903
Levi, wid. Abigail	W 9958
Peter	S 15938
Reuben	S 16188
Samuel, Conn. & Cont., wid. Lois	W 17134
Smith	S 22904
Thaddeus	S 17584
Thomas, wid. Ellen, BLWt. 26458-160-55	W 9952
Uriah, wid. Betty, BLWt. 1775-100	W 1305
Zaccheus, wid. Deborah	W 25699
(See also MEEDS.)	
MEAKER. (See MEEKER.)	
MEARA, MAAR or MAHAR, Patrick	BLWt. 269-100
MEDCALF. (See METCALF.)	
MEECH or MEACH, Elisha, Conn. & Mass., wid. Desire	W 23950
Jacob, Conn., Privateer & R. I	S 15524
Thomas	BLWt. 1712-100
MEECHUM, Philip	S 21372
(See also MEACHUM.)	
MEEDS, Cato	S 41866
MEEKER or MEAKER, Ephraim, wid. Comfort	W 16643
(Also given as MEAKER.)	
Ichabod, Conn. & N. Y	S 13912
Joseph	S 15517
(Also given as MAKER.)	
MEGREGORY, MAGREGORY, McGRAGORY or McGREGORY.	
Joel, BLWt. 6004-160-55	S 45009
John, Conn. & Cont	S 11027

MEIGS, Abel, wid. Deborah, BLWt. 9406-160-55	W 2410
Abner, Conn. & N. H.	R 7102
John, Conn. & Cont., wid. Elizabeth	W 20255
BLWt. 1383-200, Lieut., was issued Nov. 19, 1789. No papers.	
Nathan, wid. Mabel	W 17126
Phineas or Phinehas	S 42965
Return Jonathan, BLWt. 1376-500, Colonel, was issued May 20, 1791. No papers.	
Simeon	BLWt. 44-100
Stephen	S 36122
MELONEY, John, Cont. (Conn.), wid. Betsey	W 6820
(Soldier also served in 1812.)	
(Also given as MALONE.)	
MELROSS, William, wid. Cynthia	R 7111
(Soldier never applied.)	
MENTER or MENTOR, Naomi, former wid. of Nathaniel WILLIAMS.	
Thomas	S 42973
MERCHANT, Gurdon. (See MARCHANT.)	
Thomas	S 36126
(See also MARCHANT.)	
MERICK. (See MERRICK.)	
MERIFIELD. (See MERIFIELD.)	
MERRELL. (See MERRILL.)	
MERRIAM or MERRIAN, Aaron	R 7122
Amasa	S 23317
Asaph	S 13911
(Also given as MERRIMAN.)	
Christopher	S 16959
Ephraim	S 36121
Ichabod, wid. Desire	W 15787
Marshall	S 2818
MERRICK or MERICK, Loly, former wid. of Reuben CARRINGTON.	
Luther	S 31859
MERRIFIELD or MERIFIELD, Ithamar	S 29324
MERRIL, MERRILL, MERRILS, MERRELL or MERRELLS.	
Aaron, priv. under Col. Swift; Ontario Co., N. Y., in 1818	S 42971
Aaron, Conn. & Cont., priv. under Col. Webb; Litchfield Co., Conn., in 1818	S 36698
Ashbel, Abigail Eaton, former wid. of	W 16970
Daniel, Mercy Wilcox, former wid. of	W 18451
Ephah	R 7134
Ichabod, wid. Sarah	W 17130
James, Jane Dunmore, former wid. of	W 10769
Jephtha	S 11059
Jonathan	S 23796
Mead or Medad, BLWt. 665-100	S 42969
Nathaniel	S 36115
BLWt. 6141-100, Private, was issued October 7, 1789, to Benjamin Tallmadge. No papers.	
Noah	S 5759
Noah, wid. Zulina	W 23964
Phinehas, wid. Anna, BLWt. 3798-100-55	W 18509
Reuben	S 34998
Roger, Conn. & Cont.	S 23318
Samuel, wid. Artemetia	W 20254
Solomon, wid. Jerusha	R 7127
Thomas	R 7133
William	S 11064
MERRIMAN, Asaph. (See MERRIAM.)	
Charles, wid. Anna	W 18507
Elisha, wid. Chloe	R 7135
(Soldier died in 1814 in Wallingford, Conn. Never applied for a pension.)	
George, priv. under Col. Sheldon; Clinton Co., N. Y, in 1832	S 13913
George, priv. under Cols. Ward, Douglas & Enos; Wallingford, Conn., in 1832; wid. Catharine.	W 17129
Israel	S 11007
(Also given as MERRIMON.)	
Josiah, Cont. (Conn.), wid. Lydia	W 16647
Marcus, Conn. & Privateer	S 13921
Moses, wid. Lois	W 18508
MERRIMON. (See MERRIMAN.)	
MERRITT, Ebenezer, wid. Hannah	W 17127
Reuben, wid. Mary	R 7139
(Soldier never applied.)	
MERRY, Cornelius	S 16479
MERWIN, Andrew, wid. Rhoda	W 6819
Nathan, wid. Mary	W 4282
MESSENGER, Abner	S 9022
Lemuel, wid. Abigail	W 9957
Reuben	S 36118
METCALF or MEDCALF, Dan, wid. Jedidah	W 3281
Ebenezer, priv. under Col. Hosford; New London Co. in 1832	S 18125
Ebenezer, wid. Silence	W 17128
(Also given as MEDCALF.)	
Luke, wid. Nabby, BLWt. 520-160-55	W 25702
Samuel	S 16189
MEYERS. (See MYERS.)	
MIDDILTOWN. (See MIDDLETOWN.)	
MIDDLEBROOK, John, wid. Abigail	W 804
Oliver, Navy (Conn.)	R 7159
MIDDLETOWN, Peter, BLWt. 31-100	S 36140
(Also given as MIDDILTOWN.)	

MIEL, Charles... S 28812
MIGATE. (See MYGATT.)
MILEHAM, William... S 41878
MILES, Caleb.. S 40157
    Daniel... S 16962
    Isaac, wid. Martha, BLWt. 26500-160-55.. W 19879
        (Soldier served under Col. Canfield as substitute for his father, Stephen Miles; Steuben Co., N. Y., in 1832.)
    Isaac, died in 1816 in Cortland Co., N. Y.; Serg't. under Col. Swift; never applied for pension; wid. Mary.. W 9566
    Jesse... R 7167
    John, Cont. service, but Conn. residence... S 36128
        BLWt. 1402-200, Capt.-Lieut., was issued Oct. 23, 1790. No papers.
    Lucinda, former wid. of Darius HICKOK.
    Samuel, Conn. & Conn. Sea service... S 15526
    Simon or Timon, wid. Mercy... W 17141
MILLAR. (See MILLER.)
MILLARD, Joseph, wid. Hannah... W 25705
    Leavitt or Levitt, Cont. (Conn.)... S 13935
    London.. S 13926
    Sarah, former wid. of John WHITE.
MILLER or MILLAR, Abner, wid. Ruth.. W 20259
    Benjamin... S 36146
    Caleb, Conn. & Cont.. S 18976
    Charles, Conn. & Cont.. S 36132
        BLWt. 1381-200, Lieut., was issued June 3, 1791, to Isaac Bronson, Assignee. No papers.
    Daniel.. R 7181
    David B., wid. Adah... W 16651
    Ebenezer, wid. Sarah... W 13006
    Edward... S 13942
    Elizabeth, former wid. of Amasa LADD.
    John, Conn. & Privateer, born in 1756 in Lyme, Conn... R 7209
    John, Cont. service, but Conn. residence of heir in 1830............................ BLWt. 1621-100
    John Christine, wid. Roxalana... W 25708
    Jonathan, priv. under Col. Wyllys; Detroit, Mich., in 1829...................................... S 20477
    Jonathan, priv. under Col. Wyllys; died in Nov., 1811, in Vt.; Anner Bissell, former wid. of. W 23605
        Anner's other husband was also a pensioner. (See BISSELL, Ozias, Conn., S 37764.)
    Laura, former wid. of John REDINGTON.
    Martha, former wid. of Henry KEELER.
    Rebecca, former wid. of Joshua MINOR.
    Roswel or Roswell, wid. Betsey G., BLWt. 26613-160-55... W 5375
    Sarah, former wid. of William BLAKE.
    William.. S 23324
MILLETT, Andrew Jonathan... R 7233
MILLINGTON, Samuel, wid. Christina... W 17145
MILLS, Aaron, Conn. & Mass... S 13927
    Alexander.. S 36147
    Amasa, Conn. & Cont.. S 36148
    Ann, former wid. of Benjamin DYER.
    Constantine, wid. Philecta or Philicta.. W 2151
    Elias... S 22399
    Elijah, wid. Huldah, BLWt. 9205-160-55... W 17147
    Gabriel.. S 36131
    George.. S 43002
    Jedediah, wid. Sarah.. R 7249
    John, priv. under Col. Webb; New London Co. in 1818.. S 36139
    John, priv. under Col. Webb; Tolland Co., Conn., in 1818....................................... S 36158
    John, priv. under Col. Webb; Suffolk Co., N. Y., in 1818... S 42978
    Joseph.. S 36151
        Ann Beers, wid. of above soldier, was pensioned as former wid. of her first husband, PHILLIPS, Thomas, Conn., W 25233.
    Kanah.. R 7246
    Samuel... S 28107
    Samuel F., BLWt. 26016-160-55.. S 13938
    Stephen.. S 16201
MINARD, Amos... S 33106
    Christopher, Conn. & Cont., wid. Lucretia.. W 21801
        (Also given as MAYNARD.)
    William, wid. Susannah, BLWt. 24327-160-55... W 9201
        (Also given as MINOR.)
    Zebediah, Conn. & Cont., wid. Anne.. R 7062
        (Soldier was pensioned in New London Co., Conn., in 1818 for service under Col. Huntingdon.)
        (Also given as MAYNARD.)
    (See also MYNARD and MAYNARD.)
MINER or MINOR, Aaron, wid. Hannah.. R 7256
    (Soldier was pensioned from Washington Co., Vt., in 1832 for service under Col. Wooster.)
    Amos, wid. Mary... W 16346
    Anderson, Conn. & Mass... S 21884
    Charles, wid. Rachel, BLWt. 19906-160-55.. W 21808
    Christopher... S 42991
    Clement, Anna Joy, former wid. of.. W 26682
    David, priv. under Col. Crane; Herkimer Co., N. Y., in 1832................................... S 11083
    David, priv. under Col. Smith; Tolland Co., Conn., in 1832; wid. Lydia.................... W 7463
    Ebenezer, wid. Rhoda... W 17143
    Elihu... S 36135
    Elnathan... S 41871
    Ephraim, wid. Thankful, BLWt. 26238-160-55... W 24153
    Ichabod, BLWt. 31295-160-55.. S 5765

MINER or MINOR, James, priv. under Col. Webb; New York City in 1818 .... S 23802
James, priv. under Capt. Starkweather; Stonington, Conn., in 1832...................... S 13932
James, priv. under Col. Silliman; Caledonia Co., Vt., in 1832; wid. Esther............. W 23977
John.. S 9414
Jonathan.. S 36157
Joseph, Conn. & Cont.. S 13934
Joshua, Rebecca Miller, former wid. of.. W 15081
Philip.. R 7262
Richardson, wid. Sally, BLWt. 9482-160-55... S 2414
Seth, Cont. (Conn.)... S 36152
Simeon, Conn. & R. I.. S 14857
Stephen or Steven, wid. Mary.. W 25710
  (Soldier was Gunner, and an Invalid pensioner; died in New London Co. in 1835.)
Stephen, Navy (Conn.), Mariner on ship *Alfred*. Lyme, Conn., in 1818; wid. Lydia received
  pay due him, but was never pensioned.. S 36134
Sylvester, BLWt. 652-100.. S 42985
Timothy, wid. Mary or Polly...BLWt. 34822-160-55
Titus... S 36133
William, Conn. & Privateer.. S 13930
William. (See MINARD.)
MINTER, John.. S 9027
MINUET, Peter... S 36159
MITCHEL or MITCHELL, Daniel, wid. Ruth.. R 7282
  (Soldier never applied.)
David, Cont. (Conn.).. S 42981
Elisha, Cont. service, but Conn. residence; wid. Mary........................BLWt. 512-100
George, wid. Lucy, BLWt. 38534-160-55... W 21807
Ichabod... S 41007
John Benjamin, wid. Jemima.. W 15693
Joseph, Conn. Sea service... R 7278
Joseph, Conn. & N. Y.. R 20404
Margaret, former wid. of Samuel ABBEY.
Oliver, wid. Anna... W 1632
William... S 13928
Zephaniah, Conn. & Cont... S 36155
MITTS, John. (See SMITH.)
MIX, Amos, wid. Clarinda.. W 7447
Benjamin, Conn. & Cont., wid. Esther.. W 19884
Eldad, wid. Mary.. W 20258
Elisha Corp. under Col. Swift; Northampton, N. Y., in 1818.............................. S 42977
Elisha.. R 285
Elisha, Corp. under Col. Hinman; died in Hartford Co., Conn., in 1818; wid. Amna or Anna. W 21799
Enos.. S 36141
Jesse, wid. Polly... W 20257
John.. S 13945
  BLWt. 1384-200, Lieut., was issued April 26, 1791. No papers.
Josiah.. S 2824
Levi, wid. Eunice... W 19883
Lucy, former wid. of Sharp LIBERTY.
Rufus... S 42982
Samuel, wid. Roxina... W 23986
Timothy, priv. under Col. Wyllys; Bristol, Conn., in 1832............................... S 17587
Timothy, Continental service but Conn. residence in 1818, when he was pensioned from New
  Haven, Conn.. S 36154
  BLWt. 1386-200, Lieut., was issued Sept. 24, 1790 (no papers), to Peleg Sanford, assignee.
MIZE, William... S 42983
MOFFATT, or MOFFITT, Matthew.. S 36160
MOGER, Joseph, Hulda Farlow, former wid. of... W 25567
MOLTHROP or MOLTRUP. (See MOULTHROP.)
MONGOR, Jonathan, Conn. & Cont.. S 43018
  (See also MUNGER.)
MONRO or MONROE, John, priv. under Capt. Staples; Guilford, Conn. in 1832............... S 31865
Joshua, Navy (Conn.) & Privateer.. S 9980
William... S 11112
  (In the claim of his brother, Isaac MUNROE, S 43048, this man signs himself William
  Munroe.)
  (See also MUNRO and MUNROE.)
MONROSE or MONTROSE or MANROSE, Elijah, wid. Martha...................................... W 25735
MONSON. (See MUNSON.)
MONTAGUE or MONTIGUE, Jotham or Jonathan.. S 36171
Seth, Conn. & Cont.. S 33133
MONTGOMERY, Josiah, Conn., Mass. & R. I., wid. Ruth..................................... W 15097
MONTROSE. (See MONROSE.)
MOODY, Gideon W... S 41014
MOON, Paul.. S 43028
MOOR, MOORE or MORE, Asa.. S 23817
Elisha, wid. Hannah... W 20263
Grove... S 18992
Hiram... S 7326
James... S 43032
Joel Forbus, Cont. (Conn.), wid. Rosanna.. W 17164
John.. S 41011
Joseph.. S 33118
Margaret, former wid. of Joseph B. CLINTON.
Peter, Conn. & Cont... R 20408
  (Also given as MORE.)
Philander... S 36162
Rodrick, wid. Mary.. W 9578
Simeon.. S 40181
William... S 22913

MOREDOCK. (See MURDOCK.)
MOREHOUSE or MOORHOUSE, Aaron... S 13972
   Abraham.. S 13988
   David, wid. Rebecca... R 7365
      (Soldier was pensioned in 1832, in Sharon, Vt., as priv. and musician under Col. Pease.)
   David, priv. under Col. Canfield; Steuben Co., N. Y., in 1832, where he died in 1839; wid.
     Tryphena... W 20265
   Gershom, BLWt. 34851-160-55.. S 11116
   Grummon... S 13955
   Peter, wid. Phebe.. W 21812
   Samuel, wid. Anner.. W 25723
      (Soldier never pensioned; died in 1830 in Fairfield Co., Conn.; was priv. under Col. St.
     John.)
   Samuel, wid. Mary... W 25722
      (Soldier never pensioned; died in 1830 in Fairfield Co., Conn.; was priv. under Capt.
     Nash, Coast Guards.)
   Stephen, priv. under Capt. Marvin; Norwalk, Conn., in 1832................................. S 17593
   Stephen, priv. under Col. Waterbury, N. Y. in 1832.. S 29330
   Thaddeus or Thadeus, wid. Anne. BLWt. 7093-160-55...................................... W 5393
   Thomas... S 17596
   William, wid. Ann... W 17172
MORELY. (See MORLEY.)
MOREY, Ephraim, Conn. & N. H... S 19402
   Jerusha, former wid. of Joseph GREEN.
   Robert... S 17591
   Ruth, former wid. of Wait DEMING.
MORGAN, Asahel or Ashel.. S 9032
   Asher.. S 13974
   Daniel... S 36163
   David.. S 16976
   Ebenezer, Conn. & Cont., wid. Olive... W 17178
   Ephraim, wid. Elizabeth. BLWt. 8468-160-55.. W 2625
   James.. S 20887
   Jesse, priv. under Col. Webb; Lorain, Ohio, in 1832.. S 5099
   Jesse, priv. under Col. Swift; Wayne Co., Penna., in 1832................................. S 5770
   John, Conn. & Privateer.. S 17588
   Jonathan... R 7380
   Jonathan, wid. Esther.. R 7375
      (Soldier was not pensioned; died in 1828 in Litchfield Co., Conn.)
   Joseph, wid. Hannah.. W 26287
     BLWt. 6135-100, Serg't, was issued April 13, 1798. No papers.
   Joseph, priv. Col. Grosvenor, Conn. in 1832; died there in 1834; wid. Mabel............. W 20266
   Joshua, wid. Wealthy or Welthy.. W 16658
   Lott, wid. Keziah... W 17174
   Lucy, former wid. of Jehiel GALPIN.
   Nathan, wid. Abigial.. W 17165
   Nicholas, wid. Phebe, BLWt. 6267-160-55... W 10532
   Seth, wid. Desire.. W 17156
   Timothy... R 7390
   William, wid. Lucy... S 13970
     Wid. was R. 7383.
   William A., wid. Sarah, BLWt. 6437-160-55... W 1308
MORISON. (See MORRISON.)
MORLEY, MAULEY or MORELY, Daniel... S 40180
   Dimick.. S 13992
   Elijah.. S 36078
     (Also given as MAULEY.)
   John, Cont. (Conn.)... S 40176
   Thomas.. S 18511
MORRIS or MORRISS, Andrew, Conn. Sea service, wid. Lucretia........................... W 1984
   Charles, wid. Sarah, BLWt. 26054-160-55... W 9207
   David, priv. under Col. Wells; died at Goshen, Conn. in 1833; pension paid his widow Dinah.. S 44542
   David, priv. and serg't. under Capt. Hepburn; died in 1810; wid. Mary..................... W 25728
   Edmund, Conn. Sea Service... S 17590
   James, priv. under Col. Enos; Orange Co., Vt., in 1832..................................... S 16204
   James, Rhoda F. Wheeler, former wid. of... W 2035
     BLWt. 1378-300, Capt., was issued October 7, 1789. No papers.
   John, wid. Evia.. S 13957
   Lois, former wid. of Jesse or Jose LYON.
   Robert, Conn. & Cont... S 43019
MORRISON or MORISON, James... S 13971
   Roderick... S 16205
   William Cont. (Conn.) wid. Margaret, BLWt. 93-60-55..................................... W 1058
MORS or MORSE, Abiel, wid. Lucy, BLWt. 26114-160-55..................................... W 10217
   Charles, wid. Anna, BLWt. 26237-160-55.. W 23996
Darby. (See MOSS.)
   David, wid. Sarah, BLWt. 26775-160-55... W 1982
     (Also given as MORSS.)
   Elihu... S 23812
   Isaac... S 23813
   James, priv. under Col. Durkee; Canterbury, Conn., in 1818............................... S 43039
   James, Corp. under Greene; wid. in Providence, R. I., in 1836; wid. Bethiah............. W 24156
   Jedediah... R 7440
   John, Conn. & N. H., wid. Anna or Anne... W 24019
   Moses.. S 18510
   Rufus, wid. Rebecca.. W 20262
     (Also given as MORS.)
MORTON, Alexander, wid. Ruth... W 24157

MOSES, Ashbel, wid. Esther... W 17170
   Enam, Cont. (Conn.), wid. Catharine.. W 20267
   Ezekiel, wid. Eunice.. W 4551
   Martin, wid. Lydia... W 1633
   Seba.. S 13989
   Shubel, wid. Elizabeth... W 17151
MOSHER, Joel.. S 36167
   John... S 43024
   Stephen.. S 36168
MOSS, Benoni, wid. Sarah.. W 25714
   Daniel, BLWt. 810-100... S 40174
   Darby.. R 7434
     (Also given as MORSE.)
   Elizabeth, former wid. of Reuben CARTER.
   Isaiah.. S 43738
   John, Conn. & Vt., wid. Mary, BLWt. 38538-160-55... W 25730
   Levi, wid. Martha.. W 17166
   Reuben, Esther Tyler, former wid. of, BLWt. 94-100.. W 6329
   Thomas, wid. Lucy... R 7459
     (Soldier never applied.)
MOTT, Eunice, former wid. of Henry WILLIAMS.
   Lent.. R 7464
   Lyman, wid. Rebecca... W 15100
   Samuel... S 43011
MOTTHROP. (See MOULTHROP.)
MOULTHROP, MOULTHROUP, MOLTRUP, or MOTTHROP.
   John, Conn. & Cont.. S 36081
   Moses, wid. Mary, BLWt. 35837-160-55.. W 5383
   Reuben, wid. Hannah... W 17177
MOULTON, Gurdon.. S 43010
   Salmon... S 23810
   Stephen, BLWt. 3958-160-55... S 49278
     (This soldier's widow, Nancy, was pensioned for service of her former husband, Henry
       KNEELAND, or KICKELAND, Mass., W 5681.)
   William, Conn., Cont. & N. Y.. S 43026
     BLWt. 1380-300, Capt., was issued August 8, 1789 to John Doty, Assignee. No papers.
MOWREY or MOWRY, Reuben B., Conn. & Mass... S 2875
MOXLEY, Joseph. (See claim of Prudence, wid. of Benjamin DABOLL, who was first pensioned as the former wid. of Joseph MOXLEY.)
MOYER, George, Conn., Conn. Sea service & Mass. Sea service....................................... S 18135
MUDGE, Abraham, wid. Phebe.. W 15694
MULKINS, Mary, former wid. of Joseph ROBINS.
MULLETT, Lewis. (See MALLETT.)
MUMFORD, Henry, Conn. & Mass... S 11125
MUN. (See MUNN.)
MUNGER, Bela, Cont. (Conn.).. S 43047
   Billy, wid. Deborah.. W 15931
   Eber... S 15541
   Elias... S 18996
   Jehiel.. S 31875
   Lyman, wid. Eunice.. W 18544
   Timothy, wid. Loraine... W 16352
     (See also MONGOR.)
MUNN or MUN, Asa.. S 11123
   David, wid. Lois... W 17191
   Gideon... R 7491
MUNRO or MUNROE, Daniel, BLWt. 2424-100.
   Isaac.. S 43048
   John, BLWt. 1219-100.. S 43055
   John, wid. Susannah... W 25738
   Joseph... S 36182
   Josiah... S 11105
   Leonard, Cont. (Conn.).. S 40188
   William.. S 11112
MUNSELL or MONSELL or MUNSEL, Alpheus, wid. Eunice.. W 17187
   Benjamin.. R 7497
   Calkins.. S 11124
   Hezekiah, wid. Irena... W 17184
   Levi, wid. Lucretia.. W 1917
MUNSON, Almond or Almun... S 41909
   Elisha, wid. Mabel... W 17183
   Eneas, Conn. & Cont... S 34
     BLWt. 1387-300, Surgeon's Mate, was issued May 31, 1791. No papers.
   Ephraim, wid. Deborah... W 26260
   Isaac.. S 40187
   Jonathan, wid. Sally, BLWt. 26680-160-55.. W 308
   Medad... S 17601
   Moses.. S 47547
   Orange... S 43045
     BLWt. 6139-100 was issued in 1789. No papers. BLWt. 133-60-55.
   Samuel, Conn. & Penna., wid. Martha.. W 19902
   Stephen, wid. Elizabeth.. W 13749
   Theophilus, wid. Sarah, BLWt. 185-300.
     (Also given as MONSON.)
   Thomas E.. S 36181
   William, "Hazen's Reg't. of Conn. Quota." BLWt. 1564-300, Capt., was issued Feb. 27,
     1797. No papers.
   Wait... S 13995
   Wilmot, Conn. & Privateer... R 701

MURDOCK or MOREDOCK, Daniel, wid. Lurana	W 18541
Elisha	R 7506
(Also given as MOREDOCK.)	
Jonathan, wid. Lucretia	W 20260
MURRAY, MURREY, or MURRY, Amasa	S 36184
Benjamin, wid. Lucretia	W 24021
Hannah, former wid. of Abel CLARK.	
Ichabod	S 43049
Jasper	S 1400
John	S 41022
Solomon	S 43058
Stephen	S 23329
MYERS or MEYERS, Henry, Conn. & N. Y.	R 7538
Josiah, Conn. & N. Y., Lydia Granger, former wid. of	W 17032
MYGATT or MIGATE, Elisha, BLWt. 265-100	S 36185
Jonathan, Conn. & Cont., wid. Prudence	W 17194
(Also given MIGATE.)	
Zebulon, Bathsheba Hubbard, former wid. of	W 18078
MYNARD, Lemuel	S 43060
(See also MAYNARD and MINARD.)	

N.

NAILS, John, wid. Sally	W 20274
NASH, Daniel	S 11130
Joel	S 9983
Jonathan, wid. Eunice	W 10778
Joseph	S 29344
Noah, wid. Ann, BLWt. 34976-160-55	W 26568
Peter (colored), wid. Lydia	R 7558
(Soldier never applied.)	
Silas, Hannah Tyre, former wid. of, BLWt. 28545-160-55	W 608
NEAL, William	S 4599
NEARING, Henry, wid. Jane	W 6839
John	S 43071
Joseph, wid. Julia, BLWt. 26205-160-55	W 6840
NEDSON, James	S 36188
NEEDAR, Toney, Conn. & Cont., wid. Phillis, BLWt. 19813-160-55	W 7073
(Also given as Anthony EDER.)	
NEFF, Oliver	R 7573
NEGRO, Caesar, or SHELTON, Caesar or Cezer.	
NEGRO, Caesar, or CLARK, Caesar, Negro.	
NEGRO, Cato, or KENT, Cato.	
NEGUS or NIGUS, John, Conn. Sea service, Desire Baldwin, former wid. of	W 17228
NELSON, John, Conn. & N. Y., wid. Amy	W 24340
NETTLETON, Benajah	R 7601
Caleb, wid. Lois	W 2659
John	S 14020
Josiah	S 36187
Nathan	S 11133
William, wid. Zillah	W 17399
NEVINS, David, Conn. & Cont	S 14004
NEWBERRY or NEWBURY, Amasa	S 11131
Jeremiah	S 43072
Stedman	S 14021
NEWCOMB, Azariah	R 7614
Bethuel, wid. Mabel	W 26572
Eleazer	S 36186
Luther, Conn., Mass. & Privateer	S 18527
Thomas, Conn. & Navy, wid. Sylvia, BLWt. 8388-160-55	R 7615
(Both soldier and widow were rejected as six months' service was not proven.)	
NEWELL, Daniel, wid. Nancy	W 24328
Ebenezer	S 43066
Lydia, former wid. of Ezekiel WILLIAMS.	
Mark	S 36190
Nathaniel	S 14011
Norman, Cont. (Conn.)	S 40199
Riverius or Reverius, wid. Abigail, BLWt. 34859-160-55	W 805
Robert, Conn. & Cont., wid. Lydia, BLWT. 34915-160-55	W 19917
Seth	R 7618
Theodore, wid. Hannah, BLWt. 14671-160-55	W 5417
NEWHALL, Joshua, Conn., Cont. & Navy	S 36189
NEWMAN, Abraham, Conn. & N. Y., wid. Lucinda	W 24332
Jonathan, wid. Lucy, BLWt. 44507-160-55	W 5418
Rufus, wid. Polly	W 1461
Zadoc	S 15544
NEWTON, Asahel, wid. Versalle or Versally	W 15696
David	R 7633
Elias, wid. Alice	W 4298
Israel, BLWt. 1963-160-55	S 19002
James	S 22919
Joel	S 23336
John	S 17602
NICHOL or NICHOLS or NICHOLLS, Daniel, priv. under Col. Waterbury; Kingston, N. Y., in 1832	S 11141
Daniel, priv. under Col. Elmore; Stamford, Conn., in 1818	S 36191
Daniel	R 76413
Daniel	R 76453
Daniel, pensioned as Daniel 1st in New Milford, Conn., in 1818 for service under Col. Webb; died there 1819; wid. Esther	W 17402
Ebenezer, wid. Martha	W 2231

NICHOL or NICHOLS or NICHOLLS, Eli, 58 in 1818 at Windsor, N. Y............................. S 14024
    Eli, priv. under Col. Swift; died in 1845, aged 84 yrs., in Trumbull, Conn.; his daughter, Mrs.
      Sally Smith, obtained a pension from 1832 to date of his death............................. S 43076
    Ely, Conn. & Cont... S 22418
    Enos... S 14025
    Ephraim... S 23340
    James.. R 7645
    James, Conn., Navy & R. I.. S 40206
    Jesse.. S 11142
    John, priv. under Capt. Miles; Oneida Co., N. Y., in 1832...................................... S 23338
    John, priv. under Capt. Hoyt; Stamford, Conn., in 1832; wid. Mary............................. W 2685
    Jonathan... S 39829
    Joseph, wid. Nancy.. R 7655
      (Soldier never applied.)
    Mandfield, Cont. (Conn.)... S 41032
    Noah, wid. Abigail, Conn., Cont. & N. H... W 21847
    Philip, wid. Abiah... W 17403
    Reuben, Abiah Lewis, former wid. of... W 21566
    Robert... S 40209
    Samuel, wid. Sibbel.. W 5419
    Silvanus... S 14027
    Stiles, wid. Phebe... W 2656
    William.. S 17607
NICHOLSON, Francis, Rachel Weston, former wid. of.. W 6454
NICKERSON, Jonathan... S 28824
NIGUS. (See NEGUS.)
NILES, Dan.. S 21397
    Elisha, wid. Naomi.. W 26577
    Jehiel... S 43074
    Nathaniel.. S 36193
    Robert, Conn. Sea service & Privateer... S 36194
    William.. S 19006
NOBLE, Abigail, former wid. of Timothy HIBBARD.
    Elijah... S 36198
    Gideon, Lucy Hollister, former wid. of, BLWt. 38532-160-55...................................... W 24445
    Goodman, wid. Sarah... R 7681
      (Soldier was pensioned in 1818 at Cairo, N. Y., for service under Col. Swift; dropped on
      account of property; pensioned again in 1832 at Cairo.)
    Lyman, Conn. & Boat service on Lake Champlain, Elizabeth Whiting, former wid. of......... W 22613
    Nathan... S 43092
    William.. S 43093
NOBLES, Azer... S 4620
    Roswell, wid. Anna.. R 7682
      (Soldier was pensioned in 1832 at Simsbury, Conn., for service under Col. Ward.)
NOONEY, James, wid. Sarah... R 7687
    (Neither soldier nor widow applied.)
NORMAN, John, Conn., Conn. Sea service & R. I... S 30006
NORRIS, Henry, Navy (Conn.), wid. Desire.. W 17407
    John, wid. Ruth... R 7705
      (Soldier was pensioned in 1832 at Ashtabula, Ohio, where he died in 1840, for service under
      Capt. Hatch.)
    Samuel, Conn. Sea service & Mass., wid. Lucy... W 13772
    Thomas, Conn. Sea service, wid. Sarah.. W 3445
NORTH, Abi, former wid. of Justus FRANCIS.
    Abijah, Conn. & Cont., wid. Sarah, BLWt. 28632-160-55... W 2232
    Levi, Conn. & Cont.. S 14041
    Seth... S 36197
    Simeon... S 23342
NORTHAM or NORTHUM, Asa, Conn. & Mass.. S 5834
    (Given as NORTHUM.)
    John... S 14040
    Jonathan, Conn. & Cont... S 14030
    Samuel, Conn. & Cont... S 14034
NORTHROP or NORTHRUP, Amos.. S 22424
    Andrew, wid. Clarissa... W 17410
    Elijah... S 36199
    Gideon... S 22922
    Heth, wid. Ann, BLWt. 26723-160-55.. W 17408
    Isaac.. S 36196
    Joseph, Conn. & Cont... S 23826
    Joshua, Phoebe Blackman, former wid. of.. W 10419
    Lemuel... S 18530
    Lucy, former wid. of Dan HATCH.
    Stephen, Conn. & N. Y., wid. Rhoda... R 7715
      (Soldier was pensioned in 1832 in Madison Co., N. Y., for service as Serg't. and Q. M. Serg't.
      under Col. Waterbury.)
    Willson.. S 43082
NORTHWAY, George.. S 15548
    Ozias, wid. Sarah.. W 2419
NORTON, Abel, wid. Lucy.. W 17404
    (Soldier died in 1803 at Guilford, Conn.; served under Col. Swift.)
    Abel, Conn. & N. Y., priv. under Col. Webb; Greene Co., N. Y., in 1832......................... S 14042
    Abraham... S 46429
    Ambrose, wid. Bethiah... W 16356
    Benjamin, wid. Elsey.. W 2234
      (Soldier was pensioned in N. Y. in 1818.)
      BLWt. 1581-200, Lieut., was issued October 16, 1789, to Theodosius Fowler, Assignee.
      No papers.
    Benjamin, priv. serg't. and Ensign; died in 1812; never pensioned; wid. Azubah.............. W 4299
    Charles.. S 28825

NORTON, David, wid. Lois... W 16663
    (Soldier died in 1829 in Oneida Co., N. Y., was never pensioned.)
  David, Conn. & N. Y... S 14036
  Eber... R 7717
  Elias.. S 4624
  Elijah, wid. Rebecca... W 20278
  Elnathan, wid. Ruth... W 19926
  Elon... S 43090
  Giles, BLWt. 28524-160-55.. S 29352
  Isaac.. R 7719
  Jabez.. S 36195
  Jared, wid. Sarah... W 26585
  John, wid. Lucretia... W 15134
  Jonathan.. S 14028
  Joseph.. S 11146
  Levi... R 7722
  Nathan, wid. Experience.. W 17405
  Noah W.. S 17608
  Oliver, wid. Martha... R 7724
    (Soldier was pensioned in Oneida Co., N Y., in 1832 for service under Capt. Bradley, Col. Strong.)
  Oliver, wid. Susanna.. R 7726
    (Soldier was pensioned in 1832 in Washington Co., N. Y., for service under Capt. Skinner, Col. Stowers.)
  Ozias, priv. under Col. Mott; New Haven Co., Conn., in 1832................................ S 16990
  Ozias, priv. under Col. Baldwin; Portage Co., Ohio, in 1832................................ S 17609
  Samuel, wid. Phebe.. W 26582
  Seba, Conn. & N. Y., wid. Margaret... W 19927
  Selah, wid. Anne or Anna.. W 17409
  William... S 43083
  Zadock or Zadok, Conn. & Vt., wid. Anna.. W 19928
NOTT, Abraham, wid. Abigail... W 10821
  (Also given as KNOTT.)
  Epaphras, Conn. & Cont.. S 14035
NOYES, John, BLWt. 1580-400, Surgeon, was issued May 29, 1789, to John Noyes. No papers.
NUGEN, John, BLWt. 2242-100; and S-.
NUGENT or NUGEON, John, wid. Elizabeth... W 26586
NYE, Daniel... S 21903
  David... S 18532
  Elijah.. R 7748
  Jonathan, wid. Deodama... W 17412
  Solomon, wid. Mary, BLWt. 26345-160-55... W 9607
    (NOTE.—Mary received Bounty land also on account of the services of her former husband, Samuel WOODS, Mass. S 41367.)

O.

OAKLEY, Gilbert, wid. Eleanor... W 26590
  John, wid. Catharine.. W 19934
  Miles... S 18533
O'CAIN, Anthony F., or FRANCOIS, Anthony.. R 7765
  Name also appears as Anthony FRANSWOI, FRANSEWAY or FRANSUAY.
ODELL, Isaac, wid. Grizel... W 21863
  Nathan.. S 17610
  William... S 14048
OGDEN, David, wid. Sally.. W 17414
  Edmond, Conn. & Navy, wid. Sibal... R 7777
    (Soldier never applied and died in 1799; widow's claim rejected for insufficient proof of service.)
  Joseph.. S 38277
  Sturges or Sturgess... S 14049
OLCOTT, Isaac... S 31890
  Jared... S 47577
  Jonathan.. S 16996
OLDS, Aaron... S 41035
  Daniel, wid. Lois... W 4557
  Ebenezer, Cont. (Conn.)... S 43099
  Hannah, former wid. of Thomas STEPHENSON.
  John, Conn. & Cont.. S 43102
OLMSTEAD or OLMSTED, Ashbel... S 23346
  Benjamin, wid. Content.. W 20280
  Daniel, wid. Rosanna.. W 19936
    (Also given as OLLMSTED.)
  Ebenezer, wid. Esther... W 9611
  Francis, Conn. & Cont... S 40224
  Gamaliel, Conn. & Cont., wid. Elizabeth, BLWt. 30918-160-55................................ W 5435
  Gloriana, former wid. of Aarom Keeler.
  Isaac, wid. Sarah... W 26595
  James, BLWt. 1608-200, Lieut., was issued Sept. 1, 1790, to Theodosius Fowler, Assignee. No papers.
  James, wid. Mary.. R 7779
    (Soldier died in 1811; neither he nor wid. applied for pension, but son Henry.)
  James, priv. under Col. Swift; Onondaga Co., N. Y., in 1832................................ S 5857
  John.. R 7803
  John Bates, wid. Theodosha or Adosha... R 7801
    (Neither soldier nor wid. applied.)
  Joseph.. S 11157
  Matthew or Mathew... S 14054
  Nehemiah.. S 43739
  Oliver, Conn. & Cont., wid. Mercy.. W 26594
  Roger... S 5858
  Timothy... S 43740

OLNEY, Peter, wid. Tabitha	W 21864
ORCUTT, John	S 15949
Solomon, Conn. & Cont	S 41037
Stephen, wid. Mary, BLWt. 8450-160-55	W 26598
William	S 4632
ORMS, Jonathan, wid., Lura or Laura, BLWt. 18200-160-55	W 5632
ORMSBEE, ORMSBE or ORMSBEY, or ORMSBY.	
Ebenezer, Conn. & R. I. wid. Experience, BLWt. 7076-160-55	W 21873
Elijah	S 14060
Stephen	S 45039
ORR, Alexander, Conn. & Mass	S 34456
ORSBORN. (See OSBORN.)	
ORTON, Azariah	S 11161
Darius	S 14055
Eliada	S 41933
Lemuel, Cont. (Conn.) wid. Sibbel	W 4753
ORVIS, David	S 14057
Roger	S 43751
Samuel, wid. Caroline	W 25359
OSBON, OSBORN, OSBORNE, or ORSBORN.	
Abel, wid. Annah	W 20285
Abijah	R 7821
Abraham, Conn., N. Y. & Privateer	S 14061
Ebenezer	S 15550
Edward, wid. Elizabeth	W 20282
Eli	S 43743
Eliada, wid. Abigail	W 1639
Ethan, BLWt. 34953-160-55	S 4635
Ezekiel, wid. Lucretia, BLWt. 5205-160-55	W 26600
Ezra, wid. Abigail	W 15147
Isaac, Conn. & Mass., wid. Edna., BLWt. 28579-160-55	W 26602
(Given as ORSBORN.)	
Jacob	S 29355
Jeremiah, priv. under Col. Denison; Fairfield Co., Conn., in 1832	S 31894
Jeremiah, Continental service but Conn. residence & Agency in 1818; Serg't. under Col. Lamb; Weston, Conn., in 1818	S 38278
John	S 33408
(Also given as OSBON.)	
Pensioned as John 1st in Lanesboro, Mass., in 1818 for service under Col. Webb.	
John, priv. under Col. Waterbury; Fairfield Co., Conn., in 1832 and died there in 1843; wid. Jerusha	W 21875
John, Serg't., Ensign, and Lieut., Litchfield Co., Conn., in 1832 and died there in 1833; wid. Rhoda	W 21877
Joseph	S 23348
Joshua, wid. Diana	W 4559
Josiah, Conn. & N. Y	S 4638
Levi	S 14065
Naboth, Conn. & Mass., wid. Susanna	W 21878
Nathan, teamster under Capt. Loomis, Greene Co., N. Y., in 1832	S 11164
Nathan, priv. under Col. Gould; Delaware Co., N. Y., in 1832	S 23347
Nathaniel, wid. Elizabeth	R 16862
(Soldier never applied.)	
Samuel, priv. under Col. Evans; Adams Co., Penna., in 1832	S 7284
Samuel, priv. under Col. Willet; Greene Co., N. Y., in 1832; BLWt. 28611-160-55; wid. Elizabeth	W 6862
Widow later married Moses L. PENDELL, after whose death pension was renewed.	
Shadrach, Conn. & Cont., wid. Aletta or Alletta	W 21879
Stephen, Cont. (Conn.), wid. Apame, BLWt. 18380-160-55	W 9216
Thomas, wid. Lovisa	W 17415
White, Conn. & Cont	S 14066
William, Sarah H. Taylor, former, wid. of	R 10431
(Neither soldier nor wid. applied. Sarah's other husband was pensioned on account of disability contracted in service in 1812. See case of TAYLOR, William B., S 6202.)	
Zebedee	S 30012
OSGOOD or OZGOOD, Jeremiah, BLWt. 18014-160-55	S 7283
Josiah	S 19415
OTIS, Barnabas, Conn. & Cont	S 9612
Edward	S 32425
James, Navy service; Conn. Agency and residence	S 38276
John T	S 16998
Joseph	S 27276
(In American State Papers, Vol. 9, p. 153, Joseph Otis, private, in Col. Zebulon Butler's regiment, afterwards transferred to Webb's reg't.; enlisted 1777 for the war. Wounded by musket ball Feb., 1781, at Morrisiana; res. Branford, Conn.)	
Richard, Cont. (Conn.)	S 45043
OVAITT, William, wid. Sarah	W 24376
(See also OVIATT.)	
OVERTON, Seth, Conn. & Privateer	R 7839
Thomas	S 36201
OVIATT or OVIT, or OVIUTT, Ebenezer, wid. Eunice	W 21885
Job	S 38275
(Given as OVIT.)	
Nathan	S 14068
(Also given as OVIUTT.)	
Samuel, Cont. (Conn.), wid. Mindwell or Murdwell	W 10846
(See also OVAITT.)	
OWEN, Alvin or Alven	S 43733
Alvan	R 7840
Daniel, wid. Lydia	W 18478
Eleazer or Elezer	S 30628

OWEN, Elijah, Berkshire Co. Mass., in 1832; son of Lieut. Elijah (W 13787).................. S 30013
 Elijah, Lieut. of Guard at Newgate prison in 1776; wid. Lydia............................ W 13787
 Frederick... S 43762
 Gideon, wid. Nancy... W 20288
 John, wid. Lydia... W 10221
  (Also given OWENS.)
 Samuel, Conn., Cont., Mass. & Vt... S 11168
 Thaddeus, Conn. & Cont. wid. Abigail... R 1687
  (Soldier never applied.)

P.

OZGOOD. (See OSGOOD.)
PACKARD, Asahel, wid. Priscilla, BLWt. 26228-160-55.. W 1312
 Nehemiah... S 43787
PACKER, Eldredge, wid. Sabrina... W 21888
 John, Groton, Conn., in 1818, as John 2d; 65 in 1820, and had wife, named Esther......... S 38291
 John, wid. Hannah, b. 1735, d. 1835, New London Co., Conn.; Groton, Conn., in 1832...... W 26284
PAGE or PAIGE, Ann, former wid. of Thomas DOUGAL.
 Edmund, wid. Sarah... R 7873
  (Soldier never pensioned.)
 Elias.. S 23356
 Gad, wid. Abigail.. W 17418
 Jared.. R 7871½
 John... S 41936
 Joseph, Conn., Conn. Sea service and Navy.. R 7866
 Luther... S 46329
 Luther, wid. Rachel.. R 7872
  (Soldier never pensioned.)
 Phinehas, wid. Jeruiah... W 18725
 Timothy.. S 11186
 Titus.. S 23836
PAINE or PAYNE, Edward... S 3625
 Eleazer, wid. Aurel.. R 8021
 Eli.. S 14093
 Isaac.. S 36208
 Thomas, wid. Elizabeth... R 7876
  (Soldier never pensioned.)
  (See also PAYN and PAYNE.)
PAINTER, Deliverance... S 15567
 Elisha...BLWt. 1603-400
 Thomas, Conn. Sea service & Privateer.. S 18536
PALMER, Aaron, wid. Mary... R 7895
  (Soldier never pensioned.)
 Abraham.. S 43768
 Benjamin, Branford, Conn., in 1832... S 17616
 Benjamin, Voluntown, Conn., in 1832.. S 31895
 Benjamin, wid. Sarah... R 7907
  (Neither soldier nor widow, but daughter, Sally Jakway, of Ashtabula Co., Ohio, applied in 1851.)
 Chilion, Cont. (Conn.), wid. Lydia... W 2629
 Chilleab, wid. Mary, BLWt. 11162-160-55.. W10365
 Daniel, Conn. & Privateer.. S 7298
 David, wid. Anne... W 18709
 Edward, wid. Delia... W 18695
 Elijah, Conn. & Conn. Sea service, widow Polly, BLWt. 33533-160-55....................... R 7885
 Elisha, wid. Eunice, BLWt. 36561-160-55.. W 26287
 Ephraim, Conn. & N. Y.. S 8940
 George, Chittenden Co., Vt., in 1832... S 16221
 George, wid. Hannah, teamster, Otsego Co., N. Y., 1832, d. 1835.......................... W 17419
 George, Conn. & Privateer.. R 7887
 Henry, Conn. & N. Y.. S 14102
 Humphrey, wid. Eunice, BLWt. 24151-160-55.. W 4756
 Isaac, wid. Hannah... W 21909
 James, Conn., Navy & Privateer, widow Pamela... W 19969
 Jared, Conn. & Cont., BLWt. 164-60-55.. S 23358
 Jesse, Conn. & N. Y., wid. Abigail... W 18707
 Joel... S 38979
 John, Chittenden Co., Vt., in 1832... S 17189
 John, Greene Co., N. Y., in 1818... S 43807
 Jonah.. S 41049
 Joseph, wid. Eunice, BLWt. 6274-160-55... W 13793
 Lazarus, wid. Rachel... W 19952
 Levi, wid. Sarah... W 16368
 Louisa, former wid. of Silas HOLMES.
 Marshall, Eunice Fox, former wid. of... W 17918
 Milo... R 7897
 Nathan... S 43767
 Nathan... R 20422
 Nehemiah, Conn. & Privateer, wid. Anna S., BLWt. 29012-160-55............................ W 9227
 Ozias or Osias, Conn. & Mass... S 7294
 Param or Parrum.. S 36205
 Reuben... S 14091
 Samuel, Montville, Conn., in 1832.. S 14108
 Samuel, N. Y. in 1818.. S 43769
 Samuel, wid. Thankful.. W 17420
  Soldier was pensioned in Stonington, Conn., in 1832, as private and serg't.
 Seth, wid. Deborah... W 21911
 Smith.. S 36205
 Stephen, Hannah Davis, former wid. of.. R 2721
  (Soldier never pensioned.)

PALMER, Thomas, Hartford Co., Conn., in 1818.. S 36202
 Thomas or Thomas Kinne, wid. Margaret.. W 27925
  (Soldier died 1827, Grafton, Vt.)
 Thomas, Conn., Cont. & N. Y.. S 16217
  Soldier pensioned in Madison Co., N. Y., in 1832 as priv., corp. & serg't.
  Tryphena, former wid. of William McQUEEN.
 William... R 7911
 Wyatt... S 23357
PALMES, Andrew, Conn. & Navy, wid. Sarah... W 21887
 Samuel.. S 36206
PALMETER, PALMETTER, PALMITER or PALMITTER.
 Jesse, Conn. & Cont... S 43775
 John, wid. Anna or Anne... W 5474
 Jonathan, Conn. & R. I.. S 11180
 Paul, Conn. & N. J.. S 17624
 Phinehas, Conn. & R. I.. S 5870
 William, Conn. & R. I... S 43765
PANGBURN, Adonijah... S 38290
 Zillah, former wid. of Asa PARKER.
PARDEE, Abijah, wid. Rosanna... W 21905
 Chandler.. S 20905
 Charles... S 14087
 Daniel.. S 17615
 Eli... S 23365
 James, wid. Elizabeth... R 7918
  (Soldier never pensioned.)
 Joseph, wid. Sarah.. R 7921
  (Soldier was pensioned in New Haven Co., Conn., in 1832.)
 Lemuel.. S 43800
 Nathaniel... S 43795
 Thomas, Conn. & N. Y., wid. Susanna, BLWt. 26739-160-55.................................. W 3293
PARISH or PARRISH, Eliphas, Jerusha Cory, former wid. of, BLWt. 10313-160-55.................. W 1563
 Jeremiah.. S 11215
 Nehemiah, Conn. & Privateer... S 12128
 Oliver.. S 9451
 Roswell, wid. Eunice, BLWt. 9428-160-55... W 1918
PARK or PARKE, Amaziah, wid. Sabra or Sabry or Sabrey.. W 2688
 Daniel.. S 7296
  (Also given as PARKE.)
 Ebenezer.. S 14109
 Ezra, Cont. (Conn.), wid. Anna.. W 16362
 Isaac, wid. Mary.. W 21895
  (Also given PARKE.)
 John.. S 43789
  (Given as PARKE.)
 John, BLWt. 7-100 was issued Aug. 29, 1866, for services as private.
 Jonas, Cont. & Conn. Sea service, wid. Rachel... W 19966
 Thomas.. R 7932
PARKER. Abel, wid. Lydia, BLWt. 15165-160-55... W 18706
 Abraham, Rosamon Ingersoll, former wid. of.. W 5002
 Amos, Oneida Co., N. Y., in 1818.. S 43766
 Amos, wid. Polly, Serg't. Hampshire Co., Mass., in 1832................................. W 26848
 Asa... S 23354
 Asaph... S 7300
 Ashael.. R 7935
 Benjamin.. R 7937
 Benjamin, wid. Lorinda.. W 16360
 Edward.. S 14103
 Elijah, Conn. & Cont.. R 7943
 Elisha, Hampden Co., Mass., in 1832... S 5145
 Elisha, Boston, Mass., in 1832.. S 31288
 Elisha, Conn., Cont. & N. C... S 11354
  Pensioned from Morgan Co., Ala., in 1845.
 Gamaliel, Martha Hall, former wid. of... W 17038
 Isaac, wid. Anna.. W 16365
  Soldier was Serg't. and died in 1813; wid. was pensioned from Chataqua Co., N. Y., in 1838.
 Isaac, wid. Esther.. W 19967
  Soldier died in 1821; widow resided in Windsor Co., Vt., in 1838.
 Isaac, wid. Susannah.. R 7954
  Soldier was never pensioned.
 James, priv. & corp., Oneida Co., N. Y., in 1832.. S 14106
 James, Windsor Co., Vt., in 1832.. S 21409
 John, Saybrook, Conn., in 1818.. S 38982
 John, BLWt. 112-100; Chenango Co., N. Y., in 1818....................................... S 43792
 John, Conn. & Mass., wid. Elizabeth... W 18722
  Soldier died in Tolland, Conn., in 1832.
 John, Conn., R. I. & Vt., Corp. Rupert, Vt., in 1832.................................... S 14105
 Jonathan.. S 41039
 Joseph, wid. Hannah... W 18704
  Soldier died in 1823 in Georgia, Vt.
 Joseph, Conn., Cont. & N. H., Windsor Co., Vt., in 1832................................. S 14107
 Joseph, Conn. & Va., wid. Hannah.. R 7952
  Soldier never pensioned.
 Jotham, wid. Sarah.. W 19957
 Levi, Wallingford, Conn. in 1832.. S 14083
 Levi, wid. Eunice, BLWt. 34858-160-55... W 4754
  Soldier died in Orange Co., Vt., in 1835.
 Nathan, wid. Eunice, BLWt. 1661-100, BLWt. 146-60-55.................................... W 24879

111

PARKER, Phineas.. S 9984
   Samuel, Ashtabula Co., Ohio, in 1832.. S 18541
   Samuel, Conn. & Mass., Genesee Co., N. Y., in 1832.................................... S 11190
   Stephen... S 17625
   Timothy... BLWt. 259-100
   William, wid. Ruth.. W 19954
   Wyman, Conn. & Cont., wid. Mercy or Marcy.. W 15793
PARKES. (See PARKS.)
PARKHURST, Abraham, Conn. & Cont.. S 34465
   Azel.. S 21916
   David, Cont. (Conn.), wid. Susannah, BLWt. 155-60-55................................. W 24878
   Pierce, Conn., Conn. Sea service & Cont... S 15554
   Solomon... S 34463
PARKS or PARKES, Aaron... S 43809
   David... S 43804
   Ebenezer, wid. Janette, BLWt. 16111-160-55.. W 2425
     (Also given PARKES.)
   Frederick... BLWt. 755-100
   Robert, wid. Martha... W 18710
   Rufus, wid. Lucy.. W 26288
PARMALE, PARMALEE, PARMALIE, PARMELE, PARMELEE, PARMELY or
PARMLEE.
   Bani, wid. Charity, BLWt. 31565-160-55.. W 6852
   Charles, Conn. & Cont... S 11184
   Constant, wid. Hannah, BLWt. 6021-160-55.. W 5473
   Giles... S 14097
   Hiel.. S 14088
   James, Hartford Co., Conn., in 1832... S 15950
   James, wid. Lydia, BLWt. 30701-160-55... W 5481
     Soldier was in Ontario Co., N. Y., in 1818.
   Jeremiah.. S 41048
   Joel, wid. Sarah.. W 15172
     (Also given PARMELL.)
   Luther, Cont. (Conn.)... BLWt. 337-100
   Phinehas, wid. Rachel... W 18718
   Thomas.. S 28142
PARROTT, Esther, former wid. of Jonathan WAKELEY.
   John.. S 38284
   Mastin.. S 18537
PARSONS, Abraham.. S 14110
   Bartholomew... S 33429
   Daniel.. S 11208
   David (private)... BLWt. 232-100
   David, BLWt. 1667-300, Capt., was issued Nov. 5, 1795. No papers.
   Eli, wid. Huldah.. W 3111
   Jabez... S 3644
   Jesse... S 38282
   John, Herkimer Co., N. Y., in 1832.. S 31900
   John, wid. Sarah.. W 18698
     Soldier was in Addison Co., Vt., in 1832.
   John, Conn., Cont. & Mass., Chataqua Co., N. Y., in 1832.............................. S 11185
   Joseph.. S 11207
   Mercy, former wid. of Ezra FOOT. (Also given as PARSON.)
   Osborn, BLWt. 1089-100...
   Samuel, New York in 1818.. S 40243
   Samuel, Cont. (Conn.), New Haven County, Conn., in 1818............................... S 35024
                                                   S 15552
   Samuel H., BLWt. 1665-1100, Major Gen., was issued August 23, 1790. No papers.
   Solomon... S 4646
   William... S 14090
     (See also PEARSON.)
PARTRIDGE or PATRIDGE, Asa, wid. Anna... W 16053
   James, wid. Amy... W 16668
   Samuel, wid. Anna... W 15164
   Stephen, wid. Sarah... W 17423
PASCO, Jonathan... S 5140
PATCH, William.. S 11196
PATCHEN or PATCHIN, Azor, wid. Abigail, BLWt. 1378-100, BLWt. 37-60-55...................... W 6854
   Daniel.. S 14089
   Ebenezer, wid. Sarah.. W 16672
   Elijah, Conn. & Cont.. S 36207
   Freegift, Conn. & N. Y., wid. Molly... W 21910
   Isaac, wid. Rebekah... W 17425
   Jacob... S 38986
   Josiah, Eunice Keator, former wid. of... W 21510
   William... R 7993
     Wolcott, Bettey Bennett, former wid. of BLWt. 278-60-55.
     NOTE.—This woman's other husband was also a pensioner. (See Bennet or Bennett,
     Benjamin, Conn. S 38529.)
PATRICK, Abel... R 7995
   Jacob, Conn. & Privateer, wid. Sarah, BLWt. 24992-160-55.............................. W 19960
   James, Conn. & R. I., wid. Temperance... R 7998
     Soldier was pensioned in 1818 while living at Scipio, N. Y.
   Ralph... S 2883
PATRIDGE. (See PARTRIDGE.)
PATTEN, Asa... S 19743
   John, BLWt. 7294-160-55... S 19745
   Thomas, wid. Mary... W 18795
   William, Conn. & Cont., wid. Abigail.. W 26293
     (See also PATTON.)

PATTENGELL, Jacob.	S 43780
(See also PETTINGALE and PETTINGILL.)	
PATTERSON, Ansel, wid. Polly, BLWt. 10015-160-55.	W 6855
Sherman, wid. Huldah.	W 19959
William, Cont. (Conn.), wid. Lois.	W 18691
PATTISON, Sunderland, Cont. (Conn.).	S 43786
PATTON, Christopher, Conn. & Mass.	S 8662
(See also PATTEN.)	
PAUL, James, wid. Zeruah.	W 26835
Kiles, wid. Abigail, BLWt. 82541-160-55.	W 572
PAULK, Ammi.	S 11199
Ephraim, wid. Eunice.	W 18727
PAYN or PAYNE, Edward.	S 3625
Eleazer, wid. Aurel.	R 8021
Rufus, Chenange Co., N. Y., in 1832.	S 28841
Rufus, Litchfield Co., Conn., in 1818.	S 36203
Solomon, wid. Mary.	W 2160
Stephen, Conn. & Conn. Sea service.	S 41040
William.	S 11198
(See also PAINE.)	
PEAGAN, Joseph.	S 33459
PEARCE, John.	S 43826
(See also PEARSE, PEIRCE and PIERCE.)	
PEARL, Frederick.	S 36215
Timothy, wid. Lois.	W 26292
PEARSE, Richard, Navy (Conn.), wid. Candace.	W 4308
(See also PEARCE, PEIRCE and PIERCE.)	
PEARSON, Jesse, wid. Lydia.	W 16677
Peter.	S 17635
William E., wid. Hannah, BLWt. 31562-160-55.	W 3592
(Given also PIERSON and PARSONS.)	
(See also PEIRSON and PIERSON.)	
PEARSONS, Joseph Jabez, wid. Hannah.	R 26148
(Soldier never pensioned.)	
(Given also as PARSONS.)	
PEASE, Abner.	S 30022
Charles, wid. Elizabeth.	W 10869
David, wid. Jerusha.	W 19979
Ebenezer.	S 41054
Edward, wid. Abigail.	W 17431
Soldier died in 1817, Hartford, Co., Conn.	
Edward, wid. Rhoda.	R 8049
Soldier was pensioned while living in Chelsea, Vt., in 1832.	
Ephraim.	R 8045
Gideon, wid. Prudence.	R 8048
Soldier never pensioned.	
Isaac.	S 18545
James.	S 14124
Joel.	S 40252
Joel, Conn. & Mass.	R 8046
John, Cont. (Conn.).	S 18544
Joseph.	S 41065
Joseph, wid. Elizabeth.	R 8044
Soldier never pensioned.	
Moses.	S 11225
Peter, wid. Desire.	R 8043
Soldier was pensioned in 1818 from Hadley, Mass.	
Phineas.	S 17630
Robert, wid. Anna.	W 17432
Samuel, wid. Lydia.	W 10873
Soldier pensioned in 1832 from Luzerne Co., Penna., where he died in 1846.	
Samuel, wid. Sarah.	W 17430
Soldier died in 1828 at Tolland, Conn.	
Silas, Conn. & Cont., wid. Rhoba.	W 6859
Simeon.	S 14151
Stone, wid. Mary.	W 26308
PEASELY or PEASLEY, Mary, former wid. of Martin TUBBS.	
PECK, Aaron, wid. Hannah.	W 21956
Abel, wid. Diadama, BLWt. 24436-160-55.	W 2846
Abijah, wid. Sarah, BLWt. 26993-160-55.	W 6856
Soldier pensioned in 1832 from New Haven Co., Conn.	
Abijah, Conn. & N. Y., Saratoga Co., N. Y., in 1832.	S 14153
Abner, Conn. & Mass.	S 30650
Asahel, wid. Anna or Anne.	W 21957
Azel.	S 11222
Benjamin, wid. Mary, BLWt. 31557-160-55.	W 3035
Soldier pensioned in 1832 from Danbury, Conn.	
Benjamin, wid. Mary.	W 16370
Soldier died in Greene Co., N. Y., in 1820.	
Benjamin, Cont. (Conn.).	S 15571
Musician, Windham Co., Conn., in 1818; dropped on account of property; restored to rolls in 1852 from Providence, R. I.	
Bezaleel.	S 14152
Calvin, wid. Sarah, BLWt. 31593-160-55.	W 1068
Dan.	S 4644
Daniel.	S 11228
David, died 1834, Fairfield Co., Conn., pension paid wid. Althea.	S 14128
David, wid. Isabel.	R 8061
Soldier never pensioned.	

PECK, David, Sandlake, N. Y., in 1832	S 14156
David, Sodus, N. Y., in 1818	S 43813
Ebenezer	S 38300
Eliphalet, wid. Abigail	W 21946
Elisha, wid. Hulda	R 8054
Soldier never pensioned.	
Elisha, wid. Lucretia	W 15183
Gad, wid. Mary, BLWt. 26885-160-55	W 8286
George, wid. Ann	W 19977
Hiel, Conn. & Cont., wid. Hannah	W 3294
BLWt. 1687-200, Lieut., was issued Sept. 15, 1790, to Harry Williams. No papers.	
Isaac	R 8059
Isaac, wid. Elizabeth, BLWt. 26212-160-55	W 9220
Jacob, Conn. & Cont., wid. Elizabeth	W 26869
Jathleel, wid. Olive	W 26873
Jedediah or Jedidiah, Madison Co., N. Y., in 1832	S 14114
Jedediah, Cont. (Conn.), wid. Tabitha	W 16674
Artificer, died in 1821, Otsego Co., N. Y.	
Jesse, wid. Sarah, BLWt. 31312-160-55	W 1922
Jesse, Continental service but Conn. residence in 1818; Lieut., dropped in 1820 on account of property	S 36213
John, Brookfield, Conn., in 1832	S 14158
John, wid. Mary, BLWt. 300-60-55	W 26301
Soldier pensioned in 1818 from Litchfield Co., Conn.	
John, Conn. & Cont., wid. Lois, priv. and Lieut., died in 1825 in Conn	W 21930
Joseph, Hampden Co., Mass., in 1832	S 29373
Joseph, Conn. & Cont., wid. Sarah	W 21939
Soldier pensioned from New London Co., Conn., in 1818, and Lyme, Conn., in 1832.	
Josiah, wid. Helen	W 17428
Judson, wid. Mary	W 17429
Lysias, Cont. (Conn.), wid. Phebe	W 26299
Moses	S 14159
Reuben, Cornwall, Vt., in 1832	S 22432
Reuben, Cayuga Co., N. Y., in 1818	S 43812
Samuel	S 17012
Simon, Cont. (Conn.)	S 7304
Stephen	S 36214
Thomas	S 23841
Ward, wid. Dorcas	W 26310
William, wid. Elizabeth	W 26875
Soldier was pensioned as Serg't. in Bethel, N. Y., in 1818 & 1832; died there in 1837.	
William, wid. Mary	R 8066
Soldier pensioned as priv. in Chenango Co., N. Y., in 1832.	
(See also PEEK and PIKE.)	
PECKHAM, Benjamin, wid. Lucy	W 21931
PEEK, Isaac	R 8060
(Also given as PECK.)	
Samuel	S 41964
PEET, Elijah, wid. Anna	W 18734
John, Conn. & Cont., wid. Sally	W 17427
Lemuel	S 36218
Thaddeus	S 22434
PEIRCE, John, Penna. in 1832	S 3691
(Also given as PIERCE.)	
Samuel, Conn. & Cont., wid. Hannah	W 26901
Addison Co., Vt., in 1818, where he died in March, 1832.	
(See also PEARCE, PEARSE, and PIERCE.)	
PEIRSON, Amos, wid. Sarah	W 4765
(See also PEARSON and PIERSON.)	
PELLON, Edward	S 36216
PELTON, Benjamin, wid. Hannah	W 9921
Daniel	S 43827
David	S 33468
Freeman, wid. Prudence	R 8083
Soldier never pensioned.	
John	S 28842
Joseph, Conn., N. J. & Privateer, Oneida Co., N. Y., in 1832	S 11229
Joseph, wid. Abigail, BLWt. 34904-160-55	W 26303
Soldier was pensioned from Lyme, N. H., in 1832. Abigail also applied for BL on account of her first husband, John Ayres or Ayers, Conn. BLRej.	
Moses, Dorothy Phillips, former wid. of	W 17441
PEMBER, Eli, wid. Clarissa, BLWt. 11417-160-55	W 2335
PEMBLETON, Jabez, wid. Lucy, BLWt. 26971-160-55	W 2557
PENDELL, Elizabeth, former wid. of Samuel OSBORN.	
PENDLETON, Daniel, Cont. (Conn.)	BLWt. 2152-300
David	S 20910
PENFIELD, Abel	R 8089
Daniel	R 8090
James, wid. Mary	W 26298
Jesse, Dorinda Shepard, former wid. of	R 9477
Soldier never pensioned.	
Jesse, Cont. (Conn.)	S 43834
Nathaniel	S 23369
Peter, wid. Hannah	W 16679
Phineas	S 15558
Samuel	S 5895
Simeon	S 18155
PENHALLOW, Richard, Conn. & Cont., wid. Huldah	W 18737
(Also given HOLLOW, Richard P.)	

PENNOYER, William.. S 17631
    Served also in 1812.
PENOYER, Samuel.. S 15573
PENTLAND, Thomas, Conn. & Cont.. S 43840
PERCY, Joseph.. R 17029
PERIGO or PERRIGO, Ebenezer, wid. Mary... W 17435
    William.. S 43818
PERKINS, Aaron, BLWt. 277–100.. S 41053
    Abraham, Serg't.; pensioned in New London Co., Conn., in 1818; dropped on account of
      property in 1820; Cert. No. 3536.
    Charles, Cont. (Conn.)... BLWt. 340–100
    Daniel, Orange Co., Vt., in 1832... S 19026
    Daniel, Fairfield, Vt., in 1818... S 41063
    Ebenezer.. S 36219
    Elias.. S 14149
    Elisha... S 29379
    Francis, wid. Saloma, BLWt. 6438–160–55... W 6865
    Isaac.. S 33448
    Israel, wid. Lydia.. W 18748
    Jason.. S 43816
    Leonard.. S 23366
    Reuben... S 14157
    Samuel.. S 9454
    William.. S 14126
PERMELE or PERMELEE. (See PARMELEE.)
PERRIGO. (See PERIGO.)
PERRIT, Peter, BLWt. 1677–300, Capt., was issued January 8, 1790. No papers.
PERRY, Abijah... S 40259
    Almon, wid. Elizabeth.. W 18740
    Arthur... S 14154
    Ebenezer, Dorcas Taylor, former wid. of (see papers in case of her first husband, Levi FAR-
      NAM or FARNHAM).. W 16572
    Eli... S 14113
    Freeman, Conn. & N. Y.. S 14121
    Hannah, former wid. of Nathaniel PETTINGALE.
    Ichabod or Jeremiah, Conn. & Navy, wid. Rebecca, BLWt. 31558–160–55.................... W 17433
    John.. S 17628
    Jonathan, wid. Hannah... W 26295
    Joseph, wid. Mary.. W 17434
    Nathaniel, wid. Eunice... W 26864
    Ozias, Conn. & Cont.. S 43832
    Reuben, wid. Sally, BLWt. 54873–160–55.. W 2663
    Samuel, wid. Alice, Willington, Conn., in 1818, where he died in 1831....................... W 15189
    Samuel, wid. Tabitha, BLWt. 15438–160–55.. W 26859
      Soldier never pensioned, died in 1821; widow lived in Maine in 1836.
    Sylvanus... S 36212
      BLWt. 1670–200, Lieut., was issued June 30, 1789. No papers.
    Thomas, Conn. & Privateer... S 14162
PETERS, Absalom... S 14129
    Galloway, wid. Nancy.. W 18736
      BLWt. 6284–100, private, was issued June 14, 1790. No papers.
    Joseph... S 11231
    Joseph P., wid. Lydia, BLWt. 38541–160–55.. W 2338
    Nathan, Conn., Cont. & Mass., wid. Lois.. W 21937
    Peter... S 36210
    Samuel, wid. Hannah... W 17437
PETTEBONE or PETTIBONE, Daniel, wid. Eunice, BLWt. 39492–160–55..................... W 26306
    Elijah... S 43837
    John, Susannah Pinney, former wid. of.. R 8262
      Soldier never pensioned. This woman's former husband, Jonathan Pinney, Conn., also
      served in the Revolution. (See papers within.)
    Stephen... BL–
PETTINGALE, Nathaniel, Conn., Mass. & N. H., Hannah Perry, former wid. of............... W 21933
    Soldier also served in French and Indian War.
PETTINGILL, John, wid. Hannah, BLWt. 26017–160–55.. W 10877
    (See also PATTENGELL.)
PETTIS, Joseph... S 14164
PEYATT. (See PIATT.)
PHELPS, Aaron, Ruth Lewis, former wid. of... W 20438
    Abel, Elizabeth Williams, former wid. of... W 2630
    Abijah... S 4648
    Alexander... S 11240
      Invalid pensioner, and Middlesex Co., Conn., in 1832.
    Alexander... S 22933
      Grafton Co., N. H., in 1832; transferred to Albany, N. Y., Agency.
    Amos.. S 18160
    Asahel, wid. Margaret, BLWt. 13718–160–55... W 6866
      Soldier served in Conn. & Cont. Line.
    Austin, wid. Deborah... W 17439
    Beriah.. S 23843
    Bissell, wid. Sarah, BLWt. 3822–160–55... W 175
    Cornelius, wid. Philena, BLWt. 11284–160–55... W 5536
    Daniel.. S 14143
    Darius, wid. Mary.. R 8174
      Soldier never pensioned.
    David, Serg't., Enfield, Conn., in 1818 and 1832; died Nov. 3, 1834.......................... S 11239
    David, Lieut. and Capt., died before 1832, Simsbury, Conn. (See papers of his son David,
      S 14141.)
    David, died Simsbury, Conn., in 1835... S 14141
    David, Vermont in 1818.. S 41069

PHELPS, Eli, wid. Rachel, Conn. & N. Y. service, BLWt. 27592-160-55........................... W 26314
    Elijah, wid. Mary.. W 15846
        Soldier died in Hartford, Conn., in 1823.
    Elijah, wid. Zeruiah, corp. Conn. Line in 1818; died in 1831 in Middlesex Co., Conn.......... W 26313
    Elisha, Conn. & N. Y... S 14135
    Erastus... S 14142
    Giles.. S 9987
    Homer, wid. Adah, BLWt. 31564-160-55... W 18754
    Ira.. S 8952
    James, no definite service given, but Conn. residence... R 8171
    Jared, wid. Rowena... W 3113
    Joel, wid. Susannah, priv. dragoons: Warren Co., N. Y., in 1832, where he died in 1836...... W 18756
    Joel, Conn., Cont. & Mass., serg't: Bloomfield, N. Y., in 1818; transferred to Michigan....... S 35028
    John, private of infantry; Litchfield Co., Conn., in 1832... S 14137
    John, wid. Catherine, Serg't and Lieut.; died in 1812 in Albany Co., N. Y..................... W 19986
    John, wid. Sarah, Litchfield Co., Conn., in 1832, where he died in 1837; priv. cavalry........ W 17447
    Jonathan, Conn. & Privateer, wid. Charity, BLWt. 26604-160-55................................ W 9594
    Joseph.. S 15575
    Joshua, wid. Elizabeth... W 21970
    Judah, wid. Abigail... W 17448
    Lancelot. (See PHILLIPS.)
    Mary, former wid. of Richard AUSTIN.
    Norman... S 29384
    Obadiah, Cont. service, artificer; died in 1799; Arminda Hebard or Hibbard, former wid. of.. W 4985
        NOTE.—Arminda's last husband was also a pensioner. (See HIBBARD, William, Conn.,
        S 13400.)
    Oliver, St. Johnsbury, Vt., in 1832.. S 15574
    Oliver, Chenango Co., N. Y., in 1832... S 22932
    Oliver, wid. Phebe.. W 5540
        Soldier was in Hartford Co., Conn., in 1832.
    Reuben, wid. Mary... W 15214
    Roger... S 14144
    Samuel, New London Co., Conn., in 1818... S 36224
    Samuel, Conn. & Privateer, Serg't & Seaman: Madison Co., N. Y., in 1832..................... S 5919
    Seth, BLWt. 1674-300, Capt., was issued July 5, 1796. No papers.
    Silas, Conn. & Cont., wid. Mary, BLWt. 284-60-55.. W 26883
    Timothy, wid. Elizabeth... W 26317
    William.. R 8178
PHILBROOK, Thomas, Conn., Mass. & Navy, wid. Abigail... W 21964
PHILIPS. (See PHILLIPS.)
PHILLEY. (See FILLEY.)
PHILIPS, PHILLIP or PHILLIPS.
    Asa, wid. Lois, BLWt. 38568-160-55.. W 9229
    Ayer.. R 8185
    Dorothy, former wid. of Moses PELTON.
    Elisha.. S 21423
    Esquire... S 14145
    Gideon.. S 14138
    James, wid. Martha Sarah.. W 17443
    Jeruel, wid. Prudence.. W 17440
    Job, Athens Co., Ohio, in 1832.. S 16225
    Job, wid. Mary, Plainfield, Conn., in 1832 and died there in Dec., 1832......................... W 17442
    John.. S 43846
    Lancelot, wid. Jerusha.. W 16372
        (Given as PHILIPS and PHELPS.)
    Michael.. S 36222
    Philip, wid. Elizabeth.. W 5532
    Samuel, wid. Lydia.. W 21965
        Soldier died in 1815 in Litchfield Co., Conn.
    Samuel, wid. Millea, BLWt. 11068-160-55.. W 5534
        Soldier pensioned in 1818 in Litchfield Co., Conn., and died in 1862 in Ashtabula Co., Ohio.
    Samuel H., Commissary Department (Conn.).. S 17018
    Thomas, Ann Beers, former wid. of, BLWt. 26391-160-55.. W 25233
        NOTE.—Ann's second and third husbands were also pensioners. (See MILLS, Joseph,
        Conn., S 36151, and BEERS, Samuel, Conn. & Mass., S 17267.)
PHILO or FILLOW, Adams... R 8216
    Azor.. S 22931
PHINNEY, Asa... S 14136
    John, BLWt. 808-100... S 41066
        (Also given as FINNEY.)
    Joseph, wid. Mary... W 16988
PHIPPENE, PHIPPNE or PIFFANY, Nehemiah... W 14179
PHIPPS, Daniel Goffe, Conn., Conn. Sea service & Privateer..................................... S 15360
    Jason... S 14131
PIATT, Lewis, Conn. & N. Y... R 8220
    (Also given as PEYATT.)
PICKET or PICKETT, Phinehas... S 23373
    Samuel... S 30031
PICKSLEY. (See PIXLEY.)
PIDGE, Otis, wid. Jemima.. R 8229
    Soldier never pensioned.
PIER, Solomon... S 43856
PIERCE, Benjamin... R 8232
    Daniel.. S 36229
        (Also given PEARSE.)
    Job, Conn., Cont. & R. I.. S 14173
    Joseph... R 8239
    Samuel, wid. Dorcas... W 5157
        (Also given PEARCE and PEIRCE.)
    William, wid. Catharine.. W 15847
        (See also PEIRCE, PEARCE and PEARSE.)

PIERPOINT, Thomas	S 32444
PIERPONT, Eveline, wid. Rhoda	W 17998
John	S 36227
PIERSON, Nathan	R 8248
(See also PEARSON and PEIRSON.)	
PIFFANY. (See PHIPPENE.)	
PIKE, Abraham. (See PYKE.)	
Barnabas, wid. Hannah	W 26904
(Also given PECK.)	
James; wid. Sarah	W 4764
John, wid. Betsey, BLWt. 18024-160-55	W 26318
Jonathan	S 40264
Willard, Conn. & Cont., wid. Molly	W 18759
PILGRIM, Thomas	S 36231
PINNEO, Joseph, wid. Azuba, BLWt. 26763-160-55	W 21978
PINNEY, Butler	R 8095
Isaac, Serg't. Hartford Co., Conn., in 1832; died there in 1833	S 14169
Isaac, Conn. & Cont., wid. Mary, Serg't. Royalton, Vt., in 1818; died there in 1842	W 26971
Jonathan, wid. Martha	W 4760
Jonathan, wid. Susannah	R —
(See case of Susannah's other husband, PETTIBONE, John, R. 8262.)	
Lemuel	S 17020
Nathaniel	S 36228
Philaster	S 43857
PINTO, Solomon, Clarissa Hall, former wid. of	W 11263
BLWt. 1673-150, Ensign, was issued June 3, 1795. No papers. Also BLWt. 1-10-55.	
PITCHER, Abner	S 43858
PITKIN, John	S 14165
Stephen	S 3675
PITTS, Richard, Conn. & Md., wid. Sarah	W 17452
PIXLEY or PICKSLEY, Elijah	S 40265
PLANT, Eli, BLWt. 26111-160-55	S 14180
Ethel	S 43870
PLATT, Daniel	S 23374
Ebenezer, wid. Anna, BLWt. 34528-160-55	W 26323
(Also given as PRATT.)	
Gideon	S 17026
Isaac, Cont. service but Conn. residence	S 36232
Jabez, wid., Jillin	W 17462
James, wid. Olive	W 10903
John, Litchfield, Conn., in 1818	S 36233
John, wid. Sarah	W 5563
Soldier died in Delaware Co., Ohio; not pensioned.	
Joseph, wid. Lydia	W 17459
Died in 1792 in Fairfield Co., Conn.	
Joseph, wid. Mary, Fairfield Co. in 1832; died there in 1844	W 9231
Nathan, wid. Charlotte, BLWt. 90012-160-55	R 8282
Olive, former wid. of Eliphalet SMITH.	
Samuel, Cont. (Conn.), wid. Abigail	W 21980
Truman	S 18549
PLATTS, Dan	S 39018
PLUMB, Hannah, former wid. of Ichabod Talmadge.	
Isaac, wid. Catharine, BLWt. 28583-160-55	W 6871
Joseph, Middlesex Co., Conn., in 1832	S 31910
Joseph	R 8280
Nathaniel, wid. Anna, BLWt. 2255-100	W 19994
Samuel	R 8237
PLUMBS, Daniel	S 38308
George, wid. Eunice	W 26909
PLUMLEY, Ebenezer, wid. Dorothy	R 8289
Soldier was pensioned from N. Y. in 1818 and 1832.	
POLK. (See PAULK.)	
POLLEY or POLLY, Daniel	S 40295
John, Cont. (Conn.), wid. Phebe, BLWt. 3133-160-55	W 10012
Jonathan, wid. Mehitable or Mehetable, BLWt. 34903-160-55	W 6872
POLLOCK, Elijah	S 40286
Mingo, wid. Molly	W 17469
POMEROY or POMROY, Amos	S 14215
Dan, Cont. (Conn.)	S 44251
Daniel	S 3721
(Also given as POMERY.)	
Elisha, Conn. & Mass., wid. Lucy, BLWt. 36552-160-55	W 26335
Medad	S 22940
(Also given as POMROY.)	
Nathaniel, wid. Martha	W 17482
(Given as POMROY.)	
Phoebus	R 8310
Ralph, BLWt. 100-200	S 36237
POND, Barnabas, wid. Phebe P., BLWt. 31559-160-55	W 5573
Bartholomew	S 23347
Beriah, Cont. (Conn.), wid. Silvia or Silva	W 18777
Charles, wid. Catherine, Conn. & Sea service	W 22005
Dan	S 14218
Elias	S 36239
Timothy, wid. Merina	W 16374
POOL or POOLE, Chester, Conn. & Vt., wid. Bridget, BLWt. 14532-160-55	W 5569
David, Navy service but paid at Conn. Agency	S 20923
John, wid. Abigail	W 26332
John, wid. Elizabeth	R 8317
Soldier never pensioned.	

POOL or POOLE, Samuel, Serg't. in 1818 in New Haven Co., Conn.	S 36234
Samuel, wid. Ruth	W 17466
Died in 1827 in Windsor Co., Vt.	
Thomas, Cont. service but Conn. residence, wid. Elizabeth	W 26922
POOLER or POOLLER, George, Conn. & Mass.	S 14198
POOR, Jonathan, Conn. & Cont	S 38313
POPE, Ezra, wid. Mary	R 8329
Soldier was pensioned in 1832 from Richland Co., Ohio.	
PORTER, Abel, Cont. (Conn.)	S 14207
Abijah, wid. Sarah, BLWt. 26327-160-55	W 1070
Alexander, wid. Zerviah	W 15261
Amos	S 44254
Benjamin	S 23376
Clara, former wid. of Isaac RAYMOND or REYMOND.	
Daniel	S 36240
David, Weston, Conn., in 1832; transferred to N. Y.	S 14216
David, wid. Sarah, BLWt. 26136-160-55	W 13821
Soldier was pensioned from Greene Co., N. Y., in 1832	
Eldad	S 44246
Eleazer	S 44253
Elijah, drummer, in Farmington, Conn., in 1818 and 1832	S 14219
Elijah, Musician; Mass. in 1818, transferred to Ohio	S 40276
Elijah, Anna Harrington or Herrington, former wid. of	R 8337
Soldier never pensioned.	
Ephraim	S 28846
Ezekiel	S 14199
Ezra	S 35568
Isaac	S 14188
Isaac	R 8342
John	R 8344
John, wid. Esther, BLWTt. 38839-160-55	R 8346
John, wid. Lucy	W 26336
Soldier died in 1813, Fairfield Co., Conn.	
John, Conn. & Cont., Grafton Co., N. H., in 1832	S 14195
John, Cont. (Conn.)	R 17154
John, Cont. (Conn.), wid. Lydia	W 8526
Artificer; Washington Co., N. Y., in 1818.	
John, Cont. (Conn.), wid. Mary	W 21988
Artificer; died in 1806 in Hartford Co., Conn.	
Joseph, Conn. & Cont	S 35572
Martin	S 14213
Moses	S 35029
Moses, wid. Sarah	R 8354
Soldier never pensioned.	
Nathaniel	S 44243
Samuel, Corp. Berlin, Conn., in 1832	S 14208
Samuel, Drummer; Coventry, N. Y., in 1832	S 14191
Simeon, wid. Sarah	W 17468
Thomas	S 17640
Truman	S 14220
Truman	R 8355
William, Conn. & N. Y	BLWt. 1519-100
William, wid. Hannah, BLWt. 3978-160-55	W 5557
Soldier was in Lyme, N. H., in 1832.	
POST, Ebenezer	S 36741
Ezra	S 14187
George, wid. Esther	W 17464
Jediah or Jedediah, wid. Isabella or Isobel	R 8362
Soldier pensioned in 1832 from N. J.	
Jimmy	S 14206
Patience, former wid. of Peter LEWIS.	
Simeon	S 22447
Stephen	S 31916
POTER. (See POTTER.)	
POTTAGE, Jabez	S 36241
POTTER, Alice or Allice, former wid. of Alvan GOODELL or Alvin GOODALL.	
Benjamin, wid. Rachel	W 26326
Borden	S 3710
Caleb, Conn., Mass. & Vt	S 19037
Daniel, wid. Martha, BLWt. 64-60-55	W 2332
David, Conn. & R. I., Herkimer Co., N. Y., in 1832	S 14189
David, wid. Hannah, BLWt. 19780-160-55	W 2242
Artificer; Stratford, Conn., in 1832.	
David, wid. Rebecca	R 8379
Soldier was pensioned in 1818 from Chenango Co., N. Y.	
Ebenezer, Conn., Mass. & N. H	S 11255
Edward	S 14209
Ezra, Cont. (Conn.)	S 35575
Israel	BLWt. 1703-200
Joel, wid. Thankful	W 26325
John	S 14203
Lemuel, wid. Lydia	W 17472
Levi, Conn. & Cont	S 11262
Medad	S 35564
Milton	S 21426
(Also given POTER.)	
Moses	S 35569
Robert	S 40269
Sheldon, wid. Mary, BLWt. 45-100	W 18775

POTTER, Stephen, BLWt. 1668-300, Capt., was issued April 11, 1792. No papers.
 Thaddeus.. S 23846
 Timothy, wid. Martha... W 17479
POTTS, Benjamin... S 44247
POTWINE, George.. S 14204
POWEL, Felix, Conn. & Cont... S 44260
POWELL, Peter, wid. Eunice... R 8395
POWERS, Aaron.. S 40282
 James.. S 35570
 John, Conn. & Cont., wid. Anna, BLWt. 14763-160-55............................. W 26337
 Nathan, wid. Sarah... W 17476
 Timothy, wid. Elizabeth... W 17483
PRATT, Abijah, wid. Mary... W 17473
 Asa, Susanna Starkey, former wid. of, BLWt. 14955-160-55..................... W 11563
 Augustus.. S 14233
 Benjamin, Conn. & Mass., wid. Sarah.. R 8433
  Soldier never pensioned.
 Cary... S 11265
 Ebenezer. (See PLATT.)
 Edmund, Conn. & Navy, wid. Sybil... R 8436
  Soldier pensioned in 1832 in Niagara Co., N. Y.; later transferred to Michigan.
 Edward.. S 5950
 Elias... S 29392
 Isaiah... S 33506
 James.. S 44262
 Jasper or Jesper... S 35581
 Jonathan, Conn. & Cont.. S 14221
 Lemuel, Conn. & Cont., wid. Mary, BLWt. 61095-160-55......................... W 5577
 Olive, former wid. of Caleb FOWLER.
 Paul, Conn. & Mass... S 9990
 Peabody, wid. Sarah... W 26936
 Phineas, Conn. & Cont.. S 40303
 Russell.. R 8429
 Samuel, Conn. & Privateer... R 8432
 William, Granby, Conn., in 1832 as priv. and Serg't................................. S 17029
 William, Zuba or Zuby Byington, former wid. of..................................... R 1570
  Soldier never pensioned.
 Zadoc or Zadock, Conn. & Cont.. S 44263
 Zimri, Conn. & Vt... S 19043
PRENTICE, PRENTIS, or PRENTISS, Elisha... S 15563
 Jesse, wid. Elizabeth... W 26608
 Jonathan... R 8443
 Nathaniel, Conn. & Privateer, wid. Margaret, BLWt. 31566-160-55............ W 6750
 Samuel, wid. Lucretia... R 8444
  Soldier never pensioned.
 Samuel.. S 5949
 Thomas... S 21931
 William, Zephrah Kenyon, former wid. of.. W 26709
PRESBREY, John, Conn. Sea service, Mass. and R. I..................................... S 18555
PRESTON, Calvin, wid. Rachel, BLWt. 26884-160-55..................................... W 2690
 Daniel, New London Co., Conn., in 1818.. S 35586
 Daniel, wid. Esther, BLWt. 6106-160-55... W 5581
  Soldier was pensioned in 1832 in Otsego Co., N. Y.
 David.. S 40291
 Hovey... S 35578
 Joseph.. S 36244
 Noah, wid. Aner or Anor.. W 20001
 Shubael... S 14230
 Zephaniah, wid. Mary... BLWt. 73547-160-55
PRICE, David, wid. Susannah... W 17493
 Eleazer, wid. Hannah.. R 8466
  Soldier never pensioned.
 Elijah, Conn. & N. Y., wid. Beulah.. R 8462
 Jonathan, wid. Jemima... W 17497
 Paul.. S 35579
 Richard... S 36243
 Rufus, wid. Ruth.. W 16685
PRICHARD or PRITCHARD, Benjamin.. S 40302
 BLWt. 6280-100 was issued May 17, 1790. No papers.
 Jared... S 8796
 Nathaniel, wid. Comfort.. W 5582
  (See also PRITCHARD.)
PRIDE, Absalom, Conn. & Cont.. S 14232
 Jonathan, wid. Anna... W 15940
 Reuben... S 44276
  BLWt. 1671-200, Lieut., was issued Nov. 6, 1789, to Reuben Pride or Price. No papers.
PRIER. (See PRIOR.)
PRIEST, John, Cont. (Conn.), Lucy Cook, former wid. of, BLWt. 1227-100..... W 16539
PRIMUS, Job, Keturah Smith, former wid. of, BLWt. 61201-160-55................ W 10256
 (Also given as LATHROP.)
PRINCE, Edward H... S 14224
 Philip.. S 35580
 Timothy.. S 41079
PRINDLE, Abijah.. S 35588
 Joel... S 35585
 Peter... S 31978
 Samuel.. S 15577
 Samuel.. R 8488
 Zalmon, wid. Polly.. W 24920

PRIOR, Abner, wid. Abigail... W 4311
    BLWt. 1666-400, Major, was issued May 20, 1791. No papers.
  Azariah, wid. Alice.. W 17496
  Jesse... S 44275
  Roswell, wid. Phebe.. W 17495
  Simeon... S 4652
  William, Cont. (Conn.), wid. Elizabeth...................................... W 18783
    (Also given PRIER.)
PRITCHARD, George, wid. Abigail... W 2342
  James.. S 23852
    (See also PRICHARD.)
PROUT, Oliver... S 14234
  William, wid. Naomi... W 22012
PROUTY, John Warner.. S 8983
PROVEOST. (See PROVOST.)
PROVORSE. (See PROVOST.)
PROVOST, Daniel... S 20296
  Samuel, wid. Anna, BLWt. 40696-160-55................................... W 26339
    (Also given as PROVEOST.)
  Thomas, Conn., N. Y. & Privateer.. S 17028
    (Also given as PROVORSE.)
PUFFER, Daniel, Cont. (Conn.)... S 43875
  Simeon, Cont. (Conn.), wid. Fanny.. W 20007
PULFORD, Elisha... S 41088
  Joseph, wid. Phebe... W 22018
PULLMAN, John, Conn. Sea service & R. I., wid. Esther................ R 8520
  Soldier never pensioned.
PURDY, Daniel, Conn. & N. Y.. S 9460
PUTNAM, Aaron, wid. Sally.. W 16146
  Daniel, wid. Catharine, Conn. & Cont...................................... W 17503
  Israel, Conn. & Cont., BLWt. 1664-1100, Major General, was issued Dec. 13, 1790. No papers.
  Reuben... S 43876
PYKE, Abraham... S 5168
  (See also PIKE.)

Q

QUACKINBUSH, Abraham.. R 20426
QUI. (See QUY.)
QUIMBY, John.. S 11273
QUINLEY, Thomas.. S 35592
QUINTARD, Evert, wid. Hannah... W 20009
  Isaac, BLWt. 18011-160-55... S 17033
  James.. S 36248
QUY, Libbeus or Lebbeus.. S 36249
  (Also given as QUI.)

R

RAINEY, Stephen, wid. Esther, BLWt. 1374-450; & BLWt. 9057-160-55........ W 3040
RALPH, Jonathan... S 36251
RAMSDELL, Ezra... S 35595
RANDAL, RANDALL, RANDEL or RANDELL.
  Amos, wid. Jemima... W 24725
  Charles... S 4754
  Elijah, wid. Judith... W 24727
  Jedediah, wid. Martha... W 20010
  John, Conn. & N. Y... S 14245
  Jonas, Conn. & R. I... S 11279
  Joseph, Conn. & Cont.. S 22453
  Reuben, Cont. (Conn.).. S 35608
  Shubel or Shubal, wid. Sarah.. W 22035
    (Given as RANDEL or RANDELL.)
  Timothy, wid. Eunice, BLWt. 40697-160-55............................... W 26350
RANEY, RANNEY or RANNY.
  Amos, Conn. & Conn. Sea service.
  George, wid. Lucy... W 16384
    BLWt. 6377-100, private, was issued July 14, 1789. No papers.
    (Also given as RANNY.)
  Seth, Conn. & N. Y.. S 11278
  Solomon.. S 43903
  Stephen, wid. Elizabeth, BLWt. 1518-100.................................. W 22036
  William... R 8593
  William, Conn. & Cont... S 15607
RANSOM, Abner, Conn. Sea service & Cont. (Conn.)..................... R 8596
  Amos.. S 15608
  Asahel... S 14244
  David... S 35597
    Pensioned in 1818 at New London Co.
  David, Conn. & Mass., wid. Anna... W 20013
  Elijah... S 35594
    BLWt. 1798-200, Lieut., was issued Feb. 23, 1799. No papers.
  Ezekiel, Conn. & Mass., wid. Lucinda..................................... W 5663
  George Palmer, wid. Elizabeth... W 2694
  Israel, wid. Lois, BLWt. 80031-160-55..................................... W 9616
  James.. S 15610
  Joseph, Azubah Blish, former wid. of, BLWt. 47614-160-55........... W 25255
    Soldier died in 1795 in Middlesex Co., Conn.
  Joseph, Conn. & Cont., Akron Co., Ohio in 1832....................... S 18559
  Samuel, killed in service July 3, 1778; BLWt. 408-300 was issued to his heirs.
  Samuel. (Alive in 1808.)
RASAR. (See RAZAR.)

RASH, Jacob, Conn. & Cont., wid. Chloe... W 5667
RATHBONE, RATHBUN, or RATHBURN.
    Asa, wid. Ruth... W 17508
        (Given as RATHBURN.)
    Benjamin.. S 19438
    Ezra... S 40314
    Jonathan, wid. Hannah... W 11103
    Moses, wid. Olive... W 22040
    Thomas, wid. Elizabeth.. W 3115
RAWDON, Ezra, wid. Sarah... W 4772
RAWLS, Aaron, wid. Hannah.. R 8608
    Soldier never pensioned.
RAXFORD, Denison. (See REXFORD.)
    Joseph. (See RIXFORD.)
RAY, Caleb, Conn. & Cont... S 15604
    Daniel.. S 43891
    Gideon, wid. Zipporah... W 17514
    John P... S 31921
    Timothy... S 14250
    Warwick... S 35602
RAYMOND, Daniel, Conn. & Cont.. S 35601
    David, Hartford Co., Conn., in 1832... S 17037
    David, Fairfield Co., Conn., in 1832.. S 35606
    Ebur... S 36250
    George, Conn. & Navy, wid. Ann... W 11111
    Isaac, Clara Porter, former wid. of... W 26334
        (Also given as REYMOND.)
    James.. S 35598
    Joshua, wid. Elizabeth.. W 17512
    Lemuel... S 43890
    Miriam, former wid. of Benjamin DIMMICK.
    Moses... S 20928
    Napthali... S 21436
    Nathaniel, wid. Dinah, BLWt. 36628-160-55... W 26356
    Nathaniel Lynde, Conn., Navy & Privateer, wid. Louisa..................................... W 26351
    Newcomb, wid. Lorinda, BLWt. 19804-160-55.. W 26360
    Stephen, wid. Mary.. W 17513
    William... S 35596
    Zacheus, wid. Sarah... W 3719
    Zadock or Zadok.. S 16233
RAYNSFORD, Joseph... S 40317
RAZAR or RASAR, Elisha, Conn. & Privateer... R 8625
READ, Amos.. S 14261
    (Also given as REED.)
    Bailey.. S 23865
    Elisha... S 11286
    Zalmon, wid. Hannah, BLWt. 8458-160-55... W 178
    (See also REED.)
REDFIELD, Ambrose... S 45100
    Constant.. S 17042
    Levi... S 14276
    Martin.. S 17650
    Nathan.. S 31923
    Peleg... S 9464
    Roswell.. S 17647
    Samuel... R 8640½
REDINGTON, John, Laura Miller, former wid. of, BLWt. 100371-160-55................ W 10498
REDWAY, Comfort, wid. Roxana.. R 8646
    Soldier was pensioned in 1818 from Jefferson Co., N. Y.
    Joel.. S 30057
    Preserved, wid. Azubah.. W 18796
REED or REID, Benjamin, Hartland, Conn., in 1818.. S 35612
    Benjamin.. S 8651
    Daniel.. R 8653
        Indefinite service claimed, but Conn. residence.
    Diodama, former wid. of Benjamin ROWLAND.
    Ebenezer, Cattaraugus Co., N. Y., in 1832... S 14275
    Ebenezer, wid. Polly, BLWt. 8185-160-55... W 18795
        (Also given as REID.)
        Soldier died in 1827 in N. Y., was priv. & Serg't; wid. lived in Vt. in 1836.
    Eli, wid. Meliscent or Melison.. W 27235
    Enoch, BLWt. 1794-300, Capt. was issued May 29, 1789. No papers.
    Ithel... S 16235
    John.. R 8663
    Joseph... S 36253
    Justus, wid. Lydia, BLWt. 34847-160-55.. W 814
    Kitchel... S 28851
    Richard... S 43908
    Samuel, Conn. & Privateer... S 11285
    Stephan or Stephen... S 43916
    Tallcot.. R 8677
    (See also READ.)
REEVE or REEVES, Daniel, Conn. & N. Y... R 8842
    Luther, wid. Anna.. W 4570
    Puryer, Conn. & N. Y... S 28852
REID. (See REED.)
REMINGTON, Abijah, wid. Silence... BLWt. 24601-160-55
    John... S 21944
    Josiah, Conn. & N. Y.. R 8700
    Simeon... S 22948

RENELS or RENNELLS, Benjamin... S 40327
RESSEGUE, RESSEQUE or RESSEQUIE.
    Abraham, Ellen Delanoy, former wid. of... W 24054
    Alexander, wid. Ruamy, BLWt. 26507-160-55... W 1483
    John, Conn. & N. Y.. S 14268
REW, Ephraim.. S 22946
    Memucan, wid. Hannah.. W 26363
REXFORD or RAXFORD, Benjamin, wid. Mary Jane, BLWt. 34529-160-55.......... W 5684
    Denison... R 8843
        (Also given as RAXFORD and ROXFORD.)
    Isaac... S 41093
    Joseph, wid. Anna... W 5708
        (Also given as RIXFORD.)
REYMOND. (See RAYMOND.)
REYNOLDS, Albrow... S 15963
    Charles, Cont. (Conn.), wid. Hannah... W 17528
    David.. S 15964
        Pensioned as David 3d in 1832 in Washington, Conn.
    David, Plainfield, Conn., in 1832; moved to R. I.. S 21939
    David, wid. Margaret... W 17523
        Soldier in Windham Co., Conn., in 1832; died in 1836.
    David, wid. Rebecca.. W 24738
        Soldier in Washington Co., Me., in 1827; died in 1832.
    Eliphalet.. S 37326
    Gamaliel, wid. Mary.. W 24729
    Jacob.. S 7378
    James, wid. Mary... W 22057
    Jeremiah, Oneida Co., N. Y., in 1832... S 14256
    Jeremiah, Bedford, N. Y., in 1832... S 23385
    John, Broome Co., N. Y., in 1818; Pittsburgh in 1832.................................. S 4762
    John, Conn. & Privateer, BLWt. 26540-160-55; Susquehanna Co., Penna. in 1832... S 22459
    Jonathan, wid. Mary.. W 16692
        Died in 1809, York, N. Y.
    Jonathan, Cont. (Conn.), Vt. in 1818... S 41972
        (See also RENNELLS.)
    Justus... S 40319
    Matthew.. R 8714
    Simeon, Mass. in 1818; transferred to Penna... S 41094
    Simeon, Philadelphia, Penna., in 1832... S 41095
REYNOLS or REYNOLDS, Solomon, wid. Elizabeth... W 17517
    (See also RENNELS.)
RHINEVAULT. (See RINEVAULT.)
RICE, Abigail, former wid. of Lemuel CARRINGTON.
    Abiram, wid. Lucy. (Also given as ROYCE.)
    Charles... S 14292
    Chauncey, Northampton Co., Penna., in 1832.. S 5990
    Chauncey, Conn. & Mass., Meriden, Conn., in 1832.................................... S 15616
    Daniel, Conn. & Cont., wid. Jemima... W 22086
    Elijah.. S 36263
        (Also given ROYCE.)
    Isaac... S 4087
    Jacob.. S 11298
    John... S 11301
    Moses, wid. Nancy, BLWt. 40687-160-55.. W 11153
    Nehemiah, BLWt. 1791-300, Capt., was issued June 18, 1790, to Nehemiah Rice. No papers.
    Samuel, Litchfield Co., Conn., in 1818... S 35631
    Wait.. S 35620
    William, Conn. & R. I... S 14313
RICH, Amos... S 43936
    Lemuel.. S 5994
    Nathaniel, BLWt. 103-100.
    Samuel, BLWt. 6404-100.
    Thaddeus... S 35626
RICHARD, Silas... S 14307
RICHARDS, Amos... S 43921
    Edmond, wid. Ruth... S 43925
        (Also given Edmund.)
    Gershom, wid. Elizabeth... W 17539
    Hezekiah, wid. Jerusha.. W 22069
    Isaac... R 8760
    Israel.. S 27383
    Jacob, wid. Mary.. S 8759
    Jesse, wid. Clarissa... W 2346
        Soldier pensioned in 1832 from New Canaan, Conn.
    Luther... R 8758
    Mark... R 8761
    Nathaniel, Navy service but Conn. residence.. S 23389
    Peter.. S 35624
    Samuel, Vt. in 1818... S 35625
    Samuel, Conn. & Cont., Lieut. in Hartford Co., Conn., in 1818..................... S 41985
    William, Conn. & Cont.. S 17652
        BLWt. 1796-300, Capt., was issued Jan. 28, 1790. No papers.
RICHARDSON, Asa or Fidelio.. S 35623
    David, wid. Sarah... S 41097
    Fidelio. (See Asa.)
    Gershom.. W 5711
    Jesse... S 16237
    John, St. Lawrence Co., N. Y., in 1832.. S 4775
    John, wid. Judith, BLWt. 88525-160-55.
    Rufus, wid. Ruth... S 23871
                                                                                             W 18816

RICHARDSON, Russel or Rossel	S 43932
Samuel, wid. Susannah	W 17533
Sanford, wid. Roxy	W 17531
Stanton, Conn. & Vt., wid. Anna	R 8764
Stephen, wid. Hannah	W 26386
William, Conn. & Cont.	S 11291
RICHMOND, Abner, Conn. & Mass., wid. Eunice	W 17584
Vail or Viall, Conn. & Navy, wid. Clarissa, BLWt. 38544-160-55.	W 1935
RIDER, Daniel, wid. Elizabeth	W 5705
Jeremiah	S 14296
RIGGS, James	R 17439
Laban, Conn. & Cont., wid. Dorcas	W 4780
Moses	S 35629
RILEY, John, BLWt. 1792-300, Capt., was issued April 22, 1790. No papers.	
John, Delaware Co., N. Y., in 1832; Lieut	S 14304
Joseph	S 4105
Roger, wid. Sarah	W 22084
RINDGE or RING. (See RINGE.)	
RINEVAULT, William, wid. Mary	R 8830
(Also given as RHINEVAULT.)	
(Soldier was pensioned in 1818 in Conn. and transferred to N. Y.)	
RINGE, RINDGE or RING, Thomas, wid. Anna, BLWt. 3522-160-55	W 26187
RIPLEY, Abraham	S 33565
Charles, Conn. & N. H.	S 43931
Epaphras, Conn. & Vt	R 8833
Hezekiah or Hezekiel, Conn. & Cont.	S 11305
Jabez, wid. Mary	R 8836
Soldier never pensioned.	
Jeremiah, wid. Mary	R 8835
Soldier never pensioned.	
John A., Conn. & Privateer	R 8834
Nehemiah, wid. Lucy, BLWt. 15196-160-55	W 1489
Pirum, Conn., Conn. Sea service & Navy & N. Y.	S 23388
RISDON, John	S 18569
RISING, Ben	S 9086
Josiah, Cont. (Conn.), wid. Huldah	W 18818
RISLEY, Allen	S 21449
Asa	S 12226
Asahel or Asahael, Cont. (Conn.).	
BLWt. 6410-100, private, was issued in 1790.	
David, wid. Cynthia	W 24768
Eli, wid. Mindwell	W 10236
Elijah	S 23391
Levi	S 35619
Moses, Conn. & Mass.	R 8839
Richard	S 23390
Samuel, wid. Stacy O., BLWt. 27587-160-55	W 26369
Stephen	S 43930
(Also given RISLY.)	
William	S 14305
RIX, Nathan, Conn. & R. I.	S 14306
ROACH, Thomas, BLWt. 26121-160-55	S 14373
ROATH. (See ROTH.)	
ROBARTS. (See ROBERTS.)	
ROBBARTS. (See ROBERTS.)	
ROBBINS, Brintnal, wid. Mary, BLWt. 26760-160-55	W 7150
Daniel, wid. Ruth, Conn., Conn. Sea service & N. Y., BLWt. 8184-160-55	W 18826
(Also given as ROBINS.)	
Ebenezer, wid. Zeruah, BLWt. 27588-160-55	W 9636
Ephraim	S 17052
Frederick, wid. Abigail, BLWt. 47767-160-55	W 26426
John, Cont. & Conn. Sea service, wid. Alice	W 17558
Joshua	R 8856
Josiah	S 35633
Lorin or Lorrin, Conn., Cont. & R. I.	S 14372
Samuel, Conn. & R. I.	S 14374
Silas, wid. Hannah	W 17565
(See also ROBINS.)	
ROBERTS, ROBARTS or ROBBARTS.	
Amos	S 6024
Ashbel	S 18580
Benjamin. (See SIMMONS.)	
Clark, wid. Sarah	W 17550
Daniel, Hartford Co., Conn., in 1832	S 31942
Daniel, wid. Asenath	W 16391
Soldier died in 1827, Genesee Co., N. Y.	
David, Cont. (Conn.)	S 36256
Elijah, Montgomery Co., N. Y., in 1832	S 14314
Elijah, Middletown, Conn., in 1832	S 14377
Elisha, Cont. (Conn.)	S 43939
Freelove, Cont. (Conn.)	S 41995
(Also given as ROBBARTS.)	
Gideon, wid. Jerusha	W 2006
(Also given as ROBARTS.)	
Isaac, wid. Sally	W 26399
Canaan, N. Y., in 1818; d. in 1836, BLWt. 29026-160-55.	
Isaac, Conn. & Mass., wid. Sarah	W 10243
Washington Co., Vt., in 1832; died in 1835.	
James	S 28862

ROBERTS, ROBARTS, or ROBBARTS—Continued.
John, Hartford Co., Conn., in 1832.	S 31939
John. Served also in French and Indian War; applied in 1809 for pension.	
John, Berlin, Conn., in 1832.	S 11329
John, Conn. & Cont.	S 36259
Invalid pensioner & 1818 from Litchfield Co., Conn.	
Judah.	S 15622
Lucretia, former wid. of Jeduthan ABBE.	
Luke, wid. Catharine or Catherine, BLWt. 41-60-55.	W 4326
(Also given ROBARTS.)	
Nathan.	S 43969
Nathaniel, Cont. (Conn.).	S 14346
Noah.	S 43974
Pearly, wid. Submit.	W 22127
Rufus.	S 44232
Samuel.	S 43961
Stephen, wid. Rebecca.	W 2860
Timothy.	S 14337
William, West Springfield, Mass., in 1818; corporal.	S 33611
William, wid. Abigail.	W 20033
Soldier died in 1797 in Hartford Co., Conn.	
William, Conn., Mass. & Vt., wid. Margaret, Trumbull Co., Conn., in 1832.	W 4784
Ziba, Mary Chase, former wid. of.	W 22759
ROBERTSON, Daniel, wid. Esther.	W 16704
Ephraim, wid. Priscilla.	W 17547
Peter.	BLWt. 1795-300
(Also given as ROBINSON.)	
Seth, wid. Hannah.	W 17553
Simeon. (See ROBINSON.)	
ROBIN or ROBINS, Brintnall. (See ROBBINS.)	
Daniel. (See ROBBINS.)	
Joseph, Conn. & Cont., wid. Elizabeth.	W 17567
Joseph, Mary Mulkins, former wid. of.	W 17181
Lorin or Lorrin. (See ROBBINS.)	
Samuel, Conn., Cont. & R. I., wid. Zeruviah.	W 17566
(See also ROBBINS.)	
ROBINSON, Abel.	S 44235
Amasa, wid. Marcia, BLWt. 1966-160-55.	W 9268
Andrew, wid. Bethiah or Bethia, BLWt. 26912-160-55.	W 2348
Asher, wid. Sarah.	W 22121
Benjamin, wid. Ruth.	R 8915
Soldier never pensioned.	
Benjamin, Conn. & Cont.	S 43980
Chandler.	S 22957
Charles, wid. Chloe D.	W 26409
Daniel, Conn. & Cont.	S 11316
Eber, wid. Lucinda, BLWt. 10257-160-55.	W 5745
Eleazer, wid. Mary, BLWt. 851-100.	W 24793
Elias, wid. Amy or Amie.	R 8893
Soldier received BLWt. 1799-200, Lieut., April 6, 1796. No papers.	
Elias, wid. Betsey, BLWt. 31578-160-55.	W 11163
Soldier pensioned in 1818 & 1832 in New London Co., Conn.	
Ephraim.	S 22474
James, Conn., Md., N. J. & Penna.	S 7432
Jared, BLWT. 1785-200.	S 43982
Jason, BLWt. 6003-160-55.	R 8904
John, Jefferson Co., N. Y., in 1819.	S 43979
John, wid. Esther.	W 24791
Soldier died in Jefferson Co., N. Y., in 1818.	
John, wid. Lucy.	W 26407
Soldier in Branford, Conn., in 1832.	
John, wid. Sarah.	W 17573
Fairfield Co., Conn., in 1832 where he died in 1834.	
Jonathan.	S 18182
Joseph, wid. Abbey.	W 17555
Joshua, wid. Chloe, BLWt. 13020-160-55.	W 2440
Levi, BLWt. 1291-100.	S 33595
Moses, Conn. & R. I., wid. Hannah.	R 8897
Nathaniel, wid. Susanna.	W 16706
Noah, Conn. & N. Y.	S 23884
Peter, BLWt. 1795-300, Capt., was issued Sept. 14, 1789. No papers.	
Reuben, Tolland Co., Conn., in 1818.	S 36269
Reuben, wid. Rosannah.	W 7152
Soldier was in Killingly, Conn., in 1832; BLWt. 7217-160-55.	
Reuben, Conn., Mass. & Vt., Windsor Co., Vt., in 1832.	S 16238
Reuben, Stonington, Conn., in 1832.	S 29421
Richard.	S 22473
Robert.	R 8914
Simeon.	S 43949
(Also given as ROBERTSON.)	
Susan, former wid. of Alva WEST.	
William.	S 14315
Ziba.	S 14332
Zophar, wid. Charity.	W 17564
ROCKWELL, Amasa, Conn. & Mass., wid. Prudence, BLWt. 12702-160-55.	W 1086
Clapp.	S 17660
Grove.	S 36268
Jabez, wid. Betsey B., BLWt. 26759-160-55.	W 3722
Soldier pensioned in 1832 in Pike Co., Penna., as private & fifer.	
Jabez, wid. Deborah.	W 22122
Soldier died in 1818 in Grand Isle, Vt.	

ROCKWELL, John, N. Y. in 1818.. S 44237
   John, wid. Abigail.. W 18838
      Soldier died in 1823 in Mass.
   Joseph, wid. Esther, BLWt. 31583-160-55.. W 11155
   Noadiah.. S 18181
   Oswald, wid. Sarah... W 17562
   Samuel, Sharon, Conn., in 1832.. S 23375
   Samuel, Oneida Co., N. Y., in 1832... S 14356
   Silas.. S 28856
   William, Conn. & N. Y., wid. Sarah.. R 8923
      Soldier pensioned in 1828 in Fairfield, Conn.
RODGERS or ROGERS, Abel.. S 14322
   Abijah, wid. Lydia... W 11160
   Bela, wid. Rebecca... W 18823
   Bixbee... S 40357
   Chester, Eunice Boynton, former wid. of... W 20744
   Daniel... S 11336
   David.. S 36274
   Ebenezer, Norwich, Conn., in 1832... S 31941
   Ebenezer, wid. Ruth.. W 17571
      Northfield, Conn., in 1832; died there in 1833.
   Howard, wid. Hannah... W 22118
      (Soldier was Captain.)
   Edward, Conn. Sea service, Medina Co., in 1832............................ S 4795
   Elisha, wid. Anna, BLWt. 6426-160-55... W 22116
   Elnathan.. S 14376
   Ephraim, wid. Martha.. W 17561
   Ethan.. S 4139
   Gideon, wid. Lucy.. W 27479
   Gurdon... S 31940
   Heman, wid. Hannah, BLWt. 316-60-55.. W 815
   Hezekiah... BLWt. 1793-300
      Capt. was issued July 21, 1789, to Hezekiah Rogers. No. papers.
   Isaac, wid. Mary.. W 11168
   Israel.. S 14383
   Jabez, wid. Sarah.. R 8959
      Soldier never pensioned.
   Jedekiah, Cont. (Conn.), wid. Sarah.. W 17570
      BLWt. 1802-300, Capt. of Col. Sheldon's Regiment of Cavalry, was issued October 2, 1789.
      No papers.
   Jeduthan, wid. Elizabeth... R 8940
      Soldier was pensioned in Windsor Co., Vt., in 1832.
   John, Conn. & Privateer, Broome Co., N. Y., in 1832..................... S 14380
   Jonah.. R 8948
   Joseph (N. Y. in 1818)... S 43978
      BLWt. 1801-150, Ensign, was issued July 21, 1789. No papers.
   Joseph, Claremont, N. H., in 1832... S 45858
   Josiah, Serg't. in Litchfield County, Conn., in 1818........................ S 36272
   Josiah (Clarkson, N. Y., in 1832), Alice Rogers Hewett, former wid. of (wid. pensioned from
      O. in 1848).. W 10099
      BLWt. 92107-160-55.
   Josiah, or Josias, wid. Ruth... W 3605
      Soldier in Luzerne Co., Penna., in 1832; died there in 1841.
   Josiah, Conn. & N. H., wid. Hannah.. R 8943
      Soldier never pensioned.
   Leonard.. S 31937
   Levi, wid. Abigail, BLWt. 26618-160-55.. W 8292
   Nathaniel.. S 23877
   Noadiah, wid. Rebecca, BLWt. 26942-160-55.................................. W 2641
   Oliver, Navy (Conn.)... S 36275
   Perley, wid. Esther.. W 57303
   Peter, Bernardstown, Mass., in 1818.. S 33582
   Peter, wid. Nancy.. W 5731
      Monroe Co., Ill., in 1834, where he died in 1849.
   Richard.. S 4784
   Samuel, Wayne Co., Pa., in 1832.. S 22482
   Samuel, Conn., Privateer & Vt.. R 8954
      Soldier never pensioned; wid. Mehitable.
   Simeon, wid. Mary.. W 27807
   Steven or Stephen, Abigail Byrne, former wid. of, BLWt. 2185-160-55.... W 25319
   Thankful, former wid. of Elihu AVERY.
   Thomas (given also as RODGERS).. S 36270
   Thomas, Rutland, Vt., in 1832.. S 22480
   Thomas, Conn., Navy, Privateer & R. I., New London Co., Conn., in 1832.... S 14343
   Timothy, Hannah Markham, former wid. of.................................. W 25677
   Zephaniah, wid. Elizabeth... W 3192
ROLF, Henry, wid. Patty... W 104
ROLLO, Zachariah, BLWt. 1448-100.. S 36267
ROLO, Joseph, wid. Polly, BLWt. 31577-160-55................................ W 26405
ROLOO, Daniel... S 4315
   (Also given as ROLO and ROOLO.)
ROOD or ROODE, Briggs... R 8979
   (Given as ROODE.)
   David, wid. Lucretia... R 8981
      (Soldier never pensioned.)
   Jeremiah.. S 44231
   John.. S 20940
   Joseph.. R 8950
   Roger.. R 8982

ROOD or ROODE, Rozzel .... S 23403
  Simeon .... S 43964
    (See also RUDE.)
ROOLO. (See ROLOO.)
ROOT, Amos .... S 14317
  Billa, wid. Polly .... R 8991
    Soldier was pensioned in 1832 in Allegany Co., N. Y.
  Daniel .... S 11321
  Eleazer, wid. Lucinda .... R 8987
  Elijah, Farmington, Conn., in 1832 .... S 14386
  Elijah, Conn. & Mass., Genesee Co., N. Y., in 1832 .... S 23399
  Erastus, wid. Lucy, BLWt. 9207-160-55 .... W 1650
  Ezekiel N., Cynthia Cowles, former wid. of .... W 4927
  Israel, Conn. & Mass .... S 15627
  Joel, Cont. (Conn.) .... S 33589
  John, wid. Polly .... W 26404
  Joseph, Albion, N. Y., in 1832 .... S 14324
  Joseph, wid. Mary .... W 4323
    Soldier died in 1816.
  Joshua .... S 11314
  Josiah, Cont. (Conn.) & Sea serv .... S 14328
  Lydia, former wid. of Joseph WATERS.
  Moses, wid. Esther .... W 24809
  Nathan .... S 47751
  Nathaniel, Onondaga Co., N. Y., in 1832 .... S 14368
  Nathaniel, Coventry, Conn., in 1832 .... S 18574
  Nathaniel, Canaan, Conn., in 1818 .... S 36277
  Nathaniel H .... S 18573
  Salmon or Solomon, wid. Bulah .... W 1084
  Samuel, wid. Dinah .... W 24779
  Seth .... S 36273
  Solomon. (See SALMON.)
  Thomas .... S 43984
ROOTS, Daniel, wid. Lucy .... W 22098
ROSE, John, Cont. (Conn.), BLWt. 1584-150 .... S 43967
  John BLWt. 1804-400, Surgeon, was issued Feb. 24, 1797. No papers.
  Jonathan, wid. Hannah, BLWt. 12565-160-55 .... W 26395
  Levi, wid. Mary .... W 22114
  Peleg, wid. Mary .... W 22120
  Peter, Conn. & Cont., Esther Edmonds or Edmunds, former wid. of .... R 3244
    Soldier never pensioned.
  Prosper .... S 35
  Samuel .... R 9011
  William .... S 11324
  Winthrop .... S 43968
ROSETTER. (See ROSSITER.)
ROSS, Perin .... BL
ROSSETER, ROSSETTER, ROSSITER or ROSETTER.
  Benjamin .... S 23595
  Bryan, wid. Sarah, BLWt. 435-100 .... W 24782
    (Given as ROSSETTER.)
  Noah, Conn. & Mass., wid. Amanda, BLWt. 26230-160-55 .... W 7156
  Timothy, New Haven Co., Conn., in 1832 .... S 17062
  Timothy, Conn. & Cont., BLWt. 1604-100; N. Y. in 1818 .... S 44233
    (Given as ROSETER.)
ROTH or ROATH, Daniel, wid. Hannah .... W 17559
  Silas .... S 36260
    (Given as ROATH.)
ROUNDY, Uriah, wid. Lucretia .... R 9034
    Soldier never pensioned.
ROWE, David .... S 42214
  Ezra, Conn. & Cont .... S 15970
  Isaiah, wid. Mary .... R 9043
    Soldier never pensioned.
  John, Conn. & Cont .... S 14358
ROWEL, Philander. (See ROWLEY.)
ROWLAND, Benjamin, Conn. & Cont., Diodama Reed, former wid. of .. W 24741
  Daniel .... S 36271
  David .... S 14379
  Hezekiah, wid. Grace .... W 4328
  Jack .... S 17058
    (Also given FREEMAN.)
  Jesse .... S 36264
  Luke, wid. Elizabeth .... W 9271
  Sherman .... S 36262
ROWLANDSON or ROWLINSON, Joseph .... S 42218
  Rubn, wid. Eunice .... W 9272
ROWLEY, Abijah, Conn. & Cont .... S 32493
  Eli Smith .... S 11312
  Joseph L., Conn., Conn. Sea service & N. Y .... S 7408
  Philander .... S 14327
    (Given also as ROWEL.)
  Seth, Conn., Cont. & N. Y., wid. Innocent, BLWt. 5110-160-55 .... W 24777
  Silas .... S 14326
  Thomas, wid. Mary .... W 15277
ROWLINSON. (See ROWLANDSON.)
ROYCE, Aaron .... S 45126
  Abiram. (See RICE.)
  Asa .... S 31936
  Elijah, Woodstock, Vt., in 1818 and 1832 .... S 23397

ROYCE, Elijah, New Haven Co. in 1818. (Also given as RICE.)
   Isaac, wid. Abigail... R 9056
      Soldier never pensioned.
   Samuel, Conn. & Cont.. S 12256
ROZELL, Jeremiah, Conn. & Cont.. S 42219
   BLWt. 6391-100, Private, was issued March 1, 1797. No papers.
RUDD, Andrew, Conn. & Cont.. S 30077
   Daniel, Conn. & Navy, wid. Abigail, BLWt. 7209-160-55.............................. W 22137
   William, wid. Eunice.. W 22138
RUDE, Ezekiel, wid. Phebe.. W 26417
   Isaac.. S 17066
      (See also ROODE & ROOD.)
RUGGLES, Benjamin A., wid. Betty... W 26418
   Bostwick, wid. Lucy... W 17576
   Joseph... S 14392
RUICK, Owen.. S 36034
RULAND, Thomas W., Mary Deforest, former wid. of, BLWt. 12834-160-55.... W 2663
RUMSAY or RUMSEY, David... S 42225
   Jeremiah, wid. Asenath.. W 3461
   John... S 41970
   William.. S 41970
RUNDEL, RUNDELL or RUNDLE, Henry... R 9073
   John, wid. Rachel, BLWt. 2170-100... W 11194
      (Also given RUNDLE.)
   Joseph... R 8582
   Phinehas... S 18191
   Reuben, Conn. & N. Y... S 9298
RUSCO or RUSCOE, David.. S 41115
RUSS, Asa.. R 9093
   Epaphras.. S 42224
   Jonathan.. S 42210
RUSSEL or RUSSELL, Abigail, former wid. of James McDONALD.
   Asher or Ashur, Conn. & Cont., BLWt. 1195-100.. S 40368
   Cornelius, BLWt. 248-200.. S 41112
   David, Burlington, Vt., in 1832.. S 15972
   David, wid. Eunice... W 26419
      New Haven Co., Conn., in 1832; where he died in 1836.
   Ebenezer.. S 14387
   Eleazer... S 42223
   Elmore, Cont. (Conn.)... S 14391
   Gideon.. S 7434
   Ichabod, wid. Hannah... R 9101
      Soldier never pensioned.
   John, Warwick, R. I., in 1818... S 39836
   John, wid. Lovice... W 17578
      Soldier died in 1826 in Tolland Co., Conn.
   Jonathan... S 10000
   Josiah, Conn. & Cont.. S 42226
   Riverius or Riverus, Conn. & Cont., wid. Charity; both sold. & wid. Rej... R 9105
   Timothy, wid. Elizabeth.. R 9100
      Soldier pensioned in Chatham Co., Conn., in 1832.
   William, Chloe Folker, former wid. of.. W 7313
      Soldier pensioned in Cornwall, Conn., in 1818 as drummer.
   William, Otsego Co., N. Y., in 1818.. S 42221
RUST, Abel... S 42231
RUSTIN, William.. S 36278
RUTTY, Jonah, wid. Mary... R 9116
   Soldier never pensioned.
RYAN, Jeremiah, Conn. & Cont., wid. Mary... R 9122
   Soldier pensioned while living in Conn. in 1824, and N. Y. in 1832.
RYON, John... S 40377
   BLWt. 6364-100, private, was issued Sept. 8, 1790. No papers.

S.

SABEN or SABIN, Billings... S 42247
   Eldad.. S 14395
   Elihu, wid. Hannah (Conn. & Cont.).. W 17769
   Hezekiah, wid. Sarah.. W 13870
   Israel... S 11340
      (Given as SABEN.)
   Jonathan... S 31950
   Nathaniel, wid. Deborah.. W 26428
   Timothy... R 9133
SACKET or SACKETT, Benjamin, wid. Mercy, BLWt. 31317-160-55............... W 1940
   Buel or Buell.. S 14396
   Daniel, Conn. & N. Y., wid. Martha.. W 17770
   Samuel, Conn. & Penna.. S 4811
   Skeen or Skeene Douglass, wid. Lorrilla, BLWt. 18019-160-55................... W 4619
      (Given also as DOUGLASS, Skeen.)
   William, wid. Parthena, BLWt. 11282-160-55.. W 26956
SAFFORD, David.. R 9137
   Gideon.. R 6081
   Rufus, wid. Mary... R 9138
      (Soldier never pensioned.)
SAGE, Abraham, wid. Candace.. W 24887
   Daniel, Conn., Mass. & N. Y.. S 17069
   Epaphras, wid. Elizabeth.. W 26430
   Harlehigh, wid. Lucinda, BLWt. 35724-160-55... W 5972
      NOTE.—Lucinda's first husband, William PRATT, also served in the Revolution.

SAGE, Nathaniel, Cont. (Conn.)	S 33624
Stephen	S 30080
Zadoc	R 9142
ST. GEORGE, George, Conn. & Ga.	S 39090
ST. JOHN, Adonijah, Cont. (Conn.)	S 36802
David, wid. Mary, BLWt. 38542-160-55	W 25104
Enoch, wid. Maria, BLWt. 9076-160-55	W 11566
Jesse, Wilton, Conn., in 1818	S 36804
Jesse, Williamsburgh, N. Y., in 1828	S 42418
John, wid. Hannah	W 19125
Matthias	S 18200
Samuel	R 9147
SALMON, Asahel	S 36292
Gershom	S 14411
SALTONSTALL, Gurdon Flanders, Conn. & Navy	R 9159
SAMPSON or SAMSON, Zephaniah, Conn. & Cont., wid. Tamar	R 9164
Soldier was pensioned in 1818, as resident of Windham Co., Conn.	
SANDERS, Thomas	S 17661
William	S 41128
(See also SAUNDERS.)	
SANDERSON, Reuben	S 45142
BLWT. 1961-200, Lieut., was issued April 19, 1791, to Asa Worthington, Assignee. No papers.	
Silvanus or Sylvanus, Conn. & Mass., wid. Charlotte	W 24882
SANDFORD, SANDIFORD or SANFORD, Archibald	S 14412
(Given also as SANDFORD.)	
Daniel W., Conn. & Conn. Sea Service	S 29435
(Given as SANDIFORD.)	
David, wid. Abiah	W 22151
David, wid. Hannah, BLWt. 45718-160-55	R 9195
Soldier never pensioned; widow could not prove six months' service.	
Ebenezer, wid. Mary	W 11382
Elihu, wid. Nancy	W 5974
Elisha, wid. Rhoda	W 17772
Ezekiel	S 43103
Holsey, wid. Miriam, BLWt. 31714-160-55	W 586
Jairus	S 15207
James, Saratoga Co., N. Y., in 1818	S 43104
James, Conn. & Cont., Fairfield Co., Conn., in 1832	S 14410
Jesse, wid. Eleanor	W 17774
Jonathan	S 46068
Joseph	S 29434
Kingsbury, Cont. (Conn.) & Privateer	S 14398
Liffe, wid. Huldah	W 17773
Moses, wid. Elizabeth	R 9196
Both soldier and widow were rejected.	
Samuel, BLWt. 1947-300, Capt., was issued Oct. 30, 1789. No papers.	
Samuel	S 4810
BLWt. 26242-160-55; Portage Co., Ohio, in 1832.	
Samuel, wid. Ruhamah	W 19313
Fairfield Co., Conn., in 1832; died there in 1834; widow in Chemung Co., N. Y., in 1836.	
Strong	S 36289
Zacheus or Zaccheus, or Zacheous, wid. Eunice	W 22154
SANGER, Daniel	S 30081
Pearley	R 9199
SAP. (See LAP.)	
SARDAM, Henry, wid. Sylvia	W 17775
SARGEANT, Jacob, Conn. & Cont	S 15208
Sarah, former wid. of Elijah CARPENTER.	
(See also SERGEANT.)	
SATTERLEE or SATTERLEY or SATTERLY.	
Elisha, wid. Cynthia	W 2967
James, wid. Desire, BLWt. 405-100	W 4508
John, Conn. & R. I., wid. Hannah	W 18996
Samuel, Conn. Sea service	R 9212
SAUNDERS, Cuff, former widow, Phillis Tatton	W 18103
(Also given as WELLS, Cuff.)	
Peter	S 36288
Robert, Navy (Conn.)	S 36286
Samuel	S 36287
(See also SANDERS.)	
SAVAGE, Abijah, Conn. & Cont	S 36281
BLWt. 1954-300, Capt., was issued Jan. 28, 1790. No papers.	
Gideon, Cont. (Conn.), wid. Sarah	W 16064
John	S 11337
Luther	R 9225
Selah	S 17071
Seth, Conn. & Cont	S 15211
Solomon, wid. Lydia	R 9227
Neither soldier nor widow applied.	
Thomas, Conn. & Vt	S 14402
SAVY, Stephen, Conn. & Cont., N. H. & Vt.	R 17664
SAWYER, Asa	S 36283
Asahel	S 15210
Azariah, wid. Esther	W 26429
Conant	S 41129
Cornelius, wid. Sarah, BLWt. 18023-160-55	W 8704
Ephraim	S 36284

SAWYER, John, Ridgeway, N. Y., in 1818 & 1832. ... S 9472
    John, BLWt. 1771-100, private, Continental service; died 1804 at sea; heirs resided in Conn. in 1830.
    Samuel, wid. Mary. ... R 9236
        Soldier was invalid pensioner.
    William. ... S 13709
SAXTON, John. ... S 42252
    Zephaniah, Conn., Green Mt. Boys & Vt. ... S 14405
SCARBOROUGH, Elisha, wid. Prudence. ... W 26962
    John. ... S 17079
SCARRITT, James, wid. Eliza, BLWt. 19913-160-55. ... W 1942
    Nathan. ... S 45144
SCHELLENGER, SCHELLENEX or SCHELLENX, Abraham, wid. Jane. ... W 16724
    (See also SKELLENGER.)
SCHOFIELD or SCHOLFIELD, Jesse. ... S 31349
    (See also SCOFIELD.)
SCHOOLCRAFT, Samuel, wid. Mary, BLWt. 1108-100. ... W 5999
SCHOVIL, Jacob, Conn. & Green Mt. Boys. ... S 36294
    (See also SCOVILL.)
SCOFIELD, Asahel. ... S 23891
    Elisha, Conn. & N. Y., wid. Abigail, BLWt. 15425-160-55. ... W 11399
    Else, former wid. of Samuel COMSTOCK.
    Enos, wid. Amy. ... W 17786
        Poundridge, N. Y., in 1818; died there in 1830; widow in Fairfield Co., Conn., in 1837.
    Enos, Conn. & N. Y., Chataqua Co., N. Y., in 1832. ... S 15219
    Ezra, wid. Milly. ... W 1896
    Gershom, wid. Lydia. ... W 22166
    Gideon, Abigail Garret, former wid. of. ... R 3922
        Soldier never pensioned.
    Hart, Conn. & Cont. ... S 17665
    Israel, Conn. & N. Y. ... S 6052
    Jacob, wid. Abigail. ... W 17779
    Jared. ... S 16242
    Josiah Weed. ... S 17662
    Neazer. ... S 23892
    Reuben. ... S 11355
    Seely or Selah. ... S 10004
    Stephen. ... S 42266
    Sylvanus, wid. Sarah. ... W 17781
    William. ... S 28871
    (See also SCHOFIELD.)
SCOTT, Amasa. ... S 42258
    Caleb. ... S 42267
    Daniel, wid. Esther, BLWt. 3762-160-55. ... W 9511
    Eleazer. ... S 27450
    Elisha. ... R 9293
    Ethiel. ... S 41132
        Franklin Co., Vt., in 1832; served in 8th. reg't. Conn. Line.
    Ethiel. ... ELWt. 46-100
        3d reg't. Conn. Line; Addison Co., Vt., in 1800.
    Ezekiel. ... S 15220
    John. ... S 42254
    Joseph, Tolland Co., Conn., in 1832. ... S 15644
    Joseph, Glastonbury, Conn., in 1818. ... S 36295
    Justus. ... R 9305
    Lucy, former wid. of John FENTON.
    Moses, wid. Eunice. ... W 15313
        Soldier died in 1817; wid. resident of Franklin Co., Mass., in 1837.
    Moses, wid. Matilda. ... W 2176
        BLWt. 6475-100, private, was issued Aug. 3, 1790. No papers.
        Soldier was in Waterford, N. Y., in 1818; died 1853.
    Oliver, Indiana Co., Penna., in 1818; died in Ohio in 1845. ... S 41143
    Oliver, wid. Ruth. ... W 19327
        Soldier died in 1830 in Tolland Co., Conn.
    Stephen. ... S 23895
    Thomas, wid. Ruth. ... W 17780
    Uri. ... S 15217
    William, wid. Susannah. ... R 17700
        Soldier was pensioned in 1830 while resident of Fairfield Co., Conn.
SCOVEL, SCOVELL, SCOVIL, SCOVILL, or SCOVILLE.
    Abijah, wid. Rebecca. ... W 2628
    Abijah, Conn. & Mass. ... R 9319
    Amasa, Cont. (Conn.). ... R 9322
    Amasa. ... S 18592
        Pensioned in Trumbull Co., Ohio, in 1832 as private and musician.
    Benjamin, wid. Eunice. ... R 9320
        Soldier was pensioned in Galway, N. Y., in 1818.
    Ebenezer. ... S 42259
    John. ... S 14420
    Jonah, wid. Sarah. ... R 9318
        Soldier was Invalid pensioner; wounded in 1777.
    Joseph. ... S 23412
    Matthew, Conn. & Conn. Sea service. ... S 14414
    Michael. ... R 9321
    Michael. ... S 30691
    Moses, wid. Rachel. ... W 4796
    Samuel, Litchfield Co., Conn., in 1818; Broome Co., N. Y., in 1832. ... S 11360
    Samuel, wid. Lydia. ... W 16714
        Pensioned as Samuel, Jr., and sergeant in N. Y. in 1818.

SCOVEL, SCOVELL, SCOVIL, SCOVILL, or SCOVILLE—Continued.
Solomon	S 15214
Stephen, N. Y., in 1818	S 42265
Timothy, wid. Chloe	W 19006
Westol or Westole	S 23897
(See also SCHOVIL.)	
SCRANTOM or SCRANTON, Abraham, Durham, Conn., in 1832	S 49288
Abraham, wid. Lucy	W 17787
Soldier was pensioned as private & Sergeant in 1832, at Guilford, Conn.	
John, Conn. & Sea Service	S 17664
Thomas	S 15222
Timothy, wid. Sally, BLWt. 56-60-55	W 8707
Torey or Torry	S 15230
SCRIBNER, Ezra, wid. Nancy, BLWt. 40686-160-55	W 26433
Jared	R 9324
Jonathan, Conn. & N. Y	S 15215
Levi, wid. Esther	W 26961
SCRIPTER or SCRIPTURE, John	S 42264
SCRIVEN, James, Conn. & R. I	S 14417
SEAGER, Darius	S 13713
SEALEY or SEALY, George, wid. Lois	W 19339
(See also SEELY & SEELYE.)	
SEAMAN, Andrew	S 28872
SEAMAN, S., James, Conn. & R. I	S 15229
SEARS, David, Middlesex Co., Conn., in 1832	S 17539
David, Conn., Sea service & Mass., widow Martha	W 17795
Soldier was pensioned in Windham Co., Conn., in 1832 as private & serg't.; died 1841.	
Hannah. (See Obadiah.)	
Isaac, Cont. (Conn.), wid. Grace	W 16401
Obadiah	S 43121
Hannah Sears, widow of above soldier, was pensioned as former widow of Elias WILCOX, Cont. (Conn.), W 17792.	
Willard	S 17667
SEDGEWICK or SEDGWICK, Asher or Ashur, wid. Temperance, Conn. & Cont. service	W 15026
Ebenezer, wid. Martha	W 17799
John, wid. Sally	W 2007
Samuel	S 43120
Timothy, wid. Lucy, BLWt. 38547-160-55	W 26440
William	S 36298
SEELEY, SEELY or SEELYE, or SELEY.	
Abraham	S 2944
Benjamin, Cont. (Conn.), wid. Sarah	W 2358
Pensioned as Benjamin 2d in Salem, N. Y., in 1818; died in Warsaw, Wyoming Co., N. Y., in 1842.	
Benjamin, wid. Sarah	W 3463
Soldier was pensioned as private in Steuben Co., N. Y., in 1818; moved to Tioga Co., Penna., where he died in 1828.	
David	R 9363
Denton	S 17081
Ebenezer, wid. Betsey, BLWt. 7077-160-55	W 6013
Soldier was in Weston, Conn., in 1832.	
Ebenezer	S 13734
Pensioned in 1832 as fifer, Tompkins Co., N. Y.	
Ebenezer, Conn. & Cont., wid. Mabel	W 3308
Soldier pensioned in Tioga Co., Penna., in 1818 as private in Sheldon's Dragoons; died there in 1837.	
Isaac	S 11369
John, wid. Abigail	W 22173
Soldier pensioned in Goshen, Conn., in 1818, where he died in 1833.	
John, Betsey Campbell, former wid. of	W 4419
Soldier died in 1813; widow in Tioga Co., Penna., when pensioned.	
Joseph	S 36296
Seth, Cont. (Conn.)	S 43109
(See also SEALEY.)	
SEGER, Elijah	S 21962
Joseph, Conn. & Cont	S 15228
SELBY, David Melville, wid. Hannah, BLWt. 61196-160-55	W 10249
SELDEN, Benjamin	R 9371
Elijah	S 36297
Ezra, Conn. & Cont	BLWt. 687-300
SELEY. (See SEELY.)	
SELKRIG, Jeremiah	S 29443
SELLACK, SELLECK or SELLICK, Henry	S 41149
James, wid. Chloe. BLWt. 26231-160-55; BLWt. 57783-160-55	W 2256
Soldier was in Vermont in 1832; died in 1851 in Silver Creek, Mich.	
James, wid. Phebe	W 19331
Soldier died in 1803 in Saratoga Co., N. Y.	
(Also given as SILLICK.)	
Jesse	R 9379
Joseph, wid. Phebe	W 17796
Peter, Conn. & Cont	S 15226
Stephen, wid. Ann	W 7170
(See also SILLICK.)	
SERGEANT, Isaac, Elizabeth Taylor, former wid. of	R 10414½
Soldier was never pensioned. Widow was pensioned as widow of her other husband, Josiah TAYLOR, Conn., W 824.	
(See also SARGEANT.)	
SESSIONS, Abijah, wid. Hannah	W 26434
Robert, wid. Anna	W 24925

SEWARD, Jedediah, wid. Susan... W 1943
   Job, wid. Lois.. W 16716
   Nathan, wid. Martha.. W 9283
   Silas... S 43118
   Stephen, Sarah Lewis, former wid. of.. R 6329
      Soldier never pensioned.
   Timothy, Albany Co., N. Y., in 1818.. S 43111
   Timothy, widow Rebecca, BLWt. 38558-160-55... W 11416
      Soldier was in Guilford, Conn., in 1832; and died there in 1849.
SEXTON, Elijah, wid. Thankful, BLWt. 26879-160-55.. W 2444
   Ezra.. S 3879
SEYMOUR, Anne, former wid. of Kingsbury TILLEY.
   Asa... S 6072
      Granville, Mass., in 1832. (Given as Mass. service in report of 1834.)
   Asa, wid. Elizabeth... W 17798
      Soldier died in 1810 in Hartford, Conn.
   Eli.. R 9403
   George, Conn. & Cont., wid. Mabel.. W 17800
   Henry.. R 9404
   James, wid. Hannah.. W 11415
      Soldier died in 1814; was priv. & corp.; widow died in 1837.
   James, wid. Rebecca.. W 22172
      Soldier pensioned at Norwalk, Conn., as Quartermaster Serg't. in 1832.
   John, wid. Sally, BLWt. 26124-160-55.. W 24923
   Joseph... S 43116
   Nathaniel... S 15225
   Noah, wid. Miriam.. W 22171
   Samuel, private of Cavalry, in N. Y. City, and died there in 1834....................... S 28873
   Samuel, wid. Rebecca... W 17797
      Pensioned as private & serg't. died in Litchfield, Conn., in 1837.
   Seth, wid. Sally, BLWt. 36536-160-55.. W 26438
   Stephen... S 43107
      (Also given as SEYMOR.)
   Stephen... R 9406
   Thomas Young, Cont. (Conn.), wid. Susan.. W 19008
   William.. S 20951
      Invalid pensioner; living in 1824, when pension was changed to "18."
   William, Conn. & N. Y., wid. Sarah... W 19012
      Saratoga Co., N. Y., in 1832.
   Zachariah, Conn. & Cont., wid. Elizabeth.. W 26441
   Zadock... S 29440
SHAILER, Hezekiah, Conn., Cont. & Navy.. S 17675
   (See also SHAYLOR.)
SHALLIESS or SHALLEISS, Francis, wid. Anna... W 24943
SHANDLER, Robert. (See CHANDLER.)
SHARP or SHARPE, Caleb, Conn. & Cont... S 11380
   Daniel, wid. Jemima.. W 26465
   Isaac, Conn., Cont. & Green Mt. Boys, wid. Amey.. W 19358
   Reuben, Conn. & Cont... S 14450
SHATTOCK or SHATTUCK, David... S 36308
   William.. S 17670
SHAW, Benjamin.. S 36305
   Ichabod, Conn. & N. Y... S 40398
   Richard, Albany Co., N. Y., in 1832... S 22986
   Richard, Conn. & Cont.. S 40402
      Addison Co., Vt., in 1818; transferred to Ohio in 1836.
   William.. S 42284
SHAY, Timothy, wid. Hannah.. R 9447
   Soldier pensioned in 1828 in Westchester Co., N. Y.
SHAYLOR, Joseph, BLWt. 1960-200, Lieut. was issued Sept. 16, 1791. No papers.
   (See also SHAILER.)
SHEFFIELD, Joseph... S 42272
   Samuel, Navy (Conn.) & R. I.. S 39842
SHELDON, Caleb.. S 19087
   Ebenezer, wid. Love... R 9466
      Soldier never pensioned
   Elisha, BLWt. 1936-500, Colonel, was issued Dec. 12, 17—(no papers) to Theodosius Fowler, assignee.
   Ephraim.. S 14442
   James, wid. Abigail.. W 22184
   Moses, Cont. (Conn.)... S 15639
   Remembrance wid. Phoebe... W 24955
   Roger, wid. Elizabeth.. W 22189
   Samuel... BLWt. 36654-160-55
SHELLENX. (See SCHELLENGER.)
SHELLEY or SHELLY, Abraham, Cont. (Conn.), wid. Hannah................................. W 26463
   Ebenezer.. S 11391
   Medad.. R 9469
   Samuel, Jefferson Co., N. Y., in 1828; living in 1832.................................... S 42271
   Samuel, New London Co., Conn., in 1818; BLWt. 1287.................................... S 36306
SHELP, William.. S 17672
SHELTON, Caesar or Cezer... S 19764
   (Given also as NEGRO, Caesar.)
SHEPARD, SHEPEARD, SHEPHARD, SHEPHERD, SHEPPARD or SHEPPERD.
   Amos... S 33647
      Pensioned as corporal in Conn. in 1818; transferred to Mass.
   Amos, wid. Laminta, Chatham, Conn., in 1832.. W 22193
   Asa... S 14435
   Daniel... S 17671

SHEPARD, SHEPEARD, SHEPHARD, SHEPHERD, SHEPPARD, or SHEPPERD—Con.
Dorinda, former wid. of Jesse PENFIELD.
Edward Sears	R 9481
Henry	S 14448
James, Cont. (Conn.)	S 33646
Jesse	S 36307
(Given as SHEPPERD.)	
John, Cont. (Conn.), wid. Sarah, BLWt. 74-60-55	W 11452
Jonathan	S 41154
(Given as SHEPPARD.)	
Joseph, Cont. (Conn.)	S 33659
Phineas, Conn. & Cont.	S 3895
Samuel, Canterbury, Conn., in 1832	S 17674
Samuel, wid. Sabra	W 19351
Soldier was pensioned in Orange Co., Vt., in 1832.	
Stephen	S 30700
Thomas	S 36311
(Given as SHEPHERD.)	
Whitman	S 17087
(Given as SHEPHARD.)	
William	S 22505
SHERMAN, Benjamin, wid. Lydia	W 17806
Elijah, wid. Betty	R 9494
Soldier not pensioned.	
Enoch, wid. Catharine	W 15321
Isaac, Conn., Cont. & Mass.	S 33662
BLWT. 1938-500, Colonel, was issued Aug. 7, 1789, to Richard Platt, Assignee. No papers.	
John, wid. Nancy	W 8721
BLWt. 1962-200, Lieut, as issued March 7, 1792 to Jonas Prentice, Assignee. No papers.	
Nathaniel	S 14456
SHERWIN, Ahemaaz or Ahimaas, Conn. & Mass.	S 40424
SHERWOOD, Abel, wid. Mary	W 26458
Asa, wid. Molly	W 26468
Daniel, wid. Polly	W 17812
Eliphalet, wid. Abigail	W 22187
Jane, former wid. of David BURR.	
Jedediah or Jeddidiah	S 41156
Jonathan	R 9503
Lemuel	BLWt. 1739-100
Nehemiah, Steuben Co., N. Y., in 1832	S 11374
Nehemiah, Ridgefield, Conn., in 1818	S 36309
Nehemiah	S 40426
Venango Co., Penna., in 1820; suspended later for lack of identity with soldier.	
Reuben	S 14455
Seth	S 14431
Seymour or Seymore, Conn. & Navy	S 42289
Thomas, Conn., Cont. & N. Y	S 15637
Zachariah, Conn. & Cont., BLWt. 467-100	S 36313
SHETHAR, John, Cont. (Conn.)	S 11385
SHIPMAN, Benoni	S 36310
BLWt. 1955-200, Capt. Lieut., was issued June 28, 1790. No papers.	
George, wid. Mary	W 24946
James	S 33645
John, wid. Mercy or Marcy	W 17808
Samuel, wid. Sarah, BLWt. 9523-160-55	W 2670
Silas, wid. Sarah	W 17807
SHIPPEY, William, Conn., N. Y. & Penna.	S 1103
SHIRLIFF or SHIRTLIFF, John	S 21966
Noah, Conn. & N. Y	S 7478
SHOLES, Carey Wheeler	S 36314
Jabez or Jabish	S 11378
Miner	S 14457
SHOPP, Peter	BLWt. 1210-100
SHORT, Samuel, wid. Mary, BLWt. 35731-160-55	W 26454
Seth	S 17673
Siloam	S 11384
SHUMWAY, John, Conn. & Cont.	S 41157
BLWt. 1946-300, Capt., was issued Dec. 19, 1799, to Israel Harris, Assignee. No papers.	
SIBLEY, Ezra, wid. Ann or Anna	W 15337
Moses	S 29456
SIKES, David, wid. Nancy, BLWt. 24442-160-55	W 11425
Gideon, wid. Mercy, BLWt. 26482-160-55	W 6066
Jacob, wid. Sarah	W 6217
(Also given as SYKES.)	
John, Conn. & Vt., wid. Lucy, BLWt. 26020-160-55	W 19133
(Also given as SYKES.)	
(See also SYKES.)	
SILL, Andrew, Conn. & Cont	S 10014
David F., BLWt. 1940-450, Lieut. Colonel, was issued Jan. 28, 1790. No papers.	
Elisha N., wid. Chloe	W 6057
Isaac, Sarah Brockway, former wid. of	W 17358
Jabez	9570
Richard, BLWt. 1950-300, Capt., was issued Dec. 15, 1790, to Eliza Sill & others. No papers.	
Samuel, Cont. (Conn.)	S 36344
SILLICK, Benjamin	BLWt. 436-100
(See also SELLECK.)	

SILLIMAN, Issac, wid. Mary, BLWt. 35722-160-55	W 19033
James, wid. Huldah	W 17818
Samuel, Conn. & Navy, wid. Roxillana, BLWt. 27687-160-55	W 1266
SIMMONS, Benjamin, wid. Patty	W 24974
(Also given as BLACK or ROBERTS.)	
Benoni, Conn., Cont., Navy & R. I., widow Nancy, BLWt. 18376-160-55	W 13899
Chapman, Conn. Sea service, widow Elizabeth	W 19362
John, wid. Rachel	W 24965
Peleg, wid. Amy, BLWt. 26549-160-55	W 11428
Samuel, Jay, Maine, in 1818, as corporal	S 37394
Samuel, wid. Sarah	W 24967
Grafton Co., N. H., in 1818; died in 1841. BLWt. 341-60-55, BLWt. 2155-100.	
Stephen	S 32521
(See also SIMONDS & SIMONS & SYMONDS.)	
SIMON, Cummy	S 36315
SIMONDS or SIMONS, Aaron, wid. Mehitable	W 17816
Andrew	S 42300
Arad, Conn., Conn. Sea service & Cont., wid. Bridget	W 15339
Asa, Conn. & Mass	S 7519
Eli	S 33668
Elijah, Greenwich, Conn., in 1832	S 15647
Elijah, wid. Lucy	W 17813
Soldier died in 1831; widow in 1837, in Windham Co., Conn.	
Isaac	R 9583
Isham, Conn. & Cont., wid. Deborah, BLWt. 5102-160-55	W 1898
Jeduthan, wid. Mary, BLWt. 56917-160-55	R 9582
Soldier rejected; did not serve six months.	
John, wid. Ann	W 16406
Soldier served as serg't.; died in Cayuga Co., N. Y., in 1814.	
John, Navy	S 15203
Enlisted on frigate *Confederacy* in 1779, in Columbia Co., N. Y., in 1820.	
Joseph, Delaware Co., N. Y., in 1818	S 42305
Joseph, wid. Prudence	W 17814
(Also given as SYMONS.)	
Soldier pensioned in Hartford Co., Conn., in 1818; died in 1830.	
Joseph, Conn., Cont. & Mass., Chemung Co., N. Y., in 1832	S 14460
Joshua, wid. Elizabeth	W 24960
Lycus, wid. Julia	R 9584
Soldier pensioned in 1818 in New London Co., Conn.	
Nathan	S 17094
Paul G	R 9585
Sarah, former wid. of David VIBBARD or VIBBIRD.	
Thomas, Rebecca BARBER, former wid. of	W 20679
William, wid. Beulah	W 17817
(Also given as SEMONS.)	
(See also SYMONDS.)	
SIMPSON, John, BLWt. 1942-400, Surgeon, was issued Sept. 2, 1789. No papers.	
SINNOTT, Partick, wid. Mary	W 4585
SIP, Jesse, Navy (Conn.)	S 36316
SIZER, Anthony, wid. Lucretia	W 24550
Daniel	S 36317
Jonathan	S 14459
Lemuel, wid. Elizabeth	W 22215
William, Cont. (Conn.)	S 33672
SKEEL or SKEELE, Amos, wid. Lucy	W 6070
Phebe, former wid. of Robert HUBBARD.	
SKEELS, Simeon, Cont. (Conn.), Asenath Amedon, former wid. of	W 20605
SKELLENGER, Daniel	S 4844
(See also SCHELLENGER.)	
SKIFF, Stephen, wid. Abah	W 19039
SKINER or SKINNER, Adonijah, wid. Abigail	R 9631
NOTE.—Adonijah was son of Capt. John Skinner, and John's commission is on file in the Department.	
SKINNER, Ashbel, wid. Rhoda	W 17819
Benjamin, Conn. & Vt., wid. Sarah	W 17820
Beriah	S 42306
Daniel, Conn. & N. H., wid. Hannah	W 24976
David, wid. Ruth, BLWt. 6422-160-55	W 2448
(Given as SKINER.)	
Elisha, wid. Achsa	W 17822
Ira, wid. Hepsibah	R 9633
Their son Riley B. Skinner, of Trumbull Co., Ohio, applied for pension in 1855.	
Isaac, wid. Lucy	W 24975a
Soldier in Windsor Co., Vt., in 1820; died there in 1843.	
Isaac, wid. Mabel	W 22220
Soldier died in Hartford Co., Conn., in 1816; widow living there in 1836.	
Israel, wid. Lovisa	W 17821
John	S 42310
Pensioned as Lieut. in Ballston, N. Y., in 1818.	
John, Catharine Emerson, former wid. of, BLWt. 7097-160-55	W 24120
Soldier served as artificer and died in 1801; widow living in Cortland, N. Y., in 1836.	
John, wid. Cleopatra	W 24980
Soldier pensioned in 1832 in Hartford Co., Conn., where he died in 1833.	
Jonathan, wid. Judith	W 22222
Luther, wid. Sarah	W 22219
Washington Co., N. Y., in 1818; died there in 1827; widow in Franklin Co., Vt., in 1842	
Luther, wid. Temperance	W 24978
Soldier pensioned in Windsor Co., Vt., in 1832; died there in 1838.	

SKINNER, Richard... S 14471
  Samuel, wid. Elizabeth... W 22221
  Stephen.. S 31965
  Thomas, BLWt. 1943-400, Surgeon, was issued Dec. 3, 1789 to Daniel Watrous, Assignee. No. papers.
  Thomas.. S 42307
  Timothy, BLWt.. 946-100
  Uriah... S 22991
  Zenas.. S 14468
SLADE, Abner, Conn. & Cont... S 16248
  Jacob... R 9644
  William, BLWt. 15418: 160-55... S 23921
SLASON, Jonathan.. S 22513
  Nathanial, wid. Hannah.. W 24982
    (Soldier died May 1, 1835.)
SLASSON, Deliverance... S 29461
SLATE, Thomas.. R 17896
SLATER, Amos, wid. Rachel... R 9651
  Neither soldier nor widow applied; daughter, Martha Spies, of Livingston Co., N. Y., in 1850 was rejected.
  James, wid. Esther.. W 17825
SLAUSON, Ezra.. S 17701
  (See also SLAWSON.)
SLAUTER, Ephraim, wid. Ruth.. W 6079
SLAWSON, Eleazer, Conn. & N Y.. S 23420
  Nathan, wid. Hannah, BLWt. 8017-160-55.. W 22226
    Soldier died in Oct., 1844.
    (See also SLAUSON.)
SLEAD, John.. S 36331
SMALLIN or SMALLING, Jacob, Conn. & N. Y., wid. Mary........................... R 9671
  Soldier was pensioned from Windham, Greene Co., N. Y., in 1832.
SMITH, Aaron.. S 20966
  Invalid pensioner; died 1824, Haddam, Conn., aged 87 yrs.
  Aaron... R 20435
    Was of N. Y. City in 1830 and Litchfield Co., Conn., in 1831.
  Aaron, Conn. & Cont.. S 42346
    (Also given as Aron.)
    Enlisted from Washington, Conn.; was in Middlefield, Otsego Co., N. Y., in 1818, aged 63 years.
  Abel, wid. Sarah.. W 11479
    Soldier born in Brookfield, Litchfield Co., Conn., May 20, 1757; enlisted there, and died there Apr. 27, 1849.
  Abel, Conn., Cont. & Mass... S 43156
    Soldier born Oct. 18, 1750; enlisted from Mass. and resided in 1818 in Windham, N. Y.
  Abel, Conn. & R. I... S 43154
    In N. Y. City in 1820, aged 56 yrs.
  Abijah, wid. Judith... R 9783
    Soldier never pensioned.
  Abisha, Conn. & Cont.. S 18226
  Abner... S 18232
  Abraham.. S 18225
  Allen... S 43161
    Enlisted from New Haven Co., Conn., was in Plattsburgh, N. Y., in 1820, aged 63 yrs.
  Allen, Conn. & Privateer.. S 17686
    Born East Haven, Conn., 1750; died 1834, Branford, New Haven Co., Conn.
  Amos.. S 22518
    Born Lyme, Conn., & enlisted there; in 1832 was in Greensboro, Vt., aged 75 yrs.
  Amos.. R 9685
  Amos, wid. Lydia.. W 24989
    Soldier born New London Co., Conn., May 8, 1757; enlisted there, and died Mch. 17, 1836, at Schoharie, N. Y.
  Andrew.. S 17097
  Anthony, wid. Esther.. W 17844
  Asa, Conn. & Cont.. S 32528
  Asaph, Cont. (Conn.).. S 36323
  Asher, wid. Sarah.. W 17834
  Austin.. S 23426
  Azariah, wid. Alathea.. W 17843
  Benjamin... S 14530
    Born Dec. 31, 1761, at Canterbury, Conn.; enlisted there and was living there in 1832.
  Benjamin... S 17099
    Born Apr. 20, 1747, in Fairfield Co., Conn.; enlisted there and was living there in 1833.
  Benjamin, wid. Amelia... R 9684
    Soldier died in Windham Co., Conn., in 1834, not pensioned.
  Benjamin, Conn. & Cont... S 41175
    Enlisted from Pomfret, Conn., in 1818; was in Bethel, Vt., aged 64 yrs.
  Benjamin, Cont. (Conn.), widow Lydia... R 9792
    Soldier was born in East Haven, Conn., and died in 1794; never pensioned. Lydia was 84 in 1838, at East Haven, Conn.
  Bill, Conn. & N. Y.. S 14528
    Born New London Co., Conn., Feb., 1753; enlisted from Middletown, Conn., & New Lebanon, N. Y.; in 1832 was in Rome, N. Y.
    (See also SMITH, William.)
  Caleb, Conn. & Conn. Sea service, wid. Sarah... W 17837
  Calvin, wid. Anna... R 9688
    Soldier never pensioned; died in Hampshire Co., Mass., in 1832.
  Charles.. S 15983
  Cuff.. S 36321
  Dan, wid. Betsey... W 5174
    Soldier enlisted at Sharon, Conn., & in 1818 was in Rutland, Vt., aged 60 yrs.; died Feb. 15, 1833; widow died Sept. 23, 1845.

SMITH, Daniel... S 17681
   Born East Haven, Conn., Sept. 23, 1762; enlisted there & in 1832 was in New Haven, Conn.
Daniel.. S 36319
   In 1820 was in Preston, Conn., aged 74 yrs.
Daniel, wid. Mary, BLWt. 26754-160-55... W 19070
   Resided Stamford, Conn., & died in North Castle, Westchester Co., N. Y., Dec. 15, 1831.
Daniel, Conn. & Cont... S 45154
   In 1818 was in Marcellus, Onondaga Co., N. Y., aged 62 yrs.
Daniel, Conn. & R. I.. S 11416
   Born Stonington, Conn., Oct. 7, 1753; & in 1832 was in Columbia, Herkimer Co., N. Y
David, BLWt. 1941-400, Major, was issued Sept. 16, 1789. No papers.
David... S 17683
   Born Feb. 16, 1763, at Stamford, Conn.; lived there until after 1832.
David... S 31968
   Born Mch. 26, 1764, Vernon, Conn.; there in 1832.
David... S 40468
   In 1818 was in Washington Co., Ohio, aged 72 yrs.
David... R 21792
   In 1829 was in Wayne Co., Ohio, aged 75 yrs. & had a wife, Mary.
David, wid. Hannah.. W 6123
   Soldier enlisted from Derby, Conn., & in 1832 was in Auburn, Geauga Co., Ohio, aged 69 yrs.; died there Nov. 19, 1852.
David, wid. Lois... W 25016
   Soldier born in Fairfield Co., Conn., June 16, 1757, & enlisted there; died May 31, 1835, at Patakill, Ulster Co., N. Y.
David, wid. Mary.. R 9797
   Soldier born in 1758, Canterbury, Conn.; enlisted there, & in 1832, when pensioned, was in Braintree, Vt.; died Mch. 23, 1840; widow died Oct. 23, 1843.
David, wid. Mary.. R 9798
   Soldier born Nov. 20, 1756, at Milford, Conn., & enlisted there & lived there when pensioned in 1832; died Nov. 7, 1841; widow died Dec. 7, 1843.
Dow... S 14519
Ebenezer... S 17108
   Born July 27, 1762, at Stamford, Conn., living there in 1832.
Ebenezer, wid. Elizabeth... R 9722
   Soldier born Ridgefield, Conn., Oct. 3, 1761, & enlisted there; in 1832, when pensioned, in Elmira, N. Y., died Apr., 1844.
Ebenezer, Conn. & Cont. & N. Y... S 42343
   In 1818 in Onondaga Co., N. Y., & in 1820 in Cortland Co., N. Y., aged 66 yrs.
Ebenezer, Conn. & Cont., wid. Naomi... W 11471
   Fairfield Co., Conn., where he died Aug. 14, 1832.
Edmund.. S 20964
Eli, wid. Deborah.. W 17833
   Soldier died May 29, 1824, Litchfield Co., Conn.
Eli, Phebe Gouge, former wid. of.. W 19520
   Soldier was born Oct. 8, 1760; enlisted from Brookfield, Conn., & died in Bridgeport, Conn., July 17, 1819.
Elijah... R 9717
   Died Scipio, N. Y., in 1848, aged 88 yrs.
Elijah, wid. Betsy, BLWt. 33755-160-55.. W 17835
   Soldier was born Sept., 1763, in Norwich, Conn., & in 1832 was in Lebanon, Conn.; died Mch. 24, 1848.
Elijah, wid. Prudence... W 17829
   Soldier was pensioned in 1818, at Granby, Conn., aged 61 yrs., and died there Nov. 21, 1824.
Elijah, Conn. & Mass., wid. Hannah.. R 9740
   Soldier died Oct. 2, 1824, in Sempronius, N. Y., not pensioned; widow applied in 1844 & said soldier enlisted in 1775 from Stafford, Conn., & in 1778 from South Brimfield, Mass.
Elijah, Conn. & N. Y.. S 14493
   In 1832 in Saratoga Co., N. Y., aged 74 yrs.
Eliphalet, Olive Platt, former wid. of, BLWt. 26996-160-55........................... W 2241
   Soldier was born Feb. 25, 1761, at Fairfield Co., Conn.; in 1832 was in Norwalk, Conn., & died Apr. 26, 1836.
Eliphalet, Conn., Cont. & Green Mt. Boys.. S 40457
   Was pensioned from Bedford Co., Penna., in 1820, aged 69 yrs., and died Dec. 31, 1839.
Elkanah... S 36320
Elnathan, Cont. (Conn.), wid. Mary... W 24984
   BLWt. 6518-100, Serg't., was issued April 7, 1790. No papers.
Enoch, Conn. & Conn., Sea service, wid. Hannah, BLWt. 28542-160-55......... W 17842
   Soldier born Dec. 29, 1759; d. 1824, N. Y. City.
Enoch... S 17106
   Born 1753, Chatham, Conn.; died there Mch. 19, 1833, leaving no widow.
Enos.. R 9729
Ephraim... S 23423
   Born Aug. 28, 1759, Cheshire, Conn., & enlisted there; in 1832 was in Mendon, N. Y.
Ephraim, wid. Deborah... R 9711
   Soldier was born Sept. 5, 1762, in Lyme, Conn., & enlisted there; in 1833, when pensioned, was in LeRay, Jefferson Co., N. Y., & died Aug. 21, 1837.
Ethan, wid. Hannah... W 17845
Ezekiel... S 18599
Ezra, BLWt. 1959-200, Lieut., was issued Dec. 18, 1789, to Joshua Henshaw, Assignee. No papers.
Ezra, Cont. (Conn.)... S 42319
   Enlisted in Conn., & in 1820 was in Stamford, Conn., aged 67 yrs.
Francis, Conn. & N. H... R 9733
Frederic or Frederick... S 23428
   Born in 1762 in Norwich, Conn., & in 1832 was in Colchester, Conn.
Frederick... S 19470
   Born Jan. 10, 1765, at Middletown, Conn., & enlisted there; in 1834 was in Manchester, Vt.

SMITH, Frederick, Conn. & Privateer.. S 11410
    Born Mch. 1, 1760, Haddam, Conn., & enlisted there; pensioned in 1832 in Jefferson, Schoharie Co., N. Y.
Gabriel.. S 16251
Gideon, Conn., N. H. & Vt.. S 11409
Gregory, Cont. (Conn.), wid. Hannah... W 16408
Heman.. S 23427
Henry, wid. Huldah... R 18007
    Soldier never pensioned. Was married in Fairfield Co., Conn., & died Jan. 9, 1828. Children resided in Conn. & N. Y.
Henry, Cont. (Conn.).. S 43155
    Born in 1758; enlisted from Middletown, Conn., in 1818; was in Lee, Mass., & in 1820 in Tioga Co., N. Y.
Ira... S 11417
    Born in 1763, East Haven, Conn., & enlisted there; in 1832 was in Ulysses, Tompkins Co., N. Y., and died in 1837.
Ira, wid. Chloe... R 9704
    Born Sept. 7, 1757, in Wallingford, Conn., & enlisted there; in 1832 it was called Prospect; died April 22, 1835.
Isaac... S 14517
    In 1818 was at Greenville, Greene Co., N. Y., aged 56 years., and in 1820 at New Canaan, Conn.
Isaac... S 34516
    In 1820 was in West Boylston, Mass., aged 65 yrs.
Isaac... S 42340
    Born in 1758; in 1818 was in Chittenden Co., Vt., & in 1831 in Penna., & in 1834 in N. Y. state.
Isaac, wid. Mary, BLWt. 75106-160-55... W 11485
    Soldier was 63 yrs. in 1820 at Greenwich, Conn., where he died July, 1829.
Isaac, wid. Sarah... R 9853
    Soldier never applied for pension; died Oct. 6, 1828.
Isaac, Conn. & N. Y., Abigail Finch, former wid. of... W 3537
    Soldier died Feb. 15, 1805, at Stamford, Conn.
Isaac Sheldon, Conn. & Mass.. R 9745
Isaiah, Conn. & Cont., wid. Nancy or Ann... W 17826
Israel.. S 16531
    Born in 1759, Lyme, Conn.; enlisted there & in 1832 was in Dempster, Sullivan Co., N. Y.
Israel, wid. Eleanor, BLWt. 69-60-55.. W 502
    In 1818 soldier was in Cazenovia, N. Y., aged 54 yrs., & died Dec. 6, 1836, in Chataqua Co., N. Y.
Israel, Conn. & R. I... S 14534
    Born Sept. 22, 1754, at Gloucester, R. I.; enlisted there & at Thompson, Conn.; in 1833 was in Brookfield, Mass.
Ithamar, Conn. & Cont., wid. Deborah.. W 19068
Jabez.. S 14506
Jacob, Conn. & Cont., wid. Hannah, BLWt. 26335-160-55.. W 22240
    Soldier enlisted from Stamford, Conn., where he was born, & died in N. Y. City Sept., 1811.
Jacob, Conn. Sea service, Cont. & Mass.. S 34503
    Born in Dedham, Mass., in 1752; in 1818 in Orrington, Maine, & died May 11, 1834.
Jairus, wid. Sarah.. W 25032
James... S 11440
    Born 1762 at Old Haddam, Conn.; enlisted there; in 1832 at Harpersfield, Delaware Co., N. Y.
James, wid. Marcy, BLWt. 28582-160-45... W 19372
    Soldier was born July 18, 1765, & died in Otsego Co., N. Y., Aug. 2, 1827.
James, wid. Phebe... W 27567
    Soldier was born in 1762 in New London Co., Conn.; enlisted there; in 1834 in Westmoreland, Oneida Co., N. Y., & died Jan. 16, 1836.
James, Conn. & Cont.. S 42349
    Enlisted from Lyme, Conn., in 1820 in Kent, Putnam Co., N. Y., aged 62 yrs.; had wife, Mary.
James, Conn. & N. Y., wid. Ruth Ann.. W 26488
    Soldier was born in 1757, White Plains, N. Y.; enlisted in Wyoming Co., Penna., & in 1832 was in Hector, Tompkins Co., N. Y.
James, Cont. (Conn.), wid. Sarah H., BLWt. 26502-160-55.. W 11482
    Soldier enlisted from Southington, Conn., where he died Mch. 3, 1819.
James A.. R 9750
    Born Mch. 16, 1763, in Groton, Conn., & in 1840 was in West Stockbridge, Mass.
Jedediah, wid. Esther, BLWt. 125-60-55... W 22233
Jeffery.. S 16250
Jehiel, wid. Rachel.. W 22246
Jeremiah.. S-
    Born Dec. 24, 1746, at West Haven, Conn.; enlisted there & in 1832 & died July 19, 1835, there (then called Orange).
Jeremiah, wid. Anna... W 26481
    Soldier born June 30, 1762, at Norwalk, Conn.; enlisted there; in 1832 at Nevisink, Sullivan Co., N. Y., & died there July 25, 1851.
Jeremiah, wid. Temperance... W 22268
    Soldier born July 29, 1758; in 1818 at East Haddam, Conn., & died there Dec. 20, 1837.
Jesse.. S 36768
    In 1820, aged 63 yrs., was at Woodbridge, Conn.; died Aug. 15, 1831.
Jesse.. R-
    Born, lived, & died in Stamford, Conn.; died in 1801, 1802, or 1803.
Jesse, wid. Susanna.. R 9861
    Pensioned as Jesse 2nd in 1819, Great Barrington, Mass., aged 62 yrs.; enlisted at Stratford, Conn.; died May 24, 1841, Mexico, N. Y., where widow died in 1846. Neither soldier nor widow rejected, but children.
Job, wid. Esther.. W 17831
Joel.. BLWt. 198-150
    In 1802 was resident of Owego, Tioga Co., N. Y.

SMITH, Joel, wid. Sarah.. W 19066
    Soldier was born Nov. 10, 1756, at Redding, Conn.; enlisted there; in 1832 was at Butternuts, Otsego Co., N. Y., where he died May 19, 1837.
John.. S 29468
    Born June 11, 1757, at Springfield, Mass.; enlisted at Suffield, Conn., & in 1832 was at Granville, Hampden Co., Mass.; died Sept. 3, 1835.
John.. S 34493
    Enlisted from East Haddam, Conn.; in 1818 at Middlefield, Hampshire Co., Mass.
John.. S 42352
    Born 1742; enlisted at Stamford, Conn.; in 1818 at Locke, Cayuga Co., N. Y., & in 1820 had wife, Tamer.
John, wid. Anne.. W 17830
    Born in 1744; died Aug. 5, 1827, at New Milford, Litchfield Co., Conn.
John, wid. Betsey... W 22244
    Born 1741; enlisted at Conn., & died in 1835 at Lewis, Essex Co., N. Y.
John, wid. Lydia.. W 3724
    Born Apr. 27, 1760, Montville, Conn.; enlisted there and died in 1852 at Montville.
John, wid. Mary, BLWt. 26722-160-55... W 26965
    Born June 14, 1756, at New Haven, Conn.; enlisted at North Haven; in 1832 at the latter place & died there Nov. 3, 1847.
John, Nancy Ann Wilbur, former wid. of... R 11510
    Invalid pensioner, who died in 1813 at New Lisbon, N. Y.
John, Conn. Sea service, wid. Tabitha.. W 13915
    Soldier was born in 1750 and died at sea Sept. 20, 1783; widow at Providence, R. I., in 1836.
John, BLWt. 1990-200, Lieut., in Col. Lamb's reg't. Artillery was issued May 18, 1790, to Isaac Guion, Assignee. No paper.
John, Cont. (Conn.).. S 14497
    Born Mch. 19, 1756, at Farmington, Conn., where he enlisted; in 1818 was at Bristol, Conn., with wife, Chloe.
John, Cont. (Conn.).. S 36772
    In 1820 was at Haddam, Conn., aged 64 years, with wife, Anna; died May, 1834, at Haddam.
    BLWt. 13776-100, private in Artillery Artificers, was issued Dec. 6, 1799. No papers.
John, Cont. (Conn.).. S 36774
    Enlisted from Stratford, Conn., where he was living in 1818, when pensioned.
    (Also given SMITTS & MITTS.)
Jonathan... R 9776
    Born Groton, Conn., in 1746; in 1833, at Geneva, Cayuga Co., N. Y.
Jonathan, wid. Polly or Molly, BLWt. 7436-160-55.. W 19373
    Soldier enlisted at Ashford, Conn., & died May 2, 1824.
Jonathan, wid. Rebecca, BLWt. 6107-160-55.. W 24990
    Enlisted from Haddam, Conn., where he died Aug. 16, 1812.
Jonathan, Conn. & Navy... S 34497
    Enlisted in New Haven Co., Conn.; in 1818 at Sheffield, Mass.
Jonathan, Jr., wid. Rebecca... R 9835
    Soldier never applied; widow claimed that he performed sea service, applying while a resident of Rock Co., Wis.; in Feb., 1850; in May, 1850, she had died.
Joseph... S 14 11
    Born in 1756 in New London Co., Conn.; enlisted there & was pensioned there in 1832.
Joseph, Elizabeth Chapman, former wid. of... R 1865
    Soldier was born, Hebron, Conn., 1760; in 1821 was in Ontario Co., N. Y.
Joseph, wid. Eunice.. W 6121
    Soldier enlisted from Derby, Conn., & in 1820 lived there, aged 65 yrs.; died there Apr. 28, 1834.
Joseph, wid. Rebecca... W 17827
    Soldier born, lived & died at Stamford, Conn.; died Aug. 6, 1828.
Joshua.. S 42329
Josiah.. S 14533
    Born Dec. 20, 1747, Windham Co., Conn.; enlisted there & pensioned in 1832 there.
Josiah.. S 42330
    Born & enlisted in New London Co., Conn.; in 1833 at Tamworth, N. H., aged 83 yrs.; died Mch., 1838.
Josiah.. S 47992
    In 1787 at Cheshire, Conn., aged 28 yrs., living there in 1824; in 1830 in Geauga Co., Ohio; died Nov. 7, 1833.
Josiah, wid. Sarah.. W 25023
    Soldier born July 12, 1750; in 1788 at Poundridge, Westchester Co., N. Y., & died Nov. 29, 1830, at Stamford, Conn.
Josiah, Conn. & Privateer, wid. Anna... W 25012
    Born Aug. 3, 1759, & enlisted in New London Co., Conn., & in 1818 was in Philipstown, Putnam Co., N. Y.; died Jan. 8, 1842, in Richmond Co., N. Y.
Josiah, Continental service.. S 36759
    In 1818 in Berlin, Conn., aged 62 years.
Keturah, former wid. of Job PRIMUS or LATHROP.
Laban, Conn. & Privateer... S 14525
Lemuel... S 14502
Lewis, wid. Ann, Conn. & Navy Service... W 19509
Lucy, former wid. of William FRENCH.
Lue or Lewee... S 36722
Luther, wid. Ruth... W 26486
Martin.. S 18598
Matthew or Mathew.. S 31379
    Born May 12, 1753, at East Haddam, Conn., & enlisted there; in 1832 at Middlefield, Hampshire Co., Mass.
Matthew, wid. Susan.. R 9860
    Soldier died at Vernon, Oneida Co., N. Y., Nov., 1815. Never pensioned.
Matthew, Conn. & Vt., wid. Emma, BLWt. 27585-160-55... W 2010
    Soldier was born Jan. 13, 1760, at Pomfret, Conn., where he enlisted; his third enlistment was at Hartland, Vt., & in 1832 he was at Chaplin, Conn., where he died Dec. 25, 1841.

SMITH, Michael, wid. Mary... W 17846
    Miner, wid. Submit, BLWt. 3612-160-55... W 25010
    Nathan... S 17680
        Born Feb., 1735, at Lyme, Conn.; enlisted at Montville, Conn., & in 1832 was at Hebron, Conn.
    Nathan, wid. Rachel... W 26477
        Soldier was born at Holden, Mass., & lived there in 1818, aged 55 yrs.; died there Aug. 23, 1824; enlisted "in Susquehanna River in N. Y."
    Nathaniel.. S 36764
        In 1820, aged 59 yrs., was at Lyme, Conn., with wife, Lucinda.
    Nathaniel, wid. Lucy... W 17832
        Born Aug. 11, 1761, at Canterbury, Conn., & died there July 21, 1835.
    Nathaniel, Conn. & Cont... S 36761
        In 1820, aged 66 yrs., was in Litchfield Co., Conn.
    Noah, wid. Hannah... R 9819
        Both soldier & widow rejected.
    Oliver... S 21980
    Peter... S 36767
    Philemon, Conn. & N. Y... S 14503
    Phineas, Conn. & Vt.. S 19471
        Grand Isle, Vt., in 1832.
    Phinehas, wid. Abiah.. W 26487
        Soldier died in 1812 at Fairfield Co., Conn.
    Phinehas, wid. Deborah Ann.. W 11480
        Litchfield Co., Conn., in 1832; died in 1839.
    Ralph, wid. Anne.. W 17841
        New Milford, Conn., in 1818; died there in 1825.
    Ralph, wid. Hannah... W 15945
        Died in 1807 in Albany Co., N. Y.
    Ralph, wid. Mary.. W 819
        Middlesex Co., Conn., in 1832.
    Richard.. S 14520
    Robert, Conn. & Cont.. BLWt. 1267-100
    Robert, Cont. (Conn.).. S 11421
        Meriden, Conn., in 1832.
    Roger... S 14529
    Roswell.. S 17684
    Samuel... S 31971
        Private, corporal & Serg't.; in 1832 was in Savannah, Ga.
    Samuel, wid. Anna... W 22265
        New Haven Co., Conn., in 1832.
    Samuel, Conn. & Cont... S 14494
        Southington, Conn., in 1832.
    Samuel, Cont. (Conn.)... S 17107
        Norwalk, Conn., in 1832.
    Samuel B... S 17104
    Sarah, former wid. of Robert STOGDILL.
    Seth... S 14507
    Sherman, wid. Amarillas... W 25005
    Silas... S 18597
    Simon.. S 11411
    Sparrow, wid. Eunice... W 26489
    Stephen... S 17100
        Haddam, Conn., in 1832.
    Stephen, Conn. & Conn. Sea service... S 14523
        Branford, Conn., in 1832.
    Stephen, Conn. & Cont.. S 42337
        Butternuts, N. Y., in 1818.
    Sylvanus... S 40469
    Sylvester, wid. Hannah.. W 24983
    Theophilus M.. S 14532
    Thomas, wid. Thankful.. W 26474
    Timothy.. S 42314
        Pensioned as Timothy 3rd. in 1829, at Collins, Erie Co., N. Y.
    Timothy.. S 41164
        Tinmouth, Vt., in 1818.
    Wells, wid. Elizabeth.. W 17848
    William, BLWt. 1956-200, Lieut., was issued Aug. 5, 1789. No papers.
    William, wid. Esther... W 25018
        Captain; died in 1816 in Windham Co., Conn.
    William, Conn. & Cont.. S 14508
        Bozrah, Conn., aged 67 yrs., in 1823.
    William, wid. Hannah.. W 17839
        Born in North Kingston, R. I., in 1758; Voluntown, Conn., when he died July 4, 1839. (See also Bill SMITH.)
    Zachariah.. S 41177
    Zebina, wid. Martha... W 19047
SMITTS, John. (See SMITH.)
SNELL, Joseph... S 36776
SNOW, Abraham, wid. Lavina, BLWt. 26727-160-55.. W 504
    Amaziah, wid. Sarah.. R 9916
        Soldier not pensioned.
    Ezra, wid. Lavina.. W 25036
    Isaac, Conn. Sea service & Mass.. S 19098
    Ivory, Conn. & Mass... S 11434
    John.. R 9913
    Jonathan... S 16256
        Tolland Co., Conn., in 1832.
    Jonathan, wid. Mercy... W 25038
        Norwich, Vt., in 1818; died in 1833.

SNOW, Joseph.. S 14536
   Levi.. S 17688
   Nathan, Conn. & Mass... S 21495
   Nathaniel, wid. Mehitable.. R 9915
      Soldier pensioned from Chatham, Mass., in 1818, & Barnstable, Mass., in 1829.
   Robert, wid. Anna, BLWt. 2180-160-55.. W 25041
   Shubeal, wid. Rachel, BLWt. 45717-160-55................................... W 26492
   Silas... S 14544
   Thomas, wid. Lucy... W 17849
SOLLACE, Eliza Whitney, former wid. of David WHITNEY.
SOLLEY, Thomas, Cont. (Conn.), wid. Eunice................................ W 17853
SOPER, Jesse, Conn. & N. Y... R 9935
   Prince, Conn., Cont. & Green Mt. Boys, wid. Elizabeth.................. W 25044
   Timothy.. S 17691
SOUTHMAYD, Daniel.. S 14547
SOUTHWARD, Andrew... S 36778
SOUTHWELL, Asahel, wid. Hannah.. W 3363
SOUTHWORTH, Elijah.. S 10022
   Isaac... S 22525
      (Also given as SUTHARD.)
   Joseph, Cont. (Conn.)... S 33693
   Lemuel.. S 41180
   Samuel Wells, wid. Marcy... W 15802
   William.. S 40479
SOWL, David.. S 14546
SPALDING, Barzillai or Brazillai, Conn. & N. H................................. S 19101
   Darius, wid. Mary, BLWt. 27684-160-55....................................... W 1879
   John, wid. Wealthy Ann... W 3312
   Joseph... R 9952
   Joseph, Conn. & Vt... S 22529
   Josiah.. BLWt. 75115-160-55
      Soldier was son of Josiah, a soldier who had a disability pension.
   Philip.. S 14567
   Reuben... S 17695
   Silas... S 22530
   Simon, BLWt. 1948-300, Capt., was issued Dec. 15, 1791. No papers.
   Wright... S 43168
      (See also SPAULDING.)
SPARKS or SPARKES, Ebenezer, wid. Margaret................................ W 19395
   Joseph, wid. Eleanor.. W 20063
SPARROW, Stephen, wid. Lydia, BLWt. 10247-160-55....................... W 2366
SPAULDING, Oliver, Conn. & N. H.. S 14558
   (See also SPALDING.)
SPEAR, Elijah... R 20436
   Joshua... S 4875
SPELMAN, Jemima, former wid. of Joseph CLARK.
SPENCE. (See SPENCER.)
SPENCER, Aaron, wid. Mindwell or Mindel..................................... R 9980
      Soldier not pensioned.
   Ancel or Ansel, wid. Loly, BLWt. 26048-160-55............................. W 11522
   Daniel... R 9976
   Daniel... S 3961
      In 1832 was living in Penna.
   Daniel, Cont. (Conn.), BLWt. 53-100.. S 29475
   David, BLWt. 334-200.. S 14563
      Pensioned as 2nd Lieut. in East Haddam, Conn., in 1818 and 1832.
   David... S 36780
      Pensioned as private in Windham Co., Conn.
   Elam.. S 23938
   Elihu, wid. Ruth, BLWt. 11396-160-55... W 26496
   Elijah... S 11453
      Saratoga Co., N. Y., in 1832.
   Elijah, Conn. & Conn. Sea service, wid. Hannah........................... W 25062
      Soldier was in Canterbury, Conn., in 1832 and died there in 1838.
   Emmons... S 14561
   Ephraim... S 36779
   Gardner, wid. Mary... W 17856
   Ichabod, wid. Hannah.. W 22283
   Isaac... S 15653
   Israel, wid. Temma... W 6154
   Jabez, Conn., N. Y. & Vt., wid. Patience..................................... W 22295
   James, Conn. & Cont., wid. Elizabeth, BLWt. 50889-160-55.......... W 1328
      (Also given SPENCE.)
   James, wid. Thankful.. W 4811
      Soldier died in 1802 in Ashtabula Co., Ohio.
   James, Cont. (Conn.), wid. Rachel, BLWt. 19621-160-55................ W 27667
      Soldier was pensioned in Somers, Conn., in 1832 & died there in 1845; widow was living
         there in 1853.
   Jared Wilson, wid. Margaret.. W 16419
   Jehiel, wid. Anne P... R 9975
      Soldier never pensioned.
   Jehiel, wid. Naomi.. R 9981
      Soldier never pensioned.
   Joel, BLWt. 13898-160-55.. S 36781
   John, wid. Mary... R 9979
      Soldier never pensioned.
   John, Conn. & Cont., wid. Eunice... W 6157
      Rej. BL.
   Noah.. S 28892
   Peter, wid. Jerusha, BLWt. 31584-160-55..................................... W 7198

SPENCER, Reuben, **wid.** Mehitable... W 17857
   Samuel, wid. Eunice... W 22286
      Soldier was in Worcester, N. Y., in 1832 & died there in 1838.
   Samuel, Cont. (Conn.), wid. Sarah.. W 22288
      Soldier was in Windham Co., Conn., in 1818; and died in 1826 in R. I.
   Samuel B., Conn. Sea service... S 23935
   Seth... S 23004
   Theodore, Cont. (Conn.), wid. Nabby... W 26497
   Thomas, wid. Huldah, BLWt. 49-100... W 2186
   Walter.. S 16533
   William... S 6143
      Chenango Co., N. Y., in 1832.
   William, wid. Phebe.. W 17859
      Soldier died in 1804 in Middlesex Co., Conn.
   Zaccheus.. R 9989
SPERRY, Army... S 42367
   Benjamin.. R 9991
   Ebenezer.. S 15652
   Elijah, Conn. & Cont., wid. Polly... W 3885
   Jacob... S 17603
   Job, wid. Rebecca... W 17862
   Jonathan, Conn. & Cont.. S 11443
   Joseph, wid. Abigail.. W 16734
SPICER, Abel, wid. Sarah, BLWt. 15420-160-55..................................... R 9995
      Soldier never pensioned as he did not serve six months.
   Asher, wid. Rebecca... W 16418
   John, wid. Mary... W 22284
SPOONER, Nathaniel, wid. Ruth.. W 2015
   William, Cont. (Conn.), wid. Jerusha, BLWt. 28591-160-55........................ W 25071
SPRAGUE, Dan.. S 14553
   Dyer, wid. Faith.. W 15365
   Ebenezer, Conn. & N. Y.. R 10010
   Frederick, Conn. & Mass., wid. Rebecca.. R 10012
      Soldier was pensioned in 1818 from Washington Co., Ohio.
   James, Conn. & Cont... S 40482
   Samuel H., Conn., Cont. & Mass.. R 10013
SQUARES. (See SQUIRE.)
SQUIER, SQUIRE or SQUYER, Abner... S 17718
   Asa... S 42024
      (Given as SQUYER.)
   Calvin, wid. Mabel, BLWt. 26204-160-55.. W 6160
      (Given also as SQUARES & SQUIRES.)
   Daniel.. S 42376
      (Given also SQUIRES.) BLWt. 26463-160-55. Washington Co., N. Y., in 1818.
   Daniel.. S 22531
      (Given also as SQUIRE.) Rutland Co., Vt., in 1832; priv. & drummer.
   Edward Adam, wid. Mary.. R 10025
      Soldier never pensioned.
   Ebenezer, wid. Lucy... W 17864
   Elisha, Cont. (Conn.), wid. Huldah.. W 4342
   Ephraim, Conn. & Mass., wid. Priscilla.. R 10026
      Soldier pensioned in 1832 from Windham Co., Conn.
   Isaac, Conn. & Conn. Sea service, wid. Susanna.................................. W 17863
   Philip.. S 36785
   Thomas.. S 11454
   William, wid. Esther, BLWt. 26555-160-55.. W 20960
SQUIRES, Abiathar, wid. Mary.. W 4591
   Ezra, Conn. & Vt., wid. Betsey.. W 4812
   Justus, wid. Polly.. W 17865
   Phinehas.. S 46401
   Samuel, Ellen Turney, former wid. of.. W 22458
      NOTE.—This woman's second husband, James CHAPMAN, Conn. S 37831, was a pensioner; and her third husband, Aaron TURNEY, Conn. S 18633, was also a pensioner.
   Selah or Seley, wid. Hannah... W 17866
SQUYER. (See SQUIER.)
STAFFORD, Thomas, BLWt. 469-100.
STALKER, Peter, wid. Achsah, BLWt. 1381-100..................................... W 19098
STANARD, William, wid. Hannah... W 19120
   (See also STANNARD.)
STANBROUGH, or STANBRAUGH, Lemuel, wid. Jane, BLWt. 9543-160-55................. W 2453
STANCLIFT, Comfort.. S 23949
   John, Conn. & Cont.. S 14612
   Lemuel, wid. Mehitabel or Mehitable, BLWt. 2086-160-55.......................... W 3733
STANDISH, Amasa, Conn. & Mass... S 14600
STANDLY. (See STANLEY.)
STANLEY, Elisha... S 29481
   Frederick... S 7610
   Jesse. (See STANLY.)
   Noadiah, wid. Hannah.. W 19413
      (Also given STANDLY.)
   Noah, wid. Naomi.. W 25143
   Salmon.. R 10055
   Timothy... S 11475
STANLY, Jesse... R 10052
STANNARD, Abel, wid. Phebe.. W 19114
   David, wid. Ruth, BLWt. 36530-160-55.. W 25142
   Eliakim, Conn. & Cont... S 7596
   Elijah.. S 17709
   Ezra.. S 7606

STANNARD, Jasper... S 31981
    Job... S 17700
    John.. S 17702
        Middlesex Co., Conn., in 1832.
    Joseph... S 41199
    Libbeus, Conn. & Green Mt. Boys & Vt.. S 14619
    Samuel, wid. Elizabeth... W 19119
        (See also STANARD.)
STANTON, Daniel... S 20978
    Ebenezer, Cont. (Conn.) & Privateer, wid. Mary.. W 25105
    Edward, wid. Martha.. W 2481
    Elijah, Conn., Cont. & Mass... S 14623
    Jason, wid. Sally, BLWt. 8152-160-55.. W 505
    Joseph, wid. Priscilla... W 22302
    Nathan... R 10061
    Samuel, wid. Hannah... W 23305
STAPLES, Abel... S 14595
    Asa... S 21997
    Ebenezer.. S 17710
    John, wid. Lydia... W 6212
STARK, Abraham... S 42407
    John, Conn. & N. H., wid. Tryphena, BLWt. 26308-160-55................................. W 15405
        (Also given STARKS.)
STARKE, Aaron.. R 10073
    (Also given STARK.)
STARKEY, Susannah, former wid. of Asa PRATT.
STARKS, Ebenezer... R 10074
    Nathan, Cont. (Conn.).. S 33723
    Samuel.. S 23959
STARKWEATHER, Elijah... S 46072
    Ephraim, Conn. & R. I., wid. Rachel... W 22308
        (Also given STARKWATHER.)
    John, wid. Hannah.. R 10075
        Soldier pensioned from Conn. in 1832.
    Prince, wid. Marcy.. R 10076
        Soldier never pensioned.
        (Also given as WILLIAMS, Prince.)
    Thomas... S 17126
STARLING, Jacob.. S 36797
STARNES. (See STEARNS.)
STARR, David, BLWt. 1949-300, Capt., was issued Nov. 19, 1789. No papers.
    Dumill, Navy service but Conn. residence.. R 1418
    Eli.. R 10078
    Jehosaphat, wid. Mary.. W 22298
    Jesse, Cont. (Conn.), wid. Polly... W 19415
    Jonathan.. R 10081
    Joshua.. S 14609
    Josiah, BLWt. 1935-500, Capt., was issued Oct. 7, 1789. No papers.
    Josiah.. R 10082
    Robin.. S 36810
    Samuel Moor, wid. Abigail... W 6209
    Thaddeus.. S 14606
    Thomas, wid. Lois... W 17887
        Soldier died in 1801 in Fairfield Co., Conn. BLWt. 1957-200, Lieut., was issued May 29,
        1792. No papers.
    Thomas, Conn. & Mass... R 10083
    William, Deerfield, Mass., in 1819... S 33711
    William, wid. Eunice... W 8756
        Soldier was pensioned as Lieut. in Baltimore, Md., in 1818.
STAUGHTON. (See STOUGHTON.)
STAUNTON. (See STANTON.)
STEARNS, Charles, wid. Sarah... W 6176
    (Also given as STARNS.)
    Levi.. S 30716
    Roswell.. S 23439
STEBBINS, Ebenezer.. S 41203
    Joseph... R 18144
    Samuel, wid. Ruth.. W 25135
STEDMAN, Isaac, wid. Lucretia... W 2264
    James... S 28898
    Levi, Conn. & Cont., wid. Anna, BLWt. 20-160-55... W 19108
    Lucy, former wid. of Adriel HUNTLEY.
    Nathan, Conn. & Privateer.. R 10093
    Philemon.. S 33742
    Selah.. S 11491
    Thomas... S 17121
        St. Lawrence Co., N. Y., in 1834
    Thomas... S 36809
        Hartford Co., in 1818.
STEEL, Elijah, wid. Hannah.. W 25124
    John... R 10095
    Joseph, wid. Olive... W 19105
    Josiah.. S 36791
    Perez, wid. Hannah... W 28035
        NOTE.—Lucy Steele also applied for pension as widow of above soldier and was rejected
        (R. 10096). See papers in this case.
STEELE, Ashbell, wid. Eunice.. W 25162
    Bradford, wid. Ruth, BLWt. 7085-160-55.. W 17869
    David, wid. Hannah.. W 25102

STEELE, Isaac, wid. Lavinia .... W 17888
    James, wid. Jemima.. W 26448
    John.. S 36790
        Hartford Co., Conn., in 1818.
    John, Sarah Hillard, former wid. of.. W 21331
        Soldier died in service.
    Josiah, wid. Phebe.. W 871
    Lucy. (See note to STEEL, Perez.)
    Moses, wid. Amanda.. W 15372
    Samuel, wid. Sarah, BLWt. 57524-160-55.
        Soldier not pensioned; died at Sharon, Vt., in 1849.
    Samuel... S 17129
        Pensioned as drummer and sergeant in New Haven Co., Conn., in 1832.
    William, wid. Rebecca Renea.. W 22056
    Zadock or Zadok, Conn. & Vt... S 14571
STEEVENS, William. (See STEPHENS.)
STENT, Eleazer, wid. Rhoda... R 10110
    Soldier never pensioned.
    Othniel.. S 18221
STEPHENS, James, Conn. & Vt... S 23951
    William, Conn. & Cont... S 11470
        (Also given STEEVENS.)
        (See also STEVENS.)
STEPHENSON, Thomas, Hannah Olds, former wid. of.................................... W 15143
STERLING, Seth.. S 15994
    Thaddeus... S 17714
STERRY, Silas, wid. Olive... W 22342
STEUBEN, Jonathan, Conn. & Cont., wid. Lucy... W 22344
STEVENS, Aaron, BLWt. 1945-300, Capt., was issued Apr. 10, 1795. No papers.
    Abel... S 11476
    Adams or Adam, Conn. & R. I., wid. Rena, BLWt. 9439-160-55........................ W 5185
STEVENS, Amos... S 31986
        Fairfield Co. Conn. in 1832.
    Amos, wid. Rachel, BLWt. 38543-160-55... W 11556
        Soldier died in New Haven Co., Conn., in 1831.
    Asa, wid. Lois... R 10132
        Soldier never pensioned.
    Benjamin, Conn. & Cont.. S 15665
    Caleb, wid. Mary.. W 19102
    Daniel, wid. Pollyphena or Polyphena.. W 11562
    Ebenezer, Cont. (Conn.).. BLWt. 625-150
    Elias, wid. Lucretia.. W 9314
        Killingworth, Conn. in 1818 & 1832; BLWt. 6022-160-55.
    Elias, Conn., N. H. & Vt.. S 14621
        Pensioned as Lieut. in Royalton, Vt., in 1832.
    Elkanah, Conn. & N. Y... S 15664
    Elnathan... S 9486
    Ephriam... S 41198
    Forward, wid. Mary.. W 6185
    Henry... S 36805
        Plymouth, Conn., in 1818.
    Henry, wid. Polly, BLWt. 5104-160-55... W 821
        Windsor Co., Vt., in 1832.
    Hubbel... S 42404
    Israel, wid. Love.. R 10134
        Oneida Co., N. Y., in 1832.
    James, Cont. (Conn.), wid. Esther, BLWt. 9442-160-55................................. W 6187
        BLWt. 13775-100, private, was issued Jan. 25, 1796. No papers.
        (Also given as STEPHENS.)
    Jeremiah.. S 17698
    John, BLWt. 1944-300, Capt., was issued June 18, 1791. No papers.
    John, Chloe Smith, former wid. of, BLWt. 3609-160-55................................. W 28034
        Soldier died in 1822; widow was in Watertown, Conn., in 1851.
    John, Conn. & Mass... S 42431
        Dutchess Co., N. Y., in 1818.
    Jonathan, wid. Elizabeth, BLWt. 6277-160-55... W 2674
    Lemuel, Conn. & Cont.. S 18217
    Moses.. S 6148
        (Also given STEPHENS.)
        Otsego Co., N. Y., in 1832.
    Moses, Conn. & N. Y.. S 11474
        Cayuga Co., N. Y., in 1832.
    Nathaniel, wid. Amy.. W 17883
        Cont. service, but Conn. residence & Agency of widow.
    Oliver, wid. Nancy.. R 10137
        Soldier never pensioned.
    Peter.. S 41186
        Wells, Vt., in 1818.
    Peter, Conn. & Vt.. S 19109
        Pawlet; Vt., in 1832.
    Phinehas or Phineas... S 42411
    Reuben, wid. Jerusha... W 17870
        Litchfield Co., Conn., in 1818; died in 1822.
    Reuben, Conn. & N. Y., wid. Molly.. W 19409
        Greene Co., N. Y., in 1832; died there in 1842.
    Safford, Conn. & N. H.. S 41209
    Silvanus, wid. Sarah.. W 19096
    Solomon, wid. Abelinah.. R 10121
        Soldier pensioned in 1832 in Greensville, N. Y.

STEVENS, Thomas... S 11492
    Litchfield Co., Conn., in 1832.
  Thomas.. S 36792
    Grandy, Conn., in 1818.
  Thomas, wid. Lucy.. W 3471
    Huntingdon, Penna., in 1818; died in 1841.
  Timothy, wid. Prudence... W 17882
    Soldier died in 1823 in Litchfield Co., Conn.
  Timothy, Conn. & Cont. BLWt. 1286-100.. S 36796
    (Also given STEPHENS.)
    New Haven Co., Conn., in 1818.
STEWARD, Albert, wid. Reuana.. W 19100
  Eliphalet, Conn., N. Y., & R. I... S 6156
  Elisha.. S 11488
  William... S 4890
    (Also given STEWART.)
STEWART, Andrew, Conn. & N. Y., wid. Lucretia, BLWt. 27683-160-55................................ W 19099
  Charles, BLWt. 1922-150, Ensign, was issued Mch. 1, 1797; also recorded as BLWt. 2677. No papers.
  Charles... S 41196
    (Also given STUART.)
  Daniel, wid. Lovisa, BLWt. 26253-160-55.. W 9673
  Henry... S 23950
  James, Conn., N. J. & Penna.. S 40520
  John.. S 28902
  Joseph.. S 11484
    Steuben Co., N. Y., in 1832.
  Joseph, Anna Harvey, former wid. of.. W 13348
    East Haddam, Conn., in 1818; died 1823.
  Oliver, wid. Rebecca, BLWt. 27657-160-55... W 26444
  Samuel.. R 10168
  William... S 42398
    Greene Co., N. Y., in 1830
  William, wid. Amanda or Manda... W 8760
    Voluntown, Conn., in 1832.
STILES, Asa, Conn. & War of 1812, wid. Olive.. R 10182
  Asahel.. S 31987
  Beriah.. S 14610
  Gould... S 19108
  Jeff. (See BRACE, Jeffery.)
  Joseph.. BLWt. 1043-100
  Lewis... S 28894
  Martin, wid. Candace or Candice.. W 25079
  Reuben, Cont. (Conn.), wid. Submit... W 22301
  Robert.. S 42392
  Sarah, former wid. of Isaac COFFIN or COFFING.
STILLMAN, Joseph... S 31988
  Nathaniel... S 14603
  Roger, Conn. & Cont.. S 14588
STILLWELL, STILWELL, STILLWILL, Elias.. S 36806
  BLWt. 1952-300, Capt., was issued Sept. 29, 1790 to Elias Stillwell. No papers.
STILSON, Ebenezer.. S 1114
STIMSON, David... S 14627
  Joel, wid. Susanna... W 19095
STOCKER, Thaddeus.. S 15992
STOCKING, Amasa.. S 30137
  Eber, BLWt. 581-100... S 36793
  Moses, Navy (Conn.), wid. Elizabeth.. W 15384
STOCUM, Reuben... S 11456
STODDARD, Clement, Conn. & War of 1812, Esther Carpenter, former wid. of........................ R 10202
  Soldier never pensioned.
  (Also given STODDART.)
  Cyrenius or Cyrenus.. S 42383
  Daniel, wid. Lucretia... R 10204
    Soldier pensioned in 1832 in New London Co., Conn.
  David, wid. Elizabeth... R 10201
    Soldier never pensioned.
  Frederick... S 36800
  James... S 14591
  Nathan.. BLWt. 106-300
  Philo, wid. Polly, BLWt. 14952-160-55.. W 2676
  Robert.. S 14577
  Samuel.. S 42377
  Simeon C. or Simon C... S 43176
  Wells... S 18212
  William... S 17716
STOEL, Asa, wid. Judith.. W 11535
  (See also STOWELL & STOYELL.)
STOGDILL, Robert, Sarah Smith, former wid of.. W 22245
STOKES, Jonathan, Conn., Conn. Sea service, Navy & Privateer; wid Sally......................... W 25123
  Richard, wid. Jerusha, BLWt. 6020-160-55... W 11541
STONE, Albernarle, Conn. & Navy, wid. Sally or Sarah, BLWt. 6117-160-55......................... W 2483
  Andrew L. Mary Hoit, former wid. of.. W 18056
  Betsey, former wid. of Andrew DEWY.
  Bille, wid. Rachel.. W 2879
  Daniel.. S 36813
  John Evarts... S 18614
  Levi.. S 31989
    Thompson, Conn. in 1832.

STONE, Levi, wid. Mary... W 17875
    Kent, Conn., in 1832; died 1836, Artificer.
  Samuel... S 17708
    Tolland Co., Conn., in 1832.
  Samuel... S 42401
    Onondaga Co., N. Y., in 1818.
  Thomas, Conn. & Cont... S 36795
    BLWt. 6482– was issued Oct. 7, 1789, to Benj. Tallmadge, Assignee. No. papers.
  William.. S 42429
STORER, Nehemiah, Navy (Conn.)... S 36801
STORES. (See STORRS.)
STOREY, James... S 15658
  (See also STORY.)
STORRS, Augustus, wid. Anna... W 16152
  Chipman, Conn., R. I. & War of 1812... R 10231
  (Also given STORES.)
  Ebenezer... S 15995
  Justus, BLWt. 1925–300, Surgeon's Mate, was issued July 14, 1797; also recorded as above under
    Wt. 2692. No papers.
  Lemuel, Conn. & Cont., wid. Elizabeth... W 25136
  Prentiss, Conn. & Cont... S 11468
STORY, John, Conn. & Cont... S 15657
  Oliver, Conn. & Cont., wid. Lois.. W 25082
  Solomon.. S 36812
  (See also STOREY.)
STOUGHTON, Alexander.. S 14596
  (Also given STAUGHTON.)
  Augustus, wid. Cylinda or Celinda... W 3315
  Jonathan, wid. Hitta.. W 17874
  Russell... S 14622
  Shem, wid. Flora... W 17878
  William, wid. Eleanor.. W 17885
STOVER, William.. S 17705
STOW, Elihu, Cont. (Conn.), wid. Mary... W 20071
  Jedediah... S 14593
  John... S 11480
  Joshua, wid. Ruth.. W 26447
  Samuel, Conn. & Cont.. S 36819
    New Haven Co., Conn., in 1827; died in 1831.
  Samuel, Cont. (Conn.).. S 48632
    Serg't., Windsor, N. Y., in 1818.
  Stephen, wid. Mary... W 22311
  Zacheus.. S 36811
STOWELL, Nathaniel, Aurelia Fisk, former wid. of, BLWt. 45666–160–55............................... W 7266
  Samuel... S 42432
  (Also spelled STOEL & STOWEL.)
STOYELL, Stephen... S 11465
  (Also spelled STOELL.)
STRATTON, Samuel.. S 23013
  Stephen.. S 23435
  Thomas.. S 17131
STRAWBRIDGE. (See STROWBRIDGE.)
STREET, John.. S 17712
STRICKLAND, David... S 35084
  (Also spelled STRICTLAND.)
  Jonah.. R 10263
  Seth, wid. Anna, BLWt. 9469–160–55... W 17889
  Simeon, wid. Mary.. W 17880
  Stephen.. R 10265
STRONG, Anthony.. S 36814
  Barnabas or Barnabus.. S 40498
  Chloe, former wid. of Eli KING.
  David, BLWt. 1951–300, Capt., was issued Oct. 17, 1789. No papers.
  David, BLWt. 26346–160–55.. S 14573
  Elnathan, wid. Margaret, BLWt. 29060–160–55... W 8753
  Ephraim... S 18013
  Israel.. S 11467
  Jacob, wid. Elizabeth, BLWt. 3139–160–55.. W 25146
  Joel, Conn., Cont. & N. Y., BLWt. 26526–160–55... S 11466
  John... S 15659
    Norfolk, Conn. in 1832.
  John... S 31984
    Pensioned as John 2nd. in Woodbury, Conn., in 1818 & 1832.
  John... S 36818
    Pensioned as Serg't. in Middletown, Conn., in 1818.
  John, wid. Martha.. R 10274
    Soldier never pensioned.
  John, Cont. (Conn.)... S 14587
    Pensioned as musician in 1832, at Oneida Co., N. Y.
  Joseph, wid. Hannah.. R 10272
    Soldier never pensioned.
  Joseph, Conn. & Cont... S 7598
    Pensioned in Copiah Co., Miss., in 1832.
  Josiah.. S 42428
  Nathaniel, Conn. & Privateer... S 15993
  Phinehas... S 41187
  Roger, Conn. & Cont... S 14575
  Selah.. S 29483
  Seth, wid. Rachel.. W 17879
  Solomon.. S 41213
  Stephen.. S 18216

STROWBRIDGE or STRAWBRIDGE, George, wid. Bethsheba (see claim of widow, as former widow of Jason CRAWFORD, Conn.)	W 19110
STUART, Joseph	S 3974
Samuel, Conn. & Mass	S 17713
(See also STEWART.)	
STUDWELL, Henry	S 14617
STUDEVANT, Caleb	S 35645
James	S 46076
(See also STURTEVANT.)	
STURGES, Aquilla	R 10288
Augustus, wid. Mercy	W 17884
Benjamin, wid. Thankful	W 25073
David	R 10289
Hezekiah	S 14601
Lewis	S 17704
Moris Simmons, wid. Lois	R 10290
Soldier never pensioned.	
Moses	S 36815
STURGIS, Aaron	S 31389
Abram, wid. Anna, BLWt. 38561-160-55	W 19407
STURTEVANT, Zebedee	S 14615
(See also STURDEVANT.)	
SUMMERS, David, wid. Mary	W 2877
Neram or Nirum	R 20186
Sylvester	S 16263
SUMNER, Ebenezer, Cont. (Conn.) & Sea service, wid. Jemima	W 19418
George	R 10311
John, BLWt. 1939-450, Lieut. Colonel, was issued April 9, 1790, to Elizabeth Sumner, Administrator. No papers.	
Robert, wid. Jemima	W 22350
Shubell or Shubill	S 42436
William	S 36820
SUNDERLAND or SUNDERLIN, Daniel, Conn. & R. I.	S 17718
(Given as SUNDERLIN.)	
Samuel	S 41221
SUTHARD, Isaac. (See SOUTHWORTH.)	
SUTLIEF, Gad	S 23961
Janner or Jonner or Jonah, Conn. & War of 1812, Hepsibah Joiner, former wid. of	R 5682
Soldier never pensioned.	
SUTLIFF, David	R 10319
SUTLIFFE, Benjamin, BLWt. 1681-200.	
SUTTON, Benjamin, Cont. (Conn.) & Green Mt. Boys	S 42434
Edward, Abigail Lawrence, former wid. of	W 2897
SWADDLE or SWADLE, John	S 36822
SWAN, Adin	S 28903
Elias, Conn., Navy & R. I., wid. Anne	R 10331
Soldier never pensioned.	
John, wid. Sarah	W 19422
SWANEY, John, wid. Abigail	W 22352
SWEATLAND. (See SWETLAND.)	
SWEET, James	S 21518
John, wid. Anna	W 19131
Jonathan	S 14635
SWEETLAND or SWETLAND, Aaron, Conn. & Cont. wid. Lois	W 19423
Ebenezer Leach	S 15235
(Given also as SWEATLAND.)	
Luke, BLWt. 477-100	S 40546
SWIFT, Charles, Conn. & Vt., wid. Johannah	W 16431
Haman, BLWt. 1937-500, Colonel, was issued Oct. 7, 1789. No papers.	
John, wid. Anna	W 22353
Soldier died March 12, 1838; was pensioned in 1832 in Onondaga Co., N. Y.	
John, Conn. & War of 1812 from N. Y., Hepzibeth T. Buck, former wid. of, BLWt. 2505-100.	W 872
Widow was pensioned in 1858 while a resident of Detroit, Mich.	
Nathaniel	S 36823
Philetus, Conn. & War of 1812, wid. Fawnia	W 501
Roland or Rowland	S 42437
William	R 10363
William, wid. Eunice	W 19420
SYKES, Ashbel, Conn., Mass. & Vt	S 18618
(See also SIKES.)	
SYMONDS, Ashna or Ashney	S 17679
(Also given as SIMONDS.)	
(See also SIMONDS and SIMONS.)	

T.

TABER, William, wid. Lucinda	W 16749
TAFT, Abel, Conn. & Vt	S 19117
TALBUT, Ebenezer	S 17723
TALCOTT, Aaron	S 36332
Abraham	S 23452
(Given as TALLCOTT.)	
Daniel	R 10379
(Given as TALLCOTT.)	
Elizur, wid. Dorothy	W 18108
Soldier was son of Col. Elizur Talcott, and served as priv. & Serg't. in Revolution, dying in 1831 in Tioga Co., N. Y., where his widow died in 1838; pension issued to date of her death in 1846 to George Talcott, heir.	
Elizur or Eleazer, Sally Frisby, former wid. of	W 27522
Soldier was pensioned in 1832 in Trumbull Co., Ohio, as private, and died there in 1835.	
NOTE.—Sally's other husband, was also a pensioner.	
(See FRISBIE, FRISBEE or FRISBY, Luther, Cont. (Conn.), S 42731.	

TALCOTT, Joseph, wid. Rebecca... W 22377
   Justus, wid. Lydia, BLWt. 28574-160-55... W 6247
   Phineas... S 16001
TALLMADGE, TALMADGE or TALMAGE.
   Benjamin, Conn. & Cont.. S 46412
      BLWt. 2171-400, Major, was issued Oct. 7, 1789. No papers.
   Daniel, wid. Rebecca, BLWt. 26647-160-55... W 3737
   Ichabod, Hannah Plumb, former wid. of.. W 17460
   John... S 11523
   Nathaniel.. S 18024
   Samuel... S 14653
   Seymour... S 16268
   Solomon... S 11524
TALLMAN, Peleg, Navy (Conn.), wid. Eleanor, BLWt. 35689-160-55............................... W 26509
   Peter, Conn. & Mass., wid. Margaret.. R 10382
      Soldier was pensioned in 1832 from Onondaga Co., N. Y.
TAMBLIN, Timothy, Conn., Cont. & Mass., wid. Susanna... W 19428
TANNER, Ebenezer, wid. Lydia... W 22372
      BLWt. 2174-200, Lieut., was issued Dec. 14, 1795. No papers.
   Tryal... S 6189
TARBOX, Temperance, former wid. of John ABBOTT.
TATTON, Phillis, former wid. of Cuff WELLS (colored.)
TAYLER & TAYLOR, Abraham.. S 7689
   Absalom, wid. Sabra... W 18118
   Augustine, Conn. & War of 1812, wid. Huldah.. W 26502
   Azariah.. S 14C50
   Chiles, wid. Rhoda... W 4597
   David, Conn. & Cont.. S 15675
      Canton, Conn. in 1832.
   David, wid. Ester or Esther, BLWt. 520-160-55.. W 4827
      Cont. service, but resided in Berlin, Conn., in 1818; transferred to Mass.; widow pensioned
      from N. Y.
   Dorcas. (See Thomas.)
   Eleazer or Eleazar.. S 14639
   Eli... S 14646
   Elias... S 14642
      Jefferson Co., N. Y., in 1832.
   Elias... S 17725
      Warren, Conn., in 1832.
   Elijah, Conn. & Cont., BLWt. 1485-100.. S 36335
   Elisha.. S 17722
      Litchfield, Conn., in 1832.
   Elisha.. S 17726
      Portage Co., Ohio, in 1832.
   Eliud... S 14044
   Elnathan, wid. Lydia.. R 10419½
      Soldier never pensioned.
   Gad, wid. Abigail... W 6227
   George... R 10415½
   Isaac... S 11516
   Jesse... S 36336
   Jesup, wid. Sarah, BLWt. 26675-160-55.. W 1509
   Job, wid. Mercy... W 26969
   John... S 14652
      Tolland Co., Conn., in 1832; pensioned as private and sergeant.
   John... S 29496
      Otsego Co., N. Y., in 1818 & 1832.
   John... R 10419
   John, BLWt... 533-100
      Westchester Co., N. Y., in 1810.
   John, wid. Hannah.. W 18102
      Ellington, Conn., in 1832 & died there in Oct. 13, 1832.
   John, wid. Elizabeth.. W 22384
      Elizabeth was in Onondaga Co., N. Y., in 1845 & died in 1849 in McHenry Co., Ill. Pen-
      sion given her four children in 1850 to date of her death.
   Jonathan... S 23448
      Westchester Co., N. Y., in 1832.
   Jonathan, Conn. & Cont., wid. Hannah.. W 18107
      Middlesex Co., Conn., in 1818; died there in 1821.
   Jonathan, wid. Nancy... W 18105
      Fairfield Co., Conn., in 1832; died there in 1834.
   Joshua, wid. Eunice... W 22375
   Josiah, wid. Elizabeth... W 824
      NOTE.—Elizabeth also applied on account of service of her first husband, Isaac Sergeant
      or SARGEANT, R 10414½.
   Lemuel, wid. Ada... W 11604
   Levi.. S 17724
   Martin... R 10420
      (Given also TAYLER.)
   Nathan, wid. Mehitable, BLWt. 98565-160-55... W 11596
   Niles... S 42447
   Noah... S 46513
   Obadiah, Cont. (Conn.), wid. Rhoda, BLWt. 1476-100... W 3373
   Phineas.. S 14655
   Reuben, Conn. & Cont., wid. Anna.. W 16433
   Russel.. S 11509
   Samuel... S 11521
      Hampden Co., Mass., in 1832.

TAYLER & TAYLOR, Samuel.. S 14649
   Danbury, Conn., in 1832.
  Sarah H., former wid. of William OSBORN.
  Simeon, wid. Olive.. W 22385
   Litchfield Co., Conn., in 1832; died 1840.
  Simeon, wid. Sibilla.. W 16753
   Batavia, N. Y., in 1818; died in 1820.
  Solomon, wid. Abigail.. W 26513
  Stephen, wid. Prudence.. W 22365
  Theodore... S 36333
  Thomas.. S 46202
   Dorcas, widow of the above soldier, was pensioned as the former wid. of Levi FARNAM or FARNHAM, Conn. W 16752.
  Timothy, BLWt. 2172-300, Capt., was issued May 21, 1789. No papers.
  William.. S 36334
   BLWt. 6569-100, Serg't, was issued Sept. 4, 1789, to Ezekiel Case, Assignee. No papers.
  Zalmon, wid. Hannah... W 25470
TEAL, Joseph, wid. Hannah.. W 18119
   Died in 1795 in Hartford Co., Conn.
  Nathan, wid. Polly, BLWt. 18221-160-55.................................. W 19438
   (Also given TEALL & TEEL.)
TEALL, Joseph.. S 46473
   Herkimer Co., N. Y., in 1828; died in 1837.
  Oliver... S 11529
TENEYCK, Henry, BLWt. 2173-300, Capt., was issued March 7, 1792. No papers.
TENNANT, John... R 10453
TERREL, Elihu... S 3773
  Jared.. S 18625
TERRELL, Asahel, Conn. & N. Y., Hannah Blackman, former wid. of............ W 17311
   (See also TERRILL and TURRELL and TIRRELL.)
TERRILL, Ephraim.. S 11528
   (Also given TERRIL.)
  Hezekiah, wid. Betsey, BLWt. 36668-160-55................................ W 22393
   (Also given TYRELL.)
  Joel, wid. Eunice... W 4353
  Nathan, wid. Dorothy.. W 4083
  Stephen... S 41234
TERRY, Asaph, wid. Nancy, BLWt. 26938-160-55.............................. W 6249
  Ebenezer.. S 11525
   Hartford Co., Conn., in 1832.
  Ebenezer, Conn. & N. H.. S 10661
   Chenango Co., N. Y., in 1832.
  Gamaliel, wid. Susannah... W 16755
  Josiah, wid. Deborah.. W 19437
  Julius... R 10466
  Martin.. S 14661
  Solomon.. S 14662
  Stephen.. S 17140
  William N. or William, wid. Eleanor..................................... R 10461
   Soldier pensioned at Pontiac, Mich., in 1832.
  Zeno, wid. Tabitha.. W 22392
THACHER, Benjamin, Phebe Buel or Buell, former wid. of, BLWt. 26736-160-55. W 2521
  Eliakim, Cont. (Conn.).. S 23970
   (See also THATCHER.)
THARP, Abel, Hannah Austin, former wid. of................................. W 20641
  Earle or Earles, Conn. & Cont., wid. Lydia.............................. W 19444
   (See also THORP.)
THATCHER, Asa, Cont. (Conn.).. S 41242
  John... R 1439
  Josiah.. S 14670
  Samuel, Conn. & N. Y... S 11542
   (See also THACHER.)
THAYER, Asa... S 43199
  David, Cont. (Conn.).. S 36338
  Jerijah, Conn. & Cont., BLWt. 3768-160-55............................... S 41252
  Joseph, Conn. & Cont., wid. Abigail..................................... W 18133
THOMAS, Aaron, Cont. (Conn.).. S 35098
  Caleb... S 35353
   New Haven Co., Conn., in 1818.
  Caleb, wid. Polly, BLWt. 28573-160-55................................... W 6273
   Ashtabula Co., Ohio, in 1832; enlisted from Tolland, Conn.
  Daniel.. S 11536
   Groton, Conn., in 1818 and 1832.
  Daniel, wid. Eunice... R 10495
   Soldier died in 1825, not pensioned.
  Elijah... S 42485
  Enoch, wid. Anne... W 16756
  James... S 18245
  Jesse.. S 23454
  John, BLWt. 6371, issued 1790.
   NOTE.—This may be identical with the following, W 18136, but the data is so meager it is impossible to tell.
  John, Conn. & Cont., wid. Mary... W 18136
   Priv. & corp. in Woodbridge, Conn., in 1818; died in 1843.
  Joseph, wid. Esther, BLWt. 71188-160-55................................ W 19452
  Noah, wid. Mary.. W 18121
  Simeon, wid. Lucretia... W 18139
  Stephen, wid. Ann.. W 25479

THOMPSON, Abraham.. S 36341
    Conn. in 1818.
Abraham, wid. Dorcas B., BLWt. 34599-160-55.. R 10521
    Both soldier and widow rejected for pension.
Amos.. S 22016
Asa, Conn. & Cont.. S 11541
    (Also given THOMSON.)
David... S 35351
David... R 10527
Epaphras, Cont. (Conn.)... S 40566
    (Also given THOMSON.)
Henry... S 17727
Hugh.. S 23021
James... S 14681
    N. Y. in 1818. Also given as THOMSON.
James, Conn. & N. H... S 42487
    Sullivan Co., N. Y., in 1818.
John.. S 11534
    East Haven, Conn., in 1832.
John, wid. Ellis, BLWt. 26720-160-55.. W 25480
    Stratford, Conn., in 1832; died in 1836.
John, wid. Mabel.. W 3317
    New Paltz, N. Y., in 1818.
John, wid. Mary, BLWt. 100290-160-55... W 503
    (Also given Jonathan TOMPSON.)
    Saratoga Co., N. Y., in 1833; Washtenaw Co., Mich., in 1842.
Jonathan. (See John.)
Joseph, BLWt. 1705-100... S 42491
    N. Y. in 1818.
Joseph, wid. Ruby, BLWt. 26862-160-55.. W 2488
    Coventry, Conn., in 1818; died in 1829.
    (Also given TOMPSON.)
Joshua, wid. Hannah... W 22400
Matthew, Conn. & Navy, wid. Betsey, BLWt. 3140-160-55................................. W 25478
Nathan, Betty Warner, former wid. of.. W 22519
Nathaniel.. S 41241
Nehemiah, wid. Esther, BLWt. 33531-160-55... W 827
Samuel... S 11537
    Bath, N. Y., in 1832.
Samuel... S 43998
    Newport, N. H., in 1818 & 1832.
Samuel, Hannah Waldo, former wid. of... W 18298
    Captain, died in Tolland Co., Conn., in 1793.
Stephen.. S 42478
    Onondaga Co., N. Y., in 1818.
Stephen, wid. Abigail.. R 10519
    Soldier never applied.
Thomas, wid. Lydia.. W 19453
    Oneida Co., N. Y., in 1832; died there in 1840.
Thomas, wid. Lucy.. R 10547
    Soldier died in 1831, not pensioned.
William, wid. Thankful B., BLWt. 1530-100... W 2275
Zebulon, wid. Lucy.. W 18134
    (Also given THOMSON.)
THOMSON, Edward... S 14683
James... S 17731
John, Cont. (Conn.), wid. Parmelia.. W 26472
Joseph.. S 23022
Moses... S 11177
Nathaniel.. S 14695
Rufus, wid. Sally.. W 3621
Samuel... S 35352
THORNTON, Elisha.. S 14676
THORP, Amos... BLWt. 382-100
Amos, wid. Naomi.. R 10573
    Soldier pensioned in New London Co., Conn., in 1818; died in 1820.
    (Also given as THARP.)
Daniel.. S 23023
David, wid. Elizabeth.. W 15427
Ezekiel... S 36339
Ezra, Conn. & Cont.. S 11545
James, wid. Lydia.. W 26525
Joseph.. S 6237
    Livingston Co., N. Y., in 1832.
Joseph, wid. Loly, BLWt. 26419-160-55... W 15423
    (Also given THARP.)
    Bennington, Vt., in 1832; died in 1842.
Nathan, wid. Huldah... W 6259
Peter.. S 11511
Thaddeus.. S 15673
THRALL, Lemmy.. R 10575
William... S 43198
THRASHER, Bezaleel or Bazaleel, wid. Elizabeth, BLWt. 26224-160-55................... W 2372
THRESHER, Ebenezer, wid. Hannah... W 18124
THROOP, Benjamin.. S 42492
    BLWt. 2170-400, Major, was issued Jan. 28, 1790. Name spelled THROPP. No papers.
Dan, wid. Mary... W 20088
THROPP, Benjamin. (See THROOP.)
THURBER, Samuel, Conn. & R. I... S 22018

THWING, James	S 22553
TIBBALS, Samuel, wid. Miriam	W 6285
Stephen, Conn. & Cont.	S 11559
Thomas, wid. Elue	W 25482
(Also given TIBBLES.)	
TIBBITTS, Abner, Cont. (Conn.)	S 14698
TIBBLES. (See TIBBALS.)	
TIFF, Major	S 35354
TIFFANY, Amasa, wid. Sarah, BLWt. 26603-160-55	W 15433
Asa	S 17733
Isaiah, BLWt. 2175-200, Lieut., was issued August 22, 1789. No papers.	
Nathaniel	S 16005
Philemon	S 42498
Simon, Conn. & Cont.	S 11554
Timothy	S 17149
Walter, Cont. (Conn.), wid. Osee, BLWt. 78-60-55	W 2976
Soldier enlisted under Col. Sheldon; was in Williamson Co., Tenn., in 1832; wid. pensioned from Kentucky.	
Walter, Sally or Sarah Durkee, former wid. of, Cont. (Conn.), BLWt. 2169-100	W 19205
Soldier died in 1791 in Lee, Mass.; served also under Sheldon.	
William	S 7728
TIFT, John	S 23455
Solomon	S 14703
TILDEN, Daniel, Conn. & Cont.	S 4683
Ebenezer, wid. Elizabeth, BLWt. 15415-160-55	W 25486
Elisha	S 33202
Joshua	S 36342
Stephen, wid. Dorothy	W 26537
TILLETSON, TILLISON, TILLOTSON or TILOTSON.	
Abraham, Cont. & Conn., wid. Abigail	W 22424
Asahel	S 43999
Ashbel	S 11558
Daniel	S 14705
Elias, Cont. (Conn.), wid. Experience	W 18142
George, wid. Sila, BLWt. 31729-160-55	W 25489
Isaac, wid. Sarah, BLWt. 40929-160-55	W 1002
Jacob, wid. Lovena or Lovina	W 25490
Simeon	S 36343
TINKER, Absalom, wid. Mary	W 18139
Amos, wid. Hannah	W 3624
Waterbury, Conn., in 1818.	
Amos, wid. Mary	W 26535
Soldier died 1808 in New London Co., Conn.	
Benjamin, wid. Lucy	W 25483
Ezekiel, Elizabeth Gardiner, former wid. of	R 3902
Soldier was pensioned from Waterford, Conn., in 1832.	
John	S 6245
Nathan, Conn. & Privateer	S 17413
Polly, former wid. of Samuel BECKWITH.	
Samuel, wid. Sally, BLWt. 33762-160-55	W 4606
Silas	R 10615
William, wid. Elizabeth	W 25488
TIRRELL, Samuel	S 17148
(See also TERRELL, TERRILL, and TURRELL.)	
TITUS, John, Conn., Vt. & War of 1812, wid. Mehetable	W 25484
Joseph	S 14706
TODD, Benjamin, wid. Phebe	W 26540
Eli	R 10627
Jehiel	S 14708
Jonathan, wid. Sally., BLWt. 8160-160-55	W 2197
Samuel, wid. Jane, BLWt. 19507-160-55	W 2276
Thaddeus	S 36346
Timothy, wid. Phebe	W 25495
Yale, Cont. (Conn.), Phebe Davenport, former wid. of	W 17710
TOHN. (See TOME.)	
TOLLES, Jared	S 11565
TOLMAN, Lyman, BLWt. 26348-160-55	S 22020
(See also TALLMAN.)	
TOMLINSON, Agur	S 14713
Benjamin, Cont. (Conn.)	S 36347
Curtis or Curtiss, wid. Lucy, BLWt. 26315-160-55	W 25494
David	BLWt. 1314-150
Eliphalet, wid. Polly, BLWt. 89-60-55	W 18152
Henry	R 10638
Jabez H., wid. Phebe	W 6305
Joseph, wid. Bathsheba, BLWt. 13419-160-55	W 11638
William Agur, wid. Phebe	W 18151
TOMPKINS, Solomon, wid. Deborah	W 19462
TONE, John F.	S 43986
(Also given as TOHN.)	
TOOCKER, James	S 36349
Phillip	S 36348
(See also TUCKER.)	
TOPLIFF, Calvin	S 23028
James	S 16275
TOPPING, William	S 13766
TORRANCE, Joseph, wid. Sarah	W 26547
TORRENCE, Thomas	S 23457

TORREY or TORRY, Amos, wid. Sarah, BLWt. 38344-160-55	W 22437
Asa	S 42501
Bill	S 14710
Jesse	S 42509
John, wid. Abigail	W 26542
TOTTENDEN, John	S 35355
TOURTELLOT or TOURTELOTT, Joseph, wid. Abigail	W 25491
TOUSLEY, William, Conn. & Cont., wid. Sally	W 22433
(See also TOWSLEY.)	
TOWER, Gideon, Conn., R. I. & Vt	S 17735
TOWLES. (See TOLLES.)	
TOWN, William	S 32020
Thompson, Conn., in 1832.	
William, Cont. (Conn.), wid. Mary	W 31
Stamford, Conn., in 1818; died in 1828; widow in N. Y. in 1836 & Tenn. in 1843.	
TOWNER, Elijah	S 11570
Greene Co., N. Y., in 1832.	
Elijah	S 22558
Bradford, Penna., in 1832.	
Samuel, Conn. & Mass., BLWt. 3389-160-55	S 28913
TOWNSEND, John	S 11563
John	R 10659
Jonathan, wid. Miriam	W 18149
TOWNSLEY. (See TOWSLEY.)	
TOWSLEE, Nathaniel, Conn. & N. Y	S 22022
TOWSLEY, Moses, wid. Abigail	W 6301
(Given also TOWNSLEY.)	
(See also TOUSLEY.)	
TOZER, Jared, Conn. & Cont	S 42506
John	S 42513
Julius, wid. Elizabeth J., BLWt. 26986-160-55	W 25493
Richard, Conn. & Privateer	R 10664
TRACY, Calvin, wid. Elizabeth	W 19465
Cyrus	S 19130
Daniel, Conn. & Cont	S 19823
Dudley, Cont. (Conn.), wid. Sarah	R 10667
(Given also TRACEY.)	
Soldier pensioned in Franklin, Conn., in 1818.	
Eleazer, wid. Hannah, BLWt. 31724-160-55	W 11652
Elias	S 6269
Elijah, Conn. & Vt., wid. Deidamia, BLWt. 26805-160-55	W 829
Elisha, wid. Hannah	W 18163
Ezekiel, wid. Patience	W 18161
Gamaliel R., wid. Sarah	W 11660
Gilbert, wid. Deborah	W 4088
Giles	S 30748
Hezekiah	BLWt. 547-200
Jedediah	BLWt. 1535-100
Jeremiah	R 10668
John, wid. Esther	W 16448
Levi	S 28915
Moses, wid. Mary	W 26555
Philemon, Cont. (Conn.), wid. Abigail	W 3625
Solomon, Conn. & Mass	S 32025
Jefferson Co., N. Y., in 1832.	
Solomon, Conn. & Conn. Sea Service, wid. Phebe	W 20097
Pensioned as Serg't. in Rutland Co., Vt., in 1818; died there in 1819.	
William	S 35362
TRAVIS, Philip, Conn. & N. Y	S 42525
TREADWAY, Alpheus	S 15680
David	S 11578
(Given also TREADAWAY.)	
Elijah	S 16007
Jonathan	S 41265
Josiah, wid., Rana	W 18158
TREADWELL, Abel	S 23458
Benjamin, wid. Rachel, BLWt. 21832-160-55	W 2376
Cato. (See TREDWELL.)	
Daniel, wid. Sarah	W —
Note.—This woman was also pensioned as former wid. of Daniel HOYT, W 18155.	
TREAT or TREET.	
James, wid. Anna, BLWt. 26621-160-55	W 606
John, Cont. (Conn.), wid. Elizabeth	W 18156
Jonathan, wid. Caturah or Katurah	W 14051
Joseph	S 35360
Philo	S 35361
Robert, wid. Content	R 10691
Soldier never pensioned.	
Russell	S 35359
(Also given as TREET.)	
Samuel P	S 42526
Theodore, Cont. (Conn.), wid. Zippora, BLWts. 486 & 2275-100; also 48-60-55	W 2460
Thomas, wid. Rachel, BLWt. 29007-160-55	W 25502
TREDWELL, Cato	S 35358
(Also given as TREADWELL.)	
TREMAIL, Nathaniel, Conn. & Mass	S 30168
TRIM, Ezra, Conn., Cont. & N. Y	S 14729
TROBRIDGE or TROWBRIDGE, Benjamin	S 42530
Benjamin H	S 40592
(Given as TROBRIDGE.)	
Billy, Rhoda James, former wid. of	W 20173

TROBRIDGE or TROWBRIDGE, Ebenezer, wid. Parnel .... W 4607
    (Given as TROBRIDGE.)
Elihu .... S 36350
    John, BLWt. 2176-200, Lieut., was issued Sept. 13, 1790, to John Trowbridge. No papers.
John, Conn. & Cont .... S 36352
Philemon, Cont. (Conn.), wid. Eunice .... W 18162
Samuel, wid. Lydia .... W 18154
Stephen .... S 14721
    Washington Co., N. Y., in 1832.
Stephen, Conn. & Cont., wid. Isabel .... S 46494
    Soldier pensioned as Serg't. in Vt. in 1818.
Thomas .... S 17738
William, wid. Dorcus .... BLWt. 36549-160-55
TRUAIR, Manuel, Conn., Cont. & R. I. .... S 42533
TRUEMAN or TRUMAN, Shem .... S 42524
TRUMBULL, David, Cont. (Conn.), wid. Sarah .... W 14052
Ezekiel .... S 36353
John .... S 14178
    Jonathan, BLWt. 2169-450, Lieut. Col., was issued Aug. 7, 1789. No papers.
Robert .... S 21543
William, wid. Rachel .... W 22456
TRYON, Elizabeth, former wid. of William BROWN.
Ezra .... S 40586
Isaac, Cont. (Conn.), wid. Elizabeth .... W 25500
Salmon .... R 10724
Thomas .... S 14716
    Glastonbury, Conn., in 1832.
Thomas .... S 32023
    Oneida Co., N. Y., in 1832.
William .... S 36351
TUBBS, Cyrus .... S 38448
Enos, wid. Sarah, BLWt. 24981-160-55 .... W 25506
    (Also given as TUBS.)
Isaac, Eunice Cross, former wid. of. .... W 16937
John .... S 14370
Lemuel .... S 15687
Martin, Mary Peasley or Peasly, former wid. of .... W 19978
Samuel, BLWt. 378-100 .... S 40603
Simon, Conn. & Cont .... S 41272
Thomas .... R 10729
TUCKER, Benjamin, wid. Polly, BLWt. 31329-160-55 .... W 6317
    Orange Co., Vt., in 1832.
Benjamin, Conn., Cont. & Mass .... S 42549
    Schenectady Co., N. Y., in 1818.
Elisha, wid. Elizabeth .... S 17159
John .... S 42550
Joseph, Conn. & R. I., BLWt. 1101-100 .... S 42542
Reuben .... R 10740
Wait, Conn. & Vt. .... S 15681
Zepheniah, wid. Huldah .... W 18166
Zoeth, wid. Mary .... W 11677
TUELL or TUELLS, Benjamin .... S 22026
TUFTS, John .... S 18635
TULLER, Augusta, daughter of WAY, Isaac.
Elijah, wid. Polly .... W 18167
Israel .... S 35959
Jacob .... S 35960
TULLY, Elias .... S 32028
TUPPER, William .... S 36356
TURNER, Andrew, Conn. & Md. .... R 10750
Asa .... S 23975
Asenath, former wid. of Samuel DUNHAM.
Bates .... S 41275
Enoch .... S 48697
Henry, Conn. & Cont., wid. Esther, BLWt. 34992-160-55 .... W 25504
Jabez .... S 31440
John, wid. Hannah .... W 3626
    Norwich, Conn., in 1832; died there in 1837.
John, Conn. & N. Y., Sarah Lynn, former wid. of. .... R 6550
    Soldier never pensioned.
Moses .... S 41270
Nathaniel, Conn. & Cont .... S 42544
Selah, wid. Rebecca .... W 18173
Seth .... S 35365
Stephen .... R 10765
Thomas .... R 10766
Thomas, Conn. & Privateer .... S 11586
William .... S 35104
    Steuben Co., N. Y., in 1818; transferred to Michigan.
William .... S 35104
    Killingworth, Conn., in 1818; transferred to Chataqua Co., N. Y.
Zebedee or Zebade .... S 11590
TURNEY, Aaron .... S 18633
    Ellen, wid. of Aaron, was pensioned as former wid. of her first husband, Samuel SQUIRES, Conn., W 224458.
Abel, Conn. & Navy .... S 15682
Asa .... S—
    No papers.
Clarissa, former wid. of Burr GILBERT.
Ellen. (See Aaron.)

TURREL or TURRELL, Amos..	S 14735
TURRIL or TURRILL, Isaac..	S 14736
John, wid. Polly...	R 10770
Soldier never pensioned.	
TUTHILL, Daniel, Conn. & N. Y..	S 14738
David..	S 42554
Olive or Olivet, former wid. of Joseph CRUMB.	
TUTTLE, Aaron...	S 6284
Hamden, Conn., in 1816; invalid pensioner.	
Aaron, BLWt. 1496-100..	S 46519
In 1828 a resident of Southbury, Conn., and died in 1841; member of "Congress' Own" regiment.	
Abel..	S 33838
Abner, wid. Elizabeth...	W 18169
Abraham..	S 41268
Andrew, wid. Betsey...	W 22464
Asahel...	S 17160
Benjamin, Conn. & Mass..	R 10775
Caleb..	S 33844
Charles, War of 1812.	
Lucy Hitchcock, former wid. of, was pensioned for his services in the War of 1812, and also as the wid. of Ichabod HITCHCOCK, Conn., W 11293.	
Clement...	S 16276
Edmund...	S 17741
Enos...	S 17740
Hezekiah...	S 35366
Jared, wid. Roxana..	W 22461
Joel..	S 42555
Joseph, wid. Sally..	W 3627
Joseph..	R 10778
Josiah...	S 11589
Lemuel, Cont. (Conn.)...	S 14734
Levi..	S 36355
Lucius...	S 14731
Moses...	S 11588
Peletiah, wid. Elizabeth...	W 15805
Solomon...	S 42539
Thaddeus, Conn. & Cont...	S 19488
TWICHEL or TWICHELL, Benoni..	S 33848
TWISS, Joseph, Cont. (Conn.), wid. Lois...	W 26566
TYLAR or TYLEE. (See TYLER.)	
TYLER, TYLAR or TYLEE, Abel..	S 16009
Amos, Cont. (Conn.).. BLWt. 1371-100	
Bishop..	S 17162
Daniel, wid. Sarah..	W 18177
Capt.; died in April, 1832, in Windham Co., Conn.	
Daniel, Conn. & N. H..	R 10789
David...	R 10787
(Also given TYLEE.)	
Esther, former wid. of Reuben MOSS.	
Jacob, wid. Abi or Abigail, BLWt. 26939-160-55.........................	W 4839
Schoharie Co., N. Y., in 1832; transferred to Ohio, where he died.	
Jacob, wid. Julia..	W 18176
Fife major; died July, 1832, at Southington, Conn.	
James...	R 10792
James, wid. Sarah..	W 19479
John, wid. Anna...	W 18178
Branford, Conn., in 1832; died there in 1837; also given TAYLAR.	
John, wid. Ruth. (See FYLER.)	
John, wid. Waity..	W 3890
Lenox, Mass., in 1818; died in 1840; widow moved to Lee Co., Va., to be with son Henry & was pensioned from there.	
John, Cont. (Conn.), wid. Mabel..	W 18175
New Haven Co., Conn., in 1818; died in 1829.	
Major, wid. Hannah, Conn. & N. Y...	W 20102
Nathaniel..	S 42563
N. Y. in 1818.	
Nathaniel, Conn. & Cont...	W 24450
Mabel Hotchkiss, former wid. of, BLWt. 12571-160-55. Mabel was also pensioned as wid. of her last husband, Jeremiah HOTCHKISS (q. v.).	
Nehemiah, wid. Prudence..	W 25508
Oliver...	S 19137
Peter..	S 23460
Reuben...	S 14740
Stephen, wid. Polly..	W 18181
TYRELL. (See TERRILL.)	
TYRER, Hannah, former wid. of Silas NASH.	

U.

UFFORD, Samuel M..	S 17163
UNCAS or UNCOS, John, wid. Martha, BLWt. 1288-100; BLWt. 509-160-55..	W 26610
UNDERWOOD, Betsey, former wid. of John WHITE.	
Josiah, wid. Lucy...	W 20101
Shadrach, BLWt. 1223-100...	S 33849
Timothy...	S 35371
UPHAM, Chester..	S 35372
UPSON, Asa, wid. Ruth..	R 10809
Soldier never pensioned.	
Ashbell, Conn. & Cont..	W 18084
Mary Hungerford, former wid. of, BLWt. 3994-160-55.	

UPSON, Ezekiel.. S 42566
    James, wid. Mary.. R 10808
        Soldier never pensioned.
    Jesse... S 768
    Joseph, Conn. & Mass... S 9493
    Noah, wid. Rachel.. W 18222
    Simeon, Conn. & Privateer.. S 19139
UPTON, Sybil, former wid. of Abner LILLY.
USHER, Robert, wid. Anna.. W 3628
UTLEY, Samuel, Conn. & Cont., wid. Sally...................................... W 20100
    Thomas, wid. Abigail... W 19565
UTTER, James.. S 14747
    Jesse, Conn. & N. Y., wid. Sarah.. R 10815
        Soldier pensioned as fifer in 1832 from Otsego Co., N. Y.

V.

VAGHAN, William... S 14751
    (Also given VAUGHN.)
VAIL or VAILL, Peter, Conn. & Privateer, widow Nancy.......................... R 10817
    Soldier was pensioned in 1832 while a resident of Suffolk Co., N. Y.
VAILS, Nathaniel, Conn. & N. Y.. R 10819
VAN DUERSEN, William, widow Martha.. W 22480
VANORMAN, Isaac, Conn. & N. Y... R 10886
VAN WOMER or WURMER, Peter.. S 23464
VARGISON, Elijah, wid. Margery M. M... W 19576
    (Also given VERGASON.)
VAUGHAN, Benjamin, Conn., Cont. & Vt.. S 14755
    Frederick.. S 32565
    (Also given VAUGHN.)
    John... S 42570
VAUGHN, William. (See VAGHN.)
VERGASON. (See VARGISON.)
VERGESON, Daniel, wid. Phebe.. R 10929
    Soldier was pensioned in 1818 in Bradford Co., Penna., then transferred to N. Y. State; then
    to Lycoming Co., Penna., where he died.
VERY, or VERRY, Jonathan.. S 35373
VIBBARD or VIBBIRD.
    David, Cont. (Conn.), Sarah Simons former wid. of........................... W 22214
    Jesse. (See VIBBERT.)
    John, Conn. & Cont., wid. Hannah... W 18223
VIBBART, VIBBERT or VIBBARD, Jesse, Cont. service but Conn. residence......... S 35374
VICKERY, Timothy.. R 10944
VINTON, Seth, widow, Polly.. W 611
VOGUE, Publius V.. S 46024
VORS or VORSE, Jesse.. S 35375
VOSE, Charles, wid. Elizabeth... W 6375
    BLWt. 6598 was issued in 1791. No papers. BLWt. 132-60-55.
    William.. S 35376

W.

WACK, Frederick William... S 40647
WADE, Timothy, widow Sabra.. W 19585
    (See also WAID.)
WADHAM, Abigail, former widow of Heman ALLEN.
WADSWORTH, Epaphras... S 22567
    Hezekiah... S 6335
    Israel... S 19146
    John, widow Nela... W 18273
    Joseph, Conn. & Mass., widow Chloe, BLWt. 39489-160-55...................... W 9155
    Reuben... S 32042
    Roger, widow Ann... W 22529
    Thomas, BLWt. 11080-160-55... S 11645
WAGGONER, Michael or Michal... S 40636
WAID, Abraham... S 35381
    Henry.. S 33705
    Increase, widow Freelove... W 18293
    John... S 35378
    (See also WADE.)
WAINWRIGHT, Thomas.. S 36361
WAIR, Elias... S 33226
    (See also WARE, WEARE, WIER and WIRE.)
WAKELAND, James, Conn. & Cont., widow Mercy................................... W 25845
    (Also given WAKELEE and WAKELEY.)
    BLWt. 13877-100, private, in Hazen's regiment, was issued April 15, 1796, to Nathl. Ruggles,
    Assignee. No papers.
WAKELEE, David, widow Mary.. W 6422
    (Also given WAKELEY.)
WAKELEE, John, widow Elizabeth.
    (See WAKLEE.)
WAKELEY, James, widow Mercy.
    (See WAKELAND.)
    Jonathan, Esther Parrott, former wid. of................................... W 26286
    (Also given WAKELEE.)
WAKELIN. (See WAKELY.)
WAKELY, Abel.. BLWt. 1337-100
    Henry, Cont. (Conn.), wid. Deborah... W 20113
    (Also given WAKELIN.)

WAKEMAN, Gershom, widow Lucy Ann, BLWt. 27590-160-55........................... W 2282
    Gideon... S 14774
    Jabez.. S 11681
    Joseph, widow Rachel... R 11009
        Fairfield Co., Conn., in 1832; soldier was pensioned.
    Lyman.. S 14777
    Seth, widow Mary... W 18232
    Stephen... S 11683
WAKLE, Thomas... S 40633
WAKLEE, Benjamin.. S 44004
    John, widow Elizabeth, BLWt. 29030-160-55.. W 3479
        (Also given WAKELEE or WAKLY.)
    Joseph, Conn. & Cont... S 35377
WAKLY. (See WAKLEE.)
WALBRIDGE, Ames, BLWt. 2338-400, Major, was issued Oct. 16, 1789, to Theodosius Fowler,
    Assignee. No papers.
    Joshua, Conn. & Mass., widow Priscilla, BLWt. 19515-160-55............................ W 3318
    Porter... S 36367
WALDEN, David, Conn. residence... R 11013
    Mary, former wid. of Andrew BAKER.
    Robert, widow Lucretia, BLWt. 16123-160-55.. W 8981
WALDIN, Ichabod. (See WILLIAMS, John.)
WALDO, Daniel, BLWt. 28501-160-55.. S 14782
    Hannah, former wid. of Samuel THOMPSON.
    Jesse, widow Martha... W 25891
    Joseph, Conn. & Cont... S 11649
    Nathan, widow Deborah.. W 22522
    Zaccheus or Zacheus... S 16013
    Zachariah, widow Abigail, BLWt. 3805-160-55.. W 25890
WALER. (See WALLER.)
WALES, Ebenezer... BLWt. 1895-200
    Eleazer.. S 11653
    Eliel... S 40650
WALKER, James.. S 43231
    Joanna, former widow of Cordilla FITCH.
    Joseph, BLWt. 1218-300, Captain, was issued to his duaghter Catherine & two other heirs
        (grandchildren) for his services as Captain.
    Joseph... S 11672
        Private, pensioned in 1832, while a resident of Canada.
    Joseph, Eunice Eaton, former widow of.. W 17740
        Soldier died in 1798. Eunice was in Hartford Co., Conn., in 1836.
    Joseph, widow Sela.. W 3368
        Soldier was in Erie Co., Penna., in 1818, and died there in 1843.
    Nathaniel... S 6328
        Mill Creek, Erie Co., Penna., in 1832.
    Nathaniel... S 35380
        Stafford, Conn., in 1818.
    Obadiah.. S 36384
        BLWt. 6631-100 was issued Oct. 6, 1797. No papers.
    Peter.. S 23473
    Phineas, widow Susan... W 22534
    Samuel.. S 21556
    Simeon.. S 23993
    Simons.. S 17763
    William, widow Hannah... W 22518
    Zebulon, widow Hannah.. R 11057
        Soldier never pensioned.
WALL, John, Conn. & N. Y.. S 29529
WALLACE, John.. S 22031
    London, Phoebe Freeman, former widow of... W 18290
        (Also given WALLIS.)
    Richard, Conn. & Vt.. S 46659
    William, Cont. (Conn.), widow Sarah... W 18277
        (See also WALLIS.)
WALLER, Ashbel or Asbel, widow Jane, BLWt. 49744-160-55................................ W 25861
    (Also given WALER.)
WALLIS, Hammond, Conn. & N. Y., widow Rebecca.. R 11086
    Soldier never pensioned.
    Zebulon, widow Eleanor... R 11083
        Soldier never pensioned.
        (See also WALLACE.)
WALMSLEY, William, Conn. & Cont... S 36368
    BLWt. 2355-150, Ensign, was issued June 27, 1789, to William Walmesley. No papers.
WALTER, Charles.. S 36840
    Elijah.. R 11098
    John... S 11673
        Caledonia Co., Vt., in 1832.
    John, widow Rhoda.. W 2381
        Onondaga Co., N. Y., in 1818; BLWt. 11259-160-55.
WALTON, George, widow Mary.. W 15971
    John, Conn. & Privateer, widow Mary.. R 1107
        Soldier not pensioned.
    Silas... S 44017
WARD, Aaron.. BLWt. 1311-100
    Benjamin.. S 7810
    Ichabod... S 40646
        Susquehanna Co., Penna., in 1818.
    Ichabod, Conn. & R. I... S 14775
        New London Co., Conn., in 1832.

WARD, Jacob	S 35111
James	S 22568
Jedediah	S 22566
John, wid. Abigail	W 22516
Joshua, wid. Mary, BLWt. 34535-160-55	W 18276
Moses, Cont. (Conn.)	S 36838
Nathan, Conn. & Mass	S 40629
Samuel, widow Anna	W 4843
St. Lawrence Co., N. Y., in 1832; died 1835.	
Samuel, Conn. & Mass	S 17754
Hampshire Co., Mass., in 1832.	
Thomas	S 35379
Urial. (See BASCOM, Urial.)	
William, widow Martha	W 25848
WARDELL, Samuel	S 44010
(See also WARDWELL.)	
WARDEN, Benjamin. (See WORDEN.)	
Ichabod, widow Margaret	R 11132
(Also given WORDEN.)	
Soldier was pensioned in 1818 in Jefferson Co., N. Y.	
James, Conn. & N. Y.	R 11131
John. (See WORDEN.)	
WARDWELL, Jacob	S 36837
Nathan	S 29523
William, widow Catharine	W 2030
(See also WARDELL.)	
WARE. (See WAIR.)	
WARIN. (See WARREN.)	
WARING, Anthony, Conn. & Cont. widow Mahittable	W 11735
Henry	S 36372
James	S 17757
Jonathan	S 3460
Joseph	S 11689
Schuder, BLWt. 36526-160-55	S 11692
(Also given WARRING, Schudder.)	
Solomon	S 14787
(Also given WARRING.)	
Thaddeus, widow Deborah	W 18280
WARNER, Amasa	S 44209
Amos	S 36371
Benjamin, Conn. & Cont.	S 14798
Ticonderoga, N. Y., in 1832.	
Benjamin, Conn., Cont. & N. Y.	S 11644
Broome Co., N. Y., in 1832.	
Betty, former widow of Nathan THOMPSON.	
Charles, widow Sarah	W 20111
Daniel	S 14791
Pensioned as private & sergeant in Canandaigua, N. Y., in 1832.	
Daniel	S 11680
Wethersfield, Conn., in 1832.	
Daniel, widow Sarah	W 25869
Soldier pensioned as private & corporal in 1832 at Rupert, Vt., died in 1843.	
Deliverance, widow Esther	W 18278
Demas, widow Rhoda	W 18283
Eleazar or Eleazer, Conn. & N. Y.	S 28934
George, widow Nabby G.	W 25855
Jabez I., widow Mary	W 10272
Jesse, Conn. & Mass	R 11145
John	S 6329
Conn. Militia; disability pension for wounds in 1777; Litchfield Co., Conn., in 1821.	
John	S 7842
Hartwick, N. Y., in 1832.	
John	S 14786
Suffield, Conn., in 1832.	
John, widow Abigail	W 11736
New Milford, Conn., in 1832; died in 1850.	
John, widow Hepsibah	W 18243
Continental service, but resided in Norfolk, Conn., in 1818 & 1832; serg't.	
Loomis or Loome, widow Eunice	W 18297
Moses, widow Rachel	W 3742
Nathaniel	S 23990
Chataqua Co., N. Y., in 1832.	
Nathaniel, widow Ruth, BLWt. 26232-160-55	W 10271
Washington Co., N. Y., in 1832; died in 1843.	
Richard, widow Merab, BLWt. 18025-160-55	W 2829
Robert, widow Mary	W 18237
Soldier died in 1813 in Hartford Co., Conn.	
Robert, Conn. & Cont.	S 36362
Soldier was in Middlesex Co., Conn., in 1818; BLWt. 2340-400, Major, was issued April 8, 1796. No papers.	
Samuel	S 32041
Granby, Conn. in 1832.	
Samuel, widow Deborah	W 18288
Soldier was in Vt. in 1818 & 1832; and died at Pownal, Vt., in 1834.	
Samuel, Conn. & Cont.	S 11679
New Haven Co., Conn., in 1832.	
Saul	S 17747
Selden, Conn. & Privateer	S 16014
Solomon	S 11687

WARNEK, Thomas, Cont. (Conn.), wid. Belinda.. W 19584
    Soldier was in N. Y. in 1818; transferred to Penna. & died in 1840; widow applied from
      N. Y. BLWt. 299-60-55.
  Thomas, widow Huldah... W 20110
    Soldier died in 1818 in Madison Co., N. Y.
  Timothy.. R 11151
    (See also WORNER.)
WARREN, Abraham... S 44007
  Abijah or Elijah... R 11153
  Ashbel, widow Penelope.. W 25894
  David.. S 43230
  Edward, wid. Mary.. W 25878
  Elijah. (See Abijah.)
  Enoch.. R 11155
  Ezra... S 30774
  James. (See WORREN.)
  John... S 36370
    Tolland Co., Conn., in 1818.
  John, wid. Rachel... W 18241
    Soldier pensioned as sergeant in Hartford Co., Conn., in 1818; died at Hartford in 1827.
  John, widow Sally... W 25834
    (Given also as WARRIN.)
    Soldier was in Saratoga Co., N. Y., in 1832; died there in 1838.
  John, Conn. & N. Y., BLWt. 1341-100... S 44012
    Kortright, N. Y., in 1818.
  Jonathan, Conn. Sea service... R 11159
  Joseph, widow Hannah, BLWt. 24622-160-55.. W 4378
    Soldier served from Conn. & Mass.
  Jotham... R 11162
    Connecticut residence in 1851.
  Moses, wid. Mary... W 25876
  Nathan... S 17175
  Nathaniel.. S 14773
    (See also WORREN.)
WARRIN, Jesse... S 17749
  John. (See WARREN.)
WARRING. (See WARING.)
WASHBURN, Bazaliel, Conn., Mass. & R. I., widow Meribah............................. R 11171
    Soldier was pensioned from Bristol Co., Mass., in 1832.
  Eli, Cont. (Conn.), widow Mary.. W 2031
  Lemuel... S 44210
  Nathan, widow Anna or Annah... W 25877
  Samuel... S 43235
WASSON, John, Cont. (Conn.), widow Amea, BLWt. 152-60-55.......................... W 18268
    (Also given James WATSON.)
  Robert, Conn. sea service & Privateer.. S 17748
WATERBERRY, Nathaniel.. S 14796
WATERBURY, Daniel, Conn. & N. Y.. S 28933
    (Also given WATERBERY.)
  Deodate, widow Mary.. W 18227
  Enos, widow Amy... W 2280
  John, widow Hannah, BLWt. 51762-160-55... W 6432
  Jonathan, widow Sally... W 18282
  Joseph... S 17174
  Nathaniel. (See WATERBERRY.)
  Samuel... R 11177
  Thomas.. R 11178
  William, Darien, Conn., in 1832.. S 17177
  William, Greenwich, Conn., in 1832.. S 35697
  William, widow Sally.. R 11179
    Soldier never pensioned.
WATERHOUSE, Jonathan, Conn. & Conn. Sea service.................................... S 18258
  (See also WATROUS and WATEROUS.)
WATERMAN, Abram or Abraham, widow Hepsibah or Hepzibah, BLWt. 9405-160-55......... W 2287
  Asa, Anna S. Lilley, former widow of... W 21577
  Calvin, widow Priscilla, BLWt. 26934-160-55... W 8985
  Charles, widow Sarah.. W 4611
  Chester.. S 43221
  Darius, Conn., Conn. sea service & Cont. & Privateer, widow Rhoda, BLWt. 7207-160-55.... W 1336
  Elijah.. S 7825
  Glading, Conn. & Conn. sea service, widow Charlotte................................. W 15814
  Ignatius.. S 40644
  John... S 43218
  John O. Faith Foster, former widow of... R 3684
    Soldier never pensioned.
  Joseph... S 23054
  Luther, Conn. & Cont., widow Phebe... W 4379
  William.. S 19838
  Zebedee.. S 17555
WATEROUS, Benjamin, widow Elizabeth.. W 22527
    (Also given WATROUS.)
  Josiah, Conn. & Cont... S 3483
  Samuel, Conn. & Cont., Sarah Eddy, former widow of................................ W 21045
  (See also WATROUS.)
WATERS, Benjamin... S 18642
  Bigelow.. S 11667
  Daniel, widow Sarah, BLWt. 27568-160-5... W 23542
    (Also given WATTERS.)
  John, widow Mindwell... W 15464
  Joseph, Conn. & Cont., Lydia Root, former widow of................................. W 17543

WATERS, Oliver... R 11184
    Phebe, widow of above soldier, applied for pension as the former widow of her first husband,
      Samuel JUDD, Conn.
  Richard. (See WATROUS.)
  Theodore.. R 11185
WATKINS, Boadwell, Boadewell or Badwell... S 41294
  Ephraim... S 43220
  Jedediah, Conn. & French and Indian War, widow Abigail... R 11188
    Soldier never pensioned.
  Nathan... S 41304
  Robert... S 43226
    (Also given WATKIN.)
  William, widow Lois... R 11193
    Soldier never pensioned.
WATROUS, Allen... S 4715
  Ambrose... S 32043
  Benjamin. (See WATEROUS.)
  John R., Conn. & Cont., Lucretia W. Hubbard, former widow of... W 3018
    BLWt. 2343-400, Surgeon, was issued Jan. 28, 1790. No papers.
  Richard... S 36364
    (Also given WATRUS and WATERS.)
  William... S 41292
    (See also WATERHOUSE and WATEROUS.)
WATSON, Amariah.. S 4717
  Caleb... S 44009
  James. (See WASSON, John.)
  John.. S 32037
  Levi.. S 32039
  Sipeo, widow Juda or Judah.. W 18240
  Thomas.. S 11685
    Tolland Co., Conn., in 1832.
  Thomas, widow Sarah, BLWt. 10221-160-55... W 22505
    Soldier was pensioned from Washington Co., R. I., in 1818; died in 1822.
  Timothy, widow Anne.. R 11201
    Soldier never pensioned.
  Titus, widow Mercy... W 18271
WATTERS. (See WATERS.)
WATTLES, Charles... S 14799
  Dan, widow Cynthia.. S 3743
  David... S 44028
  Joshua, widow Sarah Ann, BLWt. 3797-160-55... W 26618
  William, Conn. & N. Y... S 14795
WAUGH, Joseph, widow Mary, BLWt. 26478-160-55... W 3745
  Samuel, Conn. & N. Y., widow Elizabeth.. W 25866
  Thaddeus, widow Ruth... W 22514
WAY, Abner, widow Eunice... W 25899
  Asa, Cont. (Conn.), widow Susannah... W 22504
  Durlen or Duren, widow Sarah... W 4612
  Elisha, widow Hannah, BLWt. 27578-160-55... W 1006
  George, widow Mary... W 18286
  Isaac, Conn. & Cont., Augusta Fuller, daughter of.. W 29943
  John, widow Mary... R 11223
    Soldier was pensioned in 1832 in Allegany Co., N. Y,. as priv. of Dragoons.
  Peter, widow Lucy.. W 18228
  Reynold, widow Irene... W 15462
  Selah, widow Lucy, BLWt. 28870-160-55.. W 1675
WAYLAND, Edward, widow Molly... W 18242
  James... S 6330
WAYLEY or WHALEY, Aaron, widow Hannah.. W 19895
WEARE, William... S 36376
  (See also WAIR and WIER, and WIRE.)
WEAVER, Lodowick, Conn. & R. I., widow Polly.. W 8323
  Samuel... BLWt. 266-100
    Hartford Co., Conn., in 1788.
  Samuel, Conn. & Cont., widow Hannah, BLWt. 13746-160-55.. W 1111
    Salisbury, Conn., in 1832; died in 1835.
  Thomas.. S 35717
WEBB, Abner.. S 14821
  Benjamin.. S 11704
  Christopher, Conn. & Cont... S 11705
  Constant.. S 6349
  Daniel, widow Luranda, BLWt. 27689-160-55.. W 2291
  David, widow Sarah... W 6443
  Ebenezer, widow Hannah, BLWt. 12836-160-55... W 18233
    Soldier was pensioned in 1818 from Conn.; transferred to N. Y. and died in Delaware Co.,
      N. Y., in 1835.
  Ebenezer.. S 14824
    Malone, N. Y., in 1832.
  Ebenezer, widow Phebe.. W 25921
    Stamford, Conn., in 1832; died in 1834.
  Isaac, widow Mary.. W 4851
  Jared, widow Prudence.. W 18300
  John.. R 11253
  John, Cont. (Conn.)... S 36374
    BLWt. 2356-300, Capt., was issued Nov. 13, 1792. No papers.
  Libbeus or Libbius... R 11250
  Moses, widow Abigail... W 25920
  Nathaniel, BLWt. 2344-300, Capt., was issued May 18, 1790, to Theodosius Fowler, Assignee.
    No papers.

WEBB, Reynolds, Conn. & Cont., widow Catherine	W 25919
Samuel, widow Abigail	W 16781
Lieut. & Brigade Major; died in 1825 in Dutchess Co., N. Y.	
Samuel, Conn., Cont. & N. Y	R 11255
Samuel B., BLWt. 2337-500, Colonel, was issued Jan. 29, 1790. No papers.	
Seth, widow Ann, BLWt. 77513-160-55	W 25922
WEBSTER, Aaron	S 14815
Abijah, widow Olive, BLWt. 36559-160-55	R 11266
Soldier never pensioned.	
Abraham	S 43272
Allen, widow Rebecca	W 25963
Amos, Conn. & N. Y	R 11259
Ashbell or Ashbil, widow Mercy	W 18313
Benjamin, widow Eve	W 2288
Schaghticoke, N. Y., in 1828; BLWt. 143-60-55.	
Benjamin, Conn. & Navy, widow Lydia	W 22562
Soldier was pensioned in Allegany Co., N. Y., in 1832, and died in 1840.	
Charles, Hannah Loomis, former widow of	W 20503
Daniel	S 43273
Eleazer	S 33890
Elizabeth, former widow of Isaac GOODSELL.	
Isaac, Conn., Cont. & Green Mt. Boys, widow Anna	W 20122
Israel, Conn. & Cont., widow Mary Sophia	W 18307
James	R 11262
John	S 11728
Joshua	S 43277
Michael	S 3521
Nathan	S 14817
Soldier was in Geauga Co., Ohio, in 1832, aged 79 years; transferred to N. Y.	
Nathan	S 26888
Soldier was born 1760; was in Chatauqua Co., N. Y., in 1825; transferred to Ohio and back to N. Y.	
Obed, widow Lucy, BLWt. 26921-160-55	W 613
Samuel, widow Margaret	W 18318
Simeon	S 35715
Timothy, widow Sarah	R 11267
Soldier never pensioned.	
William, widow Anna, BLWt. 31773-160-55	W 4848
WEED, Abishai	S 17191
Alexander	S 11717
Benjamin, Conn. & Cont., widow Hannah, BLWt. 11398-160-55	W 8986
Charles, widow Mary	W 2501
(Also given as WEEDS.)	
Daniel	S 17768
Daniel, widow Elizabeth	R 11271
Soldier never pensioned.	
David	S 14825
Eleazer, Conn. & Cont., widow Anna BLWt.	W 18302
Elnathan	S 23998
Frederick	R 11272
Gilbert, widow Margaret, BLWt. 27659-160-55	W 18326
Hannah, former widow of Joseph HOYT.	
Henry, widow Rebecca, BLWt. 51763-160-55	W 2289
Hezekiah, widow Rebecca	W 18299
Isaac, widow Hannah	W 22575
Ithamar or Ithamer, widow Delight	W 22558
Jabez, widow Hannah	W 22551
James, widow Sarah	W 19606
Jared, Conn. & Conn. Sea service	R 11275
Jesse, widow Martha	W 18327
John	S 23999
Delaware Co., N. Y., in 1832.	
John, Conn. & Conn	S 11724
Soldier was pensioned from Stamford, Conn., in 1818; and Darien, Conn., in 1832.	
Jonas, Abigail Daskam, former widow of, BLWt. 32239-160-55	W 22896
Abigail's other husband, William DASKAM, was also a Rev. pensioner. (See Conn. S 36495.)	
Jonathan, Conn. & N. Y	S 11682
Fairfield Co., Conn., in 1832.	
Jonathan, Conn. & N. Y., widow Susannah	W 20119
Soldier was in Delaware Co., N. Y., in 1832, and died there in 1837.	
Nathan, widow Mary	W 18314
Reuben	S 11720
Seth	S 6346
Smith, widow Sarah, BLWt. 13734-160-55	W 2290
Stephen, widow Elizabeth	W 25947
Thadeus, BLWt. 2345-300, Capt., was issued June 27, 1789. No papers.	
WEEKS, Micajah, widow Bersheba, BLWt. 1592-100	R 11278
Soldier was pensioned in Hancock, N. Y., in 1818.	
WELCH, Amos, Cont. (Conn.)	S 44032
Barney. (See WELTS.)	
Daniel, BLWt. 919-100	S 36841
(Also given WELSH.)	
David, widow Lurene	W 22571
Ebenezer	S 40665
Delaware Co., Ohio, in 1818, as fifer.	
Ebenezer	BLWt. 1196-100
Amity Coats, wife of Obediah Coats, of Sherman, Fairfield Co., Conn., obtained Bounty land in 1826, as daughter and only heir of Ebenezer WELCH. No date of his death given.	

WELCH, Hopestill... S 36382
    John, widow Jemima.. W 8987
        Soldier was pensioned from Erie Co., N. Y., in 1832; BLWt. 34579-160-55.
    John, Cont. (Conn.)... S 14804
        Warren, Conn., in 1818; died there in 1845.
    Robert... S 43282
    Samuel, Conn. & Cont... S 43263
    Solomon, Orpha Dygert, former widow of.. W 14664
    William.. R 11299
WELD, John... S 22578
WELDEN, Abraham... S 35713
    Isaac.. S 43258
        (Also given WELDIN.)
WELLER, Amos, Conn. & N. Y., widow Dimis... W 25952
WELLES, Benjamin. (See WELLS.)
    Noah... S 23063
        (See also WELLS.)
WELLMAN, Barnabas, Conn. & Cont.. S 29534
    John, widow Phebe.. W 18325
    Jonathan, Conn. & Vt., BLWt. 26108-160-55... S 15700
        (Also given John.)
    Paul... S 43264
    William.. S 17774
    Zadock, Conn. & Vt... R 11306
WELLS, Abner.. S 14805
    Ashbel... R 11309
    Austin.. S 32054
    Bayze or Bazze, Conn. & boat service on Lake Champlain, widow Ruth....................... W 18311
        (Also given WELLES.)
    Benjamin, Conn. & Mass., widow Sarah... W 6435
        BLWt. 23502-300, Surgeon's Mate, was issued Jan. 17, 1793. No papers.
        Also recorded as above under BLWt. 2622.
        (Also given WELLES.)
    Cuff (colored), Phillis Tatton, former widow of.. W 18103
        (Also given as Cuff SAUNDERS.)
    Daniel, Conn. & N. Y... S 6354
    Elisha... S 14813
        Trenton, N. Y., in 1832.
    Elisha... S 36377
        Hartford Co., Conn., in 1818.
    Gideon.. S 18273
    Hannah, former widow of Henry MAIN.
    Hezekiah, widow Sarah... W 25967
        (Also given WILLES.)
    Israel.. S 40664
    James... S 17764
    Jedediah F., widow Hannah.. W 22576
    Jonathan... S 16018
    Josiah... S 28938
    Noah. (See WELLES.)
    Robert.. S 16188
    Roger, BLWt. 2349-300, Capt., was issued April 22, 1796, to Jemima Wells, Adx. No papers.
    Samuel, widow Isabel Catharine.. W 6439
    Simon, Conn. & Cont.. S 14809
    Thomas... S 11721
    Timothy... S 40651
WELSH. (See WELCH.)
WELTON, David, widow Sarah.. W 18250
    Eben.. S 16577
    George.. S 18282
        (Also given WILTON.)
    Joel... S 35714
    Josiah.. R 11319
        (Also given WETTON.)
    Shubael... S 43283
    Solomon.. S 36380
WELTS, Barney, Cont. (Conn.) & Penna.. S 40670
    (Also given WELCH.)
WENTWORTH, Alpheus, Conn. & Cont., widow Polly.. W 22582
    (Also given WINTWORTH.)
    Amos, Conn. & Conn. Sea service, widow Lydia... R 11325
        Soldier never pensioned.
        NOTE.—A list of men sent on by Lieut. GOODELL, from Norwich, Conn., July 6, 1780,
            giving place of abode, date of enlistment, number of regiment, and term for which
            enlisted, was forwarded the War Department from this case, Jan. 16, 1913.
    Daniel.. S 30776
    Elijah... S 41311
    Ezekiel... R 11323
    Gibbens.. R 11324
    Josiah W... S 23062
    Levi W., BLWt. 55-100... S 37511
WERDEN, Jesse, Conn. & R. I., widow Ruth... W 19655
    (Also given WORDEN. See also WORDEN.)
WESCOAT, Joseph... S 43281
WESCOTT, Daniel... S 17767
    (See also WESTCOTT.)
WEST, Aaron, widow Susanna.. W 19607
    Alva, Cont. (Conn.), Susan Robinson, former widow of....................................... W 17557
    Amos, widow Helen, BLWt. 31762-160-55... W 11772

WEST, Anthony..	S 44034
Benjamin..	S 29537
Caleb..	S 11723
David..	S 43275
Ichabod, widow Lovina...	W 1113
Ira...	S 32052
Joseph, widow Sally, BLWt. 47836-160-55.......................................	W 9157
Moses, Mary Wright, former widow of..	W 18387
Richard..	S 11709
Samuel...	S 17773
WESTBROOK, James, Conn. & N. J..	R 11350
WESTCOT or WESTCOTT, Amos, Conn. & R. I., widow Abigail...............	W 18330
(See also WESCOAT & WESCOTT.)	
WESTLAND, Joseph..	BLWt. 2311-100
Robert...	S 36378
WESTON, Abraham, widow Naomi...	W 19597
Benjamin, widow Mary...	W 18320
John, widow Margaret, BLWt. 31769-160-55....................................	W 4852
Rachel, former widow of Francis NICHOLSON.	
Zachariah...	S 43257
WETHERLY. (See WITHERILL.)	
WETHY, Henry, widow Esther..	W 22574
Jeduthan, Conn. & N. Y...	R 11752
(Also given WITHEY.)	
WETTON. (See WELTON.)	
WHALEY, Aaron. (See WAYLEY.)	
Hezekiah..	S 36387
Jonathan, Mercy Lord, former widow of, BLWt. 13744-160-55................	W 2739
Theophilus, widow Lois..	W 2038
WHAPLES, Samuel, widow Huldah..	W 19613
WHEADON. (See WHEEDON.)	
WHEATLEY, Andrew, widow Rubie, BLWt. 7059-160-55......................	W 19614
WHEATON, Andrew, widow Avis..	R 11372
Soldier never pensioned.	
Jeremiah...	S 23486
(Also given WHEATEN.)	
Jonathan..	S 40687
Roswell, Conn. & N. H...	S 36383
Rufus..	S 35721
(Also WHEDON and WHEEDON.)	
WHEDON, Abraham, widow Lydia, BLWt. 12719-160-55.....................	W 11802
(Also given WHEADON & WHEEDON.)	
Rufus. (See WHEATON.)	
WHEELER, Aaron..	S 28941
Volney, N. Y., in 1832.	
Aaron..	S 11748
Schoharie, N. Y., in 1832.	
Benjamin, widow Loly or Loby, BLWt. 39-100..................................	W 6483
Beriah, Conn. & Conn. Sea service, widow Eunice............................	W 25968
Chauncey, Conn. Sea service & Navy, widow Caroline Matilda............	W 25998
Comfort, Conn., N. Y. & War of 1812, widow Parmelia or Amelia.........	R 11385
Soldier was pensioned in 1832 in Caledonia Co., Vt.; BLWt. 105622-160-55.	
Daniel, widow Amy...	W 18390
David..	S 44046
Dimond..	S 24006
Edward, Conn., Mass. & N. Y..	S 16292
Hezekiah, Conn. & Cont., widow Meribah, BLWt. 95-60-55.................	W 6486
James, widow Elizabeth, BLWt. 31776-160-55.................................	W 2295
Job...	R 11381
John...	S 40672
Genesee Co., N. Y., in 1818.	
John, widow Almira..	W 25997
Windham Co., Conn., in 1818; BLWt. 36820-160-55.	
John T...	R 11382
Jonathan..	S 15245
Joshua...	R 11383
Josiah...	S 36388
Stafford, Conn., in 1818.	
Josiah, widow Hannah...	W 19628
Washington Co., Vt., in 1818; died in 1828; enlisted from Plainfield, Conn.	
Nathaniel, widow Ellen..	W 18408
Prosper, widow Sarah..	W 22604
Rhoda F., former widow of James MORRIS.	
Rufus, Conn., Mass. & N. Y., Sarah Wood, former widow of, BLWt. 99516-160-55.........	W 11881
Sally, former widow of Jabez BREED.	
Samuel, widow Julia, BLWt. 26531-160-55......................................	W 26002
Simeon..	S 17776
Thomas..	S 33903
William, widow Anna...	R 11376
Soldier never pensioned.	
Zadock, widow Martha...	W 19620
WHELPLEY, Ebenezer..	S 29541
James..	S 41332
WHIPPLE, Benjamin..	S 11766
Caleb, Conn. & War of 1812, widow Polly......................................	W 1965
Elijah, Conn. & Cont..	S 3552
Joseph, widow Mary...	R 11389
Soldier never pensioned.	
Zebulon, widow Lydia, BLWt. 31778-160-55....................................	W 6491

WHISTON, Joseph, widow Elizabeth	W 16469
WHITAKER, Abraham	S 6375
Catharine, former widow of Silas BEARDSLEY.	
Ephraim, BLWt. 1902-300	S 9526
(Also given WHITTAKER.)	
Nell	S 32588
Philip	S 15255
Stephen	S 34527
WHITCOMB, Hiram, widow Sarah W	W 19896
John or John Skinner, Conn., Cont. & N. Y., widow Sarah	W 3371
WHITE, Abijah	S 20943
Adonijah, widow Hannah	W 22601
Anna, former widow of William JOHNSTON.	
Caleb, Conn. & Privateer	S 11758
Charles	S 11745
Consider, widow Sarah T., BLWt. 13196-160-55	W 320
Daniel	S 15238
Hebron, Conn., in 1832.	
Daniel, widow Sally	R 11443
Soldier pensioned in 1821 for disability, while resident of N. Y.	
David	S 43302
Pompey, N. Y., in 1818.	
David, widow Hannah, BLWt. 26577-160-55	W 18403
Soldier in N. Y. in 1832; died in Otsego Co., N. Y., in 1837.	
David, Hannah Wilcox, former widow of	R 11521
Soldier never pensioned.	
Ebenezer	R 11407
Elisha, widow Abigail, BLWt. 18370-160-55	R 11408
Both soldier and widow rejected as service was not six months.	
Elisha, Conn. & Cont	S 18279
Ephraim, BLWt. 1765-100	S 40676
Penna. in 1818.	
Ephraim, Conn., Cont. & Mass., widow Hope	W 1680
Soldier was pensioned in 1832 in Hartford Co., Conn., as Corporal.	
Ezra, widow Lucy	W 22605
Israel	S 6382
Jacob, widow Esther	W 18407
Jedidiah or Jedediah	S 36386
Joel	S 11775
John, BLWt. 2353-200, Lieut., was issued July 6, 1795, to Eneas Munson, Jr., assignee of Sam GOULD, Admr. No papers.	
John	S 32589
Wabash Co., Ill., in 1832.	
John, Betsey Underwood, former widow of	W 3739
Soldier died in 1802; widow applied from Colchester, Conn., in 1853.	
NOTE.—Travel roll of Capt. John Isham's Co., Col. Chester, dated N. Y. Aug. 10, 1776, was sent the War Department from this case.	
John, Sarah Millard, former widow of	R 7172
Neither soldier nor widow applied; but Josiah WHITE, son of Sarah by her first marriage.	
John, Conn. & Continental	S 3532
Athens Co., Ohio, in 1832 as private and sergeant.	
John, Cont. (Conn.), widow Martha	W 16786
Soldier died in 1812; widow in Cortland Co., N. Y., in 1837.	
Joseph, widow Mary	W 18392
Lawrence, Cont. (Conn.), widow Eunice	R 11411
Soldier was pensioned in 1818 & 1832 while residing in Cincinnatus, N. Y., as member of Sheldon's Dragoons.	
Lemuel	S 10045
Matthew, widow Esther	W 18409
Nathaniel	S 44040
Niagara Co., N. Y., in 1818.	
Nathaniel, Cont. (Conn.), widow Abigail	W 4532
Erie Co., N. Y., in 1826; died in 1830.	
Obadiah	S 15243
Oliver	S 24004
Peregrine	R 11434
Philip, widow Olive, BLWt. 119-60-55	W 25969
Samuel, widow Betsy	W 25976
Solomon, Conn. & N. Y	S 15250
Thomas	S 15244
William	R 11450
William	S 36384
Chatham, Middlesex Co., Conn., in 1818.	
William	S 40684
Killingworth, Conn. (Middlesex Co.), in 1818.	
William, widow Zilpha	W 22596
Soldier died in Tolland Co., Conn., in 1837; widow was pensioned by special act of Congress in 1848.	
WHITEHEAD, David, widow Judith, BLWt. 26405-160-55	W 10278
WHITELEY, John, Cont. (Conn.), widow Rebecca	W 25978
William	S 43308
(See also WHITLEY.)	
WHITING, Elihu	S 11176
Elijah, Cont. (Conn.), widow Anna, BLWt. 245-60-55	W 18412
Elizabeth, former widow of Lyman NOBLE.	
Francis, BLWt. 2440-200, Lieut. of First Regiment Light Dragoons, was issued August 25, 1789. No papers.	
Frederick J., BLWt. 2358-200, Lieut. Sheldon's Regiment of Horse, was issued August 23, 1790. No papers.	

WHITING, Harvey, widow Olive ... W 11801
  John ... S 15241
    New Hartford, Conn., in 1832.
  John, widow Alida ... W 19618
    Madison Co., N. Y., in 1818; died there in 1823.
    (Also given WHITTING.)
  Joseph ... S 35724
  Joseph ... R 11462
  Nathan, Conn., Navy & R. I., widow Sarah ... W 22595
  Nathan H., BLWt. 2351-200, Lieut., was issued Feb. 22, 1790, to Theodosius Fowler, Assignee.
    No papers.
  Samuel, Conn. & Mass ... S 17777
  William ... S 11746
WHITLEY, Joseph ... S 44039
  (See also WHITELEY.)
WHITLOCK, Abel, widow Phebe ... W 18413
  Hezekiah ... S 15706
  Justus, Conn. & Privateer ... S 18648
  Nathan ... S 6368
WHITMAN, John ... S 35719
  Lemuel ... S 43319
  Samuel, widow Abigail ... W 18402
WHITMORE, Hezekiah ... S 32056
  Jabez, BLWt ... 1537-100
WHITNEY, Cornelius, widow Hannah ... W 14136
  Daniel, widow Hannah ... W 25995
  David, Eliza Whitney Sollace, former widow of, BLWt., 105237-160-55 ... W 2013
    Soldier was in Addison Co., Vt., in 1832; died in 1850.
  David, widow Nancy, BLWt., 38341-160-55, ... W 3636
    Soldier was in Delaware Co., N. Y., in 1834, and died there Sept. 7, 1834; widow was in
    Cortland Co., N. Y., in 1854.
  Ebenezer, widow Ruth ... W 22609
  Enos ... S 22580
  Ezekiel ... S 44036
    Saugerties, Ulster Co., N. Y., in 1818.
  Ezekiel, widow Phebe ... W 19626
    Saratoga Co., N. Y., in 1818; died in 1835.
  Hezekiah, widow Olive ... W 18406
  James R., Conn.& Navy ... S 44037
  John ... S 17192
  Joshua, Conn. & Green Mt. Boys ... S 41326
    BLWt., 2354-200, Lieut., was issued May 31, 1790, to Theodosius Fowler, Assignee. No
    papers.
  Josiah, widow Sally, BLWt., 51764-160-55 ... W 2297
  Peter ... S 41330
  Samuel ... S 35723
  Walter ... S 11737
  William ... S 35720
    (Also WHITNY.)
WHITON, Joseph, widow Amanda ... W 14145
  Thomas ... S 44049
WHITTAKER. (See WHITAKER.)
WHITTING. (See WHITING.)
WHITTLESEY, Charles H ... S 17197
WIARD, Darius ... S 28946
WICKES, Alexander ... S 44090
  (Also WICKS.)
WICKHAM, William, widow Sarah ... W 26026
WICKS. (See WICKES.)
WICKWIRE, Grant ... S 11785
  James, Conn. & Cont., widow Sarah ... W 22629
WIDGER, Andrew ... S 36390
  Eli, Conn., Cont., Navy & Privateer, widow Lucy, BLWt. 3618-160-55 ... W 18425
  Samuel ... R 11497
WIER, James R ... S 30802
  (See also WIRE, WEARE and WAIR.)
WIGHT, Jacob ... S 33934
  William ... S 15711
WILBUR, Josiah ... S 44220
  Nancy Ann, former widow of John SMITH.
WILBY. (See WILLEY.)
WILCOX, Abraham, Conn. & Cont., widow Lucretia, BLWt. 26255-160-55 ... W 27505
  Billy, widow Rebecca ... W 18423
  Chloe, former widow of Isaac ISAACS.
  Eleazer ... S 16023
  Elias, Cont. (Conn.), Hannah Sears, former widow of ... W 17792
    NOTE.—Hannah's other husband, Obadiah SEARS, was also a Rev. pensioner. See
    Conn. S. 43121.
  Elijah, widow Lois ... W 18419
  Elisha, Conn. & R. I ... S 24011
  Ezekiel. (See WILLCOX.)
  Ezra, widow Rebecca ... W 18420
  Hannah, former widow of David WHITE.
  Hosea ... S 40709
  Jacob, widow Rachel ... W 18442
    (Also given WILLCOX.)
  James. (See WILLCOX.)
  James, Conn., Green Mt. Boys, Mass. & Vt ... S 19162
  Jehiel, widow Catharine ... W 2211
    Delaware Co., Ohio, in 1832.

WILCOX, Jehiel, widow Thankful.. W 6542
    New Haven Co., Conn., in 1818 & 1823.
       (Also given WILLCOX.)
  Joel... S 40695
  John... S 32068
  Jonathan.. S 11844
  Joseph.. S 32073
  Josiah, widow Rosannah... W 26051
      (Also given WILLCOX.)
  Lemuel, widow Anate.. W 22663
  Mercy, former widow of Daniel MERRELL or MERRILL.
  Nathan.. S 36391
      (Also given WILLCOX.)
  Rebecca, former widow of Richard DOUD.
  Reuben.. S 11859
  Stephen... R 11528
  Timothy. (See WILLCOX. See also WILLCOX.)
WILCOXEN, David.. S 36389
WILCOXSON, WILCOXON or WILLCOXSON & WILLCOXON.
  Finathan... S 15715
  Ephraim J., widow Mary, BLWt. 27694-160-55... W 2392
WILDER, Aaron.. S 18655
  Elijah... S 11779
  Jonathan.. S 11793
  Thomas, widow Taphnes or Zaphenes... W 22642
WILDMAN, Matthew, widow Polly.. W 18452
WILEY, Eleanor, former widow of David CROUCH.
  James. (See WYLIE.)
WILKESON or WILKINSON, Abel, Conn. & R. I.. S 14842
  Edward M. or Mott, BLWt. 26349-160-55.. S 24015
  Ichabod... S 40710
    Butler Co., Ohio, in 1819.
  Ichabod, widow Anna Taylor.. W 3202
    Soldier died in 1817 at Erie Co., Penna.
  John... S 11830
  Joseph.. R 11550
  Levi, Conn., Cont. & Mass... S 7913
  Malachi, widow Sally.. W 4866
    (Also given as WILKESON.)
  Mott. (See Edward M.)
  Peter.. R 11551
  Reuben or Reubin... S 44214
WILLARD, Elisa, widow Lois.. W 4715
  Joseph.. S 6432
  Lizur.. S 14850
WILLCOX, Benjamin, BLWt. 31770-160-55.. S 14852
  Ezekiel... S 34556
    (Also given WILCOX.)
  James, widow Elizabeth... W 18417
    Soldier was in Middlesex Co., Conn., in 1832; died in 1838.
    (Also given WILCOX.)
  James, Conn. & Cont., widow Lucretia... W 9019
    Soldier pensioned in N. Y. in 1818; widow pensioned in Mich, in 1852; BLWt. 3192-160-55.
  John, widow Lois... W 10283
  Joseph, BLWt. 2350-200, Lieut., was issued Jan. 28, 1790. No papers.
  Nathan.. S 19167
  Roger, widow Elizabeth... W 18453
  Stephen, Conn. & R. I.. S 6412
    Madison Co., N. Y., in 1832.
  Stephen, Conn. & R. I., widow Sabra.. W 18454
    Serg't, Chataqua Co., N. Y., in 1828.
  Timothy... S 41336
WILLES, Hezekiah. (See WELLS.)
  John... S 36848
  Silvanus, Conn. & N. H., widow Eunice.. W 22619
    (See also WILLIS.)
WILLEY, Abraham.. S 24016
  Ahimaaz or Ahimaas or Ahimaz... S 34560
  Barzillai.. S 16299
  Ephraim, widow Bethia.. R 11559
    Sold. in Washington Co., Vt., in 1832.
  Jonathan.. S 35734
    New Hartford, Litchfield Co., Conn., in 1818; son of Jonathan WILLEY, a Rev. soldier
    for three years.
  Jonathan, Conn. & N. Y., widow Irene or Irena, BLWt. 517-160-55........................... W 6827
    Torrington, Conn. in 1832; moved to Ohio.
WILLFORD, Joseph... R 11537
WILLIAMS, Alexander... S 35740
  Andrew.. S 44213
  Anna, former widow of Isaac GALLUP.
  Asa... S 14846
    East Hartford, Conn., in 1832.
  Asa, widow Prudence, BLWt. 26182-160-55... W 2040
    Soldier in Mass. in 1818; died in 1834; widow in Hampshire Co., Mass., in 1855.
  Asahel... S 6411
    Otsego Co., N. Y., in 1832.
  Asahel, widow Hannah.. W 26053
    Rutland Co., Vt., in 1832; died in 1841.
  Asher, widow Elizabeth... W 18445
    Soldier died in 1812; widow was in Orange Co., Vt., in 1836.

WILLIAMS, Asher, Conn. & N. Y., widow Elizabeth... W 2216
   Soldier in St. Lawrence Co., N. Y., in 1832.
  Bartholomew, Cont. (Conn.) widow Mary, BLWt. 3754-160-55........................... W 2627
  Benjamin.. S 11855
  Caleb, Conn. & Cont., widow Eunice, BLWt. 38337-160-55............................... W 9165
  Daniel.. S 23077
   Schoharie Co., N. Y., in 1832.
  Daniel.. S 32074
   New London Co., Conn., in 1832.
  Daniel, widow Hannah.. W 6512
   Trumbull Co., Ohio, in 1832; died in 1835.
  Davenport... S 11813
  David... S 11781
   East Hartford, Conn., in 1832.
  David, Conn. & Cont., widow Lucy.. W 22632
   Rome, N. Y., in 1832; died in 1837.
  Durell.. S 14838
  Ebenezer.. S 35729
   Saybrook, Conn., in 1818; died in 1819
  Ebenezer.. S 28950
   Albany, N. Y., in 1832.
  Ebenezer.. S 32072
   Canandaigua, N. Y., in 1832; private & serg't.
  Edward, Conn. Sea service, widow Mary... W 22633
  Elisha.. S 14839
  Elisha S.. S 30796
  Elizabeth, former widow of Abel PHELPS.
  Ezekiel, Lydia Newell, former widow of, BLWt. 4681-160-55.............................. W 5409
  Henry, widow Electa... W 2889
   Oswego Co., N. Y., in 1832; transferred to Penna.
  Henry, Conn. & Cont., Eunice Mott, former widow of..................................... W 24163
   Soldier died in 1781; widow in Onondaga Co., N. Y., in 1837.
  Hiel, widow Abigail, BLWt. 26176-160-55.. W 6513
  Isaac... S 44224
   Athol, N. Y., in 1818.
  Isaac, widow Nancy, BLWt. 26371-160-55... W 6500
   Soldier in Stonington, Conn., in 1832.
  Isaac, Conn. & Cont... S 15719
   Soldier in Norwich, Conn., in 1832.
  Jacob, widow Frances.. R 11580
   Soldier never pensioned.
  Jacob, widow Mary... W 18422
  James, widow Grace.. W 19640
  John.. S 11809
   Paris, N. Y., in 1832.
   (Also given as Ichabod WALDIN.)
  John.. S 11851
   Pensioned as serg't. in Chataqua Co., N. Y., in 1832.
  John, widow Polly... W 26067
   Delaware Co., N. Y., in 1832; BLWt. 29008-160-55.
  John, Conn. & Cont.. S 14873
   Pensioned as private & corp. in Rome, N. Y., in 1832.
  John, Conn. & Navy.. S 23072
   Pensioned as private & teamster in Darien, N. Y., in 1832.
  Joseph.. S 40704
   Waterford, Penna., in 1818.
  Joseph, Conn. & Navy.. S 14868
   New London Co., Conn., in 1832.
  Nathan.. S 49269
  Nathaniel, Naomi Menter, former widow of.. R 19136
   Soldier never pensioned.
  Obed.. S 35741
  Peter... S 11829
   Saratoga Co., N. Y., in 1832.
  Peter, widow Mary... W 18435
  Prince. (See STARKWEATHER.)
  Robert, Hannah Fitch, former widow of... W 10990
   New London Co., Conn., in 1818; died there in 1822.
  Robert, Conn. & Cont.. S 17200
   Groton, Conn., in 1832.
  Robinson.. S 23493
  Samuel William, Conn. & Cont., widow Emily.. W 26071
   BLWt. 2347-300, Capt., was issued May 14, 1796. No papers.
  Silas, Conn. & Vt... R 11620
  Simeon, widow Prudence.. R 11609
   Soldier never pensioned.
  Solomon... S 14862
   New London Co., Conn., in 1832.
  Solomon, widow Lucy... W 20133
   Soldier served as serg't. and died in 1807; widow in Broome Co., N. Y., in 1847.
  Solomon, Conn. & Cont... S 14867
   Oneida Co., N. Y., in 1832.
  Sophia, former widow of Enos CRANE.
  Thomas.. S 6428
   Soldier served between six and seven yrs. in Revolution, and received wounds for which
   in 1806, while resident of East Haddam, Conn., he rec'd pension of $20,00 per annum.
  Thomas.. S 6421
   Lorain Co., Ohio, in 1832.
  Thomas, BLWt. 1275-100.
   Wilkes-Barre, Penna., in 1828.

WILLIAMS, Thomas, widow Content... W 19645
    Soldier died at Hartford, Conn., in 1817.
  Uriah, Cont. service but Conn. residence in 1818, widow Johannah or Jehannah............. W 22665
  Veach.. S 17789
  Warham or Wareham, widow Anna... W 11856
  Weeks or Wilks, widow Tamer.. W 26059
  William, BLWt. 26352-160-55... S 14832
    Fairfield Co., Conn., in 1832.
  William or William R... R 11624
WILLIAMSON, Nathan.. S 11789
WILLIS, Daniel, Cont. (Conn.)... S 44064
  Silvanus. (See WILLES.)
  (See also WYLLIS and WYLLYS.)
WILLISTON, Payson, BLWt. 23118-160-55.. S 17787
WILLMOT, Timothy. Conn. & Cont., widow Polly.. W 26036
  (See also WILMOT and WILMOTT.)
WILLOUGHBY, Bliss.. S 7914
  Salmon, widow Ruby, BLWt. 28598-160-55... W 2634
  Samuel, Conn. & Privateer... S 11807
WILLS, Joel... S 19166
  Jonathan, Conn. & Cont., widow Lydia... W 19644
WILLSON, John... S 15713
    Born 1764; Fairfield Co., Conn., in 1832.
  John... R 11668
    (Also given WILSON.)
  Joseph, widow Eleanor.. W 18443
    (Also WILSON.)
  Sarah, former widow of Samuel DIX.
  Thomas... S 44091
    (Also WILSON.)
WILLYS, Thomas, Conn. & Cont.. S 17784
  (See also WILLIS & WYLLIS.)
WILMOT, Timothy. (See WILLMOTT.)
  Walter.. S 35736
    (Also WILLMOTT.)
WILMOTT, Elijah... R 11648
WILSON, Abiel... S 35739
    (Also given Abial WILLSON.)
  Asa, widow Joanna.. W 26037
  Calvin, widow Submit.. W 18424
  Daniel S.. S 14837
  Elnathan... S 24014
  George... S 23079
  Jacob, Conn. & Cont., widow Ruth... W 22621
  James, Cont. (Conn.)... R 11658
  Javin.. S 35738
  Joab... S 17783
  John, widow Sally, BLWt. 13736-160-55.. W 2679
    (Also given WILLSON.)
    Soldier was born in 1762; in Thompson, Conn., in 1818, and died there in 1838.
  John... S 16296
    Born in 1760; in Clinton Co., N. Y., in 1832.
  John, Conn. & N. Y... S 32075
    Born in 1762; in Sharon, Conn., in 1832.
  John, Conn., Cont. & Penna.. S 44069
    Born in 1755; in Cayuga Co., N. Y., in 1820.
  John, Conn. & Privateer.. S 14847
    Born in 1749; in Thompson, Conn., in 1818 & 1832. (Also given WILLSON.)
  Jonathan... S 17791
  Lewis... R 11673
  Moses... S 17792
  Nathaniel, Conn. & Navy, widow Ruth... W 26062
  Nehemiah, widow Rachel.. W 18437
  Peter.. R 11681
  Samuel... S 15709
    Hartford, Conn., in 1832.
  Samuel, widow Eleanor.. W 18438
    Fairfield Co., Conn., in 1832; died in 1842.
  Thomas, Conn. & N. Y., widow Sarah, BLWt. 61162-160-55...................................... W 10280
  (See also WILLSON.)
WILTON. (See WELTON.)
WINCHEL, John.. S 17790
  William, widow Elviry.. W 19651
    (Also given WINCHELL.)
WINCHESTER, Jabez... S 14871
  Richard, widow Lydia.. W 9027
WINDHAM, Thomas, widow Sarah.. W 9020
WINSHIP, Jabez, widow Hannah... R 11725
    Soldier never pensioned.
WINSLOW, Hannah, former widow of Oliver BROWN.
WINTER, Abner, widow Anna... R 11733
    Soldier never pensioned.
  Asa, widow Lydia... W 14158
  Jonathan W... S 17202
  Nicholas.. S 11797
WINTERS, Juvenil, widow Amelia, BLWt. 3818-160-55.. W 2217
  (Also given Juvenal WINTER.)
WINTON, Joseph, Conn., Cont. & Privateer... S 11814
  Nathan... S 39899
WINTWORTH. (See WENTWORTH.)

WIRE, Samuel, Cont. (Conn.), widow Eunice	W 18441
(See also WAIR, WARE, WEARE, WIER.)	
WISE, William, Cont. (Conn.)	S 11791
WITHERILL, David	R 11750
(Also given WETHERLY.)	
WITHY. (See WETHY.)	
WITTER, Ebenezer, Conn. & Mass	S 11802
Jonah	S 17793
Josiah, Conn. & Mass	S 41359
William	R 11757
WOLCATT, Solomon. (See WOLCOTT.)	
WOLCOTT, Abiel	R 11761
Benajah	S 40729
(Also given WOLCOT.)	
Elijah, widow Mary	W 22678
Erastus, BLWt. 2346–300, Capt., was issued Feb. 23, 1799, to Chloe Wolcott, guardian to Erastus, Chloe Jr., Edward, Julius, otherwise called Julah, and Helen Wolcott (minors), the only surviving heirs. No papers.	
John, Conn. & Boat service on Lake Champlain, widow Martha	W 20137
(Also given WOOLCOTT.)	
Joseph, Sarah Hixon, former widow of	W 21336
(Also given WOLCUTT.)	
NOTE.—Sarah's last husband, Elkanah HIXSON, was also pensioned. (See Mass. S 39694.)	
Josiah, widow Elizabeth, BLWt. 17733–160–55	W 9034
Oliver	R 11763
Samuel, widow Jerusha	W 22535
Soldier died in 1813 at Hatford, Conn.	
Samuel, Conn. & R. I., widow Sarah	R 11765
Soldier was pensioned from Lexington. N. Y., in 1818.	
Solomon, widow Cornelia, BLWt. 26527–160–55	W 26096
(Also given WOOLCOTT & WOLCATT.)	
William, widow Huldah, BLWt. 11070–160–55	W 26090
WOLCUTT. (See WOLCOTT.)	
WOLF, Levi. (See De WOLF, Levy.)	
Seth. (See D'WOLF.)	
WOOD, Abner, widow Betsey	W 18377
Asa	S 17798
Benjamin	R 11779
Benjamin	S 40732
Charles	S 39916
Daniel, Conn. & Vt	S 14898
David, widow Electa, BLWt. 12848–160–55	W 6564
Eli, Conn. & N. Y., widow Rhoda	W 16480
(Also given WOODS.)	
Elisha, Conn. & R. I	S 14902
Jacob	S 44095
Putnam Co., N. Y., in 1818.	
Jacob	S 44102
Pensioned as Jacob, Sen., in Orange Co., N. Y., in 1818.	
Jared, Conn. & N. Y	S 11882
Joel, Conn. & Cont	S 17206
John, widow Nabby or Nebby	W 26110
Serg't. died in 1832 in New London Co., Conn.	
John	S 18663
Lyme, Conn.. in 1832.	
(Also WOODS.)	
John, Conn., Cont. & Privateer	S 11868
Serg't in East Windsor, Conn., in 1832.	
John, Conn. & N. H	R 11790
John, Conn. & Vt., widow Abigail	R 11774
Soldier never pensioned.	
Joseph	S 23094
Lemuel, widow Elizabeth or Elizebeth	W 4106
Levi, Conn. & Vt	S 6446
Mary, former widow of Jonathan KNEELAND.	
Nathan	S 11870
Nathaniel, Conn., Green Mt. Boys & Vt., Lois Collins, former widow of	W 16928
Samuel	S 35748
Fairfield Co., Conn., in 1819.	
Samuel	S 44101
Camden, N. Y., in 1818.	
Sarah, former widow of Rufus WHEELER.	
Silas	S 35747
Solomon, Cont. (Conn.), widow Christiana, BLWt. 31764–160–55	W 2427
Thomas, widow Abigail	W 27506
Soldier pensioned from Springfield, Mass., in 1818; widow pensioned in 1836.	
Thomas, Conn. & Mass	S 14879
Schuyler, N. Y., in 1832.	
(See also WOODS.)	
WOODARD, James. (See Josiah.)	
Jesse, Conn. & Vt	S 14967½
Josiah or James, widow Jane	W 26100
(See also WOODWARD.)	
WOODBRIDGE, George, Conn. & Privateer	S 11877
Theodore, BLWt. 2339–400, Major, was issued April 14, 1790, to William Wells, Assignee. No papers.	
WOODBURN, Moses	S 22605
WOODCOCK, John	R 11812
Samuel, widow Rhoda	W 9169

WOODDIN. (See WOODIN.)
WOODEN. Charles... S 15722
    Jeremiah. (See WOODIN.)
WOODETH, Benjamin, Cont. (Conn.).. S 16025
WOODFORD, Bissel.. S 11873
    Joseph... S 29561
    Timothy.. S 41370
WOODHOUSE, Samuel, widow Abigail.. W 26108
WOODIN, Aner, Cont. (Conn.), widow Ruth..................................... W 18365
    Jeremiah.. BLWt. 1891-100
    (Also given WOODEN and WOODDIN.)
    Philo... S 45161
WOODRUFF, Amos.. S 14901
    Baldwin, Cont. (Conn.), Bede Hough, former widow of..................... W 14926
    (Also given Nathaniel Baldwin.)
    Gedor, widow Sarah... W 26102
    Jason... R 11819
    John, widow Sarah... W 16483
        Berkshire Co., Mass., in 1832; died in 1834; widow in Columbia Co., N. Y., in 1836.
    John, Conn. & Privateer... S 15721
        Torrington, Conn., in 1832.
    Joseph, Cont. (Conn.)... S 14889
    Lambert.. R 11821
    Nathaniel Baldwin. (See Baldwin.)
    Noadiah, widow Dorcas.. W 18366
    Oliver, Conn. & Privateer... S 14885
    Philo... S 15720
    Samuel.. S 7964
        Bradford Co., Penna., in 1832.
    Samuel.. S 14875
        Litchfield Co., Conn., in 1832.
    Samuel.. S 39915
        Chenango Co., N. Y., in 1818; transferred to Penna.
    Samuel, widow Chloe, BLWt. 36545-160-55................................ W 4406
        Soldier in Windsor Co., Conn., in 1832.
    Selah, widow Caroline... W 11882
    Solomon, widow Chestinah or Christina.................................. W 18367
    William, widow Ruth.. W 20136
WOODS, Justus... S 35746
    (See also WOOD.)
WOODWARD, Aaron... R 11836
    Abner... S 11866
    Asa... S 41371
        Fairlee, Vt., in 1818.
    Asa, Conn., Mass. & Vt., widow Ruth.................................... W 6579
        Licking Co., Ohio, in 1832.
    Asa, Conn., Conn. Sea service & Cont., widow Sally..................... W 26129
        Lyme, Conn., in 1832; died in 1840.
    Ebenezer.. S 41372
    Frederick... R 11838
    Gideon.. S 11897
    Hezekiah, widow Aseneth.. W 3640
    James. (See WOODARD, Josiah.)
    John, Conn. & Vt.. S 14877
    Joshua.. S 11879
    Noah.. S 11874
    Oliver.. S 40727
    Reuben.. S 11864
    (See also WOODARD.)
WOODWORTH, Abel, Navy (Conn.)... S 23496
    Benjamin.. S 11881
    Darius.. S 36851
    Dyer, Conn. & N. Y.. S 17799
    Ezra.. S 4733
    Ichabod... S 32080
    Jedediah, widow Adah... W 18362
    Joseph, Cont. (Conn.), widow Wayty..................................... W 6584
    Josiah, Cont. (Conn.)... S 14890
    Roger... S 41373
    Roswell, Conn. & N. H., widow Phebe.................................... W 18369
    Samuel, widow Sally, BLWt. 26922-160-55................................ W 26095
    Swift... S 29560
    Timothy, widow Lydia, BLWt. 6290-160-55................................ W 2475
    William... S 29559
    Ziba, widow Lucy... R 11848
        Soldier was an Invalid pensioner.
WOOLBRIDGE. (See WOOLDRIDGE.)
WOOLCOTT. (See WOLCOTT.)
WOOLDRIDGE, William, Conn. & War of 1812; Catharine Austin, former widow of......... W 10359
    (Also given WOOLBRIDGE.)
WOOLSEY, Gilbert.. S 14884
    John.. S 10047
WOOLWORTH, Ebenezer... BLWt. 1023-100
    Levi.. S 45456
WOOSTER, Benjamin, widow Sally.. W 2396
    David, BLWt. 2285-850, Brigadier General, was issued July 27, 1789, to Thomas WOOSTER, Admr.
    Ephraim... S 14883

WOOSTER, Lemuel... S 14887
    Moses, Conn. & Cont. BLWt. 1806-100... S 46333
    Thomas, BLWt. 2360-300, Capt., was issued July 27, 1789. No papers.
    Walter, widow Ursula... W 26106
WORDEN, Benjamin.. S 40724
    (Also given WARDEN.)
    Billings... S 14886
    Elizabeth, former widow of Obed HOLCOMB.
      (Also given WORDIN.)
    Ichabod, James and Jesse. (See WARDEN.)
    Joseph... S 35749
    Roger, Conn. & N. Y... S. 14891
    Sylvester or Silvester... S 45463
    Thomas, widow Jemima.. W 4407
    Wait, widow Diannah... R 11864
      Soldier pensioned in 1832 from Remsen, N. Y.
    William. (See WORDIN.)
WORDIN, Elizabeth. (See WORDEN.)
    John, Conn. & N. Y... S 14776
      (Also WARDEN.)
    William, widow Dorcas... W 22679
      (Also WORDEN.)
WORNER, Abner... S 34569
    (See also WARNER.)
WORREN, James, Conn. & Cont.. S 45452
    (Given also WARREN.)
WRIGHT, Abijah, widow Sally, BLWt. 26876-160-55.. W 2477
    Abraham, Conn. & Conn. Sea service, widow Rebecca................................. W 22699
    Asher, widow Bulah... W 22700
      Killingworth, Conn., in 1832; died in 1833.
    Asher, Cont. (Conn.)... S 36854
      Coventry, Conn., in 1818.
    Benjamin... S 36852
      Killingworth, Conn., in 1818.
    Benjamin, Cont. (Conn.), widow Susanna.. W 19662
      Genesee Co., N. Y., in 1818 & 1832.
    Charles, widow Betsey, BLWt. 6391-160-55.. W 3486
    Cornelius.. S 45467
    Daniel... S 32086
      Wethersfield, Conn., in 1832.
    Daniel, widow Mabel.. W 26133
      Hartford Co., Conn., in 1818; died in 1831.
    Deborah, former widow of Samuel BATES.
    Ebenezer.. ——
      Wethersfield, Conn., and died in 1808.
    Elijah, widow Jane... W 26135
    Ephraim.. S 19515
    Francis... BLWt. 1118-100
    George, widow Elizabeth, BLWt. 7062-160-55....................................... W 22702
    James, widow Elizabeth.. W 9038
      Soldier died in 1813 in Ashtabula Co., Ohio.
    James, Conn. & Navy... S 36857
      Killingworth, Conn., in 1818.
    Jeremiah... S 36856
    Joab, widow Peninah... W 6598
    John... S 36858
      Saybrook, Conn., in 1818.
    John... S 45464
      Unadilla, N. Y., in 1818.
    John... S 45466
      Greene Co., N. Y., in 1818.
    Jonathan... S 11908
      Litchfield Co., Conn., in 1832.
    Jonathan, widow Margaret or Pegga... W 11895
      Granville, Mass., in 1832; died in 1837.
    Joseph Allyn, Conn. & Cont.. S 36855
      BLWt. 2342-400, Major, was issued October 30, 1789. No papers.
    Mary, former widow of Moses WEST.
    Moses, widow Abigail.. W 18385
    Reuben... S 17212
    Roswell, widow Abigail.. W 26134
    Roxavene, former widow of Martin DENSLOW.
    Samuel... S 14904
      Oneida Co., N. Y., in 1832.
    Samuel, Conn. & Mass., widow Jemima... R 11890
      Soldier never pensioned.
    Simeon, widow Sarah... W 16797
WRISLE, George.. S 17800
WRISLEY, Samuel... S 32085
WYLIE, James.. S 11816
    (Also WILEY.)
    Peter.. S 41392
WYLLIS, John Palsgrave, BLWt. 2336-400, Major, was issued July 27, 1789. No papers.
WYLLYS, Samuel, BLWt. 2341-500, Colonel, was issued October 12, 1789. No papers.
    (See also WILLIS, WILLES and WILLYS.)

Y.

YALE, Daniel	S 11912
James	S 11914
Waitstill or Wate	S 36860
YARINGTON, Daniel	S 45478
(Also given YARRINGTON.)	
YEOMANS, Edward, wid. Gratiss, BLWt 8181-160-55	W 11902
(Also given YOMANS.)	
Joshua, wid. Elizabeth	W 20145
Samuel	S 22612
YOMANS. (See YEOMANS.)	
YONG. (See YOUNG.)	
YORK, Allen	S 17217
Elisha, wid. Sarah, BLWt. 1959-160-55	W 18246
James	S 17218
Jeremiah, widow Thankful, BLWt. 27662-160-55	W 2045
Sawney	S 36862
(See also CROSBY, Sawney.)	
YOUNG, Ebenezer, widow Elizabeth	W 22713
(Also given YONG.)	
Eli	S 11920
Isaac	S 22615
John, Conn. & N. Y	S 14912
Joseph. (See YOUNGS.)	
Joseph, Conn. & Mass	S 11926
Robert, Conn. & N. Y., wid. Abigail	W 20150
Solomon	S 14911
(Also given YOUNGS.)	
Stephen, Conn., Cont. & R. I	S 22072
William, Conn., Navy & Privateer, widow Mary	W 20148
YOUNGLOVE, John, Conn. & Cont	S 45486
Moses, Conn. & N. Y., widow Polly	W 4410
YOUNGS, Benjamin	S 36863
Joseph	S 24032
(Also given YOUNG.)	

Z.

ZIBBERE, Bristo, wid. Silvia	R 11986

NOTE.—Soldier never applied for a pension. Widow was a resident of Norwich, Conn., when she applied and stated that they were married in 1781 in that town, where they had lived as boy and girl.

www.ingramcontent.com/pod-product-compliance
Lightning Source LLC
Chambersburg PA
CBHW030552080526
44585CB00012B/355